Sketch map of movements of 2nd Regiment RHA 1940-1945

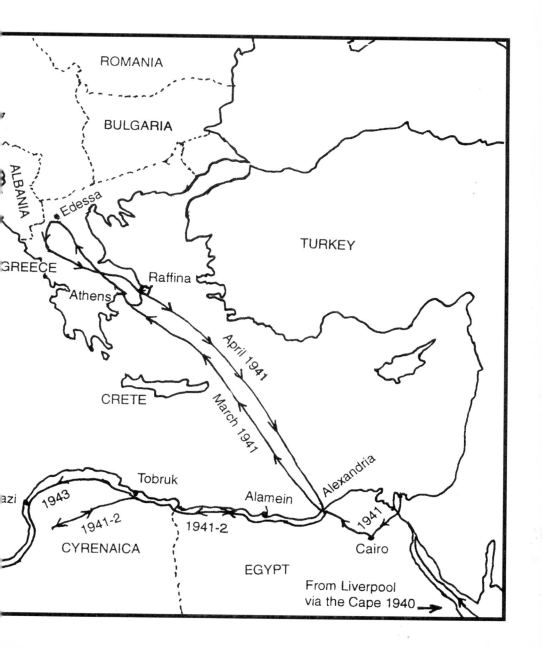

ROMANIA

BULGARIA

ALBANIA

Edessa

GREECE

Raffina

Athens

TURKEY

April 1941

CRETE

March 1941

Tobruk

Alexandria

...azi

1943

Alamein

1941

1941-2

1941-2

CYRENAICA

Cairo

EGYPT

From Liverpool
via the Cape 1940

DUNKIRK – ALAMEIN – BOLOGNA

Letters and Diaries of an Artilleryman 1939-1945

by

Christopher Seton-Watson

Foreword by
Michael Howard

Buckland Publications Ltd.
125 High Holborn, London WC1V 6QA

To all those of all ranks in the 2nd Regiment RHA
who shared with me all the experiences described in this book.

British Library Cataloguing in Publication Data
H. Seton-Watson
   Dunkirk, Alamein, Bologna: Letters and
     Diaries of an Artilleryman, 1939-45
   I. Title
   940.54

ISBN 0 7212 0833 9

Printed and bound in Great Britain by
Buckland Press Ltd., Dover, Kent.

CONTENTS

5

ILLUSTRATIONS

Plates 1, 3, 4, 5, 6, 8, 9, 12, 13, 15, 18 are reproduced by kind permission of the Imperial War Museum. Plates 10, 11, 16 and 17 by Bob Banks.

MAPS

Note: Dotted lines on the maps show 2 RHA's movements.

PREFACE

This book is not intended to be just one more addition to the long list of published Memoirs and Reminiscences of the Second World War. Nor is it a history of the 2nd Regiment Royal Horse Artillery, in which I served, with three interruptions, for six years. Its purpose is rather to present a selection of extracts from my letters to my parents (every one of which they preserved), and from the diaries which I wrote up intermittently from contemporary 'shorthand' notes. It therefore describes the immediate reactions of a young regimental officer to a wide variety of wartime experiences.

I have been able to fill one long gap in my diary for 1944-45 by quoting extensively from the 'Battery History' of I Battery RHA, written by myself while I was its Commander, with the exception of one chapter composed by Bob Banks, one of my Troop Commanders and later my Battery Captain. I greatly regret having lost touch with him some twenty years ago, and having failed to retrace him in recent months.

For an account of the last days of the North African campaign I have used the official War Diary of the Regiment, written by me as its adjutant and now located in the Public Record Office.

Because it was possible to include only a very small fraction of my diaries, many of those with whom I fought appear in them briefly and then disappear, without explanation. I hope that they, and the many others who do not appear at all, will understand the reason. All of them who stayed on in the army after the war received promotion, in some cases to dizzy heights. I hope they will forgive me for referring to them in the rank they held when I knew them.

I wish to thank the following, all of whom read parts of my manuscript and urged me to publish them: Christopher Dowling; Michael R. D. Foot; Sir David Hunt; Richard Lamb; Robin Lorimer; Margot Mayne; Elspeth Ogilvy-Wedderburn; my cousins Brian and Prunella Power; Enrico Serra; Julian Vranek; and the late John Whiskard. In addition I owe a special debt of gratitude to Sir Michael Howard, who was the first to suggest publication and has now contributed a Foreword; to Majors Gavin Kilgour and Jonathan Lee, recent commanders of I Parachute Battery (Bull's Troop) RHA, who allowed me to borrow three volumes of the Battery History and make unrestricted use of them; to my sister Mary, for her unfailing support; and to Christine Carus-Wilson, for decyphering my handwritten effusions and typing (and sometimes re-typing) them with infinite forbearance.

London. July, 1993.

FOREWORD
by Michael Howard

Christopher Seton-Watson is a distinguished historian who comes from a family of distinguished historians. His father, R. W. Seton-Watson, had written studies of South-Eastern Europe which were deeply influential in shaping British opinion and policy towards the Balkans throughout the first half of the twentieth century. His brother Hugh extended his range to cover the whole of Eastern Europe, including the Soviet Union. Christopher shifted the family focus to cover Italy, to the study of whose history and politics he has devoted his life. This book will go far to explain why.

It will also show how remarkably lucky he was to have a life to devote to anything, given his record of front-line service from the beginning to the very end of the Second World War. Statistically his chances of surviving those six years with a whole skin must have been small. In 1939 he enlisted straight from Oxford into the Royal Horse Artillery, a regiment notorious for placing its batteries at the point of maximum danger almost regardless of cost. Posted to France in December, he served throughout the Dunkirk campaign and was evacuated over the beaches. In November 1940 he was posted to Egypt, and in March 1941 took part in the short-lived and disastrous Greek campaign, during which he earned a Military Cross. Back in Egypt, he served in the Western Desert, where he was caught up in yet a third chaotic retreat, that from Tobruk in the summer of 1942. He was wounded in the bitter fighting for Ruweisat Ridge in July that ultimately stemmed Rommel's victorious advance. He recovered in time to take part in the Battle of Alamein, and was in at the death during the final days of the Battle of Tunis.

He was then out of the line for almost a year, returning to the front at Cassino in April, 1944. When the breakthrough came in May he was attached as liaison officer to the French forces whose successful attack through the trackless Aurunci mountains made the entire operation possible. Now a major and battery commander, he took part in the arduous advance through central Italy that drove the Germans back to the Gothic Line north of Florence. During the winter of 1944-45 he was stuck with the rest of the Eighth Army in the flat plains south of Ravenna; reaping his ultimate reward in the breakthrough that cleared the Germans out of Italy altogether and brought the war to an end.

Then he returned to Oxford and spent the next thirty-six years as a Fellow and Tutor in Politics at Oriel College. There in due course our paths crossed.

11

When Christopher showed me his wartime diaries and letters and wondered, with typical modesty, whether they were likely to be of the slightest interest, I begged him to publish them. Two generations have now elapsed since the events he describes. The outlines of the campaigns have remained clear, and military historians have mulled almost to excess over the strategy behind them, and the reasons for their success or failure; but people have almost forgotten what it was like to take part in them, and those who do remember are becoming fewer. I myself served in the Italian campaign, and was thankful to have done so. If one had to be involved in the Second World War at all, that was the place to be: much more interesting than North-West Europe, much more comfortable than Burma. But Christopher's experience spanned, in addition, France, Greece and the Western Desert, and he describes it all with a vividness and accuracy that brings those campaigns into sharp focus. As descriptions of war experience, these are classic.

I deliberately say 'war' rather than 'battle' experience. There is no lack of battle description here. The fatigue and confusion of retreat – indeed of three retreats; the horror of being caught under shellfire and seeing the men for whose lives one was responsible blown to pieces; the test of endurance and skill in trying to control one's own corner of the action, and the exhilaration of doing so successfully: all this is described here as well as I have ever seen it, without either exaggeration or understatement. But there was so much more to the war than this, though today it may not be fashionable to say so. There was a great deal of boredom, the most difficult of all experiences to describe. I suspect that Christopher, with his huge inner resources and lively interest in all that was happening around him, suffered less from this than most people, but suffer he did, kicking his heels in transit camps and rear areas waiting for something to happen. There was also a great deal of *fun* if you were fortunate enough to be in the right place with the right people at the right time, and there seems to have been more of this in wartime Cairo than in most places. But wherever you were, and however humble your rank, there were windfalls of happiness, when suddenly food and drink became unexpectedly abundant, or you met up with long-separated friends, or simply the sun shone and larks sang in the sky and you realised how good it was to be young and alive and, in a curious way, *free*.

For some unfortunates, the war was probably an experience of unremitting boredom or unremitting horror. But Christopher Seton-Watson had a good war in every sense of the word. It was a good war in the military sense, for he performed with consistent efficiency and courage. Had he so wished, he could have become a professional soldier and done extremely well. It was a Good War in the moral sense, for he was fighting evil, and never doubted it; and no amount of historical revisionism has yet proved him wrong. And it was a good war in the human sense: his positive experiences and achievements far outweighed the negative aspects inseparable from all military activity. These were for him good years, and his chronicle of them makes a fine book. It is a privilege to be associated with it.

Michael Howard.

CHAPTER ONE: THE PHONEY WAR
October 1939 – May 1940

When Britain went to war on 3 September 1939, I was on vacation at the family holiday home, Kyle House, in the Isle of Skye, preparing to return for my final year at New College, Oxford where I was studying Philosophy, Politics and Economics. I was just over twenty-one years of age. In October 1937 I had, together with several of my friends, voluntarily joined the horsed artillery section of the Senior Officers Training Corps, and subsequently passed the 'Certificate B' examination which entitled me to an immediate commission in the event of war. My wartime military career therefore began on 7 October, when I reported to the School of Artillery, Larkhill, for a crash course in gunnery.

Letter, 8 October

There are about 100 of us here, almost all from Oxford or Cambridge, but some as old as twenty-five, doing this Officer Cadet Reserve course – it is to last four weeks, until November 4th. By day life is extremely comfortable, by night extremely unpleasant. "A" mess is roomy and warm, comfortable chairs and a liberal supply of newspapers. The food is magnificent, and if they continue feeding us like this, at the end of four weeks I shall have put on weight considerably. On the other hand, we are sleeping in 'barrack-rooms' which are still in the process of being built – no handles to doors or windows, wet paint, no hooks for clothes, no heating. That will improve in the next few days, though I'm afraid the beds won't. They are of the worst army type, with three cushions of unequal height instead of a mattress, and so penitentially narrow that at least two of my room-mates fell to the floor with a resounding crash in the course of last night. But I've no doubt we'll get used to it. I've at least managed to get a bed against the wall, so the risks of capsizement are halved. But life by day is what matters, and it is going to be very comfortable.

12 October

I've quite settled down to the routine here by now. We work hard, and there is a good deal of 'prep' which will get gradually stiffer. We are apparently doing the same course as young officers just out of Woolwich: and they take five months over what we are expected to do in four weeks. So far it has all been elementary, but will soon require concentration. We still don't know what is to become of us at the end of four weeks. The Colonel in charge of our course is reputed to have said that we may be sent over to France immediately after the end of our course. I myself think that is unlikely, unless Hitler invades Belgium: everyone seems to take that for granted, however.

31 October

Time passes very quickly here, Last week we had two days of shooting and fired 18-pdrs on the ranges behind the school. We had the interesting, but at first mildly frightening, experience of shooting at ourselves. Half our party sat in a splinter-proof observation post and directed the fire, and the other half fired the guns. We scored a direct hit and knocked lumps of concrete off our roof. We also burst shrapnel shells within fifty yards of where we were sitting. It gave one some idea of what it must be like to come under fire, Tomorrow we set out in the morning with a bewildering multiplicity of instruments and spend the whole day putting into practise what we have learnt in the last three weeks. That is the climax of our course, and only frills are left for the last two days.

I was not immediately sent to France at the end of the course, but was instead posted, after a short leave, to 9th Field Training Regiment RA at South Camp, Pennypot Lane, Harrogate.

14 November

This camp, like all military camps, is on the top of a hill about three miles from the centre of the town. It is brand new – the first troops came here in September. But it's already very comfortable and will soon be luxurious. We sleep in huts, two in a room, with stoves and running water. The C.O. is Colonel Colman, of Colman's mustard, reputed to be fabulously rich. We have two elderly majors of some experience and an odd collection of subalterns, some regulars, some territorials and three of us from the Larkhill course. I find I know as much as most of the theory and more advanced stuff. But unfortunately, as I feared, there's going to be little opportunity of displaying or improving my knowledge. This morning I supervised a squad taking engines to pieces and learning to ride motor bikes. When I protested gently that I was quite incapable of doing any such thing, the reply was that there was no officer who knew anything about the subject, and anyhow it didn't matter. So that's how I earn 11/- a day from a proud and grateful country.

Soon afterwards I was given a week's embarkation leave, and early in December received an order posting me to the 2nd Regiment RHA in France. On the night of 5 December I crossed over from Southampton to Cherbourg, and after several days of travel in unlit, unheated trains, and hanging around transit camps in soaking rain, I arrived in a railcar at midday on 9 December at Allennes-les-Marais, a small village about 15 miles southwest of Lille. I left my luggage at the station and set off into the unknown, to find the regiment just arriving from its previous location at La Bassée. In the main street I ran into Captain W.D. Blacker, 2nd in Command of H/I Battery. He assigned me to

Battery HQ, allotted me a billet and showed me round. This was the beginning of one of my closest army friendships.

The regiment had two batteries, H/I and L/N, each consisting of two troops [H and I, L and N] of four 25-pdrs, converted from old 18-pdrs and drawn by tracked vehicles called Dragons.

12 December

We are in a fair-sized ugly village of three or four streets, with very few modern conveniences, and cobblestones down which lorries constantly rumble, and as soon as it rains, a liberal sprinkling of mud. Anywhere off the road there are seas of it, and gum boots are a godsend. We wear battle dress all day, and I find it very comfortable: canvas leggings round the top of one's boots keep one's trousers clean of the worst of the mud. I have a perfect Jeeves of a servant: he cleans and brushes and presses my clothes, helps me in my struggle to get my web equipment on the right way and when I'm in doubt, can tell me exactly what I can and cannot do, what is and what is not done. My billet is admirable – a comfortable bed in a spotless little downstairs room, complete with aspidistra, peacock feathers, certificat d'études primaires, picture of papa as a poilu in '70[1], etc. Madame sends me hot coffee every morning before I get up, and yesterday evening Jeeves (his name is Smith) and I drank with Monsieur and a crony, to the Entente Cordiale – in gin and coffee. The inhabitants put up with us nobly: all the billets have of course been commandeered by the government, but the willingness and good humour with which they voluntarily sacrifice their front parlours for some temporary emergency is really wonderful. They are amused at our antics, but also, I think, impressed.

Sunday 17 December

We've been back in these billets for several days now, since we returned from a three days' exercise. It went well, though it was not exciting, apart from watching long columns of lorries and guns and tanks of every description crawling (and often thundering) down narrow French cobbled roads. I think some very serious lessons were learnt. A lot of those three days were spent in sitting or standing around at a Command Post established in a draughty barn. We were lucky, however, in finding a farmhouse just across the road, where Madame offered us a large room where we ate and slept. Since we've been back, the weather has been bitter, though so far no snow has lain. I spend all the morning outside, inspecting trucks and guns, checking petrol consumption and batteries, and trying hard to learn the elements of wireless. Most is quite in vain, but in time I hope I shall learn a little, both about wireless and telephones and motor transport. Sunday afternoon is a time of somnolence for everybody. The village has gone to sleep, the men are mostly asleep, either in their billets or the local estaminets, and we are sitting round a fiery stove, with a thick fug on the

1. As an infantryman in the 1870 Franco-Prussian War.

windows, writing letters and listening to an orchestral concert from Germany. The trouble is that there is little news to tell you: all the interesting things would be jumped on by the censor. It's a very busy, but very varied and often amusing life. I'm gradually learning the names of the men and getting to know some of them: but it's a big job, as you can imagine. The trouble about this place is that it is *so* typical a French village, with no amenities except the bistros (where a nightly torrent of grouses against French beer can be heard), very primitive sanitary arrangements and only about three baths in the place. We have a regimental institute, which has a piano and sells good English beer, tobacco and food, but it's not very gay, and there's no cinema, and no transport, except on rare occasions, to larger towns nearby. On the whole I think Tommy Atkins is bitterly disappointed with France, particularly with the female population. That is no doubt the result of flaming accounts of Parisian life (night) in the more vulgar weeklies. The only things about which there is some bitterness are Hore-Belisha's[1] speech about everyone getting leave before or after Christmas, and the glowing accounts in the British press of all the Ensa and other entertainments which the troops have been having. These advertised concerts are no doubt splendid, but only about fifteen men per regiment get a chance to go. There is a mobile cinema which appears at intervals, but the last show was apparently a complete flop – no one could either see or hear. In short, Mr Leslie Hore-Belisha has lost a good deal of popularity.

I just missed the King's inspection of the regiment: it had happened three days before I arrived. All went off very well, but there were many grouses because he didn't look at each individual as he walked down the ranks. A lot is expected of royalty. The King must have passed within a half a mile of me on my way here, but I had no opportunity of giving him one of my reverberating salutes.

I'm enjoying myself very much out here. It's becoming less strange and less confusing and I'm learning every day, not only of my own small and rather specialised job, but of other more important things. 'I'm being educated in the hard school of life' – I think that's the correct conventional phrase. With all its drawbacks, a military career has one great virtue: one learns a lot about human nature. I know that is always said in eulogies of an army career, but I hadn't really appreciated it before. Our regiment is on the average rather old, and contains a high proportion of reservists: that's a pity in many ways. I liked the youthful atmosphere of Harrogate immensely. It's difficult not to feel rather embarrassed when at the raw age of twenty-one one finds oneself in command of veterans of thirty-five and over, some of them already grey-haired. The NCOs, on the other hand, are mostly very young, having been promoted quickly during recent expansions: they are an admirable lot, and with more training will be first-class. I mentioned my Jeeves in my last letter – he's a reservist, a conductor on No. 15 bus service, Ladbroke Grove and East Ham.

1. Secretary of State for War.

23 December

We have finished stunts now for some little time – Hitler permitting – and are having a lazy lull over Christmas. I have spent the last two days buzzing round the countryside in trucks of various sizes – buzzing is the wrong word, for the mist enforced an average speed of 8 m.p.h. – and buying Christmas dinners, pork and apple sauce and Brussels sprouts and Christmas puddings, for our troops.

It's a very queer war – queer for you, but queerer out here. If I hadn't such an immense amount to learn, I should no doubt be bored. Many of the troops are. It's very difficult for everybody. It's neither peace nor war. The routine life is not unlike peacetime, and apart from extra precautions and certain details of an unpleasantly realistic kind, it is hard to imagine the war (such as it is) is so near. In such conditions it's only natural that there should be a lot of grumbling. From what I've seen of it, the spirit and morale of the B.E.F. is admirable: but it may need some encouragement during this winter. I fancy the same applies to the French.

We shan't know what's going to happen until the spring – at the earliest, of that I'm quite sure. You of course must know a good deal of the internal situation in Germany, though I'm sure one can't sufficiently mistrust 'reliable reports from inside'. My own opinion is that Germany will not crack up for a *very* long time indeed, *without a severe military defeat*. Hitler knows this: his game is therefore to wait, and keep intact, as far as possible, his army and air force. I believe he realises he can't *win* – unless we make a colossal blunder either in the naval or diplomatic fields.

I'm afraid I shall have less and less news for you, as time goes by, if life goes on as at present. I enjoy our contacts with the civil population – they are very cordial, even with the farmers in whose orchards we dig trenches and gun pits, and whose hedges we mercilessly hack down. Among our troops there is immense enthusiasm for gossip with the locals, and we are going to start voluntary French classes, in which I expect I shall have a hand. Well over half the regiment has volunteered to attend them – though I suspect that, as with lectures at Oxford, the faithful will be few on the last day.

The 'stunts' in which we were involved were rehearsals, as far as practicable, of the operation which we would have to carry out in the event of a German offensive. 2RHA was part of the 3rd Division, commanded by General Bernard Montgomery. Its role would be to advance into Belgium as far as Louvain and take up defensive positions on the River Dyle. Our exercises therefore consisted of moving in formation, often by night, for distances up to 40 miles, in a south-westerly direction, taking up defensive positions on the rivers Authie or Canche (in the St. Pol area), digging gunpits and setting up all the communications which a real battle would involve.

30 December

Our brief and enjoyable spell of idleness and merrymaking is over, and now we start working again in earnest – harder than ever before. It was a queer Christmas, but great fun in its own way. For three days before Christmas we had seen no further than 20 yards. Frenchmen complain of London fogs, but I've never seen anything to beat their own last effort. The thick white mist greeted us on Christmas morning. It had frozen during the night, after a mild thaw the previous evening. You can imagine how treacherous the cobbles of the village street were, covered with a thin film of ice. I told everyone that I would be the first to fall over, and sure enough I was. Having mercifully kept my balance throughout Church parade, I forgot myself coming out after the service, and fell with a resounding crash in the gutter – no bones broken. We had the service in our spacious regimental canteen. The padre turned up three quarters of an hour late, his truck slithering the two miles from his last service at 5 m.p.h., his cap and greatcoat crusted with frost, even from so short a drive. The troops had meanwhile been sitting blaspheming. But 'Hark the herald angels sing' and 'While shepherds watched' went with a swing, the Woolworth streamers swaying above our heads in the gusts of hearty song. The only awkward moment was when the padre started his sermon by wishing everyone a "happy Christmas." I expected mutiny, but there was only a low grumble. The padre looked pained, then saw the humour of the situation, and went on to give a most delightful, simple talk on the spirit of Christmas, which soothed all the grumbles and quite 'got across'. I had never hoped to hear so sincere a sermon, such restraint and lack of pomposity, in an Army Christmas Day service. Communion followed, and the incongruous surroundings made it all the more meaningful. If I forget everything else that I have seen and done out here in the past few weeks, I shall remember that strange service in the French parish hall, with the fog oozing through the cracks of the window, dart boards hanging on the walls at one end, above boxes of bottled French beer; at the other end, above the improvised altar draped with a Union Jack, and above two cheap candles and the pile of yellow army prayer books, the small stage adorned with the Chinese lanterns and lacquer screens of papier mache – never has the Communion meant so much in St. Mary's, Wimbledon or New College Chapel.

The service over, Christmas began for the troops. The altar was swept away and transformed into part of a long row of trestle tables; bottles of Guinness appeared – a free Christmas present from the management of Guinness. I spent the whole morning drinking with the sergeants and sergeant-majors – I reckoned about five pints in all, and that on a very empty stomach. But 'noblesse oblige': it was impossible to refuse, and I'll say I stood it better than many of the sergeants. In fact, one of them has since been reduced to the rank of bombardier for having failed to turn up on guard duty at 2 p.m., an hour after his lunch. But considering that the only Christmas diversions in this village were drink and darts – and sleep – all concerned behaved miraculously well. Of the three above-mentioned diversions, after unlimited roast pork and Christmas pudding, sleep was much the most popular, until the evening, when the three bistros came alive and had a record turnover. I also slept most of the afternoon, and awoke refreshed about 6 for our evening meal, which was a merry function, though turkeyless. We drank a host of toasts in champagne, and finished up with a superb cognac, though some of the bouquet was lost in our 1½d. tooth-glasses. Madame lent us her champagne glasses, but could not produce any for the brandy. A huge tin of salted peanuts and some Fortnum and Mason pâté de foie gras completed the feast. As you can see, we did ourselves well.

I have taken four days over this letter so far, but shall finish it this evening (Saturday). We have now started our 'individual training programme' in earnest. The whole regiment has been divided up into several classes – one for signalling (telephone, wireless, etc.), another for artillery survey, another for young NCOs. I'm attending the last, sometimes giving lectures, sometimes drilling with the NCOs in their squads, half learning, half teaching. At the end of it I should be able to take a gun to pieces and put it together again, to carry out a thorough inspection of a truck and its engine, and to instruct in anything that has anything to do with an RHA regiment – which means practically anything under the sun. It's going to be a most profitable course, in many ways rounding off what I learnt at Larkhill. By the spring we'll be a highly efficient unit. And meanwhile digging parties will be going out every day.

The task of the digging parties was to prepare defensive battle positions, including dugouts and command posts as well as gunpits, near Lannoy, just behind the Belgian frontier east of Lille. This was part of the plan to build a line of defences which would fill the gap between the northern end of the Maginot Line and the sea.

7 January

We continue to lead a pleasant, uneventful, but quite varied life. I spent one day last week digging trenches and gunpits, the first real exercise I've had for weeks. But most days I'm with this class for young NCOs. A few days ago I gave them a lecture on the military geography of France.

Everyone has to give a lecture, on any subject he likes to choose. One talked of the making of a fur coat, another had been a roadmaker, another in an Edinburgh papermaking and binding firm, another a miner, another used to work in Morris's works and lives in Marston, just outside Oxford.

You can imagine that Hore-Belisha's resignation[1] has aroused our curiosity. He had managed to create violent feelings in the Army, of approval and disapproval, so his disappearance has aroused mixed emotions. The French are interested also, and the local paper came out with huge headlines. But not a word of political comment is allowed to appear, on any subject, except Russia and the menace it represents to civilisation in the east.[2]

1. His dismissal was due to friction between him and the British High Command in France.

2. The French press was instructed to treat the Soviet Union as an enemy, in view of its signature of the pact with Nazi Germany in August 1939 and its invasion of Finland at the end of November.

17 January

For once I need not apologise for being three days late with my Sunday letter – the BBC and the papers will have told you why. Things are quietening down to 'normal' again, and tonight the scare seems to have passed.[1] Half the regiment packed up at three hours' notice and left for a secret rendezvous. I stayed behind here with the rear party, and the only actual discomforts I suffered were two nights on the hard floor of our office, with the telephone ringing at intervals in my ear. We could have moved in less than an hour, but the order never came through. At the time we thought 'der Tag' had come. We have learnt a great deal, and the next time we will be even more efficient and quicker off the mark. Meanwhile by tomorrow the regiment should be reunited, and our first home leave party leaves in half an hour, just three days late.

Today has been the coldest day I can remember – snow on the ground, a bright sun with no warmth in its rays, and a blasting, withering N.E. wind. More snow has fallen tonight, and there seems no prospect of a change. But I'm not complaining – that snow on the Dutch and Belgian frontiers may have been important.

One consequence of the snow was that, because of the need for invisibility from the air, digging operations had to be suspended.

4 February

We had a general's inspection at the beginning of the week. It was an amusing break in the usual routine. He was an exceptionally affable and friendly general, asking us all searching questions about our military records and life histories – I survived the ordeal quite creditably – and was suitably impressed by our efficiency and the state of our billets and troops.

That was my first encounter with Monty.

19 February

I am now able to disclose – as the best newspaper correspondents begin their articles – that for some time we have been in new billets. And what billets! Our new mess is on a palatial scale, centrally heated, and a bath with unlimited hot water. In our sitting room there is a huge brick fireplace, and in the evenings we have a roaring log fire. We're established in a small town[2] with quite decent shops – the cheeses are a marvel, and the troops have a wide choice of cafés and a cinema which shows English films (of a sort) four times a week. They really are in clover, even though the roof of the large gymnasium in which they are billeted leaks at the least provocation.

By the end of February there were signs of spring.

1. The 'scare' arose from the capture of German plans for the invasion of Belgium from two staff officers who had crash-landed on Belgian soil.

2. Seclin.

12 March

This warm spring sun has a wonderfully soothing effect on nerves and tempers. I have been a different creature since it began to shine. We are just back from a huge exercise, the first since Christmas. It was hectic indeed, and I reckon I got four hours' sleep in sixty-four. A lot of driving and quick movement and wit-sharpening. I think I acquitted myself adequately, and felt more confident of myself than ever before: at a moment of crisis I found myself commanding three-quarters of the battery. It was cold, with some snow in the middle of the first night, but we found a house where we ate in warmth and comfort, and managed to take with us part of our Fortnum and Mason hamper.

From the end of March most of my thoughts were concentrated on the prospect of home leave, and on trying to arrange for it to coincide with that of my parents, so that we could spend it together in Skye. But on 9 April the Germans invaded Denmark and Norway, and next day all leave from the BEF was cancelled.

10 April

I still refuse to believe that anything will happen here, for some time to come, but we are alert. You can imagine our state of mind. We return to the mess for every news bulletin, and tonight's accounts of the exploits of the Navy and the RAF were celebrated by a magnum of champagne. This morning's announcement about leave was a blow; but now I'm not depressed. If the test is coming, I want to be here. And while such stirring events as today's are going on, we could not enjoy Kyle. The quiet mind would be a pathetic dream, hopelessly impossible to realize.

On 11 April the Regiment was put at eight hours' notice, and on the night of the 13th/14th it moved to an assembly area at Toufflers, just behind the Belgian frontier. The next week was spent waiting at a few hours' notice for orders to cross the frontier; but they never came.

Leave was re-opened on 23 April and I reached London on the 28th, travelling up to Skye on the following night for ten of the happiest days of my life. I returned to London on 8 May and spent that night with relatives. At 0800 on the 9th I took a taxi to Victoria, expecting to be returning to a 'summer of heat and dust and increasing monotony'.

Diary, 9 May

The leave trains were drawing out every ten minutes for over an hour, and the station was crowded with soldiers of the BEF, very few with wives or friends. But the atmosphere was exactly that of the school train from Paddington in my preparatory school years. A short wait, and by 0910 I was off. The trees were much greener than a fortnight before, and Kent was at its loveliest. At Dover we all walked over to the Lord Warden Hotel, now an Officer's Leave Club, and had an abominable lunch of mutton and mint sauce, rice and prunes, for 2/-. Good old England!

We had two hours to wait, and sat in the hotel lounge – the schoolboy spirit again very evident. Some of us sat very subdued in corners reading our papers and Penguins. I read the full accounts of last night's debate in the Commons. The *News Chronicle* announced in headlines that after so unfavourable a vote the Government was bound to resign.[1] Others drank double (or treble) whiskies. Others again were hearty, slapped each other's backs, and let everyone know that they were glad to see each other again. "How did your leave go, old boy?" "Never so bored in my life," etc. The true schoolboy spirit.

We sailed at 1330 in an LMS Isle of Man steamer, large and comfortable. I paced the first-class deck and saw the white cliffs fade into the mist. It was cold and sunless, but there were no excitements except for the usual practise shots from each Lewis gun and the usual wild rumours that mines had been sighted. We had no escort – destroyers were more urgently needed over in Norway.

We were in Boulogne by 1530 and I found that the 2nd Corps train didn't leave until 2115. The sun was shining, and after strolling round the quay and taking a look at the A.A. pom-poms and a French motor torpedo-boat, I made for the Hotel Maurice, where I had an excellent dinner with a subaltern of the 1st Corps Survey Coy, R.E. Until December he'd been a lecturer in Geography at Newcastle and found himself in France in less than a week after being accepted by the army. We agreed that we were in for a trying summer of monotonous waiting, and an even more trying winter. That was 2030 on May 9th. Twenty-four hours later I was to be half-way across Belgium.

We left Boulogne immediately after the L of C [Lines of Communication] train had pulled out complete with couchettes, on its long wander to Nantes. Our engine had some difficulty in getting up the hill from the harbour to the main station; but after much puffing and slipping of wheels we reached the top and rattled away at a decent pace into the night. I slept until La Madeleine, where my only companion got out. We got to Seclin at 0100 and I found a 30-cwt waiting. Bdr. Bentley drove me, slowly but dangerously, through Lille and on to the new mess at Lannoy, to which the Battery had moved during my absence.

There in the sitting-room, asleep in a chair, I found Gerry [Hulbert] looking ill and tired and suffering from acute asthma. From him I learnt the news. He was enthusiastic over the new mess, which was complete with bath, garden and tennis court. The battery had only just got back from a night march with the 15/19th Hussars and he gave me details of the hectic training programme for the next few weeks. There was talk of my going to the KOSBs [King's Own Scottish Borderers] for a fortnight's attachment. That was too much for me. I found my valise, blew up my lilo and lay down in misery among the coats and boots and tennis racquets, under the bathroom window. As I dropped off to sleep, I was debating with myself whether arriving back from leave at 0200 was sufficient excuse for shirking parade at 0800 next morning.

1. Chamberlain resigned as prime minister on 10 May and was succeeded by Churchill. I heard the news on the B.B.C. on 12 May [see p. 29].

CHAPTER TWO: FORWARD TO LOUVAIN, BACK TO DUNKIRK
May 1940

10 May

It was soon after 0500 that I woke with a start. There seemed to be a lot of unusual noise. I soon realised that I hadn't been dreaming. It was intense A.A. fire. I was soon asleep again, but not for long. At 0700 the telephone rang and Gerry burst in on me with the news that we were at four hours' notice. Half an hour later came the message that we were to move 'forthwith'. The battle had begun.

At breakfast we were too busy to think of the wireless, and so missed the news. It was not until three days later that I next had a chance of listening to the B.B.C. The world had contracted to a small circle a few miles in diameter, outside which we had very little idea of what was happening. We first learnt of events 20 miles away by tuning into London. That morning at Lannoy the fog of war descended and didn't lift until we put foot again on English soil.

A.A. fire continued most of the morning, with few intervals. It seemed to come chiefly from the direction of Lille, but there were guns firing all round us.

The 15/19th Hussars asked us to be ready by 1300. It was longer notice than we had expected, but it was a frantic morning.

In the end we were ready before the cavalry, for they had to take the 'training tracks' off all their tanks and substitute their 'war tracks'. At 1300 we paraded in the tramway garage that had been our vehicle park for the last fortnight. Our Battery Commander, Bede Cameron, gave us all the information he knew and a few words of encouragement and good cheer. These were hardly needed, for I've never seen the Battery so alert and cheerful. Everyone was confident and thankful that the long period of waiting had at last come to an end. As for myself, I remember feeling surprised at my own calm and coherence. However horrible the future, it could not fail to be interesting and in part, I hoped, amusing. With an almost perfect ten days leave behind me, serving in such company and in a Battery as efficient as could be found in the British Army, on a glorious hot May morning, it was not difficult to decide to enjoy life (while it lasted). Not that we were under any illusions as to what was in store for us. At first sight we might have been parading for just one more divisional exercise. But Bede warned us that we must expect bombing along the whole march across Belgium, and little respite while the battle lasted. There might be sabotage on the way, for Belgium was full of enemy agents, and we must expect trouble everywhere, at any time.

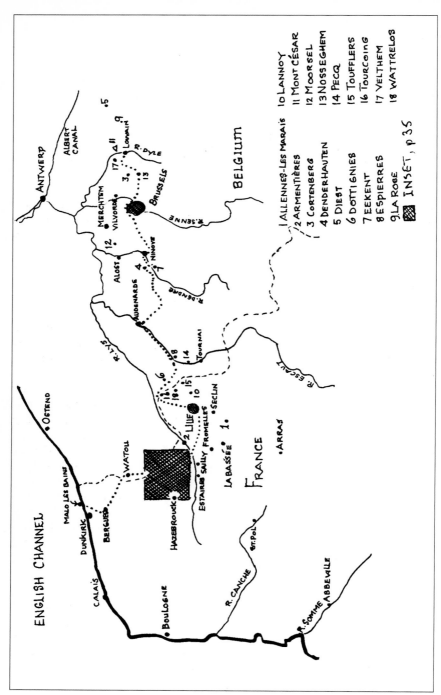

Area of operations, December 1939/May 1940.

He ended by repeating our divisional General Montgomery's advice: "Shoot first, ask questions afterwards".

We moved off at 1330. As H troop's commander, Peter Worthington, was on leave, I had to take his place and travel with the 15/19th's leading squadron and establish H Troop's forward O.P. across the River Dyle at Louvain. I drove on ahead, with Kitchen as NCO i/c Signals, and joined A Squadron's column at the stadium. The great march started badly. On reporting to Major Frith, I found him wrestling with the latest operation order just issued by 15/19th HQ. As usual, there had been last-minute alterations, which made nonsense of much of the plan we had practised so long. But all that mattered was that we were to cross the frontier at 1430. When I got back to my 8-cwt truck I found it deserted. Five minutes later Driver Wheeler and my wireless operators, Simpson and O'Brien, emerged from a café across the road, loaded with bread and chocolate and bottles of the unmentionable concoctions that had been displayed all winter in every shop window for the benefit of the BEF. They had thought my absence a good opportunity to lay in stores, having forgotten to draw their rations at Lannoy. By the time I got back I was furious – the British Army was about to move off to one of its greatest battles, the 15/19th's tanks were ticking over, and Messrs Wheeler, Simpson and O'Brien had decided to take a little walk and enjoy their last drink on French soil. I was all the angrier because in the last rush at Lannoy I too had forgotten to grab my haversack rations, and had been gloomily contemplating the prospect of indefinite hunger. How thankful I was to be for that chocolate, and even for the poisonous drinks, in the next two days.

We moved out of the stadium at 1410. The column was led by A Squadron 15/19th Hussars, and I followed in my OP truck immediately after the last tank. Behind me came the leading truck of the 41st Anti-Tank Regiment with a sergeant-major in charge – a priceless fool. We were the spearhead of 3rd Division Mobile Troops, behind which came the Middlesex Machine-Gun Battalion, and behind them the rest of one half of the division (the other half was moving on another route to our south).

All the way up to the frontier the doorsteps and windows were crowded and the whole of Wattrelos had turned out to see us go. They were quiet, and there was little of the enthusiasm with which we used to be greeted on our divisional exercises during the winter. We arrived at the frontier early and our leading vehicles were halted just the other side. I waited for ten minutes in the narrow street between the customs posts, and used my last moments on friendly French soil to load my rifle and revolver; the gesture pleased me.

At 1440 the column moved on – a hundred yards further, past policemen and an immaculate officer in a strange uniform, a sea of faces and a chorus of screaming brats, and I was in Belgium. Sappers, assisted by Belgian soldiers, were tearing down the barbed wire and removing the mines and barriers that the Belgian authorities had so painstakingly erected in the past six months. The enthusiasm of the population was amazing – but it made me feel uncomfortable. I remember wondering whether they would be as enthusiastic in a month, or even a week. The Anti-Tank sergeant-major regarded the crowds with the gravest suspicion, but couldn't help bowing to the cheers. In one village his mapboard fell out of the truck into the street. At once the crowd shouted and gesticulated and crowded round him, trying to make him stop. He must have thought it was sabotage or a hold-up, and was reaching for his revolver when a minute urchin appeared, dragging the mapboard behind him. As I said before, a priceless fool.

A gun of 2RHA crossing the Belgian Frontier, 10 May.

A mile beyond the frontier the houses ended and the bumpy French pavé turned to a broad concrete road and superb surface – "It might have been made specially for us," as Wheeler remarked. The countryside also changed abruptly: instead of the bleak undulating open fields of the Lille district, dotted with ugly factories, straggling industrial villages and smoking slag-heaps, we drove through green fields and under wooded hills, past tidy farmhouses and small clustering villages, each with its distinctive Flemish church tower. It was a most enjoyable drive: the cavalry kept up a fair pace, the sun blazed down on us, and there were few traffic blocks.

Our fears of losing our way proved unfounded. The Belgian system of signposts was first-class, and in every village and town our route was so thickly lined by the cheering inhabitants that it was impossible to take the wrong turn without mowing down the crowd. The peasants working in the fields occasionally waved to us, but seemed to show little interest; but the enthusiasm in the towns increased and the crowds grew greater the further we advanced into Belgium. At halts our trucks were immediately surrounded by hysterical children, screaming for souvenirs – the old cry uttered with new and embarrassing energy. I had to be quite fierce, and made Wheeler brandish his rifle and utter strange Anglo-Saxon cries. Fortunately these were effective: otherwise the vandals would have left few clothes on our bodies and little equipment in our trucks. The entire population seemed to rush into the streets as soon as the rattle of our trucks was heard in the distance. Later in the day it was obvious that the news of our advance had preceded us, and in the larger towns like Alost and Vilvorde we had what was almost an organised civic welcome. Fruit and packets of biscuits and chocolate were thrown into our trucks and on one occasion hurled down on us from an upstairs window. Wheeler and I were presented with huge sprays of white lilac by a charming peasant girl, who threw her arms round his neck and kissed him on both cheeks. He completely failed to register the embarrassment to be expected from a respectable married man. I might well have been next had we not moved on just in time – much to Wheeler's regret.

It was a strange prelude to battle. For the first 20 miles there was nothing to distinguish the drive from a peacetime convoy run on manoeuvres, except the Belgian surroundings. But at our first halt I was talking to a traffic control officer about the bombings early that morning in France, when we noticed two planes flying over us, at a good height, 5000 to 6000 feet. I got my glasses on them and with something of a thrill made out the iron cross on their wings. Then suddenly there was a whistle and a screaming, then another whistle, then a third, all quickly getting louder and lower in pitch. For a few seconds I thought one of the planes must have been shot down: it sounded just like the noise of planes crashing to earth produced by Hollywood in *Men with Wings* and other serial masterpieces. Then I saw two small oval eggs coming obliquely down over our heads and across the road at an angle, and a few seconds later there were three dull explosions about 300 yards away on our right. They were my first bombs, and we all stood gazing up fascinated. We were soon to learn wisdom. I was too interested to be frightened, and in any case it was a mild attack – three small bombs from a great height, and inaccurately aimed.

And so the long march continued, 15 miles in the hour, twenty-five vehicles to the mile. We had none of us dared to hope for so easy a run. The route was marked for us at every turn by civilians, special police, and in places by boy scouts. There were no parachutists to be seen, there was no sign of sabotage nor of a Fifth Column. And the roads were clear. Towards evening we met the first refugees – well fed families in high-powered Daimler and Mercedes saloons (or their Belgian equivalents), driving furiously and waving very patriotically as they sped past us on their way to safety on French soil. But humbler citizens stood watching and gossiping. We had been sitting just across the frontier all winter, practising and planning the advance: and yet our appearance seemed quite unexpected. Several times I was asked if I was French; when I replied that we were the advance guard of the British Army, they were genuinely amazed – and thrilled. Later in the day we were greeted with cries of "Vive l'Angleterre" and

"Bravo les Tommies," and my answer of "Vive la Belgique" aroused great fervour. Poor Belgium. It was all such fun that afternoon.

About 1800 we passed through Alost and crossed the Dendre. At Moorsel, a few miles beyond, came our third halt. There was a drone in the air, growing louder: then twenty-seven planes appeared, ziz-zagging, searching for a quarry. They must have seen us: we skulked in the shadow of the houses, with a queer feeling in the stomach. There were thuds not far behind us and I saw smoke when we moved on. I learnt later that the main body of the Battery had been caught on the eastern outskirts of Alost and suffered four casualties, one killed. It was amazing that so little damage was done – only one truck was hit.

At Merchtem a Belgian officer came up to me and asked, "Est-ce que le matériel est bon?", a searching question. He told us Louvain had been bombed. At Vilvorde, about 8 miles north of Brussels, big crowds still greeted us – marking our route nicely for enemy planes; but we got through safely, sirens wailing over the whole countryside. On the Brussels-Antwerp road we passed a tram – normalcy still. Another halt in the darkness at 2200, then south to Cortenberg and down the main road into Louvain, passing round the southern edge of the town about 2230. The 15/19th secured the bridges over the canal and under the railway on the far side. I was not needed, so slept a little in a barge. An Englishwoman turned up with tea, hot water and sandwiches. Very cold. Bede and Bill Blacker came up to look at me. H troop went into action on the hill above the town in the western outskirts. We waited for the Middlesex to come up and take over the canal crossings – they were much delayed.

11 May

The Middlesex came up at daybreak. The 15/19th went forward to La Rose, a small village on the Louvain-Diest road, with troops distributed on either side, patrols forward. H Troop came forward across the River Dyle in support. I found an OP to north of road, established myself by 0700: very bad visibility in heavily wooded country, the one possible position was in a tall tree. There was a troop of 15/19th just in front of me – I persuaded it to come forward with some difficulty, as it preferred a position behind me.

Bombing all day, much of it near H Troop and the bridges: waves of nine, fifteen and thirty planes, once saw fifty-four together. Sirens soon went silent because as the 'all clear' went, the next wave came over. I felt safe in my tree, looking up at them through the leaves. Could see fires in Louvain, heard continuous crashes. No sign of the RAF: occasional A.A. fire, quite ineffective. In the afternoon A Squadron HQ was bombed, with two casualties, and the village of La Rose smashed. I longed for dark. I did silent registration, got the chief landmarks identified. Telephone line arrived about midday, Dodd with a black eye acquired at Alost. Then message, prepare to withdraw. We reeled in the line, I slept for a while. Then suddenly a scare – a 15/19th report, supposed to have come from 12th Lancers who were reconnoitring out front – "Enemy 7 miles S.E. of this position". I sent it through, causing a big flap at Division HQ.

Mustard gas scare in the evening which I declined to take seriously. Line laid again in evening, very long, and maintenance was nasty owing to the bombing.

I was fed nobly by the residents in the nearby farmhouse – an excellent Flemish stew. They had many refugees from the city staying with them. I talked German to them. The farmers meanwhile calmly carried on their work. At dark I returned to A Squadron HQ, slept in a shattered house we broke into. All night Belgians trooping back: horsed wagons, mechanised artillery, lorries – all sprouting with leaves as camouflage: many on bicycles or on their feet. Also many refugees. No certain news: rumours of a German break-through across the Albert Canal, 25 miles in front of us. Great parachutist scare.

12 May

Up to the OP again at first light. At 0630 I was relieved, drove back to Battery HQ across Louvain, luckily in a quiet spell. Streets near the river bridges had been well plastered; broken glass and roof tiles, tram wires etc., littering the streets. Saw the Colonel[1] at RHQ, gave him my intelligence report, heard of the flap my report had caused yesterday – he was very nice about it. I found the Battery wagon line in a cutting behind a large monastery. We broke into a house, found hot water, gas etc, still working, and abandoned canaries and dogs. Less air activity: we saw three Hurricanes, a great thrill. Listened to BBC news at 1800, Churchill is PM – cheers! All of us in wagon line slept wonderfully in our house. Big blaze down in Louvain.

That afternoon I wrote to my parents:

1 pm Sunday 12 May – Whitsunday, incredible! I certainly returned in medias res! Only three days ago I was in London: since then years have gone by. It would hardly be adequate to say that I've been 'busy'. I got my first rest and quiet this morning, and heard the news for the first time since Wednesday. You can imagine my surprise and relieved delight when I heard the announcement 'The Prime Minister, Mr. Chamberlain, Sir Archibald Sinclair, etc., were received by the King this morning'. If we are to have our backs to the wall at last, it will be comforting to have such solid granite behind us. You will know roughly what I'm doing: by piecing together the news and the scraps I told you at home and by looking at the map, you'll get a shrewd idea. All is as yet so obscure that I could tell you nothing even if I were allowed to. To find out what is happening we have to tune in to the BBC.

But certain hard facts are not obscure. By today's mail came my *Spectator*, in which I found, to my delight, an article entitled 'Where is Germany's airforce?' I spent yesterday in the top of a tree, watching waves of Heinkels ceaselessly dropping their bombs all round us. That isn't as frightful as it sounds, for I've learnt in the last two days how little damage need be caused by a bomb. But I'll remember those sixty hours. And now we're settling down and adapting ourselves. Thank God man is so adaptable a creature.

So don't worry, and write often. I'm lying on a grassy bank under a tall,

1. Lt. Col. David F. Aikenhead.

feathery, green poplar, with the sun blazing and the north breeze gently rustling. The countryside is at its loveliest, almost as lovely as England, the birds are singing, the cuckoo is shouting just as loud as that day in the glen above Erbusaig – and its very good to be alive.

It *has* begun. Let's brace ourselves and finish this Schweinerei.

Our ten days together are a heavenly dream, a dream of constant joy and inspiration. So fortified, I could fight twenty Hitlers.

I've no time just now to write all the letters that I owe so many at home. Perhaps you will make copies of this and send it on. But please don't fail to send a copy straight away to Hugh [my brother], with all my love and regrets that it is so short – and of course to Mary [my sister].

And to you both, all that love which is so hard to express, from your strangely happy and tranquil son.

Diary 13 May

After breakfast up to monastery where the Battery Command Post was operating in the cellar; food and shelter, huge kitchens, comfort for all. I organised the officers' mess. After lunch drove back through Louvain to establish an OP in the ten-storey Philips Radio Factory on the eastern outskirts of the city. It overlooked the railway which formed the front line, held by KOSB: very exposed, but a grand view. Belgian troops still coming back. I did silent registration. We found beer in the factory but no radios in working order. Less bombing. Back to H Troop in the evening. A second gas scare. Stayed up till 0300 relieving Hunter [Greig] as CPO [Command Post Officer].

14 May

Back up to the factory OP soon after first light. No troops forward of it. Little activity, though bombing very close: houses ablaze in the main streets of Louvain, and incendiaries falling on the hills behind. Our fighters *occasionally* visible: A.A. incessant, its performance improving – some of its shells even got within a mile of their target! Demolitions continuing. At 1430 the 12th Lancers and the 15/19th came back across the Dyle and the bridges were blown. At the crucial moment the line to the Battery broke, but my signaller, Wilson mended it. I felt distinctly unhappy, all alone with him in the huge factory. I registered both troops on key points along the road and railway. But the main road was filling up with refugees, so I asked permission to stop shooting, which was given. Other batteries were also registering, including a medium battery which scored a direct hit on me – the walls of the factory shook like jelly. Not a sign of the enemy while the light lasted. I was angry with the Battery. Could get no orders and had no idea of what was going on.

At dusk it became clear that our infantry were in contact with the Germans all along our front line: pandemonium broke out, small arms fire all round. Wilson and I nervously poked our Brens through the windows and started to talk to each other in whispers. I got through on the phone to the Battery and a truck was promised. We went down to the factory gate and waited. The KOSB were windy, there was wild firing, both ways, and reports of sniping 5th columnists at work inside the city. Noise fearful. K truck turned up at last with [2nd Lt.] Scarlett: it took an interminable time in turning round! The city was being subjected to continuous artillery bombardment, shrapnel and shell splinters were dropping in the dark deserted streets and we lost our way. At last reached the monastery about 2130, to find the Battery about to move: my return was welcomed. I heard afterwards that enemy infantry had got into Louvain that evening but were pushed out again by the 2nd Royal Ulster Fusiliers.

We moved at 2200, about two miles northwards, through bad traffic jams and shelling of our road. Into action near Velthem, H Troop forward, I in the rear, CPs in cellars and a nearby windmill. We were now in support of the 7th Guards Brigade, and the 2nd East Yorks, who were in reserve, were all around us. It was nearly 0500 when the move was finally completed, but I was *worn out* and slept soundly through all the noise.

15 May

A day of digging. The enemy resumed his attacks, and I sat in the Command Post, dealing with urgent measures from RHQ, calls for concentrations, smoke screens, etc. Later I relieved George [Potts] as I Troop's GPO [Gun Position Officer]. For a time the 1st Coldstreams were forced back, and we fired in support of a counter-attack by the 5th Inniskillings, which was successful. Watty [Scott-Plummer] liaised all day and the following night in a front-line trench with the Grenadiers. More parachutist scares – we are beginning to be bored by them. I got to bed at midnight.

16 May

At first light, 0345, drove up by winding tracks onto the ridge of the Roesselberg, found an OP on the edge of a fir plantation near a Guards company HQ. Despite the many trees there was a good view of Mont César, on the far side of the valley, and of the Dyle, with the towers and spires of Louvain in the distance. The ridge was being shelled pretty continuously and the Guards had serious casualties. There were periodic signs of enemy movement and I could have had some good shooting had my telephone line not broken. Watty remained with the Coldstreams, who kept calling for SOS fire and were delighted with the Regiment's support. When the line was at last repaired, I was recalled to Battery HQ, just in time to eat a lunch of looted chicken. I acted as CPO while Hunter rested, then myself settled down to three hours' sleep, in preparation for relieving Watty for the night with the Guards. But at 1600 come orders to move at once about ten miles back along the main Brussels road to Nosseghem, where we were to report to the 15/19th. As we discovered next day, this was not because the enemy had made any progress on our front but because they had broken through the French line on the Meuse, far to our south.[1]

1. German tanks broke through the French defences at Sedan on the River Meuse, north of the termination of the Maginot Line, on 14 May.

Night 16/17 May

The Battery moved off at 1730 under heavy shelling, which hit the windmill, but there were no casualties. We had to dump a lot of ammunition, but BQMS Higdon had time to kill a pig and load it on his truck. At Nosseghem there was no sign of the 15/19th. After a long wait and a vain search, we eventually received orders to move 35 miles back to Eekent, on the west side of the River Dendre about 20 miles west of Brussels. It was a nightmare march, round the northern outskirts of Brussels, past the royal Laeken Palace. The Belgian Government had left the capital, but the population was calm. An old Belgian man rushed up to me and tried to present me with the Uhlan sword which he had acquired in the First World War, evidently wishing to be rid of it before the Germans arrived for the second time. March discipline was appalling, with trucks of other units and Belgian civilian cars cutting into our column, and at one stage we were driving three abreast down the main road. There was some bombing and machine-gunning from the air, but we suffered no damage. The sappers were mining all the bridges and there were traffic blocks at every canal crossing. After dark a further problem arose: when moving off after one of the innumerable halts, one or several vehicles would hold up the column because all its occupants had fallen asleep. After crossing the Dendre at Ninove we lost our way because we were off the maps we had been using at Louvain. At 0130 we found ourselves in a field at the end of a cul-de-sac, where every vehicle had to turn round on boggy ground. I was given the job of supervising the chaotic operation, which was made worse by many drivers falling asleep. We were in fact within a mile of Eekent, our destination, but it was 0500 before I finally brought the last vehicle into the pleasant orchard where the Battery was parked, and settled down to sleep.

17 May

A quiet day of rest and maintenance. We set up our Officers' Mess in the orchard and fed outside – eggs, chickens etc., were plentiful and we ate well.

18 May

We slept very well. I talked to Battery HQ about the German breakthrough in the south, which appeared to be threatening our lines of communication. A huge meal of roast pork. At 1400 orders were received to move five miles north to Denderhautem, to support the 7th Guards Brigade on the Dendre line. The traffic congestion was appalling but both troops were safely in action before dark. A jumpy night, with spy scares and sentries shooting wildly at every slight noise or movement, whether human or animal.

19 May

I got only 1½ hours sleep. From 0300 to 1030 I Troop fired 150 rounds per gun at targets taken off the map. The Battery started moving back at 0930 towards the river Escaut [Scheldt], which was to be the new main line of defence. We did a series of leap-frogging actions, taking up successive positions about 6000 yards behind each other for about 20 miles. We were covering the rearguard of 3 Div, and we passed and re-passed lorries of Guards on the way. At times it seemed almost a farce, like playing at soldiers, because after about midday there was no contact with the enemy. Great anxiety in the afternoon about crossing the Escaut: our route was over the bridge at Pecq, just north of Tournai, but there were reports, which proved true, that it had been blown. After a long wait we were suddenly ordered to turn right and make for Audenarde, which we had watched being heavily bombed, as rapidly as we could: but all went well, and we were almost the last to cross. Then a long clear run up the Escaut valley, along the road on which we had advanced nine days before, to an area of orchards east of Dottignies, arriving about 2200. We all had a night of blessed peace and long sleep: but news came that the Germans were still advancing rapidly towards the sea, behind our backs.

20 May

A day of rest and maintenance, very hot sun. I slept for hours. Our troops getting rather out of hand with looting and wanton destruction – but in the circumstances difficult to restrain them. In the afternoon positions were reconnoitred north of Dottignies in the grounds of a farm named Brasye: a beautiful building, with courtyard, moat, barns and stables, timber doors, slits in the wall. We had to turn refugees out of the cellar – a nasty job. One old man was impossible to move – he just repeated over and over again, "I stay with the animals". The guns moved into action by moonlight, and gun pits and slit trenches were dug all night. I spent an excellent night on a real bed.

21 May

By first light the enemy had made contact all along the Escaut, and during the day made several attempts to cross the river; but on our front the pressure on the 7th Guards Brigade was not heavy. We received the order, "We stop here till the last round". There were reports that the Germans had reached the sea at Abbeville [which was true] and had also captured Arras, the location of British GHQ [which was not true – quite yet].[1] With our lines of communication cut to our main supply bases, and no rations coming up, we were ordered to rely on local resources: sheep, pigs, hens and eggs were collected from the farms and tinned food from shops in Dottignies. The farmers in the Battery came into their own and milked the cows. Very little activity, though we heard reports that an enemy crossing at Pecq had been repulsed.

22 May

More food collection in the morning. No shelling, to our surprise. Some local residents came back to milk their cows. Bede departed, protesting, for Calais and

---

1. Arras was evacuated on 23 May.

home, to command a regiment: it seemed doubtful if he would get through.[1] Bill took over command of the Battery. I looked for OPs along the Escaut, tried Espierres church and a number of houses overlooking the villages down the valley; but none were suitable owing to the thick trees. Across the river I spotted a German working party, a lorry and what looked like a platoon moving into action, and at one point a sniper took a pot shot at me.

When I got back to Brasye I found recce parties had already left: we were not to "stay till the last round", but instead to retreat once more, ten miles back to the line of defence behind the French frontier which we had been preparing all winter. For reasons which were not clear, we were to occupy not the positions near Wattrelos on which we had worked, but positions further north, west of Tourcoing, which had been prepared by 4 Div.

Night 22/23 May

We moved off at 2300: full moon, lovely night. Guns in action by 0330.

23 May

A very quiet day. The 7th Guards Brigade had made no contact. I spent the morning in the wagon line, five miles to the rear in a brickyard, then back to Battery HQ in the afternoon to relieve Hunter in the Command Post. Everyone was digging trenches. We had our first rain in the evening since the battle began.

24 May

I started the day in the Command Post. Shortage of ammunition restricted firing. Then about 1100 came a cryptic message from RHQ, telling us to prepare for a 'change of scenery'. We soon learned that we were to leave 3 Div and move westward to meet the enemy advancing in our rear. Since Louvain we had been facing an enemy coming from the east, now we were to face him coming from the opposite direction. Our orders were to join POLFORCE, an improvised formation put together to cover BEF's right flank and right rear. At 1300 the Colonel and Bill set off to meet its commander, Col. Wood, at his HQ at Sailly-sur-Lys. The Battery started at 1400 down the main road to Lille, our CRA, Roland Tower, standing on the roadside to bid us goodbye. A clear run through what was familiar country. To our north Armentières was being bombed, there were thick columns of smoke rising from the towns to our south, and the air was acrid with the smell of burning. We reached our rendez-vous just outside Fromelles in the late afternoon. Bill arrived from Sailly about 2000 to tell us that our orders had been changed: we were to join MACFORCE, commanded by Maj. Gen. F. N. Mason-Macfarlane, and our task would be to form part of the anti-tank defence of Hazebrouck. We drove another 15 miles north-west to Borre, two miles east of Hazebrouck, where we received orders to take up anti-tank positions north of the town. But just as we were coming into action, the CO arrived with orders that we

---

1. He did get through to England, returned to France as commander of an anti-tank regiment and was killed in action soon afterwards.

were to remain on wheels all night. So we packed the Battery into two fields and a farmyard, with single guns guarding the approaches from the main road. A magnificent hot meal arrived from B Echelon and we tried to settle down to sleep in a state of utter bewilderment and confusion.

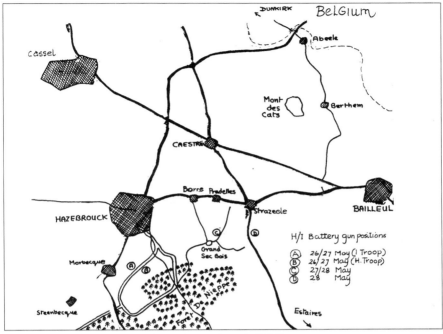

Area of operations, 24/29 May.

25 May

At 0230 George, who had been sent to Cassel to liaise with MACFORCE, returned with the news that the force was being disbanded. We stood to at 0330, but there was no sign of the enemy, so we went back to sleep. About midday we heard that we were now under command of 44 Home Counties [Territorial] Division. An uneventful day of maintenance and anti-tank drill, and a quiet night.

26 May

We stood to again at 0330, but all was quiet, so went back to sleep. In the morning we had another session of anti-tank drill. There was very little air activity over us, though we heard bombing in the distance. We watched the local residents walking to and from mass in their Sunday best – a reminder of civilisation. At 1330 Bill went off to HQ 132 Infantry Brigade, where he got orders that the Battery was to go into action north-west of the Forêt de Nieppe, near Morbecque, two miles south of Hazebrouck. I Troop moved into a forward position west of the canal which ran south from Hazebrouck, and was in action in time for Watty to do some registration before dark from his OP in Morbecque church. Heavy rain had set in during the afternoon. I took food and petrol up to the forward position, returning in the dark to the Command Post which was situated in the cellars of a farmhouse on the eastern side of the canal, close to H Troop. The Royal West Kents were in front of us. A quiet night and I slept well.

27 May

Watty moved at first light from Morbecque church to the high ground north of Steenbecque and about 0800 engaged advancing German tanks, motor cycles, troop-carrying vehicles, and later infantry on foot. At 1100 he went back to Morbecque and directed the fire of the Battery for two more hours, with the expenditure of 100 rounds per gun. I took two 30-cwt lorry loads of ammunition up to I's position. On return I found an OP near H Troop on the top of a haystack – somewhat precarious – inside a barn, from which there was a good view to the west of Morbecque and the canal running north to Hazebrouck, and of the Mont des Cats in the distance. John [Harington, Battery Captain] later joined me. We saw a convoy of British lorries ablaze. At 1300 Watty returned to his troop, which was being heavily shelled, and two hours later 200 German infantry appeared only 700 yards away: they were engaged over open sights and the troop pulled out with bullets whistling and the Germans within 400 yards. H Troop fired to cover I's retirement to a position east of the canal, from which it continued to engage advancing infantry. During the afternoon H Troop and Battery HQ came under very heavy shelling. At 1800, after laying down a small smoke screen to block the view from Morbecque church, H moved out to new positions about two miles to the north-east near the village of Grand Sec Bois. I went to meet I Troop and guided them to a position close to H. John manned an OP, from which he spotted unidentified tanks on the high ground between Borre and Pradelles, about 1500 yards to the north. They turned out to be German but fortunately didn't come our way. In the evening both troops sent out strong patrols. An officer of the Ox & Bucks from Hazebrouck told us that tanks were breaking through in our direction, so I was sent out to establish a listening patrol on the high ground to the north-west. It was an eerie experience: most of the time the only sound was the gentle hum of the wireless set, with occasional small arms fire in the distance. It was a lonely task, and not easy to keep awake. It rained.

28 May

I was glad to get back to the Battery at 0515, hoping to be able to sleep. But at 0630 came the news, which seemed almost incredible at the time, that BEF was withdrawing to the coast, and that all kits were to be immediately destroyed, only one blanket and a full pack per man to be retained. All officers' mess equipment had to be abandoned, and the cases of champagne which we had 'acquired' during our retreat were smashed. OPs were meanwhile sent out but saw no targets. It seemed that the Germans were pushing on north of us towards Cassel and Mont des Cats. In the early afternoon the Battery retired about another mile to a position just east of the main Strazeele-Estaires road. There was very little firing. Tanks were heard from the gun line, and there were rumours of tanks to our left and rear, but these were never confirmed. I Troop took up an anti-tank position and during the day our guns covered just about every point of the compass. It rained hard and everyone got soaked.

Night 28/29 May

At 2100 H Troop moved off north-eastwards to two successive rendez-vous, where we waited for orders. There was a lot of traffic, some shelling and a great deal of smoke. We were tired, wet, and cold, and the atmosphere was one of total muddle and chaos. Finally about midnight L/N's Battery Commander brought us news that we were to take part in the defence of Mont des Cats for the whole of tomorrow, then make for Dunkirk.

At 0115 we started to move on northwards, interweaving with every kind of British and French vehicle and many loose horses. After two miles we found our road blocked by ditched and abandoned vehicles. With great difficulty we constructed a detour through cut wire and hedges and across two fields: this took about an hour. At 0300 in the small village of Berthem, close under Mont des Cats, we came to a final standstill: the road for miles ahead was totally blocked. Orders were given to destroy wireless sets and sights, remove breech blocks and puncture all tyres. It was impossible to destroy the guns themselves without danger to the crowds passing by on foot.

29 May

The dismal work of destruction was completed by first light, and I set off on foot with H Troop, Battery HQ and B Echelon, a party of about seventy, for Dunkirk, about 25 miles distant. For about five miles we had to walk in single file through the solid block of British and French vehicles. We passed through one village which had been completely flattened by bombing and was littered with charred corpses. At 0530 Bill decided to lie up in a wood near Abeele, in the hope of linking up with I Troop, which had been moving on a different road. German planes were busy overhead as soon as it was light. About 0800 contact was made with I Troop, which still had some vehicles: so our party was able to ride for about another ten miles, very slowly and along side roads, the main roads being more likely to attract the enemy's attention. We crossed a small salient of Belgian territory and only with difficulty found our way round Watou, which had been made impassable by bombing. At Westhoek we had finally to abandon our vehicles and continue on foot. It was very hot. On reaching the canal which ran in a semi-circle round Dunkirk, we rested for an hour in a barn and ate. There was a mass of burning vehicles on the canal bank and all the pitiful signs of a rout. French troops were much in evidence as they were defending Dunkirk on the west, and we passed a defence post manned by the Guards: the canal was to form the last line of defence. Gerry went ahead on a motor-cycle to reconnoitre, and about 1630 we crossed the canal and marched the last eight miles across flat country, much of it flooded, towards Malo les Bains, the eastern seaside suburb of Dunkirk.

There were several air raids, with British fighters engaged, and the air was thick with bursting A.A. shells. Our spirits rose as we caught our first sight of the sea, and felt a sea breeze on our faces, at the end of a narrow street leading down to the beach. But at that very moment the dive-bombers came over again, and we witnessed two destroyers being hit and disabled, and four transports sunk. To our left thick columns of black smoke were rising from tankers ablaze in the harbour. We sheltered for a time in cellars, then about 1800 made our way to the beach where many thousands of troops were massed, waiting helplessly for information and orders. There appeared to be no organisation. Many soldiers were wading out to sea, to be picked up by small boats, but we decided to stick together as naval ships were taking substantial numbers off the eastern mole of the harbour. Meanwhile we searched some of the abandoned houses and found food and several bottles of cognac. Though the RAF was increasingly visible, the raids continued and a few bombs landed on the beach. One fell within 15 feet of Henry [Wharfedale] and killed five persons, none of them ours. It was therefore a huge relief when darkness came. Late in the evening we started moving slowly in groups along the beach towards the mole, about 20 yards per hour.

30 May

By 0300 it was clear that there was no hope of embarking before daylight. As the beach was then likely to become unpleasantly unsafe, we cleared out the cellars in a house opposite our place in the queue and installed our party in it. Bill and Watty continued their search for stragglers, from RHQ and L/N as well as H/I, and our party grew to 140. Water was obtained from a water cart (the water supply to all the houses having been ruptured), food and cookers were scrounged from abandoned lorries, and I was able to draw some meagre rations from an improvised depot commanded by a Brigadier. So everyone was able to wash and shave and eat a hot meal.

There was a fog at first light, followed by a few bombing raids, but the RAF was much in evidence and there were no casualties on the beach. One RAF plane suddenly zoomed out of the mist just above our heads and was fired on by our own A.A. Later in the day there was enemy shelling, mainly near the mole, sporadic and inaccurate. There were hundreds of rifles and Brens lying around, and unlimited ammunition, with which we armed ourselves in case we had to fight.

An effective organisation for embarkation had meanwhile been set up, and a picket established across the beach to regulate access to the mole. At 1000 we were given the serial number of 69, when no. 6 was just moving off. As a long wait was evidently in prospect, the officers set up an improvised mess in the house above the cellar which our party had taken over; a shop was raided for deck chairs and we spent much of the day comfortably eating, drinking and chatting, and falling into rather drunken sleep. We also watched the small boats arriving – yachts, launches, dinghies, tugs, barges – picking up the waders and ferrying them out to an assortment of naval and merchant vessels lying off-shore.

At 1930 we were ordered to take over the picketing. An hour later came our turn: we handed over the picket and set off up the 300 yards of the mole at the double, with shells falling 100 yards away on the far side of the narrow harbour entrance, and leapt aboard the destroyer flotilla leader HMS *Codrington*. It sailed at 2130, with a thousand aboard. The crew welcomed us with biscuits and coffee. I found a space to lie down deep in the bowels of the ship, and was only dimly conscious of the frequent zig-zagging of our course and the noise of our own pom-poms. We arrived in Dover harbour at 0130 on 31 May.

CHAPTER THREE: WAITING FOR THE INVASION
June – October 1940

On landing at Dover Marine station we entered a different world – calm, organised, normal and at peace. I described what happened to us a week later in a letter to my parents from the Devonshire village of South Zeal:

On Friday morning [31 May] as we streamed off the destroyers at Dover, they pushed us into trains and sent us off, with hardly half an hour's delay, to the four corners of England. The important thing was to get us away from the ports as soon as possible and clear the way for the rest of us coming on behind. The organisation was superb. From the time we were whisked off the beach at Dunkirk to the time when we reached this Devonshire village, we just sat back and watched other people working – no worry, no activity, no thinking required. You can't think what a relief that was. Three of us from H/I managed to stick together and found ourselves, after ten hours in the train, at Exeter. The trains from the two platforms next to ours finished at Nottingham and at Newcastle Emlyn, 10 miles from Aberystwyth. It so happened that the train after ours went to Winchester: it was a pity I didn't strike that one. But there was no choice, and none of us had any idea where we were going till we tumbled out at the other end.

And so we arrived at Exeter, a motley crown of infantry and sappers and gunners, base ordnance and police and R.A.S.C., everything imaginable. We were met and looked after by the depot of the Devonshires, and among their officers I found James Joll, who was at Kenny's at Winchester, got fourth scholarship to New College my term, and was reading Greats at the same time as I read P.P.E. The adjutant was also a Wykehamist, a year senior to me in Beloe's, and that turned out very useful. On arrival we bathed, were supplied with new clothes, fed royally, registered our names and units, and *slept*! Then gradually during the next three days they sorted us out by divisions and corps and regiments, and sent us off in driblets to our re-forming areas and depots. I enjoyed my time at Exeter very much. It was nice meeting James Joll. I had lunch in his mess one day and we talked quietly of friends and those bygone Oxford days. He lent me some gently serious books, and did a lot to soothe me. There were three of us from H/I, as I said, and we spent Sunday afternoon at Exmouth together. It's a nice little place, not too crowded or vulgar. We basked on the sand, didn't quite dare to bathe, got very sunburnt, ate Devonshire cream and ices and a huge meal at the Imperial

Hotel, and returned in a crammed branch line train, rattling through the green, peaceful countryside with the sun just going down and turning the whole estuary of the Exe into flaming gold. Next day we went to Lyme Regis and spent a heavenly afternoon on the little stone jetty at the mouth of the toy harbour. That was where I wrote my letter to Hugh and dreamt of puffins and seals at Kyle, with the water lapping the stone blocks at my feet and the sea an almost Hebridean blue. Those two expeditions restored me to sanity, and I'm glad now that I was sent off like that for the first few days to a town I'd never seen before. I was not in a state to enjoy forty-eight hours' leave a week ago. I should have spent most of it in bed, and you would have got no coherent story of our doings. I've had time since then to digest those hectic three weeks, and to think of the things I want to tell you.

Otherwise we did little at Exeter except report every three hours or so at the depot in the hope of getting further orders. I went to Communion on Sunday morning at the cathedral, a most refreshing service in that cool and beautiful building. The rest of us went to a thanksgiving service for the BEF at 9.30, also in the cathedral. I thought it was a bit early to give thanks for the BEF when, so far as was known, only a small portion of it had then got away, and so went to communion instead – not because I had no thanks to offer, but because I had a feeling that the service would be inadequate for the occasion. And I was right. The sermon was preached by the Dean – I think so, but I may be slandering him – who was most emotional, and referred in dramatic tones to 'the mangled corpses of your comrades lying in pools of blood on the sands at Dunkirk'.[1] It's amazing how little 'sense' or 'taste' or 'feeling' some people have.

On Tuesday morning we came on to Okehampton, a delightful little town sitting in a deep hole in the hills, out of which all the roads climb with fearsome curves and sweltering gradients. It is a gunner metropolis and, with Larkhill, one of the few artillery ranges in the country. We were put into a reception camp, many gunner regiments mixed up together, and told we might be there for some time. It was a lovely camp, brand new, with the tents still being put up and feeding and other arrangements still rather chaotic. But we had pleasantly little to do and spent most of the day lying under the magnificent chestnuts that surrounded the whole camp. In the evening of the day we got there, our colonel and adjutant[2] turned up, and yesterday we moved over here. We are five miles from Okehampton, in lovely country, steep and wooded, and melting in this fierce sunshine. Behind the attractive stone village is a round heathery tor called 'the Beacon', which I intend to climb one cool evening: it must be well over 1,000 feet. Our camp is on the top of a brae which catches the breeze, in a small field of clover with a wide view over the village to the Beacon. All our officers are billeted in the village and we mess at the most attractive pub I've ever seen, the Cottenham Arms. It must be very old; it's beautifully furnished with oak to match

1. The last troops were evacuated during the night 2/3 June.

2. Capt. Ainslie Miller.

the beams, has walls inches thick, and is a haven of coolness in this heat.

Of the nine officers in our Battery, eight are here already and the ninth is on his way. We have had the most amazing good fortune the whole way through, and will be able to re-form almost completely.

The future is very vague. We probably won't stay here very long, but will move shortly to some more accessible centre to re-equip and do some short intensive training before moving across the Channel again. How long we shall have to wait before being re-equipped no one as yet knows. It looks as if it won't be so long as some of us had feared, and our regiment should be one of the first to go. I sincerely hope so, for I don't relish the thought of sitting lazily in Devonshire while the French Army is hammered and bombed and blown to pieces on the Somme. We are all anxious to be off again as soon as we can – but we want some leave first! We'll all get forty-eight hours at home in due course, probably starting in a week's time. But at the moment the railways are blocked and hopelessly overworked, and inevitably several hours of the precious forty-eight would be spent on dusty railway platforms. So for the moment we are getting no leave. I'll wire you as soon as I'm given a date. I too am longing for a quiet talk in a punt on the Cher.

Yes, I've returned to a very different England. Do you remember discussing less than a year ago, I forget with whom, the theme 'England is decadent'? I remember comparing this country to a seething, ardent volcano of youthful, constructive energy, enclosed by a thick crust of complacency, short-sighted timidity and incompetent Micawber-like lack of enterprise. Now the volcano has erupted. Little do we know where we are going, but it's at least to the promise of better things. Let us pray that the terrible failure on the Meuse was the beginning, not only of victory but of a revolution comparable to 1789: a revolution not of bloodshed but of the mind and spirit. Did you see that the French military spokesman, commenting on the Meuse break-through, said "Our failure has been intellectual"? In that phrase he summed up twenty years. Failure not only to foresee German methods of totalkrieg, but failure to foresee the methods of Nazi treachery and conquest, failure to foresee the power that evil can obtain over the world. There must be no more intellectual failures, no more dazed and frightened Leopolds, no more bespattered cigar-loving counter jumpers, no more smug Chamberlains and Nevile Hendersons. We must be unflinching, not only in our Hurricanes, on our battleships, behind our Brens – but in thought and mental effort. And the greatest task of all will be, when this horror has passed, to prevent this blessed island from falling asleep again.

Meanwhile we must be prepared for the loss of Paris and many more trials, but we will win through. And so I'll come to an end – my first adequate letter for many long weeks. Yes, a different England. And a different me – perhaps! – but I hope you"ll be able to judge that for yourself very soon.

The letter from Lyme Regis to my brother, who was in Bucharest, was written on 3 June:

I expected this war to take me to odd places, but not to so unlikely a town as Exeter. I've been there three days now, doing little else but eat and sleep, with a dander in the afternoons. And now I can confidently pronounce myself sane once more. I am writing this on the end of the stone jetty at Lyme Regis, with the easterly breeze ruffling the Channel into white horses and the blue waves rolling placidly into the tiny yacht-filled harbour. The hot June sun is crinkling this paper as I write. I have been thinking of those days at Freshwater on leave-out days at Winchester, and wish there were a few puffins here today. It is a beautiful, peaceful evening, and I'm trying hard not to doze off to sleep.

I spent an hour his morning with a French captain of a tank regiment who came over the Channel on the same destroyer as me. I asked him what he thought of Exeter. His answer was "Pour ces gens la guerre n'existe pas. Voilà, ce qui m'effraie". The ladies of the suburbs still do their Saturday afternoon shopping at Marks and Spencers, the ladies of the close still go to 8 o'clock communion at the cathedral. The charabancs still pass through, loaded and labelled for Torquay. The pubs and the flicks are crammed, the pavements are blocked with prams. "Of course," you'll say: but I felt ashamed that the French captain was seeing it all. I'm used to it by now, but for the first two days it was all miraculous – walking past shops full of food, turning a tap and seeing water run, looking down streets without a single window broken or a single house in flames.

And yet just the other side of this blue, smiling Channel there is hell raging. That's the word the picture papers and the Daily Horrors love to use. But hell it is, and there is no other word. And I think it will come nearer home than Calais and Dunkirk.

I can't describe those three weeks because I haven't yet digested them. In time I'll produce some coherent account, but at the moment they seem a jangled mass of talk and noise and movement, with the pieces of the puzzle all blurred and without any relation or proportion. They were three weeks of little sleep and constant moving. We travelled just over 1,000 miles in all. I was always furiously busy, sometimes very frightened and often very angry – with myself for not being more competent, with all the exasperating nuisances (mostly human) which crop up in a battle, but chiefly with the stupid sense of helplessness with which we had to watch that green countryside and those clean, prosperous towns and villages so swiftly pounded into mangled remnants of terror, suffering and desolation. You will probably have seen accounts and photographs of the B.E.F.s triumphant entry into Belgium, the long trail of refugees, the endless bombing, our all-too-rapid retreat, and the climax on Dunkirk beach. At times I still ask myself whether I've really seen those things at first hand. It seems so preposterous that they could have happened, and Exeter and Devonshire still remain outwardly the same.

But why go on like this? I have to catch a train back to Exeter in a quarter of an hour and so must stop. I've told the parents that I'm not going to write. I don't know where to begin, and as I said before, I haven't yet digested the last three weeks. What is going to happen to me now is still vague. Our regiment will collect shortly at some depot and reform, and will no doubt soon be off once again. I certainly hope that this blank period of waiting will soon end, for now that I'm rested and restored to sanity, sitting idly in this corner of England seems a waste of precious time. In any case I feel with the French captain that our place is not in Exeter, but on the Somme.

On 13 June the regiment moved by train to the western edge of the New Forest. Regimental HQ was billeted in the village of Downton, H/I up the hill at Redlynch with our officers' mess established in the saddle room and servants' hall of Redlynch House. Our expectations to be rapidly re-equipped and sent back to France proved wildly unrealistic: on 17 June the French signed an armistice, and what was left of the BEF was withdrawn. Meanwhile Mussolini had declared war a week earlier.

Diary 16 June

At 1200 all officers met Sidney Wason, MGRA, BEF. He promised us a rifle per man, possibly a couple of Brens and Boyes, and infantry training pamphlets, in the near future. We must become infantrymen as there is no hope of re-equipment for months.

I got my forty-eight hours leave on 19 June and spent it with my parents in Oxford, where my father was working in the Foreign Research and Press Service of the Foreign Office, located in Balliol College.

24 June

We are hard at work devising a local defence scheme, with posts surrounding Redlynch village, an OP on the ridge towards Old Inn, blocks on all roads. We cooperate with the LDVs [Local Defence Volunteers] who somewhat reinforce our otherwise very thin red line. We have a rifle a man, and provide two sergeants as instructors for the LDV. They are a keen lot, old soldiers and boys under military age.

28 June

A great day. In spite of Sidney Wason's gloomy prophecies, two brand-new 25-pdrs, straight from Vickers, Newcastle, arrived for the Battery.

Shortly afterwards we received our first quads, tractors with four-wheel drive. Our infanteering days were over, and by 10 July we were almost fully re-equipped and ready to resist the invasion which most of us thought would come.

Letter 1 July

I do wish people in this island would take the war more seriously. I'm convinced that Hitler will try invasion on the grand scale. It will fail, of course. But we'll have some horrible shocks. And even now, with this government, we seem only half-hearted in our preparations.

In church yesterday we had a fiery sermon from the local vicar, a splendid old Tory. He denounced fifth columnists and defeatists as instruments of the powers of darkness working in our midst against the Holy Spirit. Rather crudely phrased, but he is maybe right. But I wish there was less talk of the righteousness of our cause, and less crude simplification of the issue into a struggle of good versus evil. Believing as I do in the existence of a God. I cannot believe that Hitler could have achieved so much without the assent of God. The righteousness is not all on one side. Let us therefore humbly pray to be considered worthy of preservation and victory. Don't let us assume that God is automatically on our side. We have got to make ourselves worthy of his help, to show our worth. Have we yet? Let us be humble, and realise our share in the world's misery today, the toil and responsibility that the asking of God's aid entails.

My phraseology is picturesque, and chosen with reluctance. But it is simply what I believe. It would be better in less biblical language, but the meaning would be the same.

Diary, 4 July

Great parachutist scare. An old woman in Downton saw 'three balloons' descending from sky. Later 'confirmed' by LDVs, etc. We and L/N sent out patrols over the downs, pursuing mysterious lights. In spite of flap, regimental cocktail party at RHQ was a great success. Being orderly officer I couldn't attend, and later had to sleep on the telephone in the adjutant's office. Woken up at 2 am by Scarlett who turned out H/I to surround wood full of scampering rabbits. Otherwise undisturbed, and sanity returned with morning.

On 11 July we moved by road, 120 miles, to Rushden in Northamptonshire, passing through Oxford on the way.
Letter, 17 July

I wonder if you got my last letter in time to turn out and watch 2RHA rumbling majestically up the Banbury Road. It was raining hard as we passed through and I hardly expected you to be there. In any case I was leading the Battery in a high-powered Humber 8-cwt truck which I was driving for the first time, and was having considerable difficulty in keeping to the official 18mph. So I had eyes for little but the road.

Rushden is not a bad little town. It has excellent shops, even Boots and Woolworths, and a lovely public park. The troops have got the best billets they've ever had, with the choice of three cinemas and innumerable pubs. I'm billeted with a charming little woman, Mrs. Jacques, who insists on heating the water for my baths, giving me early morning tea and washing my socks.

We are beginning to find out what's in store for us, and it's going to be interesting. We will be working hard, and all thoughts of leave will be in vain.

We were now part of the Support Group of 2nd Armoured Division, at eight hours' notice to move. Training was continuous and there were corps and divisional schemes, reminiscent of our winter exercises in France. Our task would be to help repel invasion from any point on the east coast from the Humber to the Thames.

Letter, 26 July

Again a long delay between letters, but this time I've a good reason. A week ago we were warned to prepare ourselves for an inspection 'by an important personage' on Wednesday last. Everyone leapt to the conclusion that it would be the King, and we put in three days of back-breaking, brain-racking work, cleaning our lorries, polishing our guns, pressing our battle dress and cutting our hair. On Wednesday we drove about 20 miles northwards, beyond Kettering, and there lined up in a huge field, together with the other four units of the Support Group of our division. The frontage from right to left must have been fully half a mile, and it was an impressive sight. We then stood for nearly two hours in driving rain, almost a Skye sou'wester. At last the long line of staff cars drove into our field, and who should step out of the first but Winston. Some of the troops were disappointed that it wasn't the King, but most of them were just as pleased to see Winston. As he passed me, he remarked in his typical way, "The right of the line and the terror of the world": being the senior regiment in the Support Group, we were drawn up on the extreme right. On our way back to Rushden we 'marched past' him in column, with all our vehicles and guns. He stood there waving his hat in acknowledgement of the cheers and smoking his cigar, and was obviously childishly intrigued by everything that drove past. He was in great form, quite undaunted by the weather, and cheered us up a lot.

On 16 August the Regiment moved out of its comfortable Rushden billets to a camp at Horseheath, three miles beyond Linton on the Cambridge – Colchester road.

22 August

Here we are under canvas, and for the last two days have all been shivering in our tents. The chief snag is that we are on chalk, which makes digging very hard work. We've been doing a lot of digging, for although there have been few bombs dropped in this neighbourhood, we get a good many warnings, and I fancy German planes are overhead most of the day.

The reason for our move is to be 40 miles nearer Hitler when he comes. I still think he'll try – it's not too late. But my conviction is being shaken, I admit. If the invasion is attempted, we'll be in the thick of it. If it doesn't, we're in for a winter of intense boredom, punctuated with intense air raids. Or, what is not at all unlikely, we'll be sent out to Egypt.

Diary, 5 September

First mass night air raid on London – we could see red glow in the sky from our mess. It was obvious that there were colossal fires in the docks area. Are things working to a climax?

7/8 September

At 2330 we got orders to pack and stand ready to move at no notice. So the Battery was aroused from its beds and worked magnificently, loading until 0300.

46

Full moon, full tide, perfect weather – the day for invasions if ever. But at 1300 'flap off' received.

This was the night of the great scare when the bells of the parish churches of England were rung to raise the alarm.

Letter, 21 September

This afternoon has been glorious. I have been sitting up on the hill above our camp, writing a few gentle letters and looking very lazily at the peaceful Cambridgeshire countryside. The only discordant sound was the drone and booming of Hurricanes and Blenheims miles up in the sky above the fleecy clouds: and there are many worse sounds than that.

Inspections are one cause of our disgruntledness. Since we arrived in this division we have been inspected by Churchill, a Brigade Commander, our divisional general, the C in C, the Duke of Gloucester and Eden. Each time it meant spending a whole day on cleaning and polishing our guns and vehicles and ourselves, and wasting valuable time which should have been spent on training. My suggestion is that we should invite the Royal Family, the War Cabinet and every general in the British, Canadian, Australian, New Zealand, French, Belgian, Dutch, Czech, Polish and Norwegian armies, not forgetting the Archbishop of Canterbury, to visit us on a given day, and that in return we should be given a solemn promise to be left alone for the rest of the war. But I'm afraid it won't be appreciated by 'them'.

27 September

I spent yesterday in Rushden, and only tore myself away with much regret. It is filling up with evacuees from London at an alarming pace. The two infantry battalions with which we are working in this division are recruited entirely from the East End. Most of them have been back for 24 hours' leave, and the efficiency of their units has increased amazingly since their return. Some, but not many, are saying, "What's the use of it all, let's have done with it". I was talking to a sergeant a week ago and discussing invasion possibilities. He, like everyone else, hoped it would be soon. "And," he said, "when they come, we'll take no prisoners. Parachute troops *can't* take prisoners. Why should we?" If an intelligent Englishman is talking like that, just think what the unintelligent Pole and Czech is saying!

On 5 October I had just had an hour's sleep in the afternoon when George burst in on me and said we were going abroad shortly. I was to be one of the advance party which would be sent off immediately on a week's embarkation leave. Next morning I took the train from Cambridge to Oxford, telephoned my father from Bletchley and was met by him at the station, where I told him of my 'bombshell'. The next week was spent with my parents and friends, partly in Oxford, partly in London. On 13 October I returned to Rushden. On the 19th I set off as commander of a convoy of sixty-five vehicles on a three day drive, mostly in soaking rain, to Dundee, where the vehicles were to be loaded for our 'unknown' destination

Letter, 25 October, Royal Hotel, Dundee

This gray, grimy city is the friendliest I've ever been in. If you ask the way, you have to stop for ten minutes' chat. In shops, trams, hotels, restaurants, everyone takes a sincerely personal interest in us all. The police are wonderful: they have sorted out all our difficulties without a murmur or sign of fuss. Our sixty-five men were all billeted in private houses or 'board residences', and although the army billeting rates are so small that any kind-hearted landlady is sure to be out of pocket on the transaction, hardly one of them has complained and they have all said how much they enjoy 'doing their bit'. My idea of a Scottish landlady, canny and crusty, has been quite exploded.

This is the first 'command' I've ever had, and it's not an easy one. But it's great fun to be away from all higher authorities, and to be entirely on my own. Last night I sent off fifty out of the sixty-five and they should be safe back in the South by now. I have stayed on to finish the job, and tonight I am alone.

I eat very well. I have found a delightful little restaurant [The Horseshoe] patronised chiefly by hard-headed Dundee business men, where the cooking is exquisite and the menu so varied that one wishes Field-Marshal Goering and his pals could see the bill of fare. I have entirely fallen for the high tea habit. Another great virtue of Dundee, at first, was the total absence of aeroplanes. But two nights ago the banshees woke me up by howling for ten minutes at 1.45 a.m., and the 'all clear' woke me again at 4.

Most of my time was spent watching the very skilled dockers hoisting the vehicles on board S.S. Bangalore *and stowing them away in the depths of the holds. My presence was in fact entirely superfluous, but I had been instructed by our adjutant to stay on until the last vehicle was safely aboard. One morning I speculated to the foreman about our destination. He laughed and pointed to one of the crates which was clearly marked, 'RAOC Depot, Abbassia, Egypt'. "So much", I thought "for strictest secrecy".*

29 October

I arrived back here in Rushden this morning from the North, for a brief breathing-space. We are really and truly off tomorrow, and this is the last letter you will have from me for many a day. I will of course write as soon as I can. I don't feel as excited as I thought I should. This is the beginning of a new life for me, truly an adventure. And who can say where it will end? But as I wrote in a letter from Louvain last May, if ever I feel down-hearted, it is the memories of the past, of our lives and thoughts and wishes and disappointments, that give me new strength and courage. My life has been so full, and will be fuller yet in the future. What I owe to you cannot, and need not, be told. Now I have another chance to prove myself worthy of you and of my past opportunities. Let us pray that we will soon be together again, united in the work, not of destruction, but of rebuilding. God bless you.

CHAPTER FOUR: ROUND THE CAPE TO EGYPT
November – December 1940

On 30 October we travelled by train to Liverpool, where we embarked on the Scythia, *a Cunard liner of 20,000 tons.*

Letter, 31 October

This is a postscript, written on board though still in port. We arrived here yesterday, in the dusk and pouring rain, amid a scene of incredible chaos and confusion. We took three hours to get on board, and many tempers were mislaid on the way. But now we are rapidly establishing ourselves. I had a wonderful night, my first good sleep for three days. This is a very comfortable boat, not, I'm thankful to say, a trooper. We sleep four to a cabin, which is crowded, but we have a private bathroom. The troops have each a bed with a spring mattress, eat in the tourist dining saloon and walk around with a stare of blissful wonderment on their faces. The food is excellent, and at H.M's expense – that means you poor taxpayers. If the sea is kind, this voyage will be a luxurious rest-cure. So intercede with the sea for me: drink tonight to Father Neptune and ask him to appease the gales.

We set sail at noon on 1 November with the sirens howling and ten Brens mounted and manned, and by next morning found ourselves in a convoy of seventeen ships. Our escort for the first three days was two cruisers and eight destroyers, then dropped to one and two. At times they were invisible, having left us, 'U-boat chasing'.

Armistice Day, 11 November

Ten days since we sailed from England and still on the high seas. Your libations to Neptune were kindly received. The sea has been gentle with us. As soon as we reached the open sea, we began to wallow in most dignified, stately motions, on the heave of the swell. I found the dining-room too much for me one dinner, and retired to my bunk for an evening and a morning. But I forced myself to get up next afternoon to perform my duties as officer of the watch, and after a stern struggle conquered the sea. For the last week I haven't faltered. As I write we are rolling and pitching more than we have felt up to now, and above my head the wind hums in the rigging. We plod gently on, with no appearance of hurry or flurry.

Never have I known such peace of mind as during the last ten days. We have been in danger, in as great danger, I suppose, as during the last three weeks last May, but outwardly there has been little sign of it, and inwardly it has hardly touched my mind. We did our boat drill several times a day, and took it seriously. We carried our lifebelts every minute of the day and slept for the first week in our clothes. Smoking on deck after dusk was a court-martial offence. But such matters seemed less real than the peaceful throb of the engines, the breeze and blue of the sea, and the lazy warmth of the sun, so welcome after the dull, smoky drizzle in which we left England. The first week was a delectable rest, such as I've not known since I've been in this army. I read slowly through Charles Morgan's *The Voyage*, a suitable name and a suitable mood. It contributed much to my peace of mind. I started on the Forsytes. I borrowed Brogan's great opus, *Development of Modern France*, and read with melancholy interest his account of the last war and of the perilous margin by which the Republic's enemies for seventy years were kept in check, those enemies who are now so nobly regenerating and re-Christianising the French soul. And I pushed ahead with my Italian, reaching Lesson 14 of the grammar in half as many days.

Today we have started working. I am learning Morse at amazing speed, brushing up my gunnery, and giving four or more lectures on the World Situation to the whole Battery. And still I will have much leisure. We feast like kings – Messrs. Cunard's first-class peacetime standard.

Continued 13 November

After I had reached the bottom of the last page, I went out on deck and stood right up in the bows watching the flying-fish leap out of the waves and skim the white horses, away from the ship, like dragon-flies glistening in the moonlight. Tonight the moon is almost full and a wonderful sight, not cold and distant like an English moon, but very warm and gentle. There were some porpoises playing around the bows this evening, and today I saw the first birds for almost ten days. They looked like fulmars, but wouldn't come near us. We are approaching land fast: tomorrow morning there will probably be gulls hovering over us, and we should spend tomorrow night in harbour.

Today has been sultry and humid and very wearying. I gave my first lecture to the Battery this afternoon on the Mediterranean situation. I had had an hour allotted to me, but in the true Seton-Watson style I spoke for 1¼, and at the end my throat was parched and the sweat was pouring off me. By day we sit on deck in our topees and the breeze cools us. But the nights are terrible. This boat was not built for hot climes, and the ventilation is inadequate. With every door shut and every window blacked out, the fug is appalling. And many pints of iced draught lager are the only remedy.

We get little news, only the BBC overseas bulletins, but the news of the Fleet Air Arm's little party at Taranto has cheered us up.[1] There was some champagne

---

1. British naval air forces sank half the Italian battleship fleet while at anchor in Taranto harbour on 11 November.

about tonight (best vintages, 10/6 a bottle!). Chamberlain's death came in a special bulletin. And that night I found this sentence in a letter I was censoring, written by one of the humblest and most likeable gunners in the Battery: "In my opinion Mr. Chamberlain died a hero." I can afford to smile now. It is hard to think back to two years ago.

We had several days in our first port of call (from which I sent the cable, which I hope has reached you), but we were not allowed ashore. There was plenty to interest us, and we sat all day on the boat-decks spying with our glasses. Niggers swarmed round the ship, singing the 'Lambeth Walk', diving for pennies and trying to sell anything from coloured silks and shawls (products of Messrs. F.W. Woolworth) to very green bananas and most attractive monkeys. I am told we have two of them on board now, somewhere in the depths of the ship: who they belong to, or what they are fed on, is not known, and were best left unknown. One day I shall be able to tell you all that we saw in port those few days, and to describe the memorable view. But censors unfortunately encourage discretion. I hope he won't mind me telling you that the first night we were there we saw our first 'tropical' thunderstorm and felt our first 'tropical' rain; and our second night was the most beautiful I've ever known – a brilliant white moon, full and straight above us, and the thick sweet scent of the jungle, drowsy and fascinating, blown to us across the still water.

The port was Freetown, capital of Sierra Leone, where we anchored above the town on the evening of the 14th. In the harbour we saw HMS Resolution, *almost on her side, repairing her Dakar wounds, and one evening a party of her officers came over to drink, and told tales (which were hard to believe) about that 'amazing affair'.[1] We sailed on the afternoon of the 17th, a cruiser and an armed merchantman escorting us.*

Letter, 25 November

Yesterday morning I gave another lecture to the Battery on 'The World Situation'. I talked about Spain and France, and suddenly, in the middle, I found myself smiling, smiling at the ludicrous improbability of the situation. Who of us would have dreamt, eighteen months ago, that in November 1940 I should be airing my views on the Spanish Civil War, to an audience of 200 gunners, with sweat pouring from my brow, in tropical shirt and shorts, rolling gently in the midst of a southern sea, in the first-class 'garden lounge' of a Cunard liner, on my way to an 'unknown tropical destination'? Ludicrous improbability. I wish you could have seen me.

We crave for news: the BBC bulletins are short and scrappy, but it seems that Coventry and other Midland towns are suffering badly. We have several men in the battery from Coventry, Leamington and Birmingham, and their unhappiness is

---

1. An attempt to land Free French Forces, loyal to de Gaulle, at Dakar in French West Africa on 23/25 September had been frustrated by forces loyal to the Vichy Government, which was collaborating with Germany since the French defeat in June.

tragic. That's the terrible thing about this war. We can have none of the easy 'we're fighting to keep them safe at home spirit' that must have cheered many soldiers in the last war. In this war there's a two-way worry. But the news from Greece is inspiring.[1]

This may reach you before the New Year. So, my best love to you all, and a happier New Year.

On 28 November we sailed into Cape Town, past the Queen Elizabeth, *drab and giantlike, and docked in the Outer Harbour at 7.30 p.m.*
2 December

We didn't get ashore at the last port, and only stopped long enough to refuel, take on water and fresh food (we had delicious crayfish yesterday for lunch). But it was a great experience to see a town looking as if it were at peace. Streams of cars, fat newspapers, advertisements for silk stockings and luxury liner sailings, full column announcements of new films. And no black-out. We made the most of it, lights blazing from every corner of the ship and every window open. The sights of the lights twinkling round the harbour, arc-lamps, headlamps, street lamps, neon lights made me feel very homesick and very war-sick.

On 3 December we sailed into Durban where we transhipped to the Dunera, *a British India Line troop carrier of 11,500 tons.*
Diary, 3 December

The Battery installed itself on No 3 Main Deck, many moans and indignations. The contrast between officers' and troops' accommodation is indecent. We have excellent cabins, air-conditioned ventilation, dining room airy and high up, colossal deck space. Troops live, sleep, eat in a cramped deck, airy by day but little ventilation after black-out.

Letter, 13 December

We had two days ashore at the port where we changed ships. I and two others rode majestically from the docks into the town in a rickshaw pulled by what appeared to be a Zulu chieftain in full war paint. We hired a car and drove a short way into the country [to Isipingo Beach] and heard monkeys chattering and tadpoles screaming – do English tadpoles scream? It was more deafening than the frogs at Mycenae. It was pleasant setting foot on dry land again, but the port disappointed me. It was so ugly, so utterly lacking in style and character.

Our two evenings ashore were spent driving in taxis from one hotel, restaurant and night-club to another, drinking far too much and working off our pent-up energy like riotous undergraduates. We sailed on the morning of 5 December, northwards, through the Indian Ocean, escorted by HMS Cornwall, *which had been with us all the way, and an armed Australian merchantman, the* Kanimbla.

---

1. The Italian army invaded Greece from Albania on 28 October and was almost immediately repulsed.

13 December

For the first time since we sailed from England I'm beginning to feel impatient with this voyage. That is the result of the recent news from the Western Desert.[1] We still, of course, don't know for certain whether we are going there or not, but in any case we feel they might have waited for us. There have been days with not a breath of wind, when the sun blazed down on us from directly overhead, and the silky sea and sky merged in one immense expanse of pale, pale, liquid blue, a glazed surface reflecting the glare of the sun in pools of brilliant white. One afternoon we passed quite close to two whales; they were lazily basking on the surface, their long backs glistening in the sun and rippling the water, and spouting half-heartedly, as if it was really too much effort on so hot an afternoon.

I imagine England was cheered up quite a lot by Churchill's last speeches – 20,000 prisoners, an advance of 75 miles in three days – it's stupendous, I hope it took some of the sting out of the recent air raids – they must have been unpleasantly severe.

Continued 15 December

I told you that I had been lecturing to the Battery on the world situation, particularly the Mediterranean, as being more likely to interest us personally. I must confess I was flattered by the interest that was still being shown after an hour by an audience sitting on a cramped and very hard deck. Since then I've lectured to L/N, our sister Battery, and three other units. In fact, soon there'll hardly be a soldier on board who hasn't heard me bray at least once. And the questions asked at the end are, on an average, very little less intelligent or less to the point than those asked after an Oxford League of Nations Union meeting – and much more intelligent than the Oxford Labour Club.

I am becoming a devotee of curry. And of course it is real curry. As on all B.I. boats the stewards, waiters, some of the cooks and most of the crew are Indians. My cabin steward is a queer little fellow called Abdul Rahim, of Calcutta. He is so efficient that I can never find anything – all is tidied away pitilessly and ruthlessly. But I haven't attempted to understand what they say. And I don't think I was ever meant to live 'out East', in spite of my ancestors. Europe is large enough to keep me entirely happy.

Continued, 22 December

We are reaching what we believe to be our destination early tomorrow morning. So this will tell you that we have safely reached the other end.

As I finished that letter we were sailing up the Gulf of Suez, with land visible on both sides. The journey north from Durban had been very uneventful: boat drill every morning, then such training as was possible in the circumstances, and I found plenty of time for reading – the Dunera's *library was well stocked. For two days we zig-zagged violently as we passed up the coast of Italian Somaliland. The news from the Western Desert continued to excite us all. On 17 December*

---

1. British forces under Wavell's command attacked the Italian forces in the Egyptian Western Desert on 7 December, and a week later reached the Libyan frontier at Sollum and Fort Capuzzo.

L/N held a fancy dress party for the whole ship's company. Next day we passed along Perim Island, saw the hills of Arabia, 'one mountain mass quite near, wicked rocks and glaring sand', and picked up a large new escort from Aden to protect us along the Eritrean coast. The RAF sent planes, mostly Blenheims, over us at frequent intervals, but, to our astonishment, there was never a sign of the Italian enemy. On the 22nd we prematurely celebrated Christmas in traditional style.

CHAPTER FIVE: TRAINING IN EGYPT
January – March 1941

At 8 am on 23 December we dropped anchor briefly for a few hours at Suez, then moved slowly though the canal and docked at Port Said at 10.30 on Christmas Eve.

Letter, 3 January 1941

Well, here we are in camp in the desert. We disembarked on the 24th, about midday, and spent the rest of that day sitting on the sand by the quayside waiting, with nothing to do but munch bully and biscuits. That night we shivered in a cramped train, and at 6 on Christmas morning we tumbled out onto the line at a tiny desert wayside station, in the cold mist through which the sun had not yet penetrated, and unloaded our baggage into waiting lorries. Then we marched up the hill the two miles into the camp. Since then we've settled in nicely. The camp was not quite finished when we arrived, but a lot of excellent work had been done on it, and we are now very comfortable. We live in Indian tents, roomy and double-roofed, which makes them cool in the heat of the day and fairly warm in the evenings. We have plenty of water, and contractors (my first experience of oriental thievery) produce enough fresh food to allow us to mess extremely well. The camp has many amenities, and the troops are far happier than they ever dreamt they would be in the middle of the desert. Meanwhile we are rapidly reassembling ourselves, inspecting our guns and vehicles, unpacking our cases and generally overhauling everything after the voyage.

The camp was Tahag no. 18, situated about 65 miles north of Cairo, just north of the railway, main road and sweet-water canal which all ran west from the Suez Canal to the Nile Valley. The station at which we detrained was El Qassasin.

3 January

The greatest advantage of this camp is that we are within a reasonable train journey of Cairo. And much to our surprise, three days after arriving, we were told that the Battery could send off four officers and twenty-four men every week for a week-end's leave. I was one of the lucky ones last week. It is an excellent idea, for just now we can afford lazy week-ends, and it is the last chance of leave for probably very many months. So four of us set off on Saturday morning for a most enjoyable week-end. It is an interesting city, the 'west end' is modern, ugly and noisy, the less reputable quarters are smelly, dark and fascinating. Apart from the black-out and the multitudes of uniforms (and red tabs), there is no sign of war. Even the black-out is mild. We went on Saturday afternoon for an hour to the racing at Gezira, an attractive garden island in the Nile. There was the elite of Cairo – Egyptians, Arabic-speaking and French-speaking, Greeks, the local British notabilities, all in their Sunday best and speaking every language of the Mediterranean. I find the attitude of the Egyptians just slightly revolting. They are hardly lifting a finger to help us in our struggle, although we are fighting for them just as directly as for ourselves. They must be making a nice pile of money out of us, for we pay for everything – we pay for being allowed to fight here. And all the time they enjoy themselves in their clubs and at the races, flaunting their wealth and most enthusiastically wishing us success in the Western Desert. Perhaps I'm being superficially unfair. It is always easy to criticise wealthy non-combatants. But ours at home at least produce the cash.

We spent Sunday morning at the Pyramids, going out there by tram, an amusing experience. I climbed to the top of the Great Pyramid, 450 feet. It was my first real exercise for eight weeks, but it was worth it. I rode round the Sphinx on a camel, in best American tourist style. My most enjoyable sightseeing in Cairo was my trip up to the citadel. It is a massive place, built by Saladin, with walls of vast height and thickness, gateways and a precipice facing the city, a ring of bastions looking out onto the desert. Another of my trips was down to old Cairo, to see the Coptic churches. Next door to them is a Roman bastion built of blocks of stone taken from Egyptian temples. In the churches the pillars have capitals from Roman temples, and the walls are also partly made of ancient Egyptian blocks, sanctified with roughly hewn crosses. I think a Coptic Church is one up to me on the rest of the family!

The train journey was as interesting as anything. Egyptian villages, even some of their largest towns, are indescribably sordid, far worse than the worst I saw in Greece, even the miserable wattle huts inhabited by the Albanians on the lower slopes of Pentelicon. The huts are made of mud, with decaying green stuff on the roofs, presumably to prevent the sun from cracking the mud. The smells are amazing. The camel is a dirty animal at close quarters, particularly when feeding on piles of garbage in the village square. From a distance, striding across the desert in the sunshine, he is more picturesque. But perhaps I'm overstressing the sordidness. One uniquely Egyptian sight is the hubble-bubble, being smoked by four tarbouched dignitaries. The cultivated countryside is amazingly green, intricately irrigated from canals and wells – the latter worked by wheels turned by patiently plodding, blindfolded water buffalos. It is amazing how abruptly cultivation ends and the desert begins. Along the canals run roads, many of them tarred with an excellent surface. Speed, however, is dangerous. The fellaheen rides his donkey without reins, and time and space being no object, the donkey's course is hardly straight. He has be to circumnavigated with care. It is a fine sight to see the family setting out along the road, sitting hard astern on the family ass, almost falling over the tail.

I have been writing a guidebook and I apologise. For more you must await my next instalment. It will take me many letters to do justice to this country. I can tell you little of what we are actually doing, but I can try to give you some idea of the fascination that Egypt has already made me feel, in spite of the discomforts. So for tonight, all my love.

Soon after posting this letter, I received my first mail from home, two letters dated 31 October and 10 November. They brought with them tantalising hints of the work that my father was doing in the Balkan section of the Political Intelligence Department of the Foreign Office, to which he had transferred in October 1940. Its 'secret' country headquarters was located in Woburn Abbey.

13 January

Balkan intelligence must be a hectic job just at present,and likely to remain so. I reluctantly take off my hat to old Codfish Metaxas [the Greek military dictator]. He has proved himself worthy of his nation. There were several Greek ships in the port where we disembarked. That morning the news of the fall of Chimarra[1] had just come through, and they were beflagged and bedecked with bunting and streamers from mast to mast and bow to stern. The Greek waiters in Cairo are childishly proud, and to see their enthusiasm makes a solid Briton like myself childishly proud of our own effort in Libya. The war moves so fast that we are wondering what will be left for us to do by the time we are ready. I don't think we need worry. There's plenty left still. I hope so, anyway, for being stuck out here and inactive would be boring. We are progressing steadily with our training, getting to know our bit of the desert and how to tackle it, and how to live in it with reasonable comfort. Little has happened since I last wrote, except for yesterday's sandstorm. It was an unpleasant experience, but one that will be repeated more often now that the warmer weather is only two months off. There was a chilly breeze when we woke up yesterday. As the sun rose, little spirals of dust began to sweep round the camp, in and out of the tents, some of them rising hundreds of feet into the air. Suddenly, at 10 o'clock the khamseen was upon us. Work was impossible, so we retired to our tents and sat praying that the pegs and ropes would hold, the air round us thick with dust, tables and chairs and books disappearing deeper and deeper under the silting sand. Outside visibility was 10 to 20 yards. I ventured out with goggles, a handkerchief over mouth and nose, and compass in hand. Without a compass one was lost, even struggling the 50 yards from the mess to my own tent. It was thicker than the thickest London pea-souper – but occasionally the sun broke through the sand-clouds feebly and turned the fog to a dense Scotch mist. It raged from 10 to 5 p.m., and suddenly died down with the sunset. We had an hour of daylight in which to shake the sand out of our sponges and pyjamas. Then a marvellous meal, completely unflavoured by sand, and we all retired exhausted to bed.

1. A town on the Adriatic coast about thirty miles inside Albania.

The desert has a certain fascination, particularly at night. This is the country in which to study the stars. There are rarely clouds. And tonight is full moon, so bright and large that one can read outside with little strain to the eyes. The sunsets are wonderful. The sand turns to pink, the horizon is yellow and gold and greenish-white, and the camp's white tents glow with red. I have spent enjoyable mornings out in the wilderness. We set off on a compass bearing, and if we make a mistake, we are late for lunch. It's an exciting feeling – in the middle of nowhere, nothing visible but sand and some patches of camel scrub, and nothing but a compass to show the way back to civilisation (comparative). One thing I miss – animal life. One day I saw what might have been a hyena, grey, slinky and dog-like, galloping away from our column. And there are foxes. The most interesting birds are the kites. They are huge hawks, as big as buzzards, and remarkably tame. They are excellent scavengers, and preserved by the Egyptians for that reason. They circle round our cookhouses and are reputed to have snatched hunks of meat from hungry soldiers' mess tins as their dinner was being dished out. This you may believe if you wish. I have been given circumstantial details. It's a good story. So you see bird life is limited. But along the canals and round the salt lakes are birds' paradises (excuse so foul a plural).

No more now. I must early to bed. We are spending tomorrow night in the open – our first bivouac in this country. It will be very cold. And there are unpleasant rumours that the stock of whisky in this country is running out. The next day we are going to fire some practice live rounds, and see what a mess our shells make of the desert.

25 January

We did a bit of practice shooting a week ago, and spent a night out on the fringe of the open desert. It was good fun, chilly but beautiful. We parked our vehicles in the 'front drive' of the local Greek merchant's villa, under the desert pines and eucalyptuses. The worthy Greek came out with all his household, laden with coffee and tangerines from his own little grove. He was a delightful old boy, rather 'gone native' and not too clean, but full of enthusiasm. He had two sons in Albania, fighting 'with the bayonet', as he told us with relish and appropriate gestures. Next morning we were off before sunrise, but he was there to say goodbye, and to supervise his camel train which was setting off for the local town, very picturesque plodding down the ridge, outlined against the yellowing sky.

11 February

Nearly a week since Benghazi fell, the whole of Cyrenaica occupied, and here we still sit, twiddling our thumbs in camp, miles away behind the fighting. It's hard not to feel impatient, as you may well imagine.[1]

---

1. A small armoured force under O'Connor's command reached El Agheila, on the Cyrenaican-Tripolitanian border, on 8 February. By then eleven Italian divisions had been destroyed and 130,000 prisoners taken.

I'm getting the feel of the desert now. Of course, our desert here is very mild. There are no rocks or ravines or flinty precipices. Soft sand is the exception, and most of it is covered with pebbles, which make excellent going for guns and lorries. Navigating is a fascinating job. The maps are vast blanks, with a few contours and tracks, but nothing else. The Regiment on a desert run, in open formation, is an impressive sight, spread out over several miles in case of bombing, trucks and lorries looming up through the dust just like ships in convoy.

There is much less time for reading now that we are training intensively again. But I have just finished *Gone with the Wind*. I'm now starting on Jane Austen.

28 February

Since I last wrote I have been on a week's gunnery course at the base on the outskirts of Cairo. The work was not strenuous, in fact it consisted chiefly of re-learning what I had been taught at Larkhill over a year ago. Every evening was free, and I lounged luxuriously in the bars and baths and restaurants of the wicked city.

It is getting hotter, and the season of sandstorms seems to have ended. The days are longer and the sun is stronger. My face this evening is painfully sore. And my nose is a regimental joke. As soon as it heals, it peels again.

It is pleasing to open one's paper every morning, knowing that one more crumb will have been broken off Musso's decrepit empire. The speed is breathtaking. We have been hearing many details of the Libyan fighting, and the more we hear, the more we regret having missed it by so little. It was good fun for almost all concerned. But not war. And bad training for sterner battles that must come soon.

That letter did not reveal that our period of frustration had come to an end. I got back to Tahag on the evening of 26 February to find white-heat speculation: we were to be ready to move on or after March 1st and no one knew where we were bound. I noted in my diary, 'I favour Volo, Piraeus, Salonika in that order'. Our packing operations were made uncomfortable by two days of torrential rain. On 2 March we set off in a blustering north-west gale, 'the camp area half-submerged', drove through Cairo, past the Pyramids and out along the desert road, stopping the night in a bivouac at Wadi Natrum, about half way to Alexandria. Next day we reached Amriya camp, 17 miles west of the port. On the 4th I noted, 'Bulgaria has joined the Axis,[1] We must hurry!'

---

1. Bulgaria formally joined the German-Italian Axis on 1 March.

CHAPTER SIX: TO GREECE AND BACK
March – May 1941

At last on 9 March the loading of our vehicles and guns began in Alexandria, and on the 11th we embarked on Hellas, *'a 1500-ton Greek passenger tub, British built as S.V.* Valiant, *rebuilt in Piraeus 1928, small and not too clean'. We were to support the 1st Armoured Brigade, which was being detached from 2nd Armoured Division, the rest of which moved up into Libya.*

Diary, 11 March

Over 600 troops on board, besides us RAMC, RAOC, Australian oddments, many New Zealanders. Most sleeping on decks, some on open deck, in the one lounge, passages etc. Not too pleasant. Seventy-two officers, mostly New Zealand, in tolerable cabins. Lavatories, washing, cooking facilities very meagre. Left quayside 1515, anchored in harbour for rest of day. Absorbing scene. Four immobilised French cruisers, the *Lorraine* (band playing Marseillaise), two aircraft carriers (*Eagle* and *Illustrious*), *Warspite,* multitude of destroyers, auxiliary ships, minesweeping trawlers, seaplanes landing, naval tugs and speedboats. Large convoy came in from north and took our berths as soon as we moved out. Watched defaulters on *Eagle*. Bugles sounding all round at sundown.

12 March

Sailed 0615 while I was still in bed. On deck at 0730 to see low coast line of Egypt on skyline. Convoy of four Greek boats, three with troops, *Aegeus* with vehicles and guns. Three destroyers escorting us.

I described the experiences which followed in two letters written in May, the censor having by then relaxed his restrictions:

The troops were packed like sardines. Every inch of deck was occupied. We fed on bully and biscuits. And we met the worst storm the Aegean has known for years – or so they told us. I spent thirty-six hours on my bunk. Never have I been so miserable. I vomited until it seemed that my stomach must burst. The noise was unbelievable – twenty-six hours of every conceivable variation in pitch, toss, lurch, clatter, bang, roll, thud, shudder, creak, smash, the hiss of the lashing spray past the porthole, which began to leak, and all the sounds of human misery around me. The waves were 30 feet high, the troops on deck were soaked to the skin, and nothing could be cooked except an occasional cup of tea. On the fourth

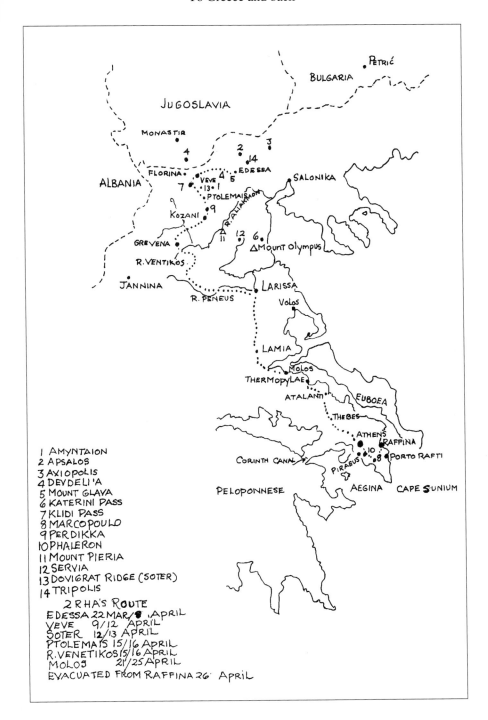

1 AMYNTAION
2 APSALOS
3 AXIOPOLIS
4 DEVDELI'A
5 MOUNT GLAVA
6 KATERINI PASS
7 KLIDI PASS
8 MARCOPOULO
9 PERDIKKA
10 PHALERON
11 MOUNT PIERIA
12 SERVIA
13 DOVIGRAT RIDGE (SOTER)
14 TRIPOLIS

2 RHA'S ROUTE
EDESSA 22 MAR/8 APRIL
VEVE   9/12 APRIL
SOTER   12/13 APRIL
PTOLEMAIS 15/16 APRIL
R. VENETIKOS 15/16 APRIL
MOLOS   21/25 APRIL
EVACUATED FROM RAFFINA 26 APRIL

day out from Egypt the storm died. I went up on deck to find a bitter north wind, the sun breaking through black clouds. We were well up the Attic coast, creeping close inshore. The sun slowly got warmer as we sailed across Phaleron Bay, the snow gleaming on the top of Parnes and Pentelicon and Hymettus, and on the hills of the Peloponnese; Lykabettus and the Parthenon were shining out brilliantly, and the sea, Salamis and every hill and island growing bluer every minute. And so we docked at Piraeus about 10 am.

Almost the first sight we saw was 600 Italian prisoners coming off a diminutive Greek gunboat, all in rags, many of them wounded, and exhausted by sea-sickness. They had presumably come the whole way round from Albania by sea. And then, as we came into dock the cheering began. Apart from the few troops, chiefly sappers and RASC (and of course the RAF) who had been in Greece all winter, we were among the first British troops to land. It was the beginning of a welcome that never failed in kindness or intensity, from the first drive through Piraeus and Phaleron to our camp under the spur of Hymettus right down to the last days when we passed through Athens on our way to the beaches, and drove through crowds cheering and clapping and crying, weeping with pride, distress and sincere thankfulness towards us for the little we had been able to do.

We spent four days in camp outside Athens. From my bed in the mornings I had that glorious blue sea, with Aegina and the hills of the Argolid floating on the water, framed in my tent door; and as a foreground the clumps of mountain pines climbing in and out around the tiny rocky ravines. I spent one afternoon shopping in Athens. Two of us bought walking sticks for our colleagues: it took us an hour, because every customer who came into the shop, on seeing us, would seize the sticks by the bottom end, cry out in savage tones "Mussolini, Mussolini", and then proceed to miss bashing out our brains with the weighted handles by ¼ to ½ inch. They were delightfully childish in their enthusiasm over their victories, their joy at seeing us, their seething, scornful indignation that the Italians, of all people, should dare to attack their country. These Mussolini demonstrations became very familiar wherever we went. On our drive north, whenever we halted, the children would crowd round our guns, pat their muzzles and dance with joy, shouting "Mussolini, Mussolini, boom, boom, kalò, kalò". But not a mention of Hitler all this time. The German Legation in Athens was of course sending minute reports back to Berlin of every gun and vehicle that landed.[1] The German military attaché, who spoke faultless English, did the rounds of the cafés talking to British soldiers, asking them their units and where they came from, until the Greek police found out what was happening. The German Legation asked for protection from the Australians. And one night a company of Palestinian Jewish pioneers got very drunk and almost broke in. It was a queer situation. I ran into Raymer, chaplain of the Legation, who arranged the tour in 1937 – you

1. As Germany did not declare war on Greece when the Italians invaded in October 1940, it maintained diplomatic relations.

remember of course.[1] He had grown a huge beard, and looked like a patriarch. He had many interesting things to say; some of them left me unhappy, and some of his hints about the behaviour of Athenian society were justified by later events. But the atmosphere in Athens was invigorating – grim indeed, but full of pride and confidence. That day I revisited the Acropolis – in battle dress, and thought back to that very different visit four years ago. And I felt thankful that I had been given a chance to do something for a valiant little nation in a great cause.

On our fifth day we set out on our four day journey. We did close on 400 miles all told. I shall never forget them. The first two days were cold and wet, but for our drive through the high mountains the sun shone brightly all day, and every hour saw the trees grow greener. The nights were bitterly cold. We used to sit at breakfast shivering in our greatcoats, watching for the sun to come over the hills. The first 70 miles were familiar. We drove down Odos Stadiou, Athens' main street, crowds lining the pavements and cheering. It was astonishing how quickly a crowd gathered, at the first faint sound of a distant lorry or motor-cycle. A gunner regiment on the march is not a bad sight, and I hope we impressed the German military attaché, who was no doubt watching our progress. It was thrilling, on our second day, to pass the steaming spring of Thermopylae and to feel that we were on the same errand as those Spartans of long ago. But though we were feeling suitably heroic, we hoped we wouldn't be invited to share their drastic fate. The third day we crossed the Thessalian plain to Larissa. That poor town was in a terrible state. In the centre the earthquake hadn't left one house intact. All were cracked or bulging, and in many the roofs had crashed to the ground. It was a nice piece of Italian chivalry to bomb the refugees trying to rescue their poor belongings. Then we headed for the mountains. The climb over the shoulder of Olympus was unforgettable. It was a sublime view – dazzling snow towering above precipitous gorges, thousands of feet deep. And the road twisted and climbed and dipped round crazy hairpins, across broad rushing rivers by narrow stone bridges, along precipices with no parapet between us and the drop. We spent our third night bivouacked in a heavenly spot close under Pieria, our tents pitched on green grass beside the broad, peaceful Aliakmon. And on the fourth day we wound down into the Salonica plain and reached our 'permanent' camp below Edessa. We arrived without a casualty, not a bad effort. It needed good steady driving to take lorries loaded with three tons of ammunition over those greasy, muddy, stony roads. Spring reconstruction had only just begun. All along the route women were carting and breaking the stones, helped by children and a handful of able bodied men. In every village the population turned out to greet us. Mussolini's throat was slit with suitably savage gestures (no reference to Hitler). And as we got further north, the children gave us the Nazi salute. This worried some of our troops a great deal, and one of our sergeants was most painstaking (and successful) in teaching them to substitute 'thumbs up'. When we stopped for the night, they swarmed round us, ready to pounce on our petrol tins,

1. I had visited Greece in April 1937 on a schoolboys' tour organised by the Anglo-Hellenic League.

empty bully tins, biscuit tins, any and every kind of tin. By the end of the campaign I think every family in Greece must have been eating out of British Army petrol tins, drinking out of them, cooking in them, growing flowers in them, shopping with them. We did well. The rate of exchange started at five eggs to a tin, 100 tins for a sheep, sixty for enough onions or leeks to feed the battery. We were able to supplement our rations very nicely. No fresh rations were issued, and one soon gets tired of bully and biscuits and eternal tinned meals twice a day.

Our fortnight at Edessa was delightful. Our tents were tucked under fruit trees just beginning to burst into blossom and among tangles of thorns with a green fluffy film that thickened every sunny day. Through the white and pink blossoms we looked across the valley to snowy peaks 20 miles to the south. Just below our camp the river made a lovely bath, rushing through huge rocky pools, almost like a Highland burn, though the water was chalky white instead of brown. The evenings in these surroundings were delightful, as you can imagine, and I used to spend Sunday afternoons lying on the grassy bank, reading and writing and basking. I bought Greek newspapers and studied them industriously. There were excellent little phrase books published specially for us, and I was beginning to make progress. Occasionally I got up into the town, by the steep path up through the orchards and vineyards, that ended by zig-zagging up the cliff on which Edessa stands. It was not a beautiful town. The old streets were amusing, but too clean to be really picturesque, and the new houses were atrocious. But there were quite good shops selling German goods, and cafés and cake shops. The wines were disappointing, for few varieties were stocked, and the local vintage varied violently. Some were syrup of figs, others tasteless cabbage water. But I enjoyed my few evenings up there. It was a very mixed population. Some of the villages were pure Bulgar, although the Bulgarian that they spoke was, I imagine, unrecognisable. We were warned that there was a good deal of espionage and 5th column work going on in Macedonia. We were even told on no account to drink from mountain streams, because German agents had poisoned the rocks. I think we were getting a 5th column complex. I doubt if there was very much anyway except in Athens. Certainly I never came across anything but sincere friendliness from everyone I met.

That fortnight was very peaceful. It was hard to believe that 80 miles away fierce battles were raging in Albania, or that 60 miles in the opposite direction German divisions were massing on the Bulgarian frontier.[1] Occasionally the sirens sounded and a plane would come over, very high, on reconnaissance. The Greeks always said they were Italian from Albania, but they probably came from Bulgaria. One German plane was shot down in March, but the Greeks kept it quiet. We did little travelling, but worked hard at gunpits, dug ourselves a perfect gun position just outside Edessa, constructed a road to it and drained a big pond nearby, to clear the area of mosquitos. I have a photo of the position and one of

1. German troops had started to move into Bulgaria immediately after 1 March [see p. 59].

64

myself and one of our 'pressgangs' working on the pond, which you shall see one day. The weather was lovely and we were all in good spirits, particularly after the news from Jugoslavia. A letter written from Edessa at that time is now on its way to you. It will show you what we were thinking.

The 'Pressgang'
Left to right: Gnr. Wix, Gnr. Deane, L/Bdr. P. Jones, Gnr. Adams, Gnr. Donald, Gnr. A. H. Evans and Sgt. Macdonald.

Diary, 25 March

Jugoslavia has signed Axis Pact 'with reservations'. How will it affect us? Much talk and flap.

26 March

Up at 0500 and posted anti-parachutists on the hill above camp. Hitler has 250 troop-carrying planes on Bulgar frontier, considerable flap at Brigade HQ. 155th Light AA Battery posted on hills all round town, one gun on top of hill just above our CP. German troops have occupied El Agheila in Libya – is this serious?[1] Riots in Belgrade and throughout country. Poor Jugoslavia.

27 March

Heard news that revolution in Jugoslavia has put King Peter on throne, army in control and mobilising, Regent Prince Paul has fled, frantic enthusiasm throughout country. And what next?

1. Hitler had decided on 11 January to send German troops to Libya, to reinforce the defeated Italians. On 12 February Rommel arrived in Tripoli to take command. The first clashes between British and German troops took place on 27 February.

Letter, 28 March

I write this from 'somewhere in Greece'. So much I trust the censor will allow me to say. As I sit at my tent door, meditating what to write, I can see the sun setting red below heavy black clouds, throwing a pink glow on the snowy peaks that ring this valley and shut off its western end.

Spring in Greece! What could be lovelier? What a delight to see mountains again, snow and trees and green grass. I go to sleep every night with the sound of the rushing burn in my ears. No more choking sandstorms, no more of that pitiless scorching glare over the desert. Egypt had a fascination of its own, and I half regret that we never saw the Western Desert of Cyrenaica. But how pleasant to be among friendly people again. And they *are* friendly, these Greeks. And one doesn't always have to count one's change. Or count the pages of a newspaper, to make sure that the Egyptian gentleman hasn't sold the other half to another mess (for the full price). I could vegetate here happily all summer. But Hitler will perhaps have something to say about that. I love the donkeys, and lizards and tortoises, and the frogs. A week ago I saw five eagles together, soaring and wheeling far below me in a deep gorge. And a pair of hoopoes are nesting quite near our camp. I've yet to find the nest, but they are always flying round together. The little town above us is great fun. Narrow streets, evil smells, shabby cafés and ultra-modern barbers shops. Have you ever eaten kokoretz? Is it Slav or Turkish? Surely not Greek, with that name. It's chicken liver roasted slowly on a spit turning over redhot ashes. It goes well with a bottle of Samian or Lesbian. Food is of course ridiculously cheap after Egypt. Beer is scarce, to the disgust of the troops, and when they try to substitute home-brewed cognac for it the results are sometimes unfortunate. But café pottering is a pleasant evening's entertainment. And the yoghurt!

But I musn't give you a false impression. We are working 6½ days out of 7, and are very much prepared for whatever is to come. You can imagine how thrilled we have been by our friends the Jugos. For forty-eight hours I had the sickening feeling that even they would be steam-rollered and snuffed out. Then that magnificent sight of a people asserting itself with total disregard of desperate dangers on every side. How I wish I could have been in Belgrade that night. I wonder if Hugh was there.[1] Even here in Greece the excitement was intense. There must have been something primitive and frightening about those demonstrations. The Greek press had long descriptions of the crowds and cheering and mobbing of the British and Greek ministers. The singing of the "Madelon" and "Tipperary" in the streets of Belgrade, the shouts of "Long live Great Britain", "Long live Russia", outside the Russian Embassy. Who can tell what the next few weeks will bring? It is a privilege to fight this war with two peoples like the Greeks and Jugoslavs. They have the fire and directness and simplicity which we, with our Anglo-Saxon diffidence and doubt and sophisticated cynicism, seem to have lost. The caricatures of Musso in the Greek

1. He *was* there, working for Special Operations Executive [SOE].

papers are refreshingly sincere, if not in very good taste. I have been reading a lot of Greek and speaking a little. Newspapers are very easy, with what I remember of ancient Greek. And that, somewhat to my surprise, is a great deal. The spoken language is quite different, but its hybrid words and exotic derivations are great fun. The pronunciation is tiresome after years spent in Anglicised recitations of Homer or Thucydides, but I'm gradually getting used to it, and the weird transliterations never fail to give me pleasure.

Diary, 31 March

Fantastic story of the naval battle in the Med. Cunningham has sunk most of the Italian navy en bloc, with superb dash and disdain.[1]

4 April

Details of tonight's manning exercise came in during morning, with hints that it was more serious than a mere exercise, and that we might stay in action positions indefinitely. At 1500 whole Battery moved out of camp. H Troop's right section went forward to the position under Tripolis hill, I went with it as Gerry's GPO. Settled into dug pits in dry river bed, very nicely hidden. A Bofors on a mound just to our left front, a noisy Lancashire crowd. They have a gun sited between us and Tripolis, Rangers have a company HQ on far side of the railway under the embankment. A populous region. Heard 7 o'clock news and learnt Benghazi has been evacuated in face of determined German-Italian push eastwards.[2]

5 April

Bad night. Awoken by AA boys returning from Tripolis revels towards midnight, one particularly vociferous, brazen-lunged sergeant. And every passing train woke me, snorting within 100 yards of my head. Stood to from 0500 to 0700, OP manned, no incidents. Worked at camouflage. Colonel came at 1200. Heard Eden and Dill[3] were in Edessa yesterday, E. convinced by his information that attack would begin yesterday morning. E. in great form, D. very tired, Brigadier[4] saw both.

6 April

Stood to again at 0500. Just before 0700 plane flew low over us, Bren gunners and Gerry at OP distinctly saw iron crosses, AA boys thought it Greek: but it was

1. This is an exaggerated description of the naval victory at Matapan on 28 March.

2. The German-Italian advance continued until the whole of Cyrenaica had been lost, except for an enclave round Tobruk. During the British retreat the 2nd Armoured Division suffered losses so severe that it was never reconstituted.

3. Eden was Secretary of State for Foreign Affairs; Dill was Chief of the Imperial General Staff.

4. Brigadier H. V. S. Charrington, Commander of 1st Armoured Brigade.

an obvious Henschel, sitting target at 3000 feet or less. Bill arrived later in morning with news that Germans declared war on Jugoslavia and Greece at 5 a.m. So that explains the Henschel. Gerry and I walked into Tripolis in evening but found no beer. A lovely still night, half moon, frogs shouting. I lay abed meditating before falling asleep, scene of complete peace. We have entered Addis Ababa. And 'the British Imperial Army has landed in Greece'. Splendid news!

7 April

Woke at 0245 with drops of rain wetting my head and pillow. Gerry and I decided to dress and roll up our beds, spent damp two hours shivering under a tree. Henschel appeared again at 0700, but out of range of Bofors, sirens sounded a little late. Today I become a lieutenant, appeared in full glory of my two pips. Extra pay almost swamped by increase of income tax to 10/- in today's budget. Tantalising lack of news from east, except intensive bombing of Thracian and Macedonian towns, small advance of Bulgarian mountain division from Petric.

On 8 April we received a Special Order of the Day from Charrington: 'The Brigade Commander has no anxieties whatever as to the determination of all ranks of the Brigade to play their part in the forthcoming struggle. He only wishes to remind them that the eyes and ears of the whole civilised world will follow with heartfelt interest during the next few days the deeds of the first British Troops to go into action against Germans since the operations in Norway and around Dunkirk'.

8/9 April

Stood to at 0600 (went forward one hour to Greek summer time last night). Heard on the wireless Jugos captured Scutari, Zara, Fiume[1]. Then message from RHQ that 'advanced elements' have captured Devdelija after thrust west from Bulgaria, possibly already in Axiopolis district. Went with Watty as far as Apsalos, looking for OPs in case of attack over mountains from north. Lashed with rain and hail in afternoon, streams and water courses turned to torrents, our tents and kits swamped. Visited police and got key of chapel from priest, we had just turned it into good dry billet when order to prepare to move at once came in. Stunning. Germans have pushed strong forces west right across Southern Serbia, have turned south and now threaten Florina pass, magnificent tactics, Jugos cut off from Greeks, wedge threatened between Albania and Salonica, thrust down main supply artery to Kozani and heart of Greece. Set to packing up at 1800, pulled out with some difficulty in mud, abandoned all our dumped ammunition, moved off at 1930, dismal drizzle, clouds low over hills. Good drive up to Agras, through narrow winding pass filled with tank obstacles, barbed wire, prepared demolitions: kept pace with westbound troop train. Frantic cheering by Greek troops, surprisingly. Many of them on march westwards. Wound over hills above Lake Ostrovo, helped by fitful moon, reached Veve about midnight, our nearest

---

1. These Adriatic towns were re-occupied by German and Italian troops within a few days.

to Jugo frontier where Colonel had been warned we might meet enemy and so be cut off. But all well, turned south, soon met our advance party that had been to Brigade for orders, turned and waited for dawn in narrow valley south of Veve, on main Florina-south road. Bitter night – I sat with mac over knees and shivered – bitterly cold dawn. Just after Veve met column of anti-tank guns and heard Aussie twang – what a relief![1] Went into anti-tank positions along road and in bottom of Klidi village, rumour that Germans have 15-ton tanks. Troop of 6 inch howitzers below us, Rangers holding mouth of pass, Australians on hilltops on either side, a strong position, though thin on the ground. Uncertain where enemy are, believed in Florina but not much further south. Watty and I pored over the map, discovered depressing possibilities of their pushing west towards Kastoria, Jannina, etc., and turning our flank. All afternoon stream of carts, soldiers on horse and foot, odd lorries, a horsed battery, wagons, a few Jugo vehicles (we'd seen them last night) but mostly weary Greeks, blocking track and filling village with clatter. Heard Churchill's speech, long account of Greek affair, Eden's attempt to visit Belgrade, German push into South Serbia, the German push in Libya, not too cheerful, warning of possible reverses. Ate huge meal in a quad, to bed in hay shed at 2200, desperately cold wind, rain, rain, rain and mud morass.

10 April

Slept well, getting up was ghastly, cutting north wind. All still quiet. After breakfast three of us walked round the four guns, all prepared for anything that came up road. Detachment in great heart in spite of cold. Sun rose and shone briefly, soon disappeared behind black clouds. An easy morning. Watched steady backward flow of Greeks, towards midday road cleared and flow ceased, the battle about to begin. Then Colonel appeared and ordered George and me back to H Troop, no work for us to do in anti-tank position. I went up to Peter's OP on 1109 feature west of pass. Wonderful view over plain to Florina, ring of snowy mountains to north up into Monastir gap. RAF very active, plastering Florina and nearby roads and villages, crumps and clouds of dust, Blenheims and some fighters. A few Heinkels, a Henschel hovered overhead, passed close to a Hurricane who took no notice. But Germans left us alone on whole, went for A.A. batteries behind us in Amyntaion plain, bombed Amyntaion itself and main road, very feebly. How unlike France! With regret left OP, returned to troop position. Still no contact in Klidi pass.

11 April

Bill returned early from conference with news that I Troop is to come out of anti-tank role, support Greek battalion holding high hills to right of Klidi. I was immediately despatched to Greek battalion HQ, part of XX Division. My truck could take me only 400 yards above village, morass impassable, very bad track. Got lift on Aussie armoured OP carrier to Battalion HQ. Arrived to hear battalion

---

1. Part of 6th Australian Division.

reporting on one company shelled by own gunners. Was lent their interpreter, very weary, full of laments, from Alexandria. As I reached Aussies, rain had turned to snow, which thickened to 20 yards visibility, dense clouds over Mount Glava as we plodded up track to desolate Ag. Constantinos church, then struck up into hilltops, following mule tracks, into narrow pine-scattered ravine, already three inches of snow, very bad going. I had on shoes and no gaiters. At last, after three miles, came on long line of bivouac tents, mules, stores covered with snow, one bell tent which was battalion HQ. Explained mission to Colonel, with difficulty found out his front and zone, got two fire tasks, discussed communications. Had two large koniaks, drank to Níke [Victory]. Colonel almost illiterate, couldn't read map properly. Koniak took me swiftly downhill to Klidi, reached Watty at 1600. Set off again at once with interpreter, in tank as far as church, found Colonel again, agreed for him to lay line to join ours at church, fixed provisional SOS lines. Armoured column has been seen on Veve-Kelle road but no infantry attack on their front. Back to Klidi Station by 1800, still snowing hard. We officers sat in fierce heat of cookhouse established in railway hut. Guns along either side of road, wagon line along railway tracks. Watty up to spend night with Greeks. I changed and ate, deliciously comfortable. George fired twenty rounds per gun into Kelle. At last through by line to Watty at 2100. I slept in Jugo train in station, shared by Rangers, B Echelon and Field Ambulance.

12 April

I was to have relieved Watty at Greek HQ, but he rang through saying NCO would be enough, all fire tasks having been arranged. Bill came up with orders for our retirement, first stage tonight, eventually back behind Aliakmon where Jumbo Wilson [Commander-in-Chief, British Troops in Greece] has guaranteed to stand! All dumped rounds to be fired before then. So I fired off ten rounds per gun at Kelle, searching and sweeping. Line to Greeks broke continually, but they were not hard pressed, helped by thick snow on their front. At 1300 sudden scare that five 15-ton tanks coming out of Veve. Switched all guns onto road and track though Klidi, got out A.P. [armour piercing] shot. Watty and I down to Rangers HQ in railway tunnel, heard they and Aussies had retired from FDLs [Forward Defended Localities] under great pressure, not helped by own shells dropping among them. Rangers swore Aussies had run at first contact. Two Rangers Companies fell back, reserve company into action on ridge 400 yards in front of us. Fired fifteen rounds per gun into Veve, according to Rangers with great effect. Also onto infantry concentrations to left on which Peter had been firing. So we shot North, West and South in one position. About 1600 battle hottened. We could see Aussies retiring from ridge to our right, German mortar shells dropping on crest to our left above us, Ranger HQ vehicles drove back, Aussie anti-tank guns retired – three left in mud, bridge blown behind them, without firing a shot. At 1700 final attack began. More rounds into Veve. Then Rangers and Aussies abandoned further ridge at north end of pass. There was danger of enemy OPs, so Souter's H sub gun fired at it over open sights, range-guessing difficult, but successful after three rounds. Our position and the station became Rangers Anti-tank HQ. About 1740 Rangers Colonel told us he'd given his company five minutes to leave nearer ridge. Before last troops had driven past, German infantry appeared 600 yards from us, in our helmets and battle dress. Watty immediately ordered F and G guns out of action, himself laid Souter onto infantry and fired about ten rounds, magnificently cool. Then rifle bullets sang past our ears from left, dust flying very near Panton's E Sub gun. Machine guns opened up from hillside above us. Panton came out, Watty continued firing till all safely away. George and I crouched under cover until Stait hit in backside. We carried him to truck. BSM Garner's helmet dented one inch by bullet above nose, luckily he was stooping for ammunition.

By time H Sub had limbered up, with superb calm and efficiency, bullets were flying thick and fast, enemy only 200 yards above us, we pulled out well after last infantry. Shells falling close on either side of road, but we drove past unscathed. And so down road, Aussie battery still firing, trucks picking up Rangers, Aussies and Greek stragglers, down into peace of plain. An hour's halt at battery position beyond Xynonero (after buying twelve loafs in village). At 1900 we moved off again, drove about five miles (I rode in the tank, which was running abominably) then turned left onto open grass and scrub. Aussies disinclined to stop, but part of a battalion took up position with Rangers on Dovigrat ridge. We went into action as dark fell 200 yards behind ridge. No cover, completely exposed, vehicles dispersed openly 200 yards behind guns. Camouflage nets up. No light for registering, and long time in settling in. Slightly warmed by meal and whiskies. We dug! We are facing Adolf Hitler Division.

13 April, Easter Day

Bitterly cold morning. I patrolled area from 0100 till 0230, occasional firing, but no excitements. Watty up in his tank to his OP on ridge 400 yards in front of the guns at first light, then ahead to Rangers Carrier Platoon HQ. I went up to his OP. Bad observation, much dead ground, but saw enemy MT concentrations on zigzags leading to the Klidi Pass, carriers, infantry debussing and coming down road in extended file. Had just begun shooting when Watty demanded troop by wireless from his tank, so I had to watch battle helplessly. NZ machine-gunners[1] and Rangers had some fun, but we did most of the damage, firing round after round of gun fire. Our front thinly held by Rangers and Aussies, latter retired in some haste almost as soon as engaged. I left at 0930 in withdrawal party, through Perdikka, past big ration and petrol dumps, deserted eerie countryside. Then through Ptolemais, where there were a few bewildered inhabitants and Greek soldiers. By now sun hot, north wind still bitter. Found position three miles south of Ptolemais, on gentle south slope of green valley. Regiment arrived about 1100, having got away safely with shells beginning to fall thickly round guns, German infantry not far from top of ridge. No casualties. Depressing signs of army in

1. Part of 2nd New Zealand Division.

retreat, ditched lorries, many Greek; ammunition and food and supplies of all kinds, harness lying by road, loose mules. Guns in action by 1200.

At 1330 I took E Sub's gun a mile forward to top of hill above guns, not far from Peter's OP. Right in open in sniping role. First-class view of Ptolemais and its main exit, of the bridge over river which had been blown by sappers and of the main road, zig-zagging down into plain from the north. At 1430 dust on zig-zags, three armoured vehicles and some motor-cycles entered Ptolemais at speed after cautious halt, emerged and stopped at exit. We fired at them, two ran very hurriedly off road, turned back into Ptolemais – our second shell very close. Then shot at the third, which was under the trees on the road nearer to us – its crew jumped in very quickly and was off. The three vehicles drove furiously back to the zigzags and on up hill to report – one stopped on hill and stuck rest of day, first blood. We laid directly for line over open sights, indirectly for elevation. Registered the exit from town, the blown bridge and a halfway point between: and then waited. Three Messerschmidts came over machine-gunning Rangers' position, some of their bullets falling unpleasantly close to Abraham's quad, though he was quite unmoved. My first direct experience of machine-gunning; the popping noise of the bursts is frightening.

At 1515 more dust, quickly becoming vast thick cloud on the zigzags. Long stream of tanks, carriers and motor-cycles entered town, started coming out. All but two light tanks stopped at the first corner of the road. I let the two get almost to the bridge, fired, short: second round fell between them. Then one of our cruisers below my hill opened up with its 2-pdr, magnificent flying of tracers, some very close shots, almost direct hits. The enemy turned and scuttled back into Ptolemais, I dropped a round close as they passed the corner. Then for three hours vehicles poured into town, amazing sight, tanks, carriers, motor-cycles, staff cars, lorries of infantry, tractors pulling mortars. Peter fired H/I, and L/N opened up also, dropping round after round of gun fire onto the main entrance to Ptolemais, the centre and main buildings. Restrictions on ammunition were a tragedy. Continuous fire would have caused chaos, and if only the RAF could have been there. I fired at any tanks I could see near the corner, skulking in the shade of houses. They moved each time. No attack down road. Periodically Messerschmidts came over and machine-gunned. Henschels spotting most of the time. RAF invisible. Heavy bumps behind, probably in Kozani and on main road to the south. By 1630 two light mortars in action among poplars on front edge of town. We fired at one, got range exactly, and I think knocked it and its tractor out. The other ceased firing and pulled out. We had used quiet periods to dig hard. Peter hit a field battery plumb, just as they were limbering up. Whole regiment firing, dust and smoke all down road. It was thrilling, sitting on limber behind gun with glasses, observing the fire. About 1740 heavy mortar in centre of town opened up on us, the flash terrific behind houses of main street, but difficult to locate accurately. Had Devine flash-spotting – when he saw flash, we dived for our trenches. We returned fire, but quite soon they got range, one round 50 yards minus, another 50 yards plus. We limbered up and pulled out after short gun-to-gun duel, firing four rounds, but observation very hard. Away just in time – they got the 30 yards bracket, then plastered the position. Back to the troop, but enemy tanks had penetrated our left flank, infantry and New Zealand machine-gunners started withdrawing, explosive bullets from tank battle over the crest falling near the guns. At 1900 pulled out, drove a fair speed down the road, we were last out except for tanks once again. Road was being shelled, but inaccurately. We dropped into action just off the road at Mavrodendri as dark fell, filled up with petrol and ammunition, got down to big meal. Enemy didn't follow up. Moved again at 2330, long delays and crawls over a hill, down to Kozani, full of Greek mule transport, lorries, soldiers demanding lifts. Then a long 30 mile drive over a high narrow pass, very cold: fortified myself with rum from my flask, bright moon helped. About 0300 zigzagged down through grey-clay gashes to the Aliakmon, across a narrow bridge, and one and a half more hours later reached harbour three miles north of Grevena, tucked vehicles into scrub and under trees and turned in to sleep in a deep green dell.

14 April

Woke at 0800 to sound of Heinkels and Messerschmidts overhead, treated to 20 minutes air circus, bombs and machine-gunning mostly on Grevena. Like Louvain and Dunkirk days. A glorious sunny day, wind warmer, ideal for Luftwaffe. We did maintenance all morning. Raids at 1000, 1430, 1700, 1830 and 2030. Our 3-tonners came up in evening with ammunition and reported nice mess of Grevena. Our camouflage pretty adequate, and we were never attacked directly – though this was largely luck, I suspect. The Messerschmidts were all around us. Bombs on the village just to our north, and aimed at the road along which Greek lorries, horses and soldiers poured incessantly. At 1900 got our orders to move south to cover Venetikos bridge and fight delaying action. Signed note from Colonel – "You will resist at all costs until your flanks are turned, then extricate yourselves and make S.E. to rejoin BTG [British Troops in Greece] on foot if necessary. Guns first, then small arms. Good luck!" To bed at 2030 very depressed!

Night 14/15 April

Moved off 2330 for most ghastly night in my life. Down to Grevena to find it full of Greeks, charred lorries in main streets, houses shattered by bombing; on other side of town our first long traffic block, in narrow valley ablaze with burning lorries, petrol and ration dumps. Greek bullock carts packed in serried rows, abandoned horses and vehicles. Heard a plane overhead but it didn't stay. Treacherous road, L/N quad ditched and held us up. We crawled all night, 100 yards every ten to twenty minutes, nose to tail, column stretching miles ahead, heart-breaking blocks. I walked up and down waking drivers, pushing broken-down Greek lorries off the road. In and out wound motor-cycles, Greeks on horse and foot, cars private and military, adding to confusion by cutting in. At last I gave in, sat down by the road and prayed. The miracle happened and we moved on, in fits. With sinking hearts watched the dawn. But enemy missed perfect target. By 0900 we were fairly spread out, wound down zigzags to the Venetikos. A Messerschmidt flew below me within 200 feet, but no attack. Across the narrow stone bridge, spanning a weird precipitous chasm, the water sluggishly eddying through rocks. Then up a steep hill and pulled into harbour in oak scrub at top.

The Greek Army in Retreat.

15 April

Bombing of the bridge and the road in front and behind us, and machine-gunning of vehicles began in real earnest at noon. But most of brigade safely across (except tanks), Charrington standing by bridge, very cool, the last across. Three of regiment's 3-tonners blown up in woods a mile to the south, but no casualties. Bill did reconnaissance and had nasty journey under MG fire back to harbour. George took F. Sub. forward onto hill to snipe across river. I took the other three guns back four miles into action in oak scrub on gentle slope, cover not too good but well off road. On way A sub. was eased off road by Greek car, tumbled 30 feet over into deep hole. All the crew injured, Nunn fatally, rest concussed and badly cut; gun, quad and trailer lost. A great tragedy and happened so quickly that I couldn't believe it – I had just turned my back for 30 seconds. At 1700 and 1830 full dress Junker 88 and Messerschmidt attacks on the road 400 yards from our position. We had a front seat, lay watching fascinated and weren't spotted. Otherwise (!) quiet evening, no contact. Huge meal reached us at 2200. News of Greek withdrawal in Albania. Fog of war is densest we've known yet.

16 April

Stood to 0600. Still no sign of enemy. At 0900 got orders to move. So once again our psychological preparations for a last stand were wasted. The brigade is in a sorry plight. Rangers lost a quarter of their personnel at Veve. Only four of the 3rd Royal Tank Regiment's tanks got across Venetikos bridge, and 4th Hussars have lost practically all theirs, so brigade is no longer armoured, can do little good by trying delaying actions on left flank. George came in with his sniping gun, having had no shooting. At 1200 we pulled out, successfully got guns up muddy track and sat by roadside for three hours, waiting for our turn in the column. Mist low over hills and thank God it didn't lift. A 30-cwt full of men with picks and shovels went ahead of each unit, road making, filling bomb craters, bridging ruts with fir trunks, wire netting. Crawled 5 mph for three hours, the road newly engineered but no surface, a mass of skiddy mud, ruts axle deep. Skid chains saved us. Many detours to avoid charred lorries. Miles of abandoned Greek lorries, captured Italian mobile workshops, Greek guns, ammunition, harness, equipment of all kinds, dead horses and mules, trucks with windscreens shattered by MG bullets. Passed most of our regimental signal section and part of its B echelon caught in yesterday evening's blitz. Uncertainty as to where the enemy were. All day drove through oak scrub, rolling hogbacked hills up to 3000 ft., snow on distant high mountains on all sides. Into bivouac as dark fell, under tall ancient oaks and planes at bottom of a deep valley. Ate well, slept in tents. Lashing rain all night.

17 April

At 0430 I drove two miles up the road to Brigade HQ, in torrential rain and with full headlights blazing, found the Brigadier eating porridge, very cheerful, but doesn't know where we're going or what we're to do, told us to move whenever ready. Moved off 0615. At 1000 reached Peneus valley and turned left down main tarmac Jannina-Larissa road. Great relief to be out of the inhospitable mountains at last, and to see encouraging signs of organisation, in contrast to the chaos of the previous weeks.

Over the next three days we made our way slowly southwards, away from the battles which the Anzacs were fighting in the Katerini and Servia passes. We moved usually by night and lay up in bivouacs, doing maintenance and sleeping, during the day. The weather was glorious. On the 18th I 'slept in the open under the pines, to the sounds of frogs, crickets and a corncrake, the sky filled with stars.' On the evening of 19 April we reached our southernmost resting place on the coast six miles north of Thebes. The fog of war was thick and most of our information came from the BBC.

Diary, 20 April

At 1000 came orders that all personnel for whom there is no room in our vehicles are to be left to be picked up by the RASC and go back with the rest of the armoured brigade to Athens, to be formed into anti-parachutist units. Two of I

Battery's officers, Rex Danks [Battery Captain who had received a bullet through his backside in the Wagon Line, but was quite unshaken] and Frank Edwards ['hopping to get back to I Troop', where he would have replaced me, 'but forbidden because his twisted ankle had not yet healed'] will go with them. The only units still battle-worthy are the Northumberland Hussars and ourselves, who are to support the New Zealanders south of Lamia on a short coast-to coast line. Battery moved off at 1115. Heinkels spotted us, dropped some bombs on the road, but most fell in the fields alongside. Machine-gun bullets uncomfortably close, but quite haphazard attacks. We kept moving, a good performance. Got into harbour in evening, dead beat and limp, a long strain. We were lucky. Heard that Hitler is 52 today.

21 April

Battery set off in dribs between 1930 and 2100 for its new position at Molos, just north of Thermopylae. On reaching Ag. Contantinos at 0030, orders came form the New Zealand CRA to get off the road to allow an infantry battalion to move back. So we bedded down.

22 April

Tucked vehicles away under olives and in farmyards behind village, safe distance from road. Bombers overhead continuously and Henschels, but all left us decently alone. Massacre of chickens and ducks, with inhabitants' smiling approval. Village mostly evacuated, peasants living in grass huts in the field, coming down with donkeys for food and belongings. Colonel in at 1200 to say we are to occupy Molos position by day – H Troop got through last night. We are to hold the line for 48 hours, then fight rearguard action the whole way back to beaches somewhere on Euboea – our second Dunkirk. Felt overwhelmingly depressed. How are we to win this war?

We left in pairs of vehicles at quarter-hour intervals and drove fast the 15 miles. Got to gun position at 1630. Camouflage poor, guns in recently planted young olive grove with standing corn, tracks hopelessly obvious from the air. Concentrated MG attack all round us at 1900. Mosquitos frightful. Slept in bivouac tent. Overlooked by high hills north of gulf.

23 April

At 1100 I was told to be ready to go out on an officers' patrol. At 1230 was fetched by Capt. Richardson of 4th New Zealand Field Artillery. We drove to Constantinos, where the CRA ordered us to report forthwith to BTG, Athens; gave us a direct order not to return to battery. A queer officers' patrol. Set off in one of I Troop's 8-cwts, with Drew and Maitland, Richardson and his BSM, at great speed and with many bumps, for Athens. We were short of petrol, saw I Battery's petrol lorry on road, windscreen shattered by MG bullets, part burnt out. We rifled its cans. I found its driver, Adams, lying under a tree, mass of blood and wounds, almost unrecognizable. Felt hopelessly depressed, longed to be back with battery, hated prospect of lone responsible job, hated war more ferociously than ever, wanted to be led and soothed. But spirits gradually revived. Saw the Luftwaffe's Piraeus evening flight overhead, Greeks and Aussies ran into fields. Pulled off road just before Eleusis, cooked gigantic meal on Aussies cookers – our primus, as well as my valise, lilo, blankets left behind. On at 2130, took two hours to Athens, tried driving without side lights, met long convoy in opposite direction with lights, knocked down one of three Greek soldiers walking abreast on side of road. War makes one callous. We bundled him in the back and dumped him, with his two pals, at big Greek hospital near Omonia. Then to Acropole Hotel to report. Athens very dark, streets deserted, air of quiet efficiency, many police, ambulances. As usual no one knew anything about us until we penetrated to canteen for tea about 0030, met gunner Major Packard, evidently organising evacuation staffs, who told us we would be embarkation staff on one of beaches. We would get orders tomorrow at 0800. Providentially we met a friend of Richardson's, NZ liaison officer at BTG, who lent us half his room at Splendid Palace in Stadiou. Left the truck outside, Drew, Maitland and NZ sergeant major asleep in it. Richardson and I slept on beds, dead tired, and were very soon asleep.

24 April

Slept badly, perhaps sudden change from open air. Up at 0700, just in time to get round to Acropole by 0800. Sirens went as we stood on balcony of Packard's office, trams stopped, many made for shelters, but quite calm, Athens not yet bombed. Packard told us outlines of evacuation from seven beaches, timed for next four nights. Our party of five is to form collecting area and beach staff at D beach, Porto Rafti, on east coast of Attica. Gave us maps and orders to report at once. Richardson and I then searched vainly for breakfast, ended up with sweet biscuits and chocolate. Bought razor, bread, oddments. Papers had news that king and government went yesterday to Crete. Shops closing down, whole police force out, but amazing calm, huge crowds walking up and down, no bitterness towards us, BTG lorries clapped and cheered, women in tears on Drew's shoulder, offers of 5000 drs. to take them with us, 'all Greeks aren't spies'. Melancholy, impressive, great pluck. At 1100 down to Phaleron, supply depot closing down, crowds outside vulturing, found petrol at last near Piraeus in rapidly emptying pump. Then out by Sunium road, church bells tolling for air raid in villages, smiling Attic countryside, with vines and raisins, peasants hard at work in fields, very different from deserted north. Turned left in Marcopoulo to P. Rafti, parked under a broad olive two miles from sea, ate vast meal. Some difficulty in finding to whom to report, at last found Aussie Maj. Shepherd from HQ 6 Div, quiet, small, most efficient, OC Port Area. Walked down to port, saw jetty and beach, back for conference at which staff gathered for instruction. By dark at 2000 we were all manning posts to deal with incoming convoy of 6 NZ Infantry Brigade Group. Vehicles had to be emptied on road, hidden under cover, all under 30-cwt destroyed, personnel guided to beach and embarked, a big task. My job of parking

500 vehicles in a small area almost impossible. Not enough cover, staff officers kept interfering, drivers liked parking in the open and rushing off to beach. Very exhausting. But the organisation worked well. By 0345 nightmare over, 3600 embarked, to bed. It was our old friend, the *Dunera*, which took them off.

25 April

Up again 0530 to walk round the MT collecting area. Pleasantly surprised, for most vehicles were nicely under cover among thick pines or under olives. We moved some, others had been smashed and couldn't be moved, so we must hope over-inquisitive planes do not come over, or tomorrow's embarkation will be difficult. Spent morning completing smashing of vehicles, and for two hours fought a fierce fire blazing in two 3-tonners, possibly caused by a short after seizing, possibly by Greek looters, careless or malicious. We collected and emptied all pyrenes in area in vain: at last damped it with shovel after shovel of earth. A tall pine also blazed, and reconnaissance bomber came over in the middle of the operation. The looters very thorough. At 0600 the procession started, by 0800 the wood black with peasants, taking bagfuls, cartfuls of rations, blankets, packs and clothes, picks and shovels, fantastic scene. Whole area horrible, covered with litter, equipment in first class condition. I acquired a jack-knife, slept under five blankets. Ammunition lying in huge dumps – but very few arms. Two hours' sleep in afternoon. At 1700 conference on night's work. Part of 5th NZ Infantry Brigade arrived from 2000 onwards, with most of 1 Armoured Brigade, half to C Beach, half to us. Richardson's regiment, Northumberland Hussars, 64 Medium Regiment, odd RASC, Cypriots, sappers, New Zealanders. I organised no 3. Area, parked vehicles nicely in olives and cypresses, guided troops up onto pine-covered hill where they spend next 24 hours. Bed by 0345.

26 April

Lovely weather as for last four days, hot sun, gentle breeze. Slept till 1100, in spite of looters' procession that started at first light. They even tried removing bits of vehicles yet unsmashed. Hitler will get little this time. After immense brunch – I've lived better these three days than ever before; stews, vegetables, bacon, fruit, soups, jams, cheese, chocolate, cigarettes in 000's, incredible variety of tinned rations – set off on brand-new NZ motor-cycle towards C Beach, trying to trace 2RHA. Jolly ride. Iron girders bedded in roads outside villages as tank blocks. Peasants friendly as ever. A few scattered vehicles and troops waiting to move down to beach tonight. Took the Marathon road, stopped by MPs just outside Raffina, found the regiment hadn't come yet, down for C Beach tonight. Then my perfect m/c let me down, back tyre punctured. Left it lying, nicely smashed, though it went to my heart. Got lift back in Greek van, on top of a fat pig, to the road fork, then in Greek quad, driven furiously, an officer and three soldiers making way to Crete. Walked from Marcopoulo. Conference on beach at 1630, programme for our final operation tonight. Troops who got in last night marched down first, having destroyed their vehicles. Embarking went slowly.

Then rest of 5 Bde came in, only a few vehicles, all crammed full, unlike Thursday's half-empty 3-tonners. Had 'last meal' at 1800, my truck parked at control point ready to be smashed, all kit buried or given to Greeks. Then at 0100 heard 4 NZ Bde is falling back from Thebes line tonight, to embark *here* tomorrow, Corinth bridge having been captured by parachutists. Spent second half of night on jetty filling up caiques. And so at 0430 to bed under old olive, with prospect of sticky morrow. Bulk of 2RHA went from C Beach. 4600 embarked by us.

27 April

Woke to chilly west wind, couldn't sleep after 0900, so moved down to signals enclosure, parked and washed and cooked huge brunch. Warm under lee of hill. Porto Rafti an attractive little place, on one side a wide bay with white villas and gardens coming down to shore and a knobbly promontory with a jetty, on the other rocky pine-clad hills falling steeply to sea, the bay closed by two lumpy islands. At 1100 came Heinkels and Messerschmidts for an hour's strafing of two abandoned Greek trawlers in bay, MT in our area, vehicles on road; bombs, long MG attacks. We are well spotted. 4 NZ Brigade took up defensive positions round port area, east of Marcopoulo. Germans entered Athens in morning. I lay under a wall with Shepherd and the naval commanding officer, Lt. Cmdr. Wilmot, discussing tonight's problems. As yet no transports arranged for us. In last resort we'll take caiques and make for Kea, then work along the islands by compass by night, to Izmir or Crete, hoping to be picked up by destroyers who will call, giving short sharp blasts on a whistle. Wilmot gave us rough sketches of the islands. We collected rations and water in case. Very romantic. I changed clothes – we are to dump our packs. Finished the letter home started at Edessa!

27 April, 4.45 p.m.

This letter will be something of an historical document, if it is ever posted. The pages you have read refer to a very distant era of peace and high hopes. And this is written in a very different mood. I'm sitting in an olive grove close under a stone dyke, 300 yards from the brilliant blue sea of a tiny port on the east coast of Attica. I have just washed – a luxury which has almost restored me to normal – and shaved. And now I'm trying to decide which of my belongings I'll crowd into the small haversack which is all we are allowed to take aboard tonight – if we ever get aboard. The Germans must be in Athens by now, probably much closer. Heinkels and Messerschmidts have been enjoying themselves almost all day without a break, bombing and machine-gunning us, our abandoned vehicles, the fishing boats that are to take us off. It seemed that they were concentrating especially on me, but perhaps that was imagination. There's a merry blaze of burning lorries behind me, and three hours of daylight still to go. I have been here five days, on a temporary staff job, assistant embarkation staff officer. I had to leave my battery at Thermopylae, just as the battle up there was beginning, much to my disgust. I hope they are all safely away by now. They should have embarked from another beach last night, guns blown up and all equipment destroyed. And I hope I shall see them again in a few days. This is better than Dunkirk, our retreat has never once yet degenerated into a rout. There is a brigade still fighting three miles behind me, covering this beach. We have got 8000 men off from here in the last two nights, 4500 should go tonight with no one left behind. The navy, as usual, are magnificent. But transports are desperately short, and I may spend the next week on a fishing boat, chugging from island to island, with a swiftly diminishing store of bully and biscuits, trying to run into a destroyer or cruiser. Playing at pirates will suit my present mood.

This is a disastrous affair, but how inevitable, when one looks back on it. Three divisions against thirty, with the Greek army worn out by five months of Albania and pitifully thin on the ground. But I still believe Dill was right to send us. We had to come. Prince Paul [of Yugoslavia], I think, bears a terrible responsibility for this. It is three weeks since I saw a paper, a week since I heard the wireless, and I know nothing of events in Jugoslavia. But the complete lack of liaison with the Jugos gave Hitler just the chance to smash across Serbia and down the Florina gap. And he succeeded brilliantly. I admire the Greeks more than ever. We saw their pitiful, broken army in retreat. There was much panic and confusion, but they stood up to the ceaseless bombing and machine-gunning better than the French or Belgians. I was in Athens the morning the public was told the King and Government were in Crete. The shops closed down, the police turned out, and huge silent crowds filled the streets. But not a trace of bitterness against us, although it was obvious we were leaving. And the leaders in the morning papers were thrilling in their tone of proud defiance. Even now they are helping us. Ten miles up the road behind us I met a dozen Greeks this morning, with two machine guns, gloriously drunk, resolved to fight it out. In spite of all their mistakes and strategic follies, I take my hat off to the Greeks.

Diary, 27 April, continued

Heavy raids at 1600 and 1830, no one hit, trawlers still afloat, naval caique machine-gunned, more MT set alight. At 2000 embarkation began. Operation on the jetty went well, on the beach very slow, no one off till midnight. Then things moved miraculously. A TLC [troop landing craft] came in, snorting diesel. It grounded twice, but took off 750 men, who marched on six abreast. HMS *Ajax* came inside bay plus two destroyers. One can count on the navy. 4th NZ Brigade formed up in units at control point, most orderly quiet embarkation. A hundred German tanks sighted in afternoon at Marcopoulo, but they made no attempt to push through, a miracle. By 0230 last rearguard platoon was on way unmolested to the jetty. I boarded last caique, declined navy's offer of a piratical voyage in the islands, out to HMS *Kimberley*. Gusty shore wind blowing, we circled round twice before getting alongside, navy impatient to be off by 0430. I crowded into wardroom, brigadiers and lance-corporals mixed up, just enough floor space for me to lie down, utterly worn out. We had embarked 13,000 in all from Porto Rafti.

28 April

Slept uncomfortably on the floor. Violent zig-zags about 0700, we fired several rounds, presumably dive bombers, but nothing dropped. Woke about 0900 for tea and sandwiches. Every inch of space crammed, wounded lying on settees. Heard news – Churchill spoke last night on withdrawal from Greece, 'Fighting still continues!' At 1000 we dropped anchor in Souda Bay, full of navy, Greek and British ships, aeroplanes; a long narrow inlet closed by boom. Off in troop landing vessels at 1200 to the quay. A two-mile dusty tramp to a reception camp for tea and luscious oranges and bully, then another weary hot suffocating three miles to the British camp, where I found a number of other stragglers from 2RHA.

No tents, men sleeping under olives in huge grove, hardly any blankets, cooking in petrol tins on wood fires, but plenty of rations, water not too distant. Organisation of camps and areas rather chaotic, many returns of arms and ration states etc. required. I am OC our representatives, which prevents me sleeping all day.

29 April

At 1100 walked into Canea, through olives along dusty tracks, buying oranges every 200 yards. Found NAAFI, but no meals served to troops from transit camps. Called at Forces HQ, gave our names and strength, saw Colonel Lloyd and other bigwigs, heard that isolated detachments like us are to embark before whole units, no warning likely.

30 April

Parachutist alarm develops. Units to stand to on alternate days 0500 to 0700, night guards, two lookouts all day. Freyberg [Commander of the New Zealand Expeditionary Force] has taken command of all troops in Crete and expects immediate invasion by air.

The next ten days were spent in anxious waiting. We were told that 'we were on the list' for evacuation and there was no point in worrying; but there was ominous talk of forming a composite RA battalion to stay and fight in Crete. Peter Bishop, Hugh Cruddas, Vernon Price and I took it in turns to walk into Canea and have a meal of omelette, chips and salad (all that was to be had) at one of the two restaurants operating, the Capris or the Piccadilly. Air raids were frequent, and on one occasion we found ourselves in a cellar with Prince George of Greece, in admiral's uniform, and his wife for company. Most of us suffered in some degree from fever or diarrhoea or headaches, and there was a lot of rain. We organised bathing parties down to the beach. Crete was at its loveliest, the gardens of Canea 'full of rambler roses, phlox and clematis, lilies, honeysuckle, delicious sweet scents, with finches and thrushes shouting'. One day I climbed the hill above our camp and spent several hours drinking in the view over the whole western end of Crete, but also watching the sky for those Junker parachutist transports. On 8 May we found a large house in which we were able to install our contingent. 'Its upper rooms were full of dry grass and made reasonable billets, though as we learnt later, excessively flea-ridden'. But we didn't have to stay there long.

9 May

Hugh Cruddas summoned to Camp Commandant at 0730, to be told we embark this afternoon in *City of Canterbury*. Officer from 2RHA detailed as 2nd in command to OC Troops, so I went straight down to Souda. Hot muggy walk, but it seemed only half as far as ten days ago. Watched *City of Canterbury* unloading battalion of marines, who marched off very smartly with full equipment. At 1430 went aboard, to find that there was a permanent OC Troops and staff. So trip will be a holiday. Suddenly heard embarkation postponed for twenty-four hours. Went ashore to meet Peter Bishop and our contingent which had been stopped two miles down the road and told to wait in nearest olives. They now had no blankets or rations, but I managed to bully Area HQ into supplying them. Then I returned to the ship, having with difficulty persuaded OC Troops to allow me to stay the night aboard. Enormous dinner. To be back in civilisation is 'a dream'.

10 May

We cast off from quay at 0800 and anchored just off it, to allow *Lossiemouth* to unload vehicles and stores. At midday moved outside the inner boom. Alarmed to hear in afternoon that numbers have been cut from 1400 to 900 because only one destroyer available to escort us, but 2RHA still on the list. All Aussies aboard went ashore at 1600. Then TLCs started arriving, full of Greek air force, Greek civilians – ministers' families, small children, old women, dogs, stacks of luggage belonging to King and Prince George. Full load of distressed seamen, many Lascars, 4th Hussars, NZ contingents, AA units – and at last, in last load, 2RHA – great relief. We sailed at 2000, out past Souda Island into a hazy evening sky. I got a mattress on cabin floor.

11 May

Sat on deck all day between meals. No land in sight. At 1200 detailed as duty officer for twelve hours, duties satisfactorily vague. All I did was to chase troops downstairs during air raid alarms. Of these we had four at least, once for two Hurricanes, once for a Swordfish that showed off its dive-bombing performance over us. Paid men 5/- in cash in afternoon. By 1900 reported to be off Sollum Bay. Lovely moon. Late to bed after many excellent beers.

12 May

Sighted land about 1200, a few sandy humps. Addressed by OC Troops on necessity for secrecy. Down the swept channel into Alexandria, lay to off harbour at 1530. Incredible naval array inside, battleships, rows of cruisers, an aircraft carrier, *Averoff* and several Greek destroyers. The quays full of merchant ships, both British and Greek. Clouds of officials, civil and military, came aboard. We disembarked soon after and were driven in lorries through Alexandria to Londonderry Camp on seafront; troops in huts, we in officers' mess of most hospitable 9th AA Regiment.

The next two days were spent in buying clothes to replace those lost in Greece, eating cakes and ices in excellent patisseries, browsing in bookshops, and seeing Charlie Chaplin in 'The Great Dictator'. We learnt that the Regiment was back at Tahag. There was no news of four of our officers, including Rex Danks and Frank Edwards. We subsequently learnt that they were prisoners of war. On 15 May we moved by train to Qassassin.

CHAPTER SEVEN: IN EGYPT AGAIN
June – August 1941

Diary, 15 May

Good to see old faces again. Most officers and all but fifty men on leave. Talk of our going to Abbassia to re-equip. Found almost all my kit rescued, including my suitcase with last year's diary, from Piraeus. And a vast pile of mail, thirteen letters from the family, written between 11 November and 18 April, the last having come by the new air service.

Letter, 16 May

Here I am again in a tent on the desert, in the same camp in which we arrived last Christmas Day and spent last winter. I set foot for the second time on Egyptian soil two months almost to the day after sailing so bravely for Europe, that precious foothold in Europe that would have meant so much had we been able to hold it. And so the old proverb comes true, "Qui Nili aquas bibit, rursus bibet". I'm off to Cairo for a week's leave tomorrow.

While in Cairo I got into touch with the Embassy, in the hope of news of my brother Hugh. I was fortunate in finding Adam Watson, 3rd Secretary, who was with him in Bucharest, and also Reggie Smith, late British Council lecturer in Bucharest, and his wife Olivia, later to become famous as the novelist Olivia Manning. They told me what I had suspected, but didn't know: Hugh had been in Belgrade on 6 April, and they presumed (correctly) that he would now be in Italy, having been captured by the Italians at Kotor with the rest of the legation staff.

On 20 May came the news that parachutists had landed in Crete. I realised how lucky I had been to get away. If the greater part of the regiment had not come straight from Greece to Egypt, but had been taken to Crete, I would have been in the thick of it now.

Letter, 25 May

I believe there was an article published in two parts in *The Times* about May 5th and 6th, giving the story of an 'armoured brigade in Greece'. And it probably mentioned a regiment of RHA in that brigade. If you saw it, you will have realised that it was us. I'm glad our story has been published, and that some people at home realise there were British troops in Greece. We were getting slightly tired of the flood of publicity showered on the Anzacs – everything they do is superhuman – and poor Englishmen and Scotsmen often get overlooked. Not that we want publicity. And if the extravagant praise of Australian achievements is necessary to keep the Empire together let's have it. But it isn't. And I think Australians are the first to be sickened by it all.

It's difficult to compare Greece with France. We weren't so lucky with the weather. We had snow for the first three days and a cruel north wind for the first week. I've never been so cold. Later we had two days' rain – but no grumbles that time, for without it we would never have been able to drive 200 miles back south with so few casualties. No one minded the mud and damp as long as the clouds were low in the valleys. After that rain the weather was almost too fine, and the Luftwaffe enjoyed itself in the clear blue sky. For two days we saw a lot of the R.A.F., then they disappeared from our area – not their fault; they fought magnificently but never had a chance. But it became a question not of German air superiority, but of air monopoly. We were lucky in France in never being directly machine-gunned from the air. This time we had plenty of it, and it is far, far more unpleasant than dive-bombing. Messerschmidts are a lovely sight. Their silver wings and bodies turn and wheel and flash in the sunshine, then they suddenly right themselves and point their evil yellow noses straight at you. You're unlucky if there's no trench or cover handy. A milky stream of bullets pours down to the ground in long straight streaks, the pop and splutter of the machine guns is deafening, and you watch with fascination the bullets kicking up the dust along the road you had been driving along. And they do damage. As we drove south, the roads were littered with all the depressing junk of a retreating army. An endless stream of Greeks, on horseback and on foot, plodded patiently on – not a trace of bitterness when we had to refuse them lifts on our guns, for we had to be ready to drop into action at any moment. Their lorries broke down one after the other, poor old requisitioned crocks from every town in Greece, from Patras to Kavalla, with five months' hard war service behind them. Many of them I helped to push over the cliff, to clear the road for us. And many Italian lorries and guns, superb mobile workshops, ambulances and tractors were left behind for their lawful masters to recover. And to add to the desolation we blew up the bridges and mountain sides and blocked the roads wherever we went. But it didn't seem to stop those amazing German tanks.[1]

31 May

Just now I'm finding life rather unsatisfactory. Since the beginning of the Cretan affair, the whole of Egypt has been waiting for the parachutists and gliders and JU52s to land. I'm glad the big-wigs are taking it all seriously, though for the moment I don't believe the danger here is very great. We get up in the morning at 4.30, 'stand to' for an hour, watching the reddening dawn sky. Then back to bed for a couple of hours. The rest of the day is hardly strenuous. We

---

1. An account by me of our Greek experience was published in 1950 in *The Royal Artillery Commemoration Book 1939-1945*, pp. 167-72.

work gently in the morning and sleep most of the afternoon. But sleep is restless and dissatisfying, and the flies are a curse. They start buzzing around one's nose as soon as the first streak of light appears. I think it's the same fly that wakes me every morning at 5. But I'll get him yet.

In one way, but only one, these days are like the month we spent after Dunkirk, exactly a year ago. We are again without guns and vehicles, and spend our time playing with rifles and anti-parachutist tactics, and trying to be efficient infantrymen – with little success. But this bleak desert is not the green lanes and shady copses of the New Forest. We hear constant rumours of imminent re-equipment. And there is *some* equipment out here, but we suspect nothing like enough to replace at once all that was lost in Greece. We are pleased with ourselves in having been able to rescue and bring back all our sights and much valuable equipment. This was possible because the evacuation, on the whole, was well organised. There was no comparison with the muddle and chaos of Dunkirk beach.

In the last few days we have lost several of our officers who are leaving the regiment for more exalted positions elsewhere. It is sad that the family circle is being broken up, but I think inevitable. We have been lucky in having so much talent and experience, and it has brought us safely through two tricky campaigns with very few casualties. But nowadays a thinning out is obviously desirable, from the point of view of the army as a whole, although sad from that of the regiment. I'm wondering how long I shall stay myself. This battery has been a delightful, sheltered haven for me. I couldn't have been luckier than in serving for eighteen months in such a unit – the best possible introduction to the army. Last February I was actually posted as staff captain to our division, and was on the point of leaving the battery when we got our orders to prepare to move to an unknown destination. I should have been bitterly disappointed if I had been torn away on the eve of a second campaign. But my Colonel put in a plea for me and said that he didn't want to lose me just before the battle. I was very grateful to him. Now the situation is different. We are marking time, and just as in England a year ago, I have time to think and chafe a bit and feel restless. It is hard to choose between the jobs of a staff officer and a regimental soldier. The latter has the opportunity of so many pleasant experiences denied to someone on the staff. It has been the personal contacts, the delight of commanding and getting to know a large number of men whom in peace I would never have met, of sharing every kind of situation, uncomfortable, pleasant or dangerous with them, of seeing their and my reactions, of talking about their families, their past lives, of finding out what they think about the war and the world, and what they hope to do with the rest of their lives – that is what I have found so satisfying and enriching. Those have been my chief gains from this war, and when the war ends, that experience will end too. That is why I feel reluctant to retire to an office and work at problems that I shall probably work at for the rest of my life, without the personal contacts – and without the common experience of danger in battle, which I admit unashamedly I have found exhilarating, and look forward to experiencing again.

You will understand what I mean. Most regimental officers, in this and the last war, have said the same.

Meanwhile I have found a new kind of employment. While military training is difficult, if not impossible (for obvious reasons), our Brigade is busy organising an educational scheme. Lecturers are being arranged from the American University and the British Council in Cairo, and the subjects proposed vary from astronomy to French and the workings of the British Parliament. The scheme is slowly taking shape, and I have been made 'Education Officer' for the regiment. We have also been having debates for our NCOs – subjects like "we consider we should not have gone to Greece" – that motion was lost by a huge majority.

On 2 June the regiment moved, mostly by train, to Beni Yusef camp, on the edge of the desert beyond Ghiza on the southern outskirts of Cairo.
Diary, 3 June

This is a very compact camp, though on soft sand which makes hard walking. Battery and regimental stores and offices in huts next door to each other, troops in dug-in 160-pdr tents, dining halls and cookhouse also in huts, regimental messing. I sleep in a hut within 20 seconds of battery parade ground, convenient for roll call. Huts are bleak and airless, not so pleasant as tents just now, but better in a sandstorm. Cinema, NAAFI, bathhouse all in our lines. Sandhills rise 100 feet both sides of camp, a desolate spot. To north the Nile valley starts at camp gates, green trees visible, and in the hazy distance Cairo's smoke, the Makottam hills, Mehemet Ali mosque.

4 June

There is a POW camp at entrance to ours, all-Italian. They pitch tents for us, sing most cheerily, cheer new arrivals and give tremendous salutes to officers.

On 7 June I went with our regimental quartermaster, 'Mac' Macrae, on a long drive to Tel-el-Kebir to collect our new guns and trailers. Vehicles were slower to be delivered, and our establishment was not complete until 17 July.
Letter, 15 June

The Nile valley and the Delta are very interesting just now. I had to do a 150 mile journey by road a week ago, starting at 7 a.m. For two hours I had a lovely fresh drive, the canals a liquid pale blue in the early sun and all the trees and green fields soft and cool, and the animals lively and moving about, goats and sheep grazing, loaded camels plodding down the dusty tracks, mules and donkeys drinking from the ponds and irrigation ditches. By midday the whole look of the countryside has changed. The crops look parched, the trees seem to droop, only the very industrious peasants keep to their work, and every man and beast who can find himself an excuse lies in the nearest shade. Driving through a village at midday is an extraordinary sight. Under every tiny tree and scraggy bush, under carts and lorries, under the cafe tables, in every square yard of shadow, lie motionless corpses, all among the dust and filth and squalour of Egyptian village life, quite indifferent.

By the evening Egypt wakes up again. The women in their black dresses come down with their huge clay chattis on their heads to fill them in the canals. The water buffaloes, who spend most of the day submerged hippo-like with only snout and ear showing above the surface, are hauled out to work on the water-wheels. The oxen tread out the corn, and the peasants toss the ground grain into the air to set the chaff flying in the wind. I suppose the Pharaohs watched just the same work being done in just the same way. Most of the corn is cut by now, but the fields are still full of beans and clover-like cattle fodder, and the cotton is just beginning to flower in the Delta. What I miss most in this country are the scents and smells of flowers and trees and grass. The sun scorches and dries them up. I miss them, especially after Greece. And the gardens of Canea and the countryside of Crete were most fragrant of all. I've never smelt such honeysuckle and lilac, such sweet roses. They were intoxicating. Crete was indeed a garden isle.

We are now within reasonable reach of Cairo, and I get in there occasionally. It's too hot for sightseeing, though there are several mosques I must visit yet. And then one spends the evening in some roof restaurant or in an open-air cinema, beguiling the time with pleasant music and many drinks. Nowadays I frequent a small French restaurant run by an ardent de Gaulliste who produces bouillabaisse every Friday and specialises in sole bonne femme – a dream dish. Last week I had a delectable meal there with Frank Thompson, son of Edward Thompson, of Winchester and New College, recently arrived from England. We had a long gossip and talked of old times.

I must apologise for all this talk of food. We eat disgracefully well and often think guiltily of sternly controlled rationing at home, and ration cards growing blanker every month. But remember that we are thinking of months of bully and biscuits that will one day soon be our lot. Many thanks for the books, Mr. Louis Levy's *The Truth about France* is great fun. I see his Penguin has now arrived in all the Cairo bookshops. Of these there are plenty, some of them almost up to Blackwell's standard, though of course new books arrive two or three months old.

My Italian progresses slowly. I think I've mastered the elements of the grammar, and my vocabulary is gradually increasing. I buy the rather interesting Cairo *Corriere d'Italia* (which last week published a sensational letter written by Matteotti's murderer,[1] captured in Derna) and find news and political articles very easily understood – as of course I should. I also read *Phos*, the local Greek paper, from time to time, to keep my hand in.

Meanwhile all our eyes are on Syria, as you can well imagine.[2] It's a tragi-comical affair. I never imagined the French would really be such criminal idiots as to fight. But it is obvious that they are fighting, and seriously. Otherwise our advance would hardly be so slow. What folly. I wonder what Hitler has up his

1. Matteotti, leader of the Italian Socialist Party, had been murdered by fascist thugs in 1924.

2. British Imperial and Free French forces moved into Syria, which had remained loyal to the Vichy regime in 1940, on 8 June.

sleeve. A nasty surprise, I know. I can't believe he'll really attack Russia. Meanwhile my best love to you all.

A week later I walked in at the door of the Gezira Club 'and there was a message on ticker that Germany attacked Russia on 1500-mile front at 3 a.m. this morning'. I dined with Frank Thompson that evening and 'we talked chiefly of Russia of course'.[1]

Letter, 30 June

For four days I have been upon the bed with tonsilitis. It was not very serious. I suspect I picked it up a week ago when I spent one of my periodical evenings in Cairo. Or it may have come from the heat and dust. This is not a country to feel ill in. One of our recent afflictions has been the taste of the water. We haven't been affected here, but in Cairo it is horrid. The official explanation is that it is due to the pressure of algae in large quantities in the Nile, this being a normal seasonal occurrence. But it's strange that so much fuss is being made by regular residents of Cairo who say they've never known such a taste before. And of course wild rumours are going around the native quarters – Hitler has poisoned the Nile, etc. I've been hearing quite a lot about the German broadcasts in Arabic. The line they are taking at the moment is, of course, "We'll go on bombing you and bombing you and bombing you in Alexandria until you turn the British out". So far it seems to have been as unsuccessful here as in Greece, which is surprising. The Alexandria raids were nasty, but the natives appear to have behaved admirably. And the government organised the evacuations and relief well (although for four days no ordinary trains ran between Cairo and Alexandria), and have now set to in real earnest to build the shelters that should have been built long ago.

After a week it's obviously too soon to judge how the battle [in Russia] is going. I can't bring myself to hope that Uncle Joe will be able to hold out till winter, but he should be able to extricate the bulk of his army and air force into the centre. And then, even if Hitler successfully overruns the Ukraine, Caucasus, Baltic States and Leningrad, his problems have hardly begun.

Diary, 9 July

At 11 I lectured to the Battery on the war situation, chiefly Russia – Hitler's motives, his chances of success, the course of the battle so far (illustrated by a rough blackboard map), Russian tactics, the chances of collapse, 5th column, patriotism, Hitler's real problem being to smash the Red Army. Our breathing space. I enjoyed it and I think lectured well – Colonel in the audience.

Letter, 15 July

We are getting used to the heat now, and only the very exceptional days worry us.

---

1. Frank Thompson later joined SOE, and was captured and executed while serving with partisans in Bulgaria.

We go out every morning before breakfast for a two hour run with our guns over the desert – very minor and elementary manoeuvres. Going to Greece made us forget a lot of our desert training, and we are busy re-learning it and fast reaching the advanced stages again. I enjoy it.

The Syrian armistice is good news. It was a senseless affair. We were beginning to wonder whether we mightn't be sent up there, if the fighting had gone on longer. It was a possibility I didn't relish, pleasant though Damascus or the Lebanon would have been after the desert. But I pray I will never be asked to fight the French. To judge from declamations heard in Cairo bars, there are plenty of British officers who would rather fight the French than the Germans. I sometimes despair of my fellow countrymen.

I manage to get into Cairo fairly often – sometimes as often as twice a week. I laze at the Gezira Sporting Club – one blaze of khaki drill, but I've given up trying to elude uniforms in Cairo. My sporting is limited to swimming in the Club's very pleasant pool, and playing highly inexpert croquet, which I enjoy very much. It is no doubt a degenerate game to play at my age. Otherwise I lie under the trees, dozing and watching the cricket. The grass and shade are a blessed relief from the glare of the sand. One can almost imagine oneself in England – white flannels, the click of bat and ball, deck chairs under the trees and the circle of semi-somnolent spectators. Only the palms and the native waiters and buzzard-like squeals of the scavenger kites overhead bring one back to Cairo.

At that time our training was reaching its climax, and on 29/30 July we did our final desert exercise. On the 31st we held a huge regimental cocktail party in the grandstand of the Gezira racecourse.

Diary, Friday 1 August

And so this diary comes to an end, for we move westwards for the desert at 7 a.m. on Sunday, and I am leaving it in the suitcase I'm depositing with Thos. Cook for safekeeping.

On 18 July I had received a telegram from my brother: "Arrived Britain Saturday after three months journey and detention". I wired back next day, "Delighted and envious your safe return." On 7 August came another telegram saying, "Arriving Cairo shortly, expect stay four days". We hadn't seen each other since November 1939, and it was maddening that we had missed each other by only a few days.

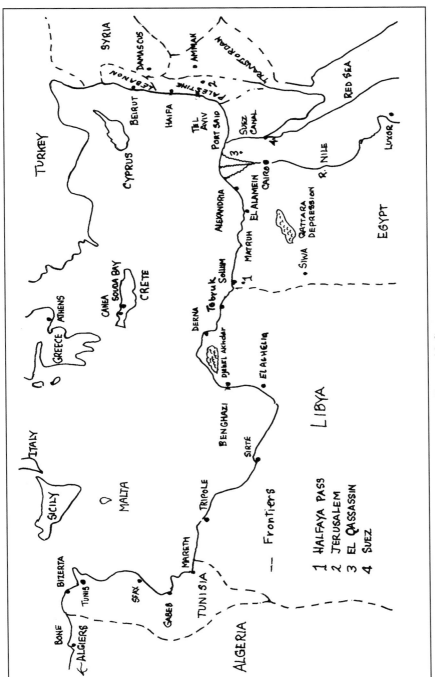

Eastern Mediterranean

CHAPTER EIGHT: THE WESTERN DESERT
August – November 1941

The Regiment left Beni Yusef on 3 August and spent a week in a training area near Mersa Matruh. On the 10th we took over positions from 8th Field Regiment about twenty miles east of the Libyan frontier, on the eastern edge of the 200ft escarpment which overlooked the coastal strip running up to Sollum. There was no front line. The most forward troops were deployed in widely dispersed columns named Brother and Sister, each of which sent out little columns fifteen miles in front. H Troop joined Little Brother column in the forward position during the night of 10/11 August, while I Troop remained behind in a wadi near column HQ. Its task was to prepare a defensive position named North Point, to which Little Brother would withdraw 'to fight a serious delaying action in the case of a heavy enemy push'. It was not to be a 'last round' position.

We in I Troop led a quiet life for the next ten days, the only sign of war being in the air, with occasional strafing by Messerschmidts and the RAF much in evidence.

Letter, 13/16 August

Life in the desert is a subject on which it is hard to be dispassionate. The discomforts need no emphasising. There is no scenery to look at, there is practically no visible life – except the flies – and the clusters of khaki drill and sand-painted vehicles. Travelling is uncomfortable; tracks are few and very misleading, for they rarely go in the direction one wishes to go in. So one works out the bearing and distance off the map and drives as straight as one's driver is capable of driving, trusting one's compass and speedometer. And nine times out of ten one finds oneself within a few hundred yards of one's destination. But the going is shocking – endless miles of wicked rough stones, sharp knobbly boulders and shallow shelving slabs, all glaring white. For miles and miles the same scene.

At the moment I am resting for a more strenuous life in the near future. The war is near, yet life is very peaceful. Rations are excellent; we even get fresh meat, though sometimes it shows too obvious signs of its sufferings on the long journey. We are restricted to one and a half gallons of water a day. Normally, this is ample; one can drink all one wants and still have enough for a fairly adequate wash once a day. And we get beer. It's miraculous, but we get it, and never have I enjoyed beer so much before, inferior though it is. Some of it is made in Egypt, some in Australia or New Zealand, some in Shanghai. So you see we don't do badly. But one thing is to be avoided – a long drive in the middle of the day with a following wind. It's only happened to me once so far. But it was agony to see my precious one and a half gallons remorselessly disappearing in clouds of steam into the bubbling, spitting radiator.

Flies are the curse of the desert. It is they who are responsible for three-quarters of the exasperation, short tempers and genuine hardship. One puts down a mug on a rock, and in ten seconds twenty flies will have settled round it, on the rim, on the sides, in the tea itself. They follow the food into one's mouth. They are hungry, persistent and merciless. And innumerable. The units that came up to live in the desert – the then virgin desert – a year or eighteen months ago, were criminally careless. Now we have evolved the strictest routine of sanitary discipline. But I'm afraid the damage has been done beyond repair.

Yet the discomforts bring their own consolations. The evenings are pleasant, when the sun has gone down and the flies are asleep, and we gather over a mug of beer to discuss the day's doings. There is satisfaction in the feeling that here is something to be defeated and mastered, nature at her worst. I suppose Kipling would call it a man's life. And for hundreds of miles around there is one occupation – war. War in surroundings that cannot suffer, where there can be no distractions. I feel I'm 'getting down to it'. That's something. All my love.

On 21 August the troops swapped round and I Troop went into action at first light. For the next fortnight life acquired a regular routine. The nights were spent in 'close leaguer', with vehicles grouped tightly together. At first light, about 0545, the guns moved into their pits not far away, and the OPs drove forward about ten miles to one of the few viewpoints, with a small escort of infantry and anti-tank guns. I spent some days with the guns, some days at one of our two OPs which were named 'Point 200' and 'Arad'. On our left was a troop of South African armoured cars [SAAC], on our right we had a telephone line to the Australian units at the bottom of the escarpment. It was a featureless landscape, marked only by the odd hummock and wrecked vehicle, the litter of previous fighting. The only signs of the enemy were one or two armoured cars, watching us as we were watching them, and occasionally a moving truck. Visibility grew steadily worse after about 1100, 'till every bush and derelict was dancing and swaying in the mirage'. Occasionally some of our guns would be brought forward within range of the enemy and brief shoots would be carried out, sometimes against the odd truck or armoured car, sometimes at an invisible target, which usually provoked return enemy fire.
Letter, 24 August

Hitler has managed to turn everyone's ideas upside down. Here am I, sitting in the front seat of my wireless truck somewhere in the desert, only a few miles from many German subalterns doing exactly the same as I, writing our Sunday letters home. And what have I – and no doubt they – been doing all day? Swatting flies, for hours and hours on end. Not the conventional idea of war. And that goes on day after day – not always quite so peaceful, but the excitements are very few and the dangers even fewer. Of course it won't last for ever, because one day one side (and let's hope it will be us) will decide to stop playing and get on with the war, and then life will become highly exciting and highly unpleasant. But it's a strange thought that in the first ninety weeks of this war I have done exactly six weeks of fighting, and the huge majority of soldiers in this army of ours have done exactly none.

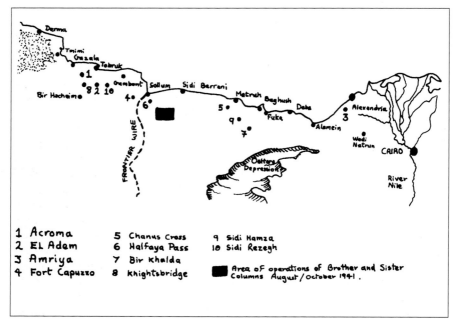

Western Desert

In this part of the desert there is a little more wildlife than in most. There are swallows and even a few house martins, arriving from the north, I suppose. A few days ago I put up a little owl, a delightful sight. And there are more varieties of the nondescript desert thrushes and finches and small plover. But the most charming sights are the gazelles – little deer, sandy brown with light patches, slender curved horns and a swift, graceful pace. In the camel-scrub they have a beautiful natural camouflage. When fresh meat fails to come up with the rations and we get sick of bully, one of us goes out a-hunting in a Morris truck with a rifle. I haven't had a shot yet and will have to be given a lot more bully before I do. They are such graceful creatures. A subaltern from another unit went out the other day with a tommy gun. But that was definitely pronounced unsporting. I think it's slightly unfair to chase them in a motor car, though over this vile boulder-strewn desert I think the gazelle has the advantage. (It's a miracle how

94

our vehicles stand up to it. I'll never hear a word against Lord Nuffield after this war. He is a wizard.) But roast gazelle is a tasty dish.

On 5 September I troop returned to the wadi and H troop went up to the forward position.

8/12 September

What can I tell you of my present doings? In my letters from Cairo six weeks ago I remember speaking of my horror at the prospect of living far in the desert, away from all the blessings of civilisation, iced drinks and daily newspapers and armchairs. But we've settled in like true Bedouin, and Cairo and civilisation are another world, quite cut off and hardly worth thinking about. I can't help feeling surprised and pleased – rather smugly pleased – at my powers of adaptability. I've often thought how adaptable an animal man is. If he weren't, wars would be impossible. Perhaps Englishmen (and Scotsmen) are especially adaptable. They certainly take to nights in air-raid shelters or days in the desert with equal amusement. When I leave this desert I shall never want to return to it, but it will be an experience to look back on. And no doubt I shall talk about it for the rest of my life. I suspect air-raid dramas also will be told and retold for many years to come. Up here the admirable organisation of supplies and the sufficiently varied routine make time pass quite tolerably fast. One gets depressed at times – 'browned off' as the army insists on putting it, and then the desert is a nightmare – the heat, the flies, the glare, the tummy upsets, the ridiculous inactivity. That is when one sits down and writes a letter full of one's martyrdom and miseries. I censor many of that kind every day. And I'm sure I've written some myself. Two days later everything has changed. Mail has arrived, there may be some roast gazelle for dinner, or Churchill has made a speech, or we are at the end of our period of 'active duty' and due for ten days' rest. Perhaps it's only that the breeze has swung to the north and has a faint faint sea tang – just enough to satisfy the imagination. Those are the good days when one can be philosophical. And as you have no doubt already guessed, my long suffering Papa and Mama, from this flood of waffle, today is one of my philosophical days. But you must continue to suffer. Next time I'll perhaps be the martyred misery. For as my moods change, so will my letters.

I'm on a new job just now. I should be resting, having just done a fortnight of more active work. But our quartermaster and one of his assistants have disappeared into the vast network of hospitals with dysentery, and so I have been sent down here [to B Echelon] to cope temporarily with distribution of rations and water and all the thousands of stores we are constantly needing. It's an interesting change and instructive. I don't have to do a great deal of work myself, but have many minions to despatch on the troublesome errands. I sit back 'supervising' – the officer's true function, I'm told. I'm a very short way from the rest of the battery, and yet the atmosphere seems quite different, and after feeling admirably fit for five weeks, as soon as I arrived here I developed tummy troubles, nothing serious and only the universal complaint. Everyone is affected by it off and on. But it's uncomfortable. It must be the quality of the sand, I think, and it's degree of dirtiness.

And there *is* a certain fascination in this life. Some bigwig in Cairo (who may never have been in the desert) said the other day that all future wars should be fought out up here. One can be single-minded about it, and that is certainly an advantage. Some of my most disquieting memories will always be of the humble, peaceful French, Belgian and Greek civilians caught and overwhelmed by the full flood of modern mobile war. It was a horrible experience to see their familiar, peacable world tumbling to the ground around them, and to feel that one was oneself adding to their wretchedness. I sometimes hate to remember how cruel and callous we had to make ourselves in those strange weeks. But here there are no civilians. Every man and every thing for hundreds of miles is concerned with only one thought and activity – the war. The poor Bedouin were cleared out months ago. They will hardly recognise their desert when they return. Their few tracks have been multiplied many thousand-fold. And what used to be virgin rock and sand is now gashed by trenches, soiled and littered with all the refuse of advancing and retreating armies – tins by the million, old worn tyres, boxes, and every conceivable form of junk. It's as well that at home you can't see it, for the cry of 'Waste', the groans of the salvage experts would rise to heaven. And rightly so, no doubt. But I should be surprised if it wasn't lying here still for the Bedouin to collect and cherish when he returns. And very soon he will have names for every burnt-out lorry and derelict tank, and will be able to find his way about from one to the other, just as happily as he wandered from scrub-patch to scrub-patch before the war.

Another part of this life that I like is the convenience of living independent and self-contained on a small truck. One's truck is one's little world, with its three days' supply of food and water and petrol, and all one's belongings tucked into the odd corners. A little time ago I went on a longish drive on official business which took me to the sea for a heavenly bathe in that deep Mediterranean blue, so restful after glaring yellow and drab grey-brown. I started home late in the evening, too late to reach 'home'. And so half an hour before dark we stopped where we were in mid-desert, lit our fire of camel grass (helped by a drop of petrol – yes, you may well cry 'scandal'), cooked up a bully stew and a large mug of tea, then unrolled our beds and in ten minutes I was asleep, my head against the front wheel, a sky of dazzling stars, and not a sound to be heard. The silence is the most amazing thing about the desert. At present the days are windy and the winter birds are arriving and sometimes even chirping, and so there is something to listen to. But at night the wind falls and one can hear nothing. It is weird and rather thrilling.

Two days after I posted that letter, the pace of life quickened dramatically.
Diary, 14 September
Woke about 0700 to hear fierce rumblings, gunfire, AA fire, every kind of loud noise, not far away, whether on coast or inland it was impossible to say. At 0730

came order 'Move to North Point at once', in midst of shaving and cooking. Pulled out in forty minutes. As we came out of our wadi, over the crest of the hill, we saw black columns of smoke. Fifteen ME 109s flew over us, having just bombed and strafed dummy tanks and other vehicles. I gave disperse signal, all dismounted and ran, but the MEs passed away, With difficulty got the guns on the move again and into action. About 1100 two enemy lorries came down main track towards us, their crew dismounted to look at the minefield. One lorry was knocked out by 3 RHA, the second was chased away by Vernon [Price] at Point 221, firing our guns. Very quiet afternoon. Heard main push was to our south, enemy having got round open left flank. About 1800 reports of MT, including many tanks, converging from north-west and south-west, made us alert. Then came full dress attack. We got 'Victoria' [the signal for withdrawal]: guns hooked in, then came 'Stand Fast': I ran cursing to give out angles again, got all guns nicely on line, then came 'Victoria' again. As we pulled out and made north-westwards, shells from tanks were bursting round us and AP ricocheting unpleasantly close. An ME110 had circled over us as we pulled out. Away to south we saw lines of tanks coming towards us, and others in distance in the setting sun. Panton's gun had both tyres punctured by a burst right under spout and had to be abandoned. As it grew dark we closed into columns, drove on in choking dust and with wearying jolts for 28 miles, then formed leaguer near Sidi Abbas. To the south 29 FSD [Forward Supply Depot] burning merrily, half the sky lit by leaping flames – ¼ million gallons of petrol, NAAFI, rations and much else, all blown on 'Victoria' – yet the enemy was miles off. Settled in by 2200. Had whisky off Colonel who was in fine spirits.

Next morning it became clear that the enemy had withdrawn. By 1500 we were back in our gun pits at North Point. Panton's gun was found untouched. After dark we moved, guided by flares, into a night leaguer.

16 September

Woken 0030. Loud rumbles had been heard to north-west, and dawn attack seemed possible. So back into action 0215, after laborious drive and much searching in the dark for the gunpits. Slept for three hours on sand with greatcoat over me. Then came order to move, before breakfast could be made ready. The rumbles had apparently been last German rearguard going north-west. Straight into familiar old Madan gunpits. Many immense tank tracks whole way up, their route quite plain. Our telephone lines cut to ribbons, our signallers were busy. But dumped ammunition intact. Only losses were Bill's despatch case, including copy of battery history with uncomfortable information in it. The Germans were after documents. So back to the old routine. Arad and Pt 200 OPs. Less sign of enemy than usual. To bed with feeling of anticlimax.

More news of battle. One German tank crew captured, three Italian tanks found abandoned without petrol. Several Italian planes came down to give themselves up, others shot down. Stukas fared badly. Our total casualties; 4 killed and 9 wounded. So we win on balance.

On 26 September we were relieved by an Australian field regiment and set off on a two-day cross-desert drive to Rakham Bay, ten miles west of Mersa Matruh.

25-pdr in action in Western Desert.

Letter, 2 October

You can imagine what a heavenly change this is. When we came to the edge of the escarpment at the end of our long hot drive in choking dust, and saw the blue below us, the surf breaking on white, clean sand, and the green of the saltings and the stray palm clusters, I knew what Xenophon felt when he shouted "Thalassa, Thalassa" – I shouted too, and halted my column for five minutes, just to gaze in anticipation. We were very lucky. This is the star resting-place of the Egyptian coast. Only the select are allowed to see it, and eight weeks in the desert is a small price to pay.

The whole Battery bathes at 7 a.m. before breakfast – compulsorily. There were squawks at first, but they died down when we found out how amazingly warm the water is, much warmer in than out in the early morning. The sound of the sea is in our ears all day, and it's lovely to be sung to sleep by the breaking waves.

On 14 October I set off for five days' leave in Cairo. On arrival next day I rang Adam Watson at the Embassy and heard that, by amazing good luck, my brother was expected within a few days for consultation with his SOE bosses. That night I was woken at 1 a.m. in my room at Shepheards by a phone message saying he had already arrived and was staying at the Continental. There, next morning at breakfast, the great reunion took place. We sent a joint telegram home. After Vernon Price, with whom I was sharing a room, left to return to the regiment, Hugh moved in with me.

Letter, 27 October

Hugh and I used to have breakfast in our room at 9. It tended to last till 11. Then he went off to his office while I shopped or did odd scraps of regimental business. We met again at lunch which lasted till 3.30, on one famous occasion in Julian Amery's flat till 4.45. A little sightseeing in the afternoons (including a visit to Sakkara), Hugh visited his office again in the evenings while I wallowed in a hot bath, then dinner about 9 to 11.30 p.m., and back to our room to lie on our beds talking till 2 or 3 a.m. That was our programme for four days. It doesn't sound exciting, but I haven't enjoyed four days so much for a long time.

I caught the return leave train on the night of 20 October. Hugh saw me off, pacing the platform with me till it left at 1.30 a.m. On the 22nd I was back at Rakham. Four days later we moved back into the desert and occupied a position south of Brother and Sister columns, which were now being run by the 4th Indian Division. Our role was to support the 44th Royal Tank Regiment in frustrating any attempt by the enemy to repeat the 'reconnaissance in force' of 14 September.

Letter, 2 November

I knew our seaside holiday was too pleasant to last. Here we are back in the middle of the desert again, and that heavenly blue and the damp sea breeze are only memories. But it hasn't been so much of a shock as our first trip west last August. We are pretty well acclimatised and consider ourselves fully qualified members of the very exclusive Desert Brotherhood – properly toughened desert rats. When we meet units that have come out more recently than ourselves, we put on very superior and knowledgable airs.

In one of your letters to Hugh which I saw when we were together, you said you felt I was being wasted in the desert and that you were disappointed at my not having got a more congenial job. I don't think there was ever any question of my being offered anything in Hugh's organisation [SOE], chiefly because I'm not qualified. Admittedly I have been born and bred in the Balkans' atmosphere, and know far more of the background and even of recent events than many in high places with great reputations. One of the chief reasons I dislike Cairo so much is that one sees so many inanities and nonentities with no knowledge and no 'sympathy' for their work, occupying jobs on which thousands of lives depend, eating and drinking well, sleeping in the afternoons, spending their lives trying to 'get away with it' and avoid being bothered, and by their negative futile harmlessness doing more damage and committing a far greater crime than any regimental commander who by an error of judgement causes the deaths of hundreds of men under his command and the loss of equipment it may never be possible to replace. I don't think I'm exaggerating. Nor am I taking the stupid line that far too many 'front-line' soldiers take, that all staff officers, and particularly those at GHQ, are idle rotters. But I have met personally several of the type in Cairo pleasantly settled in jobs which I feel I could myself perform more efficiently than they. You see I am deliberately not being modest. Hugh and I did discuss the problem, and we agreed that if the alternative to my present most enjoyable and very profitable occupation was to be a junior office boy in Cairo, introduced on sufferance into the organisation of the experts and the great ones, I am far better off where I am. I shall never become a 'stooge' if I can help it. But I don't think I'm getting into a rut. For one thing I find this life most stimulating. On the other hand, I do not believe that the end of this war will find me a subaltern, or even a captain, in the 2nd Regiment RHA. I have never had less wish to leave this battery than just now. The reason for that statement may well be clear to you by the time you receive this. But if I were offered an attractive staff job, I would not blindly refuse it. I have ambitions – healthy ambitions I hope. I do however want to win recognition on my own merit as a soldier. I'd rather that than get a Cairo job on the strength of the family reputation or that of lifelong acquaintance with the Balkan background ('lifelong' sounds grand, but I do feel older nowadays). Even though, as I said before, I know I am just as qualified for certain jobs in Cairo as some of those who are 'running' intelligence in that part of the world out here.

All around us at that time were the visible preparations for a major offensive. My guess was 20 November, and events proved me only two days out. On the 13th we were relieved by 8th Field Regiment and moved four miles south, ready to join the 4th Armoured Brigade of the 7th Armoured Division which we were to support in the forthcoming battle.

CHAPTER NINE: SCHOOLMASTERING IN CAIRO
November 1941 – May 1942

On 14 November I received a bombshell.

Letter, 21 November, Kasr-el-Nil barracks, Cairo.

I was told to pack my baggage and leave the battery within the hour, and report here to the OCTU [Officer Cadet's Training Unit] in Cairo as soon as possible. All this without a scrap of warning. The journey down took three days, and so here I am, still fretting and chafing and resentful. You can imagine how bitter I was at being snatched away, at that moment of all times. We knew that Zero Hour was very near. We had been studying the maps of Cyrenaica for weeks, we knew the role we would have to play. We were to move forward at a moment's notice. To have trained for it, discussed it and thought about it for weeks, and then, just when the long awaited day was coming, to be torn away and banished to this hatefully civilised city – well, you can imagine how bitter I still am. And now I sit over my scrambled eggs and coffee with the *Egyptian Mail* propped up against the milk jug in front of me, in the august silence of this most dignified establishment, trying to piece together the progress of the battle from the incoherent accounts of bewildered war correspondents – and I should be in the thick of it all, in the dust and smoke and roar of what must be the maddest battle any war has yet seen. I can't help thinking and thinking and wondering where the battery has got to and how it has been faring.

The Middle East OCTU was commanded by Colonel Calam Renton of the Rifle Brigade. The commander of the RA Wing, to which I belonged, was Major Tom Cavenagh, until September second-in-command of 2RHA, and it was he who had insisted on my posting to Cairo. The members of B Troop, for which I was responsible, arrived on 28/29 November and started their course on 2 December.

Letter, 5 December

It's a long time since I wrote in my last letter [of 21 November] that another, fuller letter would follow almost at once. The truth is that I am a very busy man nowadays. Much busier back here in the peace and comfort of Cairo than in the desert last summer. For though we were in contact with the enemy most of that time, it was an absurdly artificial type of fighting, in semi-static conditions. And we got some time to ourselves. This is my first attempt at being a schoolmaster and I find it hard work. The cadets work long hours. I have to be up by 6.30 every morning, and we work with very short breaks till lunch. Start again at 4.30 and finish at 7.30. Very often there is something on in the afternoons as well, and we go out on a good many all-day exercises in the desert nearby. And twice a week we do some form of night scheme. So you can see there is not much spare time, and most nights I'm ready for my bed by 9. But I'm lucky if I'm asleep before 11. The weekends are easier. But being new to this job, I have to spend a lot of my time in instructing myself and preparing lectures. As I said, I'm a busy man.

I'm already finding the job most interesting, and it's going to be a useful experience. I'm still feeling bitter about being wrenched away from the battery four days before the battle began. I am no hero, and have no wish to die a hero's death. Every day that passes, I realise more and more how much I want to survive this war – for all sorts of reasons. Chiefly perhaps because I think and hope that I shall be of some use in a topsy-turvy post-war world. But to be left out of it all like this, to be in civilisation while so many of my friends are in the thick of it, in all the frightful discomfort and danger – why go on? For of course you will understand my tangled feelings. And to write and think of it only makes my thoughts more confused. One great consolation I have all this time. I know that you know I am safe, and that you haven't that worry added to all your other worries.

In spite of the news and the lack of news I'm settling down. I have twenty-four cadets to instruct in technical gunnery, infantry tactics, map-reading; all the innumerable subjects that an officer has to know nowadays. Much of the teaching is done by NCO instructors, but I have to supervise it all, and work out the three months' programme between the time they first arrive at the OCTU to the time they go to the School of Artillery for a final two months' instruction on the technical side. It is a responsibility, but a most enjoyable one. My twenty-four are a mixed lot, the majority of them Australians and New Zealanders, and later on I may get some South Africans. That in itself makes the job interesting. And coming from units that have been in the Middle East for some time, all of them have seen active service. I have cadets who between them have been in every campaign in the last twelve months – Wavell's Libyan campaign, the April retreat – we call it the Nine Days Wonder – Greece, Crete, Eritrea, Abyssinia, the abortive June offensive in the desert, Syria, Iran – and soon there will be arriving a few latecomers for this course, straight from the present dogfight. So you can see that I learn as much myself as I teach.

The OCTU is housed in barracks right in Cairo. They are a bit gloomy and prison-like, and at this time of year windy and chilly. But I have quite a comfortable room with a wide verandah on two sides looking down onto the two barrack squares. From the desk at which I'm writing I can see the river with the sails of the feluccas moving slowly up and down, and the palms and green grass of the far bank. It still gives me a little thrill when I suddenly realise that I'm looking at the Nile. I'm not yet used to the idea that I'm in Cairo and Egypt – even after a year. It still seems too unnatural and improbable. One great advantage of these barracks is that they are far enough from the street to escape the worst of the hoots and clanks of the traffic and the Egyptians' most unmelodious cries. When the military hustle and bustle of early morning has died down, one can appreciate the peaceful surroundings and work and think and reflect in undisturbed quiet. And when one has a quiet and reasonably comfortable 'home' to return to, Cairo becomes a very different place to the frantic, noisy, dirty Cairo of five days' leave in expensive inhuman hotels and crowded clubs and restaurants. I intend to do a lot of nosing around, sightseeing and digging out old acquaintances, of whom there are an astonishing number out here. I have joined a circulating library, and for the first time since this war began am going to be able to hear good music.

My present position is that I'm here for six months, then return to the regiment. I am lent and not posted finally away. That is why you can still put R.H.A. after my name. It's slightly ironic that about the last letter I wrote you from the battery should have been a long statement of the reasons why I didn't want to leave at that time. I knew that this job was in the air, as were several other possible jobs. This was the one I was least enthusiastic about, and for a long time my Colonel and battery commander were able to do their best for me and keep me from going. But in the end they were helpless against a direct order from this end. I quite see the OCTU's point if view. They want as instructors officers who have seen some active service. But I wish they hadn't insisted on me. Wailing again!

Diary, 8 December

Huge headlines in the paper announcing Japan's sudden bombing attack on Pearl Harbour and Honolulu. This war has certainly provided some sensations. Now we will have to learn Pacific geography.

In those weeks I got intermittent news of the Regiment from those who came down to Cairo on leave or into hospital. 'Operation Crusader' had started on 18 November, and 2RHA had been in the thick of the fighting at Sidi Rezegh, just south of Tobruk. On 10 December George Potts, in hospital with a slight head wound, gave me a 'hazy account of the battle, which must have been a bewildering, chaotic fantasy, wearying and frightening'. Gerry Hulbert had been killed, and Ainslie Miller, Hugh Cruddas, Henry Wharfedale and several others missing. H/I had lost two guns and been converted to a six-gun troop. But by the end of November the battle had been won and Tobruk relieved. In mid-December 2RHA advanced with 22nd Armoured Brigade across the Cyrenaican desert to Mersa Brega, about 100 miles south of Benghazi, where Rommel made his stand.

I found myself acting as 'personal representative of H/I Battery at the base', visiting its members in hospital and making enquiries from the Red Cross about those believed to have been taken prisoner.

Letter, 21/24 December

This is the beginning of my fourth week of schoolmastering, and I have found my feet. It is interesting work, and satisfying, too, for with such keen 'schoolboys' one sees results gratifyingly soon. It's a responsible job, too. Well though the desert battle is going, there have been heavy losses. More than ever before there is a need for officers, and good officers. So none of my colleagues who feel the same as I do think we are wasting our time here. The great ones delight in telling us that this is not a base job, but a front line duty.

And bases do have their consolations. It is a comfort to be able to go to church again, a real church and not an altar made of a packing-case, sitting on the footboard of a 15-cwt truck. I go most Sundays to the Cathedral. It is just round the corner from these barracks, very new and plain, severely simple inside, but fine proportions and a great sense of space, built in Byzantine style in many respects with some consciously Moslem ornament, and a tall tower sweeping upwards from the rounded domes of the apse and transepts. The choir is a bit shaky, and one of the deacons murders Isaiah or St. Luke or St. Paul with ruthless impartiality. But there is a fine organ, the other deacon reads the prayers more simply, sincerely and movingly than anyone else I've heard except the current Bishop of Durham;[1] and the congregation is alive. At the Sunday evening service the big aisle and the transepts and the choir and galleries are packed to overflowing. Mostly khaki and RAF blue, many officers but mostly soldiers and airmen working round Cairo or on leave, all with lusty voices, that make the roof stretch and strain to fly skywards, as in the good old days in Chapel at Winchester.

Another pleasant feature of Cairo is 'Music for All'. I think I mentioned it in my last letter. It is a converted cinema where every night of the week good music can be heard by anyone in uniform for the price of three piastres, just less than 8d. The programmes are very varied. I have been four times. It is filled with comfortable easy chairs grouped round small low tables. In the intervals one orders and drinks coffee, and one can even eat sticky cakes if one likes. There is a large selection of papers and magazines to pass the time while waiting for the performance to begin, and to hear the best programmes at the weekends one has to be there early, for there is a tight squeeze. The whole atmosphere is delightfully friendly and informal.

We are having cold, raw, sunless weather, like a November in England. Probably not so cold, but I feel it more. They say that even after a year 'out East' the blood gets thinner. It is exactly a year today, Christmas eve, that I set foot on Egyptian soil. At this time we were sitting huddled in our greatcoats on the sandy quayside at Port Said, waiting for our first Egyptian train to shriek its way into the siding. Looking back I feel I've lived many years in those twelve months. I feel very adult nowadays. It must be a sign of old age that I can never remember straight off how old I am. I have to say to myself; 'I was born in 1918 and 41 minus 18 is 23'.

1. Hensley Henson.

104

Diary, 5 January 1942

In the paper another long list of Middle East New Year Honours and Awards, and there was my name among the MCs. Felt very proud and undeserving, and thought back to the day I first wore my [Winchester] College XV tie. Three of us in the mess, Philip Graves Morris and George Highland in addition to myself.

On the evening of 14 January I received a message from my brother Hugh, announcing his arrival at Shepheards. He was being transferred from Istanbul and likely to be in Cairo for some time.

Letter, 29 January

With Hugh in Cairo indefinitely, you can understand that I'm having a busy time. Now that he has been taken away from his 'odious Turks', I think he is pining to get back to Istanbul. I sympathise with his dislike of Cairo; it's worse for him than for me, for I have some sort of home in these barracks, but he lives in the dismal gloom of Shepheards. But it is splendid having him accessible, and it makes all the difference to my enjoyment of this job. We meet about every other day for a meal and a long pow-wow afterwards. I'm afraid we drink rather a lot. Before we met last October I was afraid he might be shocked by the blatant signs of moral degeneration in me since I have been absorbed in the army. But I find he is just as degenerate. I'm afraid neither of us takes any exercise, beyond strolling gently down the Nile for a couple of miles and back. I ought to be energetic, and play football or hockey, or even row – there is a rowing club in Cairo. But I'm afraid I'm too lazy. Besides I don't get very many free afternoons. Hugh is very secretive about what he is doing, and I don't try to worm secrets out of him. I'd just as soon not know – knowledge in Cairo is a dangerous thing. But I know he gets very depressed at times at the muddling and mishandling of his job.

As well as having Hugh at hand, I have had a friend from the battery [Pem Robinson] staying with me for the last week, recovering from jaundice which brought him back to hospital in the Delta from well west of Tobruk. Another of the old gang is in hospital at this moment with a minor wound in the foot from bomb splinters. The regiment has had a sticky time. Of the old members of the battery whom I left in November, two officers have been killed, my late troop commander and battery commander and one other are prisoners in Italy, and three others have been wounded. These will of course return, but many of the old familiar faces have disappeared. I feel amazingly detached, even after so short an interval. In war, events move so fast and one lives so much from day to day, that very quickly and unconsciously one transfers one's loyalties – in part at least. I feel myself part of the OCTU now and 2RHA is almost a memory.

The M.C. came as a bit of a shock. I knew my name had gone in after Greece, but naturally, after so long a delay, thought nothing would come of it. The first I knew of it was seeing the list in the *Egyptian Mail*. You may have noticed that Bill Blacker's name figures among the D.S.O.s. He was my battery commander in England, whom you once met on St. Pancras platform. He is now 2nd in command of the regiment. I feel a bit bogus sometimes when I hear stories of the M.C.s won in the desert during the last few weeks. However, it was a most gratifying surprise.

The news is a bit gloomy just now. The evening paper has just announced the fall of Benghazi. But we must be thankful for the Russians.

The enemy had counter-attacked on 21 January, and by 6 February the British forces had fallen back 250 miles to the Gazala-Bir Hacheim line, thirty miles west of Tobruk. 2RHA was with them but fortunately suffered no heavy losses.

Letter, 3 February

One great feature of this OCTU is the outside lectures. Almost every night we have a talk on a topical subject, often by most distinguished lecturers. Generals come with the dust of the desert still on their boots and give us the intimate history of their campaigns. Your humble son was cajoled and coerced into haranguing the OCTU on the subject of the Balkans, and managed to reproduce with sufficient conviction and air of authority some of the words of wisdom of his distinguished father and brother. I was afraid I had made it very dull, but it seems to have been appreciated.

10 February

I am writing this at the open window of a Greek patisserie [in Alexandria], two sticky cakes and a jug of chocolate on the table in front of me, and beyond them, not a hundred yards away, the blue waters of the Mediterranean. It is a Sunday afternoon and I return to Cairo by the evening train, after a very pleasant weekend by the sea. I was glad to get away from barracks and their atmosphere, for I was getting just a little stale. Of course they are quite right to work us hard. That's why this OCTU is so different a place from the OCTUs at home: there is a certain feeling of urgency and five months is a long time to keep even a few hundred cadets away from the desert. And yet how short a time to teach even a fraction of all the intricacies of this crazy war. I find myself teaching three subjects; first the tactics and technical details of gunnery. Secondly a smattering of the workings of other arms and services. One thing this war has shown is the need for perfect cooperation between everybody – we're only beginning to get it, by very painful experience, and cooperation must be based on knowledge. Thirdly, in addition to all this knowledge and mass of facts I throw at their heads, hoping it's not all flowing out of the other ear, I'm trying to make my troop think. A lot of them are accustomed to thinking, in others I think I can see the wheels slowly and rustily beginning to revolve. There's such a lot for an officer to think about – his own job, the relations between himself and his section or platoon, the character and psychology of the people he's looking after, how they're going to react to the noise and strain of battle, how the battle is likely to go – that brings in enemy tactics, enemy character and psychology. And above all that, why am I an officer? What's the war about, whose fault was it? Very humbly I am trying to break down the provincialism of some of these Australians (actually General Tojo has had more success than I at that particular job) and in general to encourage them all to take an interest in the world round about, to be alert and not so dumb and smug – and most of them need very little encouragement.

I have recently been taking an intense and rather personal interest in Egyptian politics. You probably know the inner story of recent events. It was all good comic opera while it lasted, and I hope has turned out as happily as it appears just now. I'll tell you an amusing tale about it all one day.

My diary reveals the nature of this recent 'personal interest in Egyptian politics':

2 February

Assembled for school lecture at 1830, waited about a long time, then the commandant arrived in something of a fluster straight from BTE [British Troops in Egypt HQ], and announced there was a political crisis in progress – the resignation of Sirry Pasha's government was in the evening paper – and that a N.Z battalion would arrive in Kasr-el-Nil in half an hour. So we set to and cleared our lecture rooms to give them room to sleep, then repaired to the mess to gossip and speculate. The N.Z. arrived later, and Peck [my room mate] and I had a subaltern in with us. The mess is going to be very crowded. Apparently the situation is that Farouk is trying to refuse the Wafd their claim to government, and is intriguing with Ali Maher and others: Sirry Pasha resigned partly as a result of increasing Wafd pressure, partly because of royal displeasure at the sudden breaking with Vichy while he was in Upper Egypt.[1] Some students were demonstrating this afternoon, and if the Wafd is refused, there may be trouble and we will be called upon to restore order. The thought of quelling students to please King Farouk doesn't much appeal to me. But I can't believe anything will happen. Early bed in case of excitements tomorrow.

3 February

All outside training cancelled. Whole OCTU paraded at 0930, all transport drawn up in North Square and allotted to wings and companies. We put twenty-four hours' rations, water, two tommy guns, one bren and plenty of ammunition on board. We are confined to barracks till further notice. Great excitement. In evening a troop of 1RHA arrived in barracks, Peter Gregson in command. Also some very ancient South African whippet tanks with .55 Vickers m.gs and no armour worth looking at – good enough for a Cairo mob. In evening we unloaded our vehicles and the transport dispersed to their garages. The mess crowded beyond a joke: two sittings at every meal, no hope of a chair. The political crisis continues but the day passed quietly enough.

---

1. Ali Maher was a leading politician with well-known pro-Axis sympathies. Nahas Pasha, leader of the nationalist Wafd, believed that collaboration with Britain was the surest way to independence for Egypt. A full account of the political crisis of February 1942 may be found in Artemis Cooper, *Cairo in the War 1939-45* (London 1989) pp. 164-74.

4 February

Usual morning of work. Transport drawn up on the square again at midday and we loaded rations and guns, etc. The mess almost uninhabitable. Towards teatime the tension appeared to increase – newspapers naturally said nothing beyond mentioning continuous political discussions. At 1800 we were told to load three days' battle rations and to stand by. Dinner at 1830, parade 1915, only to be postponed for an hour. Then Tom told me the story. Farouk has refused to let Nahas Pasha form purely Wafd government, and is still intriguing dirtily. HMG has sent ultimatum to expire at 1800, later extended one hour: Farouk allowed it to expire. So at 2040 we move off to Abdin Palace. At 2105 Lampson [the British ambassador] and Stone [new G.O.C., B.T.E.] call on the King, escorted by Majors Cavenagh, Martin and Graves-Morris, and demand Farouk's abdication, under threat of OCTU's bayonets (N.Z.battalion at one minute's notice to move in barracks, and other troops ready in Cairo area). So at 2040 we moved off, South African tanks leading, then B company of the OCTU, followed by Battalion HQ (Renton C.O., Hugh Finch I.O., etc), B Troop as local protection, and behind, the rest of the OCTU and 1 RHA. We drove up to Abdin Square, all traffic held up for us, a halt in the street with excited gyppos gradually gathering – the cadets sang "King Farouk, King Farouk!", then into the square to debus. B Troop followed Battalion HQ into centre, rest of OCTU formed cordon across all exits, while tanks forced way into courtyard and B company sent platoon to palace porch, and 1RHA trained their guns on palace and bodyguard's quarters. So took place the Battle of Abdin Square 1942, and after half an hour's wait we went home to drinks in the mess. B Company had a bit of a scuffle with an Egyptian police officer and pinched a rifle from the Royal Guards, but in quite friendly spirit. Inside Lampson read out very strong document demanding Farouk's abdication. The story went that an empty car was at the door to take F. to Alexandria and put him on board a battleship. After a while F. stopped him, retired to consult his adviser, then returned in tears, grovelled to Lampson and agreed to a Wafd government. A poor loss of face. And how he will hate us. So to bed to dream of Ruritanian comic opera.

5 February

All restrictions off and back to normal. 1RHA and South Africans left barracks in morning, New Zealanders expected to go tomorrow. Papers full of Nahas Pasha's new government in process of formation.

6 February

In evening paper text of exchange of letters between Lampson and Nahas, reaffirming complete independence of Egypt, loyalty to alliance and Britain's complete lack of interference in her internal affairs.

21 February

Tom deputised on ceremonial parade for the new commandant who arrived from Syria last night. Afterwards the General, Maj.Gen.Webster of the Marines, watched B Troop's gun drill, which went excellently. He commented on their keenness and complemented me, little as I had to do with it. Then a morning of polishing off the programme. And so ends my career with B Troop – I wish I could stay on with them at Almaza, for they are a good crowd. At 1230 was suddenly summoned to Orderly Room by adjutant and shown a letter signed by Renton, wishing to "draw attention to the excellent work done by Lt. Seton-Watson during his tour of duty" and mentioning particularly the lecture on the Balkans. It's gratifying but I feel hardly deserved.

Letter, 25 February

I am at present enjoying an idle week between courses and take the night train this evening to Luxor for a very brief change of air and respite from Cairo. I'm going to be the complete tourist – my 'all-in' tickets are in my pocket and they cover hotel, meals, fares, even taxis from the station to the hotel.

When I return at the weekend I shall have a hectic few days. A major reorganisation of the OCTU has been in progress for some months; the cadets' course has been altered a lot and we have been growing in numbers. To meet the new situation the old RA wing of the Middle East OCTU has been expanded into an OCTU of its own, and I am going to the new establishment with the exalted rank of Captain. I shall be teaching less general subjects and more gunnery.

On 1 March I moved up from Kasr-el-Nil to the RA Base at Almaza, on the northern outskirts of the city, with Tom Cavenagh who was to command the new RAOCTU. I interviewed the cadets of C Troop as they arrived, and their course started next day.

Letter, 20 March

Things are going quite well. My chief grouse against the new OCTU order is that I don't get enough work to do. But I think that will soon change. As I feared, I find my style quite cramped by being under a more rigid regime enforced by the academic gunners. The great joy of my three months down at the old OCTU was that I had thirty cadets all to myself. Up here I 'share' twenty cadets with another instructor, and much of my time is spent at the back of a lecture room listening to him giving lectures which, in all humility, I think I could do better myself. I made my cadets write an essay at the end of their first three months, stating the twelve things they would most like to remember if they had to forget everything else about that time. Every one of them put right at the top the friendships they had made. One Australian wrote: "The first thing I should like to remember is this. When I came to the OCTU I thought, like most other Australians, that an Englishman could be only one of two things – a tailor's dummy or a man on the dole. I now know he is a quiet, likeable fellow who just doesn't think it necessary to act tough". Surely that's what we must try to do after this war – bring people together, even for a few weeks, and make them work hard for a common purpose. Start with the Empire and America, then break the language difficulty and bring in other nations. I suppose the same was said and discussed in the last war, and all the high hopes came to nothing. But this time we must succeed. Provincialism seems to me to be the worst enemy of progress: the greatest attraction of the Middle East is that provincialism is impossible out here.

I don't get much time for reading, but at the moment I'm slowly making my way through Buchan's autobiography, *Memory Hold the Door*. It is delightfully written. I am developing what I'm afraid is a slightly degenerate taste for history in biography form. That is, I suppose, one aspect of the greater interest in people and character that this war has given me. Buchan devotes several pages to Raymond Asquith, and quotes one of his letters written in Egypt, describing Egyptian scenery as about as picturesque as a spittoon. Prettily put! I know only two 'natural' views worth looking at in Egypt. One was the Valley of the Tombs of the Kings at Luxor, and the other is the view from Kasr-el-Nil bridge in Cairo, looking up the river on a misty morning with the felucca sails filling the middle distance, and the ugly ultra-modern flats on the far bank transformed by the mist and haze and early sunshine into a row of fairy palaces that might be in Canaletto's Venice.

20 April

In my last letter I think I told you how I was feeling rather unsettled and frustrated. Since then I have become cynically reconciled to my situation. I am earning a vast amount of pay – 5/- a day on top of a captain's pay and Middle East allowances, and my captain's rank is entirely bogus. And I am doing no work. I have now been six weeks at this RAOCTU. For the first month my conscience was permanently troubled and uneasy. This institution is immorally overstaffed, and even if I spent all day making work for myself, I wouldn't be fully occupied. But I have made my protest and been told I'm doing all that is required of me. So that is that. And I have decided to enjoy myself while I may. I'm afraid I'm naturally lazy, and it needs little encouragement for me to drown my feeble sense of duty and make the most of my opportunities. The first fruit of my 'new policy' – Hugh, I think, feels much the same, though he has more work than I – was a most delightful day he and I spent together on Easter Sunday [5 April] watching birds in the Fayoum. A scandalously heathen Easter, for which I shall shortly make amends. But very enjoyable. The Lac Karoun in the Fayoum oasis is a most attractive place. On the southern shore is the cultivation, with the criss-cross pattern of canals and rich fields, marshes here and there full of tall reeds, shady trees along the road and the usual crumbling stinking villages. The far shore is formed by the yellow desert falling steeply to the water, and once again I was thrilled by that lovely contrast of brilliant, glaring, savage yellow against vivid blue flecked with white by the breeze. We wandered for several miles along the mudflats, stopping every few yards to look at the birds and listening to the quacking of the ducks and the familiar piping cry of redshanks or their close Egyptian kinsmen. We saw many old friends, as well as some exciting hawks that Hugh pronounced to be harriers. A flock of bee-eaters, many hoopoes, and adorable little black and white striped kingfishers who hovered and fluttered over our heads and suddenly dived precipitously for fish almost as large as themselves, which they somehow managed to push, still wriggling, down their throats. We had an excellent lunch at the Hotel de la Chasse; it had a real French country inn atmosphere, and there wasn't too much khaki. Altogether we had a most successful day, and both of us felt a bit depressed when we returned to the dusty boring hurly-burly of Cairo.

The weekend at Alexandria [10/12 April] was a great success. It's a most delightful place, as I've said before. I didn't bathe, for it was still a bit chilly, but I got my lungs full of good sea air. I went down by plane with two School of Artillery colleagues, and was very ill the whole hour's flight. Very feeble and I was furious with myself. When I did dare to look out, the view was fascinating. I spent Saturday afternoon sailing around the harbour – one of the best days I've had since leaving England. The black-out, after Cairo, was terrifying, but there was no moon and so no air-raids. I didn't risk a second trip by air and returned by train.

I must finish this, wash the dust off my face, change, take the tram into Cairo, meet Hugh for dinner and then go to what should be a heavenly concert by the Palestine Orchestra – the Water Music, a Beethoven Concerto, and Brahms 4th Symphony. Is there really a war on somewhere?

Diary, 17 April

At 8.30 p.m. B Troop's final dinner; an unbelievably long menu – grapefruit, soup, fish, duck, roast beef, pudding and ice. Sat next to Bryan and Martindale – latter made an excellent speech with home truths about us all. He mentioned as "one of the highlights of the course the exhibition we had of Britain displaying the iron fist in the velvet glove". Tom C answered, briefly and charmingly as usual. O'Sullivan sang admirably. I got away at 1.30 a.m. I'm sorry they are leaving, in a selfish way, for they have been a grand troop, and I don't suppose I shall see any of the Australians again. They were the cream.

Letter, 1 May

I have a novel excuse this week for being late with my letter. I have been house-moving. I'm writing this on the balcony of the snug little flat in Heliopolis which I'm sharing with my two colleagues, Gethyn Hewan and David Fitzherbert. I'm looking out on Sharia el Ahram [Rue des Pyramides] with its broad strip of green grass running down the middle of the road, and the jacarandas are a blaze of brilliant blue. They are a restful sight in the soft evening light, and what a change from the vista of sand and army huts and straggling lorries and telegraph poles that greeted me as I emerged from my tent in camp. This last month at the OCTU is going to be a delightful prelude to sterner things. Such is my natural sloth that if left to myself I should have stewed in my fly-ridden camp without making the slightest effort to move. But these two colleagues have five and six months at the OCTU before them, and so they talked me into sharing the flat for my last month. And very glad I am that I allowed myself to be persuaded. It will cost very little more than living in the 'Lyons' Corner House' Base Depot Mess. And here one can be quiet and eat in a civilised manner – no scrambling for food at a vast sideboard. One can talk and write and read in privacy and entertain one's friends. Heliopolis is not a bad place – entirely residential, all flats and villas, most of them with green gardens, and comparatively little noise. In the trees opposite sparrows are chattering and a hoodie is cawing persistently from somewhere behind the house. Not all the noises are so idyllic. In the flat above live a bevvy of brats who squawk day in day out, and there are endless successions of repulsively unattractive (and persevering) Egyptian gentlemen who stroll up and down the road wailing their wares, brooms, rags and bones, newspapers, razor blades; anything that one just doesn't happen to want.

Our domestic troubles started with a vengeance on the first day. We got rid of our first cook, interviewed two candidates and engaged a third, in the space of an intense half-hour. You will envy us the ease of the servant problem in Egypt. Whisper to Muhammed the dustman that you want a cook, and within the hour a dozen Muhammeds, Muhammeds' cousins, and Muhammeds' washerwoman's nephews will be hammering on the door. And surprisingly most of them can cook. Our Bakri Abdullah is a jewel, and with a boy to clean and wash up and make the beds (the boy is fifty years old at least), and my admirable Gunner Tofts (a true gentleman's gentleman) to run the household, bully the boy and wait on us at meals, we are indeed in clover. The first day was chaotic – furniture still arriving, and the kitchen full of Abdullahs and Hassan the boab, Muhammed the suffragi; and all their friends and relations and partners in crime. But now we are settled in and in a few days the flat will be complete. We have still to wangle a wireless and cushions, curtains, pictures and fly-netting out of the owner. But if we continue asking him for them at least five times a day, preferably waking him from his afternoon siesta, he will soon give up the struggle and provide them, if only to be rid of three exasperating British officers. And he'll swindle us some other way as compensation.

The only other snag is distance from camp. Fortunately Gethyn has a car – of something near 1923 vintage – but it goes. We have to start early to be on parade at 6.30, but just have time to dash back for lunch between lectures, and in the evenings can take our leisure, dressing most informally and thinking with pity of the crowd in the mess in their hot huts and tents, perspiring in collars and ties and drill jackets.

Life in Cairo is getting very grim! No drinks can be bought after 10 p.m. since ten days ago. That, of course, made little difference to the irredeemable 'boozers'. They just ordered sixteen whiskeys and sodas at 9.55 and sat drinking them until midnight. The final indignity has been the latest order by Nahas Pasha that to have alcoholic drinks in your possession after 10.30 p.m. will be considered a crime. And so, to the fury of the bar-owners and cabaret kings, war has come home with a vengeance to Cairo! It's hard on the men on leave from the desert who haven't touched a glass of beer, possibly for five months. But a much needed measure. Not only will it reduce the scandal of shiploads of canned beer still coming in from the U.S.A., and ships of whisky from England. But it will reduce the drunkenness among troops, of which there has been too much.

11 May

I am very near the end of my schoolmastering now, and my immediate future is settled, as far as anything is settled in the Middle East, or in war. My cadets are commissioned on May 23rd, and that should be the day of my release also. But they all do a week's course of observation of fire, as officers, immediately afterwards, and my boss has asked me particularly to stay on for that week. I shall be quite glad to do so, and spend a week watching my ex-cadets dropping their shells, I hope not *all* in the wrong places. It will be the real test of my humble attempts at teaching.

After that, on May 29th at 2.55 p.m., Hugh and I leave Cairo by the Palestine train on a week's leave. Almost as soon as I get back, I shall be starting up on the long trek west to rejoin the regiment. I shall go as a Captain, for my Colonel [Lindon Bolton] has been holding a troop open for me for several weeks already. It is settled that I go to Bill Blacker's battery and take over the troop I left last November. I couldn't wish for anything better. After that, who knows? It's idle to speculate. My immediate boss, Tom Cavenagh, for whom I have a great respect, gave me a most gratifying bouquet the other day. He said he'd been talking to my Colonel, and to some other higher authority unspecified, and while recommending me as a troop commander, had also expressed his own opinion that after three or four months I would be capable of commanding a battery. This was a bit staggering, for I'd never till then even dreamt of reaching the dizzy rank of Major. But after all, who knows? At the moment all I want to do is to wash six months of Cairo out of my system.

Hugh and I departed on leave on 29 May, as planned.
Letter, 3 June, Damascus

Here is the outline of our journeyings so far. We left Cairo last Friday by the afternoon train. A hot dusty three hours' run to Kantara on the Canal, across the ferry, a long wait for no apparent reason for the connection and a ghastly unorganised scramble through the Egyptian customs. At last got our comfortable sleeper, and woke up next morning well across the desert, jolting along through orange groves and green grassy fields with fat cows grazing, past the neat white-washed houses of the Jewish settlements. The last two hours in the train were puffing up a deep precipitous winding gorge, with real hills to look at once again, my first for over a year. And so we got to Jerusalem and were standing by 11 o'clock on the balcony outside the most expensive room in the most expensive hotel in the Middle East,[1] looking across the walls of the old city to the Mount of Olives behind.

1. The King David Hotel.

Next day we spent the morning at the Dome of the Rock, wandered through the old narrow streets and visited the Holy Sepulchre – where 'there were far too many sightseers, most of them in heavy army boots'. In the afternoon we drove out to Bethlehem. On 1 June we 'set out in our luxurious car, hired for six days for £30 – a huge price, but it has been worth it, and we couldn't have done what we have in any other way'. We drove down to the Dead Sea where we bathed, then across the Jordan, and spent the night in Amman. Next day we visited Jerash, then a long drive on through Irbid and back into Palestine at the bottom of the Lake of Galilee.

2 June, Tiberias

This is a delightful little place. Church bells are ringing as I write, but it is largely a Jewish population, though immediately below our hotel there is a mosque and a lively chatter of Arab tongues and the familiar wail of Arab music from the wireless in the local cafe, round which sit the worthies in their attractive white head-dresses. We arrived about tea-time and spent the evening at the Galilee-Lido – a quiet little bathing place that happily belied its name. After a jolly swim in the thick green water, quite cold out from shore with a gusty wind blowing down off the hills, we sat on the lake's edge under shady trees and drank beer – a truly European atmosphere, helped by the looks and talk of local inhabitants who were gossiping in German at nearby tables. Now, after eating well of fish straight from the lake, washed down by passable Palestinian red wine, I am very sleepy and shall retire to bed, for we have a strenuous day before us tomorrow. Hugh refuses, as usual, to go to bed at once, and I suspect he is learning his daily task of fifty Turkish words. I shall have to pour water over him to get him up in time in the morning.

On 3 June we drove to Damascus, and next day to Baalbeck and over the mountains to Beirut. 'A bathe, then back to Aley, a small resort perched on the slopes 2,000 feet up'. On the 5th we 'walked all day in the hills and got disastrously sunburnt', on the 6th drove down the coast road to Haifa and on the 7th 'back to beastly Cairo by train'.

Letter, 12 June

It was a lovely week to look back on. We spent a terrifying amount of money, a sum of a size I wouldn't have dared to contemplate even two years ago. Hotels, restaurants, transport, clothes; everything in Palestine is scandalously expensive, worse even than Egypt. Syria was much better, though we had been warned it would be worse. Hugh used to worry each time we had a bill presented to us, not because he felt he couldn't afford to pay it, because of course he is a notorious capitalist and war profiteer! But he was infuriated by the moral iniquity of the prices and wished to haggle over piastres, just for the principles involved. I took a quick glimpse at our first Jerusalem bill and resigned myself to the inevitable, refusing to be worried. But it's probably a good thing that I shall be living in the desert for some time, for even with the help of the £50 cabled from the Royal Bank of Scotland, my Cairo bank account has been reduced to very slender proportions. The biggest expense was of course the car, but we were extremely lucky. Hugh persuaded a proprietor who had done much work for his office in Jerusalem to hire us a smart new one, spacious and comfortable, for a much more modest price than rival organisations were prepared to hire us rather ramshackle taxis. In six days we never had a suspicion of a breakdown, not even a puncture on the rough roads of Transjordan. The car had five brand new tyres, a rare sight on a civilian car nowadays in the Middle East. Tyres in Palestine are strictly rationed and cost up to £40 each. Our driver was an Armenian, rather dour and melancholy. I used to insist to Hugh that this was because we never kept him waiting less than half an hour in the mornings. Actually it was probably because he didn't speak a great deal of English. However, he drove us most efficiently.

Hugh will probably have told you that I left him in hospital. It was a stupid ending to so successful a holiday, but he should be out of it by now and completely healed. I've never seen such sunburn – his arms and knees were a mass of huge blisters and raw flesh. But he was very comfortably established when I left him and already in better spirits. My knees are now almost normal and I can walk in a natural fashion once again: the soreness has gone, and they are beginning to peel over an enormous area. It was extraordinary that six hours in the sun should have done so much damage, even though it was the first time that either of us had worn shorts this year. Apparently the sun in higher altitudes is much more treacherous, and we were 6,000 feet up. And I've no doubt the strong cool wind made the sun burn even more fiercely.

A note at the end of the letter records that I finished it on 23 June 'safe and sound with I Battery'. During my absence in Cairo, 2RHA had been reorganised into three batteries, H, I and L. I, composed of R and S Troops, was commanded by Bill Blacker.

CHAPTER TEN: BACK TO THE DESERT: THE GREAT RETREAT
June – July 1942

The letter of 12 June was begun at the RA Advanced Reinforcements Camp near Fort Capuzzo, just across the Libyan frontier. I had left Cairo on 9 June by the 4.45 p.m. Desert Special train, 'whole train plastered with sand and not a pane of glass left in it', in the company of a fellow instructor at the OCTU, John Plant. We arrived at Mersa Matruh Transit Camp at 2 p.m. the next day. There I got news of the battle which had been raging all the time I had been on leave.[1] Cairo had been full of confidence when I left, and I was bidden God speed to Benghazi, 'where you will probably catch up with your regiment'. But I soon discovered that the situation was very far from cheerful.

Diary, 11 June

At 0800 about a dozen officers, a few ORs, and our mountains of baggage were driven out to the staging-point on Charing Cross road, two miles beyond the minefields. There we were dumped by the roadside, very forlornly: and to learn that no convoys were going west today didn't lighten our gloom. But we split into parties, drew lots for priorities, and waited for trucks to come by. In surprisingly short time John and I got onto an RAF 15-cwt, and sat reasonably comfortably on their and our junk and baggage. A good lunch at the Sidi Barrani NAAFI roadhouse. Sollum village a heap of ruins, bare shattered walls covered with "V for Victory" next to "Viva il Duce" and "Viva il Re". Some German graves by the roadside, neatly marked with crosses. Then up the steep hairpins of Halfaya pass to Sollum barracks, South African sappers working hard on widening the road. At the ruins of the Italian customs house and arch of welcome the tarmac began, and so I set foot on Libyan soil. The RAF truck dumped us at the Fort of Capuzzo, and an Eighth Army signals staff car gave us a lift down to the RA Reinforcements Camp, next door to the Transit Camp. Many conflicting rumours from the west, but general tone was hopeful.

12 June

Daniels, G3 RA, 8th Army, appeared at breakfast to settle reinforcements and officers' postings. Said 2RHA were shouting for me and I could go straight back.

---

1. Rommel's forces launched their offensive on 26 May.

But no transport forward today. The regiment has been doing stout work with the Guards in Knightsbridge box, and hasn't suffered too badly, though 'Bill was a bit rash on one occasion and lost five guns' – which sounds queer and not at all good. Lorries full of French troops passed down road towards Egypt in the evening. All in great heart, plenty of "Vs" and thumbs up. But it must mean the evacuation of Bir Hacheim. So all of us to bed depressed, not cheered by the stories told by stragglers from 4th Field, 72nd Field Regiments etc.

13 June

Things calmer this morning. As usual rumour has been exaggerating. But steady stream of lorries down the road eastwards to Halfaya and Sollum, and all trains seem to be going the same way. A long dull day. At last in the evening came word that transport will be provided for me tomorrow to take seventy reinforcements to the regiment, with odd officers to other destinations.

14 June

After much fussing and delay we finally left the Camp at 1100, a convoy of four 3-tonners. Ours seemed to be the only one going west; in the opposite direction was an endless stream of traffic, jammed for miles head to tail and hardly moving. Lorries full of troops, transporters carrying salvaged tanks and vehicles, including one 8-cwt with 2RHA's familiar sign on its mudguards. All most disconcerting. Miraculously not an enemy plane in sight, though I anxiously looked upwards many a time. Got to the Tobruk Transit Camp on the Derna road about 1630. The adjutant had had no warning of our arrival, had no idea where 2 RHA is, Knightsbridge box having been evacuated last night. The atmosphere of Tobruk seems to be complete chaos and uncertainty; no one knows what is happening, where anyone else is, who is commanding where and whom. Two unknown subalterns in the mess assured me 2RHA had been wiped out. Down the Derna road all evening and night came an unending stream of traffic, more and more of it South African. The Gazala line is being evacuated. Towards dark clear sounds of battle on the escarpments to south, flares not very far away and the old familiar German white verey lights. Fires burning merrily some way up the Derna road. A nightmare night and I slept little.

15 June

Up by 0500, I could stick the noise and fuss no longer. The traffic stream no thinner. The adjutant phoned 1 Armd. Div., no answer, they have gone in the night. Then tried 13 Corps RA – no answer. Finally CRA 2 South African Division – he knew nothing of 2RHA. No one had any suggestion. So after watching the traffic awhile, got lift on a water cart, then a 15-cwt, and four miles down the Derna road spotted vehicles with 2RHA markings – my instinct had been right. Soon discovered it was H Battery and found Peter Worthington and Peter Bishop. Heard their news. They came out of Knightsbridge Saturday (13th) evening, spent a sticky day near Acroma, future uncertain. But all in good heart in spite of no sleep for three days. Soon Bill arrived with remnants of I Battery – four guns, sixty men missing, just over half. We are still under 201 Guards Brigade, little known of our future, our orders are to wait and see.

I spent that night back with the regiment, dispersed in a 'rest' area on top of the first escarpment, and walked round the surviving troop of I Battery with Vernon Price, to get 'acquainted and re-acquainted'. The old faces were very few.

16 June

At 0800 message, "Move at once": we are to get out of Tobruk while the coast road is still open, leaving Guards behind. We are not making for frontier but are to help defend a FMC [Field Maintenance Centre], roughly 40 miles south of Gambut, which is supplying 7th Motor Brigade. A loathsome drive; strong following wind smothered us in our own dust, flies very persistent. Leaguered seven miles short of our rendezvous at dark, having driven 80 miles. Had an interesting though gloomy discussion on the battle so far, Dick Taylor[1] maintaining that we would have won it on Day 3 if our commanders had had the guts to attack with concentrated armour that day.

Next morning we drove the remaining seven miles to the FMC: 'a vast conglomeration of RASC 3-tonners and 6-tonners, spread over miles of desert: petrol, rations, water, even NAAFI', and spent 'a long day of much needed maintenance'. On the 18th we joined 7 Motor Bde, but our stay with them was very brief: next morning we received orders that the whole regiment was to move back at once to Sollum.

19 June

Set off at 1330 in a vast calvacade. On the whole good going. I navigated. Thirty miles to the frontier wire. We passed through in single file, South African MPs guarding it and thirsting for news. The whole organisation for distribution of information has been ghastly in this campaign, right from the first day. And so once again onto Egyptian soil. Immediately the flies got twice as troublesome and numerous. Perhaps only a coincidence! We halted three miles north of Bir Nuh – sadly returning to familiar ground: Arad visible in the distance, and slit trenches, Italian derelicts and old tank tracks all around us – traces of the activity we used to watch and harass from our OPs last August and September.

On 20 June we moved into action in the Sollum box, in support of the 5th Indian Infantry Brigade of 10th Indian Division.

20 June

Atmosphere in box is chaotic. Infantry ridiculously thin on the ground, minefields incomplete and the 1/25,000 map very incorrect; most of the mines are

---

1. Commander of the anti-tank battery of the Northumberland Hussars which was under 2 RHA's command.

enemy, pre-November. It's a very big area to defend. At 1930 with Vernon to reconnoitre our OP at Pt 207, the good old Qahah Italian strongpoint of Arad days. Vernon discovered an officers' mess underground, complete with tiled walls and floor, and traces of electric light. Italian officers have always done themselves well. Returned to guns as it got dark. Narrow escape when Webb picked up a bottle and began playing with it: it suddenly burst into flames and burnt for about two minutes, an Italian version of the Molotov cocktail: luckily he was standing ten feet from the truck. Patrols from both sides in contact round Capuzzo.

21 June

Battalion of Baluchis have taken over our sector of the box. Rumours that Tobruk has surrendered, but we refused to believe them. Talked to the battery at 1500, tried to put them into the picture, ending with a mild rebuke to the long faces. Later in the evening heard on the BBC that Tobruk *has* fallen. Long faces justified this time, I'm afraid. It explains why we have seen practically nothing of the Luftwaffe all this time. But now we can expect a serious attack quite soon. And I don't believe this box will hold out long. A gloomy outlook – let's hope big things are happening behind, and that Auchinleck [who had that day taken direct command of the operations] has situation properly in hand.

22 June

After breakfast Bill arrived from RHQ with news that we are leaving tonight for Baghush: the Sollum box is to be evacuated. So Rommel is going to see a fat piece of Egypt after all. We spent evening replenishing and raided a rations dump with enormous success, just before sappers blew it up.

During the night of 22/23 June we drove 35 miles south-east, together with the Baluchis, in four parallel columns, 'the Indians driving exceedingly dangerously and only by miracle were accidents avoided'. At 1145 reached Bir Khamsa, after another 30 miles.
23 June

Wandered round the guns and vehicles, but felt thoroughly browned off, by the weather, this constant muddling about and disorganised retreating, and desert life in general. I've been back with the battery over a week, and not a round fired yet in action. Bill also discouraged and depressed. Dick saved us both by bringing plentiful supply of beer and gin and lime juice from his well-equipped truck and we had a long talk over long drinks – and felt human again. Heard the news. There is to be a full-scale debate on Libya in the House, so Attlee announced today: much talk of the scandal of our being 'outgunned'. Unfortunately not true this time. I'm afraid the reasons for all this are many and deeper, and harder to be put right than simple technical deficiency. No news of enemy for miles around: not a sound of battle to be heard.

On 24 June we drove another 70 miles eastwards, ending up for the night about ten miles short of Baghush. At the end of the day my speedometer showed 117 miles, 'this including swanning'.

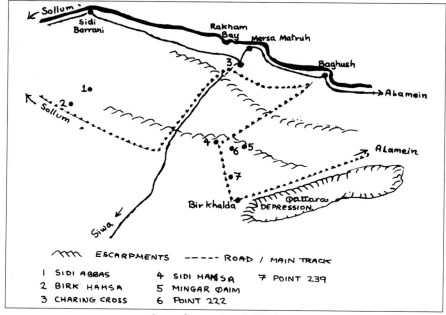

ESCARPMENTS ----- ROAD / MAIN TRACK

1 SIDI ABBAS	4 SIDI HAMSA	7 POINT 239
2 BIRK HAMSA	5 MINGAR QAIM	
3 CHARING CROSS	6 POINT 222	

Area of operations 24/28 June.

24 June

These marches are anxious affairs, for we are down to rock-bottom on vehicles, some of them falling to pieces, and even the guns are well-worn and none too happy. We leaguered very close to Baghush aerodrome: as I Battery drove in, 18 Bostons flew west, returned about ¾ hour later, another flight just before dark, and their fighter escorts twisting and gleaming in the setting sun. Most cheering sign of action and efficiency: the battery greatly heartened.

Next day we moved back westwards for twenty miles to Sidi Hamsa, with orders to join the 22nd Armoured Brigade. But we failed to find them.

25 June

All was confusion, Bill swearing lustily at lack of promised guide, no-one knowing where to go, feverishly investigating clumps of MT in panic that enemy had arrived, but they turned out to be 1 Armd. Div. HQ! By then too dark to do anything but leaguer.

Night 25/26 June

Woke about midnight to hear plane droning overhead: hoped it was RAF on patrol. At 0020 it dropped a flare, then others every five minutes or so, as it flew backwards and forwards over us, lighting us up almost as brightly as daylight and throwing jet-black long shadows from every truck. Decided our close leaguer was a most enticing target, so we dispersed to 50 yards minimum between vehicles: one of those simple operations that take so long because of general dopiness of everyone just hauled out of their beds. I then returned to mine at about 0130. Still the flares dropped. It was about 0200 that the fun started in earnest, planes diving low and machine-gunning us, bullets unpleasantly near my bed, and some lorries hit, but without damage: then bombs, smallish, but they made a big bang and the ground shook alarmingly: two fires started to the south of us, one of them a 3-tonner of L Battery, and heard afterwards they had two killed and several wounded. Could see silhouettes of planes quite clearly when they came low – one twin-engined bomber looked suspiciously like a Blenheim. At 0430 the last plane flew away. I never want to spend a night like that again.

26 June

I went up at first light to an OP at Pt 222, a high point on the escarpment named Mingar Sidi Hamsa, views excellent almost all round. Attack had been expected at 0630, but all was quiet. The guns moved forward four miles and went into action during the afternoon. I set off in the armoured car as roving OP. Mirage very bad. Enemy armoured cars and MT visible up on the Siwa track in the distance. As light got worse, sounds of biggish battle ahead, with heavy shelling, and infantry appeared in large numbers over Siwa track ridge. Soon saw they were Indians, withdrawing in some haste, and many of their lorries obviously reluctant to wait to pick them up. At one moment looked like a stampede, but situation saved in time. Soon afterwards Bill told me to come in, the whole brigade withdrew to much the same spot as we left this morning. Heard officially that our visitors last night were definitely the RAF!

27 June

Broke leaguer early, about 0800 moved back to our gun position of yesterday, a five mile drive. From the noise obviously a battle was in progress forward. I took the armoured car to watch the northern flank, where enemy were reported to be creeping up the escarpment to outflank us. Almost as soon as guns were ready, I shot them at MT and some guns behind lorries moving towards us at top of escarpment. Mirage bad: two 75s came into action 2,000 yards in front, shelled me and the dug-in 6-pdrs nearby, but not very seriously or accurately. Vernon saw their flashes in the mirage-hidden wadi and engaged them. Soon after they, and most of the MT, withdrew: three armoured cars remained moving up and down, but I did a reasonably good shoot on them and they too disappeared about 1030, leaving our right flank clear. Whole brigade withdrew at 1130, back to where we spent last night. In afternoon I went out to Pt 239, a very conspicuous lozenge-shaped hill five miles to south. Saw Gordon McFall at Pt 222, my OP of yesterday morning. Little activity. Recalled to gun position at 1800. Heard evacuation of Matruh, 20 miles due north of us, started yesterday morning. About 1900 an enemy column of hundreds of vehicles (the lorries mostly captured British) and twenty or more tanks reported moving N.E. towards us. I went out to look at them, at least 20 squat ugly tanks creeping between us and Pt 222, making towards escarpment, with acres of vehicles spreading out behind them in clouds of dust. Just as light began to go they opened up on our leading tank patrols. Absurd battle began at extreme range, tracer flew for over half an hour, a fascinating sight, but I doubt if any damage was done on either side. At 2030 we pulled out and formed leaguer in the dark. Our tanks broke off engagement and stayed nicely between us and the enemy, Vernon with them. Gordon McFall did not turn up: we heard some weeks later that he is now confirmed POW, a very great loss.

Night 27/28 June

We moved off at 2230, making for Bir Khalda, with orders to find 3CLY [3rd City of London Yeomanry] and keep with them for the long drive back to Wavell's Alamein-Qattara line. Very dark night. Not far beyond my OP at Pt 239 four tanks appeared in the gloom, sitting not 300 yards away. Dick Taylor and I stopped and lined up four 6-pdrs, sighting one on each tank. Rest of column hurried on. When we were all ready for the excitement, a man started walking towards us from the tanks. Dick and I met him halfway, escorted by one of Dick's gunners with a Bren. Turned out to be a Tank Corps subaltern with four Crusaders, one being repaired: a bit alarmed by the lining up of the 6-pdrs! Got to Bir Khalda about midnight. The moon rose, which helped. Enemy verey lights not far off, and obviously the column that attacked us at sunset was following us up. A few lorries broke down but fitters as usual did wonders. How I dislike retreats, it's such anxious work, with that constant childish fear of being left behind. We couldn't find 3CLY in the clumps of vehicles, so moved off behind 7 Armd. Div. HQ. I kept up the rear, whipping in. One of our ammunition 3-tonners had a puncture and fitters found its inner tube irreparable: luckily succeeded in borrowing wheel off H Bty. Took maddening time to change it and we were well behind the column and feeling nervous. But caught them up again at 0200 in their leaguer.

28 June

Opened out as it got light, and the 3-tonner had another puncture. I was quite glad of the halt, for I was dozing off standing upright in the armoured car. This time no spare wheel to be found, so abandoned the lorry after smashing engine, tyres, water cans, etc., but couldn't do much with the ammunition. Piled its six passengers onto the armoured car and the fitters 15-cwt and, appallingly overloaded, continued on our way.

It was not until the following evening that I met up with the regiment again, after endless enquiries from a multitude of British, New Zealand, Indian and South African units, some of them as lost as myself.

30 June

Stood to before first light. I drove south-eastwards to a ridge with a good view. Soon spotted an immense column of vehicles to the south, gradually bestirring itself from its night leaguer and getting on the move. No one knew whether it was 7 Motor Bde or the enemy. Eventually, when most of it had disappeared into the east, our tanks went out to investigate the lorries that hadn't moved, found they were enemy. Rifle Brigade went out to help, burnt many lorries, brought back several 10-tonners loaded with Italian infantry and supply personnel, and four 're-inforcing' German officers. As they drove back to us they came into the middle of a tank battle. About twenty M13s of the Ariete Division attacked us from behind. I was slow to grasp the very confusing situation and in fact only realised that the tank sitting about 600 yards from me on the hill was an M13 when it started machine-gunning me. I popped inside my Honey very quickly. About 0830 the Italians withdrew, leaving seven tanks knocked out or burning, which our sappers promptly blew up. At 0930 our column formed up 'facing the Union Bar' [in Alexandria] as Bill put it over the air. After five miles there were noises ahead and the column halted again. I went up to the front, found Bill and a bunch of senior officers clustered round the brigadier's tank: sporadic shelling, and dim splodges through the mirage directly east of us showed a German column plumb on our line of march. After much palaver a way round was found. Rising dust proved a good friend, and although the enemy can't have been more than 2,000 yards ahead, all we did was drive three miles north, then due east again, and no more trouble all day. A long hot dusty 30 mile march. Towards evening we at last hit the wire of the Alamein box, behind it serious-looking fortifications with slits of pillboxes just showing above ground and dugouts of cement well covered with sand and rubble. A cheering sight. South Africans inside. After failing to get any orders we closed up and bedded down for the night.

1 July

We sat waiting all morning after putting our guns into action. About 1600 came hurried excited orders to move west in support of an Indian box which was being hard-pressed. After a drive of about eight miles we went into action in a valley with prominent ridges on both sides. Two ME 109s skimmed close over us, almost hitting my mudguard. Bill and I sat in the armoured car on the northern ridge, afterwards to be famous as Ruweisat. Vernon on the southern ridge later named Essex. Good view of the valley between and a gigantic concentration of enemy MT to north and north-west. Saw distinctly at least fifteen tanks to the north and nine to the south. They were engaged by CLY. Bill and I shot up the MT, competing with Vernon, who had gone forward with 4CLY, for control of the guns – rarely does a gunner get such targets. Indians were meanwhile evacuating the box at high speed, skidding down the ridge on punctured tyres, the Indian drivers very scared and out of control. They had reason to be: as they came out of the box and drove over Ruweisat ridge, they were running the gauntlet of every gun the enemy could bring to bear on them. Bill and I helped to engage a

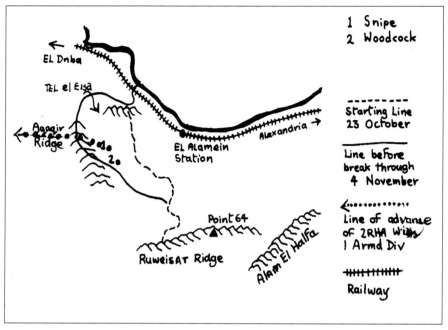

The Alamein battlefield, July/November 1942.

battery of four 75s, making them shift. Meanwhile Vernon was shooting in support of our tanks in action at the western end of Ruweisat ridge. Tracer flying, and we were getting the overs. Many Indian vehicles hit along the ridge. As light faded the CLY withdrew, leaving one Crusader and two Honeys burning, and their colonel, Frank Arkwright, killed. The Indian box completely overrun, though most of its defenders got out. Our help came too late – once again. But I doubt if the box could have been saved: it was unfinished and the minefields were full of gaps. We moved back about six miles in the dusk and dark, leagured in much the same place as last night. To bed at midnight a bit depressed. But at last, a fortnight after I rejoined the battery, we are getting down to it: tonight was only the second time I've had a shoot in all these days.

2 July

I went out at first light, to get contact with the enemy and watch him in the area where we engaged him last night. Crossed the valley and onto Ruweisat Ridge, made my way slowly and cautiously westwards, keeping under cover of the ridge on the south side. Vernon meanwhile crept westward along the Essex Ridge. Enemy MT were still in position, acres of dispersed lorries stretching away to north, west and south-west, into the dim distance. Our guns came into action quite near our last night's leaguer – this meant they could only reach nearest fringe of enemy at extreme range. From 0645 South African guns to my right rear put a series of short concentrations into the MT, moving their fire backwards and forwards, quite effective harassing. Gradually the tempo quickened. At 1045 five Mark 111s [German tanks] came into my sight, creeping very very slowly along the slopes of the ridge facing me, till by about 1400 they were about level with me on the opposite side of the valley. Meanwhile at about 1130 there suddenly emerged out of the stationary MT to my north-west a column of thirty lorries, some towing guns, and moved towards the western end of Ruweisat Ridge. It was tantalising to have such a perfect front-line view and be unable to use my guns which were out of range. About 1145 enemy started shelling the ridge pretty accurately and I moved 400 yards east. South African gunners opened up, a lovely piece of shooting, and I saw the enemy column disperse and men jump out of their lorries and run for cover and slit trenches. I chatted with an OP from 11th Field Regiment and told him all I could. His whole regiment came forward into action in the valley just east of our position last night. About 1300 I edged forward once again about 700/800 yards, crawled up onto top of ridge and saw, perhaps 200 yards away, just over the crest, a vast gun, an 88-mm, with its crew leisurely digging it in and standing around: infantry in same area, also obviously digging positions. It looked so near that I felt I could almost throw stones at it. I put Morrow out of the armoured car onto the ground with his Bren, in case infantry thought of walking up the hill to meet me, and showed the gun to the 11th Field OP, who at once started to range. Morrow highly delighted and couldn't resist shooting at some of the nearest German infantry – but not very good marksmanship. All this made us rather conspicuous and shortly afterwards we withdrew east along the ridge as shells were falling unpleasantly close.

At 1500 Bill ordered me back over the air – a grand advance by 1 Armd. Div. was planned: 22 Armd. Bde., with us following close behind, were about to start moving 16 miles west, then swing north to meet, engage and destroy the main body of enemy armour which GSI [General Staff Intelligence] are confident are concentrated in that area. The plan was utter nonsense, I at once told Bill: those Mark 111s which I had been reporting all morning were not there just for fun, and to expect us to break through them and all the acres of guns and MT, and drive 16 miles behind the enemy's lines was crass stupidity. We moved off about 1630: I did OP protection left rear. After two miles of majestic progress in disciplined open formations we came under considerable heavy shelling. Vernon, forward with the leading tanks, ordered the troop into action and did a lot of shooting into the Ruweisat valley. Three Mark 111s appeared about 2,000 yards in front of me and Dick's 6-pdrs opened up at extreme range. The tanks replied and I had to shift many times when AP tracer flew past my armoured car. Dick drove round visiting his guns in his 8-cwt, completely cool and unconcerned – what a first-class soldier he is, and what delightful company. At least one of the Mark 111s was hit by 6-pdrs though not set alight. Shelling continued. Bill joined me and we kept well away from the excitements. Towards evening all calmed down, a dullish battle, and we pulled back two miles into leaguer. Our great advance has been a fiasco: on the other hand enemy are no further forward than last night after over-running the Indians. Rommell announced this morning that he was through the Alamein line in this sector: well, he's counting his chickens too soon, and reckoning without 1 Armd Div.

On 3 July the regiment moved forward into action about two miles south-east of Ruweisat ridge in a defensive role. I spent the morning prospecting for suitable OPs on its northern slopes. There were many stationary enemy tanks and vehicles in the valley below, but it was hard to tell whether they were 'live' or derelicts from the previous evening's battle. In the afternoon came an enemy counter-attack which Dick Taylor's 6-pdrs helped to repulse, but fire from I Battery was not required. We were shelled sporadically all day.
4 July

Up to the northern slopes of Ruweisat at first light and found an excellent OP in a shallow pit which someone had dug just below the crest of the ridge. I edged the front of my armoured car into it, 'hull down', so that all but the observation turret was under cover, and as its doors were at the back, one could get in and out totally unobserved by the enemy, and my driver could brew up outside. Dick Taylor had his OP close-by. Many visitors during the day, some of them drew sniper fire; two infantry officers, despite my warnings, hit quite near me. Immediately in front of me there was some dead ground in which I suspected there might be German infantry, so I registered it. As the battery's guns were on the far side of the enemy from me, I started firing smoke at myself until I got the range. Several other regiments were firing into the valley, and I occasionally joined in, shooting at individual tanks or vehicles and forcing them to keep moving. This was also a way of identifying derelicts.

In the early afternoon enemy tanks starting moving very slowly up the valley, till Dick Taylor's guns halted them. Then at about 1500 the valley suddenly sprang to life, with infantrymen jumping out of their slit-trenches or dismounting from their troop carriers. I engaged what looked like one platoon edging obliquely up the slope towards me and made them turn round and run. Every gun within range then opened up for five to ten minutes, and our tanks began to move forward. At that moment Bill came on the air to say that ammunition was getting short and ask, was my shooting necessary? "It's a crucial moment", I replied, and he authorised me to continue. Soon afterwards, magically, the valley seemed to empty of infantry, and the tanks also moved away leaving about a dozen derelicts. There was a general withdrawal of enemy vehicles towards the west. We all, 6-pdrs and OPs, moved 2,000 yards down the ridge in high spirits, until we met resistance. Psychologically we felt it had been a decisive moment, that the tide had turned, and at dusk we withdrew to our leaguers hoping that tomorrow might bring another advance.[1]

---

1. It is now generally agreed by historians that the battles of 1/4 July were indeed decisive: Rommel had been halted and Egypt had been saved.

But these hopes were disappointed. For the next four days the position remained static: a temporary stalemate had been reached. I spent my time partly with the guns, partly manning an OP on Ruweisat, partly swanning and reconnoitring, almost like the old frontier days of summer 1941. On 5 July I was careless with my compass bearings as I returned to the guns at dusk, and two 88-mm shells passed unpleasantly close. The enemy artillery and Luftwaffe were very active (as also was the RAF) and we suffered several casualties.

On 9 July I Battery received sudden orders to move 20 miles north to the coast for special operations under the 9th Australian Division. With the enemy tied down in the Ruweisat sector, Auchinleck had decided to attack on the northern flank along the coastal strip. We were to be part of a column consisting of A Squadron of the 6th Royal Tank Regiment, a troop of armoured cars from the Royal Scots Greys, and ourselves. Our commander was Major Jim Richardson of 6RTR. The Australians were to attack next morning at first light astride the main road, with Pt 33 on the Tel el Eisa ridge as their objective, after which our 'raiding party' would pass through them and make for the Daba airfields, ten miles to the west, where we were to inflict maximum damage, then rapidly return. We were told that the Italian Trentino Division was immediately in front of us, and between Alamein and Daba was the Sabratha Division with only 20 anti-tank guns. Neither Bill nor I felt enthusiastic at the prospect: it sounded all too like the operation which had ended in disaster for the battery on 30/31 May. We spent the night in leaguer not far from the sea, just north of the main road and in front of the Australian guns.

10 July

Australian infantry attack at 0330, huge barrage. Our column dispersed at 0530. Shortly afterwards Jim Richardson, Bill and I were standing around, awaiting orders, when a stray 105mm shell dropped right beside us. Jim was seriously injured (and died of his wounds next day). Bill was hit in the arm, which began to bleed copiously. We applied an amateurish tourniquet while I did my best to put on a consoling bedside manner, and he was quickly evacuated. So I found myself in command of the four gun battery, with only Vernon Price, Danny Davis, David Boe and David Wootton. One of the 6RTR's squadron commanders, Major E.J.A. Pettman, took over command of the column.

At 1030 we moved six miles west down the road. The Australians had reached their first objective on the coast, but were held up when they turned inland across the railway towards Tel el Eisa. We dispersed outside the Alamein box while 6RTR sent patrols forward to contact the infantry. Heavy shelling from southwest, and Stuka and JU88 raids on Aussie guns, infantry and transport. For us it was a day of waiting, and at dusk we withdrew into the box which was held by the South Africans.

11 July

Woken at 0200 for new orders: we were to form part of Day Column, which was to attack south-westwards and raid Deir el Abayad, about five miles west of

Ruweisat Ridge and behind the enemy's forward troops. It sounded pretty crazy. Our start in the dark was chaotic, partly owing to the soft sand and salt marshes in which several of our vehicles got bogged down: but the mines were lifted for us at 0400 and we got as far as the Qattara track, where we went into action. The 6RTR reported men wandering around: these turned out to be Italians, who emerged in their hundreds from their trenches and ran forward with their hands up, eager to surrender and get out of the war. Later that morning they passed us, 1600 in all, many of them grinning happily, their minute escort urging them on with rude and good-natured cries.

Italian soldiers surrendering.

Confused fighting for the rest of the day. Danny and David had plenty of shooting in support of an Australian battalion which, with the help of 44RTR, captured Tel el Eisa, but then ran into heavy shelling. German units had been brought up to hold our attack and offered tough resistance, so no opportunity arose for our column to carry out our 'raid'. There was continuous shelling all around us, and several attacks by Stukas and JU88s, one of which we saw brought down in flames by our fighters. Pulled out at 1900 and returned to our last night's leaguer inside the Alamein defences.

The next five days were marked by great confusion. The enemy launched a number of counter-attacks and and we received a succession of orders to support Australian or South African units, only to have them cancelled a few hours later.

For much of the time we were out of action. This at least enabled us to carry out urgent maintenance and to get some rest.

On 15 July we moved into a nice sheltered gun position between the railway and the Tel el Eisa ridge, in support of the 26th Australian Infantry Brigade. The role of 6RTR was to reconnoitre and send out patrols on the right flank, in order to draw off some of the enemy's forces from the main sector of operations further east. I spent that day and most of the next with Pettman at his HQ, while Vernon and David went forward with the tanks and had sporadic shoots.

On the night of 16/17 July the Australian infantry made a limited advance to the south-west. At 0500 we moved out of our night leaguer to the same gun position we had occupied for the two previous days, and engaged a variety of targets in support of the Australian divisional cavalry on the right flank. We had only tanks in front of us, and no idea of what enemy forces we were facing. On the afternoon of 17 July I set off in my tank to reconnoitre. As I passed the tank of one of 6RTR's troop commanders, he warned me that there might be an 88-mm in the valley behind the low ridge immediately in front of us. I decided to try to locate and engage it, so edged very slowly up towards the crest, standing full upright on my tank, hoping to get a glimpse of it without being seen – as I had done successfully on 2 July. About 1,000 yards to my left front I had spotted what looked like a machine-gun post. In fact, as I realised later, it was also an OP for the 88-mm. Before I could see over the crest, an 88-mm shell whistled past us very close. I at once told my driver, "Back quick, quick as you can", and dropped down into the turret. But it was too late, and a second shell scored a direct hit. I climbed out and tumbled to the ground, realised that I had been wounded, but scrambled back up onto the tank to look inside. There were flames and smoke rising, and my crew[1] of three were obviously dead. I hobbled back to the 6RTR tank which I had passed earlier, and a truck soon arrived to take me back to the guns and on to a Field Dressing Station. There I was sedated, after which I was only vaguely conscious of being transported in an ambulance. I woke up next morning in a hospital somewhere near Alexandria. My wound was dressed, and that day at 1100 I was put on a hospital train which delivered me at 1900 to No. 6 General Hospital at Qassassin.

1. Gnrs Carroll, Morrow and Newton.

CHAPTER ELEVEN: IN HOSPITAL AND CONVALESCING
July – September 1942

Letter, 22 July

6th General Hospital, Egypt. Yet another change of address, and so many gaps in my correspondence that you must have given up trying to puzzle out my movements. But I'll try to explain it all now. You will have had a letter written on my way up to the desert, mostly about Transjordan. After a long delay I managed to finish it and post it, about 25th June, while with I Battery. Then you will also have had a wire saying "Safe and well July 7th". That was sent by an officer of the battery who went back to Alexandria for a short business visit. Just ten days later, on the 17th, I was out on observation for my troop when my tank got a direct hit from a largish anti-tank gun. I am lucky to be here, as my crew of three, as good soldiers and companions as any in the desert, were all killed instantaneously. As you can imagine, it was a moment that is not pleasant to look back on, and I feel a terrible responsibility for those three. I shall never forget it. And yet to win wars and battles risks must be taken. I took a risk, and in the same situation I think I should do the same again. I only pray to God that I was right.

As for myself, let me tell you exactly how I am, so that you can stop all worrying at once. There is a fair-sized hole in my left thigh, which is fearsome to look at, but which is not in the least serious. I can move my foot and toes about just as easily as if nothing had happened, and so you see, miraculously, it is only a flesh wound, although a large one. There is also what the experts call a 'small deep wound' in the back of my left hand. They seem to think that one or two minor bones have been broken. But here again, it's nothing very serious, for I can move all my fingers, even though I can't use them to lift or grip. Apart from these, all that's wrong with me is as fine a collection of bruises, on my arms and legs and back, as I've ever seen. It won't be long before they disappear. I don't know whether the wounds were caused by splinters from the anti-tank shell or from pieces of the tank, but the effect would be the same in either case. At present both the leg and the hand are in plaster, and I am pretty immobile. But very comfortable, and in *no* pain. And so there is no need for you to worry at all.

This hospital sits on what two years ago was the bare desert. It is an efficient institution. I am sitting up in a springy bed with beautiful white sheets, in a ward of about twenty-four – one of those round huts with walls and roof all in one piece, electric fans, plenty of light, and yet so built that the sun never shines directly inside. We are fed admirably; chicken, salads, black currant tart, beer for supper – for a while I ask for nothing better. But it *is* hot, very hot indeed. Not so hot as last year at just this time of year when I was in bed with tonsilitis down by Cairo. But hot enough to make the afternoons very tedious and uncomfortable. So, although it's tiresome being moved again, I shan't be sorry to leave for Palestine tomorrow – I never thought I should visit it again so soon. Nobody knows which hospital it will be, but whether it's at Jerusalem or by the sea, it will be a great improvement on this.

It was a bad time for me to get knocked out. I was the fourth officer casualty in the battery within a week, and there had been two the week before. The old faces were pitifully thin by the time I rejoined them, but they are a good deal thinner now. The first casualty of last week was Bill Blacker. Do you remember my introducing you to him on St. Pancras station almost two years ago? He had a large piece taken out of his arm by a shell splinter, but was not seriously hurt. After he was evacuated, I was commanding what was left of the battery. I actually rejoined them in Tobruk, and we were all very glad to get out of the place – although at the time, of course, none of us seriously considered the possibility of the fortress being lost. From the moment I arrived we started going back. It was my third major retreat, and the longest of them all. We all found it a great strain and it was hard not to be depressed. In France and Greece it was obvious to everyone why we were retreating. But this time it didn't make sense. It all seemed so unnecessary and inexplicable. I of course missed the early part of the battle when things were going well. I hope you read the exploits of 2RHA with the Guards Brigade in the Knightsbridge Box. I found them in Tobruk two nights after they had evacuated Knightsbridge. I suppose the military spokesmen in Cairo are being denounced by you all at home for their unwarranted, misleading optimism. But talk to anyone who went through the first five days of the battle, and he will tell you that everyone up there was convinced at the end of the third day that we had won. They *knew* they had won. And yet! So narrow is the margin between victory and defeat. I don't suppose anyone yet knows why things did go wrong. We all have our own ideas, but I doubt if any single mistake or deficiency explains it. And in any case, what is important now is the future, a future with great possibilities. But it's not going to be easy – no sudden victories and triumphant pursuits – just yet, anyhow. It will be a slow, painful process – hard slogging, and there'll be a price to pay as always. And I expect Rommel has some tricks up his sleeve yet. But no one here is gloomy – just calm and rather grimly confident. I hope to be out and about long before it's all over. And this time it will be an advance. It's got to be. It's some consolation to me that I was knocked out during an advance, slight though it was. That morning we had gone forward just about a mile and taken hundreds of Italian prisoners. So we were doing something – my first advance this war. And all this on an undulating, quite unattractive piece of desert called Tel el Eisa, which, as all the newspapers in the world have been announcing, means "Hill of Jesus".

Continued 26 July

23rd Scottish Hospital, Bir Yakub. I couldn't finish this in the desert after all; but here I am in Palestine, comfortably established and fast recovering. I think it will be well worth your writing to this address. Besides, then you'll be able to send me my birthday greetings. What a way to spend a birthday [on 6 August]. But better perhaps than in the dust and sweat and noise of battle, somewhere down by Ruweisat Ridge!

3 August

Once again you will have to excuse the pencil – ink is very difficult to manage in bed, even if I had ink to refill my fountain pen. And I'm afraid this will only be two pages, for the same reason – I think this will be the first time I have ever failed to fill all three pages of a letter-card. Life here is becoming monotonous in its peacefulness. The hospital is a good one. My ward is a long, cheerful hut with rows of windows on both sides, a verandah facing south on which some of us take our ease in the cooler mornings. It's a superior sort of hut – smooth concrete floors, walls of timber and white plaster. Much better than anything the army can afford to put up nowadays. I imagine the whole hospital was laid out during the 'troubles'[1]. They look after us well. The sisters work like slaves for us. Both they and the orderlies are Scottish. The unit was raised in Peebles, and they all come from roundabout, some from Edinburgh, but all full of a fierce Lowland pride. It's good to hear the accents and the soft singing voices. Besides the Scottish orderlies there are three Italian prisoners to do the dirty jobs. Very cheerful they are, and friendly, and they never seem to stop working. I have sent for my Italian dictionary and grammar from Cairo and intend to have quite a lot of fun with Argo, who looks after me. He comes from Rome and has a long scar on the side of his head from a wound he got in Eritrea. We have a date in St. Peter's after the war. At present he is learning English much faster that I'm learning Italian which is rather humiliating! As soon as I am up and about, I shall make for the bookshops in Tel Aviv or Jerusalem, and buy a select little library with which to amuse myself, during my stay at the convalescent camp, and then on sick leave. And I might even seriously get down to the Russian grammar Hugh presented to me some months ago, with its disquisitions on social injustice and the economics of collectivism and the life of the great leader, Comrade Joe!

You can imagine how we snap up every speech and promise and rumour on the subject of the Second Front. What a day it will be when we read in our morning paper that British and American troops – divisions of them – have made their successful landing, and that Europe is ablaze behind the German armies. Do it we must, and soon – *if* we can. But when I think of the risks I go cold all over, and humbly thank God it's not *me* that has to make the decision.

---

1. The Arab rebellion of 1936-39.

12 August

I am progressing still, rather slow but very sure. The hand has completely healed, although I can't yet use the fingers as much as I should like. Apparently it will return to normal, and I have been told to hasten the process by 'constant physical and mental exercise'. So I spend hours lying on my bed waggling my fingers in the air, and saying to myself, 'I will straighten that little finger, I will, I will, I will'. It all helps to pass the long days. The leg is very much better. The plaster was taken off some days ago and since then I have been much more comfortable. The deep wound has closed almost completely, and the doctors and sisters look at it from time to time and exclaim in enthusiastic tones, "A very nice wound Mr.Watson", or occasionally, with something approaching ecstasy, "Oh, that's lovely". From all of which I gather it is healing faster than originally expected.

I've had quite enough of this hospital existence, but am not too bored or impatient. Every day has the same comfortable routine. At 5.15 we are woken up and our mosquito nets are ruthlessly torn off us. I usually spend the next hour with my head under the sheets, only popping it out to drink my early morning cup of tea, wave frantically at the attacking hordes, maddened with hunger after a night of frustration buzzing round the net – and then down under the sheets again. About 6.15 the night sister and the orderlies have become too insistent to be ignored, and I have to emerge for a wash and shave. By the time that is finished the sun is up, the fans are going full blast, the floor is being swept, and most of the mosquitos have retired to their murky daytime crannies. About 7 Joseph the fruit man arrives, and we buy our daily hoard of grapes or figs or tomatoes, and sometimes a "sugar melon, very gooood, very gooood". Soon after comes the paper boy, and we settle down to our miserable *Palestine Posts* with their scrappy, tantalisingly incomplete news snippets and Zionist gossip. Breakfast at 8, then more sweeping, tidying, bedmaking. Probably one of the MOs comes round. The Major is a delightful person, and I'm told a very skilled surgeon: he is gentle and sympathetic, and has a sense of humour. His underling, a captain, is not so welcome. When he apppears, the whole ward groans. Some mornings he strides in looking very purposeful, and it's obvious he is on the warpath. He seems to take a delight in prodding and pulling and squeezing at all the tenderest spots. He gave me a very uncomfortable twenty minutes when I first arrived here. When the MO has gone and the dressings are done, we settle down to our books or letters or jigsaw puzzles. Tea at 3.30. During the afternoon a boy from the NAAFI comes round offering tinned fruit and chocolate and soap and oddments. So that we don't starve when the 'plain', most unimaginative hospital cooking gets too depressing. We have to have our grumbles: and it is a bit exasperating to have dished up to one twice a day for a week on end identically the same portion of an underboiled old hen, under the guise of roast chicken. At one time I found myself longing for a good thick army stew. And from our corner of the ward came a plaintive sigh, "Oh I wish they'd give me a tasty slice of bully". So quickly do one's standards and sense of proportion change. But to finish the day:

in the evenings we listen to the wireless, usually the forces' programme from London. Supper at 7, and then the worst part of the day. The doors are shut and the blackout shutters drawn across the windows and the mosquitos come out. It is very hot, and by that time I'm feeling too tired to read but not tired enough to go to sleep with the lights in my eyes. At last, about 9.30, our nets are let down, the lights are turned off, and I go to sleep, very rarely dreaming, very rarely waking till 5.15 next morning.

25 August

Last Tuesday they decided to perform a secondary suture on my leg and as a result I haven't been feeling quite myself for the last three days. The anaesthetic made me extremely sick, and the leg is now extremely sore and tender. But to my inexpert eye it looks as if a miracle of surgery has been performed on me. Instead of a broad piece of raw flesh, there is now a neat row of stitches joining the skin just where the wound used to be. The doctors are sure that the operation has been a complete success, and so I am waiting hopefully for the day when I shall be allowed up.

It has been some week, this last one! Churchill at Alamein, then a new C-in-C, then the Moscow meeting, then Dieppe. What would we do without Churchill? His visit out here has made everyone sit up. I wish I could have seen him in the desert.[1] And now it looks as if it was boiling up again.[2] Alexander comes with a great reputation. It's an unfortunate moment to swap commanders. There must have been a very good reason for it. Montgomery is an old friend – he commanded the 3rd Division in France, of which we were a part. He was an outstanding, inspiring personality, and a first-class divisional commander. It's good to be under him again.

Alexander was the new commander-in-chief, Middle East, and Montgomery was the new commander of Eighth Army.

31 August

Big events have taken place since I wrote last. On Wednesday my thirteen stitches were removed and on Saturday I was allowed out of my bed for the first time. Yesterday I was allowed even to walk a few steps. Altogether I feel in high spirits and have literally taken on a new lease of life. Your cable with the news that Hugh was in Cape Town arrived, funnily enough, by the same post as a cable from Hugh himself, giving his address as Marine Hotel. I only hope that he is on

---

1. Churchill was in Egypt from 3 to 10 August, in Moscow from the 12th to the 16th, and in Egypt again from the 17th to the 22nd. He paid two visits to Alamein, including Ruweisat Ridge and Tel el Eisa, and also visited many units in training.

Dieppe was raided by a mainly Canadian force on 19 August.

2. Rommel launched an attack at Alam Halfa on 30 August but was forced to call it off three days later.

his way home to you, and not just stuck in the Cape, neglected and forgotten after his evacuation.

My brother Hugh had been evacuated from Cairo, together with all other 'non-essential personnel', at the beginning of July when it seemed possible that a German-Italian breakthrough at Alamein would lead to the Delta being overrun.

10 September

Big news again this week. I leave hospital on Friday and go to a seaside convalescent camp about 40 miles from here for two weeks. I had a medical board yesterday and was granted 'D' for two weeks, and then 'A'; which means that unless I have a relapse or any other odd mishap, I shall be able to rejoin the battery in just over a fortnight's time. I'm much more mobile now, and have twice been down to the camp cinema, about half a mile away. This afternoon I'm taking the bus into the nearby garrison town [Sarafand] to buy clothes and books and oddments. The doctors were rather doubtful whether two weeks in category 'D' would be long enough. But I really do think that by then I shall be fit. The hand gives me little trouble, though recently I found I couldn't cut the finger-nails on my right hand, and I haven't full strength in the fingers yet. I can't move the fourth and little fingers 'laterally' at all, and apparently I may never get those muscles working again. But it's a trivial matter, and as my MO said, is hardly likely to bother me unless I decide to take up the career of a concert pianist or a cardshaper.

In the last week there have been more changes in the ward. I am now sleeping in a tent, an annexe to the ward, having been turned out of my old bed by an American bomber pilot who was badly shot up while attacking a convoy – most successfully attacking – off the south coast of Crete. We are a truly international collection. Apart from the New Zealanders and South Africans, we have an ex-officer in the Imperial Russian army who for years has been running a sanatorium in Sweden and is now a naturalised British subject and a captain in the Rifle Brigade. He is a professional masseur, with the biggest biceps I've ever seen. Then we have an Indian captain, a very cultured fire-eater with no love for either Mr. Jinnah or Gandhi & Co. There is a Czech officer, rather shy and dull, who escaped from Brno via Hungary and Jugoslavia in 1940: he is a gunner and I have had long discussions about Czech, German and British guns. He is a passionate, though not bigoted, believer in horse-drawn artillery – but not in the desert. And in addition to two more American airmen and one Canadian pilot, we have a Jugoslav naval pilot, who flew his seaplane from Kotor to Alexandria in April '41. He is a Slovene and his wife and small son are in Ljubljana. He has heard from them twice in the last eighteen months, and is naturally beside himself with anxiety. His wife's sister lives fifteeen miles north of Ljubljana, in the German 'zone', and it took them a whole year to get permission to meet. So you see, with so many nationalities, there is plenty of variety and talk, and we learn a good deal.

It will be a relief to get out of hospital, for I'm beginning to stagnate. But they have looked after me admirably, and I shall always be grateful to Maj.Lowden, who did a wonderful piece of surgery on my leg. And I shan't forget this view that I'm looking at now – the ground falling away from this verandah to the orange groves and the neat little two-storey farm houses. Beyond, at the bottom of the valley, runs the railway. For weeks, while I lay in bed, the engine whistles were my only link with the outer world. And in the distance I can just see a glaring patch of sand dunes showing above a long row of jet-black cypresses. Behind the dunes, somewhere, is the sea.

On 11 September I travelled by bus to No. 3 Convalescent Camp Depot at Nathanya, twenty miles north of Tel Aviv.
18 September
It's just a week since I came to this camp, and the sea air, good food and plenty of gentle strolling have been doing wonders to make me fit again. This is a very jolly spot. The camp is ten minutes walk from the sea, but from the verandah of the mess one looks over the sand dunes, covered with coarse grass and scrub, to a wide expanse of blue. My favourite walk is along the top of the cliffs which run all down this coast. I was told not to bathe when I arrived because of the danger of the wound opening up again if exposed to the sand and dirt of the beach. I'm going to have my first dip this afternoon, but shan't go far out till I see how strong I feel swimming. I become 'A1' on the 22nd, and will probably be discharged two days later. It may take several days to get to Cairo.

Yesterday I took a bus into Tel Aviv for the day. I thought I'd better see it while I had the chance. I'm glad I went, though I've no desire to return. I walked along the sea front, sat in a cool cafe and read newspapers, and had an excellent lunch in a small restaurant in the town. The Wienerschnitzel was superb, and I struck a good local red wine. I don't know why it should make one smile to see the 'King Solomon Hotel' in Lord Samuel Esplanade. But there are all sorts of blatant incongruities like that in Tel Aviv. The taxi-drivers speak German to each other; in the less reputable quarters, discreetly removed from the sea-front, the notices in the shops are in Hebrew and Polish – not, of course, only for the benefit of Polish soldiers, though there are plenty of them too. I suppose the Jews are right to be proud of their city. Built from nothing, it is something civilised to replace the sand dunes. But there is not a trace of taste or beauty. The streets are straight and run parallel or in geometrical regularity. But there is no plan in the building. Ten-storey ferro-concrete monsters like the Gat Rimmon stand next to one-storey tumbledown beer-parlours (with precious little beer nowadays). There are few gardens, and they are not well-kept. The whole impression the city made on me was one of shoddy pretentiousness. But perhaps I'm being too critical. Anyway, I'll remember Tel Aviv's orange-juice, and that Wienerschnitzel.

26 September
I write this in a transit camp on my way south. I arrived here yesterday afternoon from the Convalescent Camp, about twenty miles away, and get

on the train tomorrow morning for Egypt.

The fortnight at the Convalescent Camp was delightful. The sea air gave me an enormous appetite, which the admirable mess caterer never failed to satisfy, and made me feel very sleepy. My last week I bathed every day. As a result of that fortnight I now walk normally, until I get tired, when the wound starts to ache slightly and the limp reappears. But every day I walk will help to put that right. What I want almost more than anything is a job and some work to get my teeth into, after so long in hospital being merely a drag on the community and the war effort.

4 October

My last letter was written in the Palestine transit camp and posted on arrival in Cairo. I had a foul journey down: the train was three hours late in starting, eventually left the miserable wayside station at 11.30 a.m., and ambled into Cairo at 10 next morning. My carriage was crammed with Greek officers who sang ferocious marching songs most of the night. It was very hot, and I didn't improve either my spirits or my digestion by drinking bottles of what goes in Palestine by the name of lemonade.

When I reported to the Base Depot, I found that the Regiment had completed its reforming and re-equipping, and had disappeared somewhere into the desert for intensive training. And as I was afraid would happen, my vacancy for troop commander had been filled. However, Tom Cavenagh, now Commandant of the Base Depot, promised to get me back to them without fail, and said he would keep me meanwhile at Base, working in the Training Wing, until there should be a vacancy for me. And then he suggested I should have a little leave. So off I went for four days to Alexandria. I got back here last night to find a note from the Regiment saying they want me to be adjutant, and asking for me to be 'attached' straightaway so that I can learn the job.

CHAPTER TWELVE: VICTORY AT ALAMEIN
October – November 1942

Letter, 11 October

I write once again from the desert, having been picked up in Cairo in the Colonel's car and driven comfortably direct to the door of I Battery mess. Very different to my last homecoming to the Regiment last June. I'm at present commanding S Troop, the same troop as then. The suggestion that I become adjutant is still in the air.

It has been like joining a new battery. Of the officers, I knew only two before Thursday. One, Hunter Greig, now 2nd in command, was with the Battery for six months in France. The other is a subaltern in my troop, David Boe, who did magnificent work last summer. The rest are new faces, including the Battery commander [James McNaughten], who has only been out here two months, having flown fron England in a Liberator. Of the men, I suppose I know thirty to forty, most of them now being senior NCOs. I find myself constantly making comparisons and looking back to the 'good old days'. There's a lot to be done, and we must try to reach and maintain the old standard. I think we will, given time and a reasonable amount of luck.

When I rejoined the regiment it was situated in the desert about half way between Cairo and Alexandria, training hard. On 19 October we moved to another 'training area' only about 30 miles behind the Alamein frontline, through acres of tents and vehicles, workshops, dummy AA guns with realistic dummy crews, and past a mass of aerodromes with 'hundreds of fighters, Bostons and Baltimores, mostly South African'. Strict rules for camouflage by day and blackout by night.

Diary, 21 October

I was still in process of washing when a message arrived that I was to report to RHQ at 0900, to take over duties of adjutant. A fine moment for the upheaval. Spent the morning on odd jobs of coping with semi-comprehensible messages, read the operation order for the attack and with Freddy [Robertson, whom I was succeeding] dipped into his secret files. At 1100 Colonel [Hugh Cowan] talked to all officers and put them in the picture. Attack starts 2200 on Day One, 9th Australian Div. in north, then to its left 51 Highland Div, 2NZ Div, 1 South African Div: 1 Armd Div goes through 51 Div. Operation expected to take at least a week, possibly fortnight, of hard fighting. Intention – to destroy German army at Alamein. After that, an easy walk to Tripoli.

On 22 October we moved a further twenty miles forward to an assembly area ten miles from the front. Final orders came in the afternoon of next day, with a personal message from the Army Commander to be read out to every soldier: "It may well be one of the decisive battles in the history of the world".
Night 23/24 October

At 2140 the artillery bombardment began and the infantry attacked. The sky full of gigantic flashes, plus flares from RAF and Fleet Air Arm hanging in the air, and distant rumblings. We received our orders to move at 2340, with 15 minutes' notice. Route admirably well marked with lamps, quite foolproof. All the while rumblings grew louder and flashes bigger. Through a gap in the double British minefield and into action just beyond at first light. Guns settled in within a mile of where I was wounded in July (see p. 124 for map).

Early on 24 October we heard that the infantry had reached their second objective, in some cases their third, but not 2 Armd Bde. In the afternoon the infantry attacked again, but 2 Armd Bde ran into 88-mms and were largely saved by a snap smoke screen put down by one of our troop commanders, Wilf Harris.
24 October

I sat all day near the telephone and rear link set in the Scout car, shouting and coping with a stream of orders, reports, minor administrative matters, battle situations and fire-control, all of which always came in at the same moment in frantic 20-minute periods, punctuated by dull half hours. Chat round the Colonel's truck in moonlight, early bed. Bloody night. Nearby Bofors opened up just as I was going to sleep, again several times during the night, a frightful racket, and 'what goes up must come down'. Many guns opened up at 0200 in support of 51 Div and 9 Aus Div.

25 and 26 October were relatively quiet days. The Highlanders and 2 Armd Bde made slow progress and we fired almost continuously in their support. Stukas and ME 109s visited us at intervals.
Night 26/27 October

Attack began at 2300. 7 Motor Bde went forward on a two battalion front and we put heavy fire down on two enemy strongpoints named Snipe and Woodcock. The sky full of flashes and a fearsome noise, a really remarkable sight, the air full of the vibrations of passing shells. R out as FOO [Forward Observation Officer] with 2nd Rifle Brigade [2RB], he reported show successful and infantry pleased. I was awoken at intervals and never had much more than ten minutes' consecutive sleep. Much interference on the wireless, and about 0300 R went off the air altogether. We made frantic efforts with aerials, and were just deciding to send out another set half way as link when at 0530 he got through and ordered "Snipe + 1,000 1 round GF". In the middle of it came "Troop target, 1 round GF, plus 1,000". I immediately stopped the regiment and told R to send proper fire orders.

Then came "One gun smoke", then "H.E. one gun" – laboriously spelt out, and finally "check ammo" and other incomprehensions. I told the regiment to fire only on my order. At 0600 got through again, asking for details of situation, trying to ensure that R was not asking for fire on own troops, and back came, dramatically spelt out over the air, "It is dark and I am surrounded by tanks". After that could only get through faintly to the tank, R having left it to walk to battalion HQ of 2RB. Felt very unhappy over whole affair. If R was surrounded, I hadn't helped by stopping fire of regiment. On the other hand, to shoot up our own infantry wouldn't have helped R to get out of the nasty situation. I woke the Colonel, and he agreed with me. As it got light, wireless got better, and we told Bdr Blackburn at the OP that R could have all the fire he wanted, provided he could see. And so ended an unpleasant night in chilly windy morning. Found I had caught cold hanging about in pyjamas, though I wore a sweater and greatcoat over them.

27 October

CRA [Frizz Fowler] turned up at 0745 and found Hugh asleep. Brought news that we are to move forward. Reason is a big night attack which we are to support and for which we require extra range. Then we waited most of the day. Very little news from forward that made sense. 2RB reported to be in Woodcock and Snipe, but under heavy fire of every description and having extremely unpleasant time. R's whereabouts unknown, presumed with infantry and unable to get back to his scout car. Blackburn meanwhile sent back sitreps, from which it was obvious he was in front of the infantry, west of Snipe and in wonderful OP position. He shot his battery.[1] At last we moved at 1630, in clouds of dust up Moon track, through the first enemy minefield. Greeted in our new area by a short sharp burst of shelling which laid us flat on our tummies. After that plenty of digging. Ammunition headaches once again. CRA turned up at 2030, and he, Colonel, Len [Livingstone-Learmonth, 2nd in command] and I crammed ourselves into the 'bread van' [the regimental command post] and worked out the night's programme over our whisky. CRA very tired and his brain was meandering, very inconsequential. Once again I found myself lost in amazement of Hugh, who took no notice of the CRA's interruptions and just went quietly on working out the concentrations, due to begin at 2130. We were supporting 7 Motor Brigade. A colossal artillery programme, whole corps artillery plus oddments taking part, teriffic noise. Shells came back and landed unpleasantly in our area, also bombing near the batteries' guns. We all slept below ground.

28 October

Slept very well in my slit trench. Told on waking that our cook, Cox, and our

---

1. Some weeks later I was happy to recommend Blackburn for the award of a Military Medal. We also learnt that R was a prisoner of war.

storeman, Cardon, had been hit during the night, Cox killed, Cardon badly wounded. Certainly some of the shells passed mighty close above my head. Very vague news from OPs, doubtful whether we or the enemy are in Snipe and Woodcock. At least 150 Bostons, Baltimores and Mitchells went over us during the day, one flight with US markings, bombed ridge 10,000 yards from us, good brew-ups. Padre spent miserable day burying Highlanders. Nightly ammunition howl, air filled with queries about 'bottle parties' and their 'bottle men'. At last we got thirty RASC lorries late at night. At 2200 the programme started in support of an Australian attack, we fired for forty minutes onto a strongpoint NW of Tel el Eisa. Could hear shells bursting on our targets. The sky once again filled with flashes.

The next four days were a time of much confusion and hard fighting, with heavy infantry casualties and very slow progress by the tanks. For us it meant long hours of continuous firing, sometimes in conjunction with all the divisional and corps artillery and timed to coincide with RAF attacks. The Stukas came over about four times a day, 'very regular in their habits, and unfortunately our fighter sweeps always seem to be half an hour too late'. We suffered from sporadic enemy shelling, which encouraged digging. At RHQ we created a 'system of deep trenches round the nerve centre, with some room for the flocks of visitors that always seemed to congregate when the shelling began'. A cheering development was that German prisoners were beginning to come in, often 'because they couldn't stick our artillery fire'. On the night of 1/2 November the NZ and 51 Divisions launched a major attack in the Snipe and Woodcock areas, with 9 Armd Bde, accompanied by our OPs, in close support. We fired concentrations for 2¼ hours, 'a great programme'. I slept through it all, 'never heard a bang'. Next night we fired again in support of 7 Motor Brigade's attack on Aqaqir ridge.

Diary, 3 November

About midday interesting information began to come in that, pieced together, made a picture – enemy guns abandoned, infantry withdrawing, intercept of a message to 15 Panzer Grenadiers to get out of the Aussie pocket at all costs with their equipment, especially anti-tank guns; a wounded Highlander picked up who spent last night in enemy hands and was left behind 'because he would be found soon by us' etc. Enemy seems to be on the run. But how far? Moved three miles forward at 1500. The dust on the tracks appalling. Many traces of the enemy, signposts in German and Italian, unit signs, notices warning "Minen". 2 Armd Bde pushing on very gradually, situation apparently very satisfactory.

4 November

Out of action without firing a single round. The plan – 1 Armd Div to push west and break through, with us behind 2RB. Moved off 1130. The road to Aqaqir pitted with shellholes and bomb craters, truly impressive evidence of our efforts of last ten days. Many tanks in process of being blown up by our sappers, many guns shattered in their pits. Enemy reported to be making westwards ON

HIS FEET! 2 Armd Bde captured von Thoma, OC Afrika Korps, in the afternoon as he was doing reconnaisance in his tank. We close leaguered south-west of Aqaqir at dark, a tremendous relief to be in the open again, a grand night's sleep. But we all felt we should be pushing west to cut the road somewhere near Fuka. Rommel must not get away this time.

5 November

Moved forward at 0900, Daba our objective. 2 Armd Bde no longer in contact, much of the enemy having retired during the night. Len travelling ahead with Motor Brigade saw a German ambulance in distance, gave chase, captured it and handed it over to Ben [Powell, our medical officer] with an MO and orderly inside. A six-wheel affair, well appointed and good equipment. Ben now refuses to leave his new toy. I talked to the German officer who was in Russia last winter. The Russians are 'savages' he told me. In the afternoon 7 Motor Brigade entered Daba without firing a shot. A few Italian and Askari [Eritrean] infantry rounded up. Lots of valuable loot, but many of the huge drums of petrol marked "Wehrmacht-Heer" had been punctured. Enemy seems to have done a thorough job of scuttling.

Night 5/6 November

Our orders are to make for Khalda, familiar ground [from our July retreat], in an attempt to cut enemy's line of retreat, perhaps on the frontier. Moved off at 1900. Going foul and pitch black, though our route was illuminated at times quite brightly by RAF flares along the coast road. 12 Lancers ahead of the division bumped enemy, so it was decided to sweep round the opposition to the south. This we did in a frantic stampede. With a great effort we kept up with the Motor Bde, but left trucks and guns scattered over the desert. Roared through NZ leaguers, a madman must have been leading us. Came to rest again at 0615 and waited for light.

6 November

Dispersed at first light, started to move on slowly in heavy rain. Complete lack of orders. To our south a huddle of 50 disconsolate Italians seen, only too glad to give themselves up. Parties reported to be scattered over the whole desert to the south, having set out to walk to Tripoli on their flat feet. Regiment in action by 1600 in Deir Khalda. It is now out of petrol, we need 5,000 gallons, but the RASC 2nd line hadn't turned up by evening. Lashing rain, the sand fast turning to mud under our feet.

Our RASC petrol convoy finally reached us at 1600 on 8 November, and we were mobile again. The returning lorries 'picked up prisoners and drove them eastwards with no guards except the driver, but apparently no danger of bellicosity'. That day the sun came out and the ground dried fast. In the afternoon we heard that Matruh had been found clear of enemy – a petrol convoy had reached their rearguard during the night 'so they got away'. On 9 November we moved 25 miles west with 7 Motor Brigade, a glorious sunny day, 'the desert at it's best and quite dust-free'. Orders then came that the whole division was to move north of the main coastal road to reorganise.

Letter, 9 November

I am now adjutant – the vacancy suddenly fell open two days before the battle began, and I was pitched into the midst of the last frantic preparations. You can imagine the result. For the first fortnight I think I was busier than I have ever been in my life. Regimental Headquarters in the middle of a battle is reminiscent of a parrot house at the zoo. And all the parrots are screaming at one unfortunate, the adjutant. Wireless and telephones, brigadiers and battery commanders, tactical reports and ammunition returns, casualties and dumb-witted visitors – from dawn till well after dark I found myself in an incessant whirl. Sometimes I managed to get a wash in the afternoon, some days not at all. But looking back on it, it was an amazing experience, and I'm proud to have made my small contribution to a great victory. Now the desert campaign has changed to its old character and we are once again in the great spaces. And yesterday came the news I had half been expecting, and yet had not dared to hope for – the landings [of the First Army] at Casablanca, Oran, Algiers. The Eighth Army would have cleared North Africa by itself, but it will all help to make things go quicker. And so, all my love, and here's to the future.

On 10 November we started moving westward in stages, joining the coastal road at Charing Cross.

Diary, 10 November

The roadside was an amazing sight – a scene of carnage. Very few bombholes and I fancy the RAF did most of the damage by machine-gunning. All strangely reminiscent of France and especially of Greece. I didn't feel very jubilant – my first reaction was disgust at the waste of war. Heard all church bells are to be rung next Sunday in England to celebrate Eighth Army's victory.

On 12 November 'an open car flying Union Jack passed us, escorted by armoured cars. Alexander and other red hats inside'. On the 13th Tobruk was reported clear: 'the yanks in Tunisia now 690 miles from Tripoli, we are 980'. On the 14th we drove up Halfaya Pass and that night leaguered near Capuzzo, once more on Libyan soil. Next day we reached an area five miles short of Sidi Rezegh. 7 Armd Div was reported 50 miles west of Gazala – 'we are getting very far behind'. On the 16th we received the news that 1 Armd Div was to move to the Tmimi area, 30 miles west of Tobruk, 'for three weeks' training'.

Letter, 16 November

In your last card you imagined that I was not in this battle because of the phrasing of my letter of October 15th. You were wrong, for the regiment was in the thick of it from the first night. The first twelve days, the static battle on the Alamein-Qattara line, were something quite different from anything the Western

Desert has yet seen, and a completely new type of fighting for this regiment. I suppose it was reminiscent of the last war. It was certainly a great experience to stand behind a gun position during one of our many night barrages, and see the sky lit up with the flashes round three-quarters of the circle – enemy guns probably flashing in the fourth – and listen to the never-ceasing din for hour after hour, the sharp bark of the hundreds of 25-pdrs, the deeper louder bang of the mediums, and the throb and rustle that filled the air as shell after shell passed over our heads. The enemy never made an effective reply, either with guns or tanks or infantry. Some of his counter-attacks were serious and particular units had heavy losses – that was to be expected. We were shelled fairly often, by perhaps four or eight guns. Particularly at night I find shelling a terrifying experience, even if one has a deep slit trench to lie in. I cannot conceive what it must have been like for the other side under our barrages of scores and hundreds of guns. No wonder they broke and ran. I think the gunners can feel proud of their contribution. But in a sense it was a technical contribution – a matter of working out angles and ranges, and giving the right orders down the telephone: and a question of getting hold of vast quantities of ammunition in time, and shoving round after round up the barrel. For the gun crews it meant plugging away, sometimes for hours on end, loading and pulling the trigger, and sticking the unceasing noise and smoke and dust and the blinding flashes. A matter of grit and determination and considerable powers of physical endurance. But not a question of brilliant manoeuvre, or quick decision, or pointblank engagement of tanks in a surprise attack. In all the desert campaigns till now gunners have had to do those things, and have suffered heavily as a result. Last summer gunner casualties were out of all proportion heavier than either tank units or infantry. This time, I'm glad to say, they have been very slight. Infantry casualties have been high. And although the tanks did noble work in the breakthrough, and are still pursuing with efficiency and great spirit, I do think the infantry should be given their due. It was their battle, and, well supported by both guns and tanks, they bore the brunt of the fighting. The New Zealanders, the Australians and the Highlanders were magnificent. I've no doubt the rest were just as magnificent, but we never saw them on the Alamein front. Everyone deserves the credit for their own contributions, and cooperation between all arms was very fine. When all is said and done, I can do nothing better than repeat what I said in my airgraph of a week ago, that I am proud to have made my small contribution to a great victory.

And now to the future. You will have to try to guess where we are now, or what we are doing. All I can say is that we are west of Alamein. We are all speculating hard, and know very little more than you do. It looks as though Hitler has decided to hold North Africa, even at what is obviously a terriffic risk. But even if the Americans and the First Army have to fight in Tunis, and the Eighth Army is to be given another battle to win, it's only a question of time, careful organisation and determined plugging away. And then we've got him. How new and satisfying is this sensation of being conscious of one's own strength. I hope we shall never again lose it. It suddenly came on me about the third day of the

Alamein battle. I realised, with absolute and inspiring certainty, that we only had to keep on hitting hard, loading the shells and pulling the trigger, giving the enemy no rest and relaxation – and we were bound to win through. I'm sure it will be the same as far as Tripoli – and let's hope all the way beyond.

Many months later, on 7 July 1943, I sent a long-promised retrospective account of the battles to my parents, explaining that I was now allowed 'to mention places and incidents, but not other units and formations, except where these have already been mentioned in the press or on the BBC':

You have seen *Desert Victory*, so you will remember Kidney Ridge and Aqaqir Ridge. In the early stages of the battle we were firing almost every hour of the day on Kidney Ridge; and on the day of the breakthrough, November 4th, our guns followed the tanks over Aqaqir, truly 'the grave of the Panzers', as the official account has called it. That scrub-covered, sandy ridge was a terrible sight – littered with tanks and lorries and guns, still smouldering as we drove through, scattered graves in twos and threes, slit trenches filled with machine-guns and ammunition, papers and documents blowing in the wind, still unburied corpses, clothes and equipment lying in confused heaps and huddles, just as they had been abandoned a few hours ago in the panic of that first retreat. It was a great day for us, for we drove through the last minefield and got out beyond the last Alamein defences and into the open desert once again. The worst feature of that Alamein battle was the restricted space. The ground was plastered with minefields in all directions, some of them ours, some of them enemy. All movement had to be along the tracks, axle-deep in dust, and through the minefield gaps marked by barbed wire and white tapes, and by night by green and red lights. In the unmined areas vehicles and guns had to crowd together, and there were plenty of fine targets for the Stukas and enemy guns. But after Aqaqir there were no more mines, for Rommel hadn't time to lay them. We spread out and moved in open formation like a vast convoy on the sea, as in the old days of 'Jock columns' before both sides were pinned down to trenches and wire at Alamein. The greatest joy of all was that feeling of freedom of movement and space – the unique characteristic of desert warfare. In among the minefields one felt trapped, one had to watch one's footsteps every inch of the way. Out in the desert one can wheel large formations at will, disperse and baffle the bombers, and always have room to wriggle out of a tight corner. Above all as we advanced west from Aqaqir, we could once again sleep above ground. At Alamein we all slept in slit trenches, narrow and uncomfortable and dirty: whenever a shell landed, or a lorry passed, or even someone walked by within a few yards, a little cascade of sand and pebbles would fall down on to one's bed at the bottom of the trench. I used to wake up with eyes and ears and nose choked with sand, and blankets white with dust. That first night of the breakthrough, falling asleep on the clean gravel beside my wireless van, with time and peace of mind to look at the stars, no shells and mines, knowing Alamein was left behind forever and wondering how far we would push Rommel's rearguard back next day, and how much loot and how many prisoners we would take – I shall always remember the peace and content of that night.

We advanced pretty fast, with only minor opposition, did a long night march across the desert, and reached one of the main desert tracks running south from Matruh. Then we formed into 'columns', an exciting reversion to the methods of the old days. We never got definite orders, but I imagine the intention would have been for us to push on hard to the top of Sollum Hill and Halfaya, and try to cut off the rearguard and smash the last of Rommel's army before it left Egypt. Then it started to rain. Our supply columns got bogged down over their axles in mud. For four days we sat south of Matruh, unable to move without petrol. Only a few units could push on, and by the time the desert dried, Rommel was well into Cyrenaica. That rain certainly saved him. We followed gently on some way behind the leading troops, along the coast road which was littered with every imaginable type of enemy equipment, bombed and burnt out, or often just abandoned intact in panic or for lack of petrol. I had the official recognition pamphlet which contains pictures of all the German and Italian tanks and guns and lorries. I drove along with it in my hand, ticking off each type as I saw it lying beside the road. There were very few I didn't tick off during those few days.

The floods which saved Rommel.

CHAPTER THIRTEEN: IN CYRENAICA: A WINTER OF FRUSTRATION
November 1942 – March 1943

We arrived at our 'training area' south of Tmimi on the evening of 18 November. Little did we know that we would be stranded there not for three weeks but for three months, and would not fire a single round 'in anger' until the middle of March 1943.

Letter, 25 November

You ask about the functions and status of an adjutant. It's difficult to describe them. I believe officially he is responsible for the discipline and administration of the regiment. In a sense he is the staff officer of the Colonel, and has to settle all the small details of administration with which a colonel doesn't want to be bothered; and it's his job to see that the Colonel's major decisions on policy and administration are put into practical form and carried out. This means that much of his time has to be spent in an office, reading piles of General, Army, Divisional etc. Routine Orders, and working through envelopes containing every conceivable type of fatuous correspondence. If, in the middle of one of the decisive battles of the war, a letter arrives from the Base Depot asking why Gnr. Snooks has arrived from the 2nd Regiment RHA without a waterbottle, and in possession of only one pair of pants, short, cellulose - it is the adjutant who has to collect his wits and think about the answer. For you see, whatever happens to the war, whoever wins or loses it, the Army must carry on.

During the big battle I was busier than I ever want to be again. Getting the right amount of ammunition to the right place at the right time was by itself enough to keep one man busy. Besides all the administrative worries like replacing vehicles lost by shelling or on mines, arranging for rations and water to come up, compiling and sending in the numerous returns required by divisions and corps, and acting as a link between our 24 guns and higher authority, I had to sit by the wireless and telephones, keep in touch with the tactical information that came down from OPs, read the operation orders and pass on all that concerned batteries, control the fire of the regiment when big concentrations or barrages were called for, often at very short notice, and look after RHQ during moves and arrange its layout and local protection when the guns went into action. I am learning a lot about the working of the Army, particularly its higher formations, besides getting more than a working knowledge of Army officialese. I never tell anyone anything nowadays, I always notify him. Instead of writing 'I realise', I say 'it is appreciated'. This is not to say that I don't often take great pleasure in addressing a letter to some worthy Base official, written in plain English. But the system is formidable and is bound to sometimes 'get one down'.

On the whole I must admit I like the job. The chief snag is that I am largely 'office bound'. For close on three weeks I never got further than 200 yards from the telephone, and only very rarely caught a glimpse of a gun, though they were always close and at night their noise inescapable. I was very sorry to give up my troop. To have sixty men to look after, to get to know them, be near them and share their dangers and discomforts in battle, is a great experience. An adjutant has little direct contact with the men of the regiment: he knows them well on paper, and so is always in danger of getting the bureaucratic outlook - juggling with numbers and ranks and rates of pay, and forgetting that it is men's lives that are concerned. I shall miss that exhilharating sense of companionship in action. But the new Colonel, Hugh Cowan, wanted me as his adjutant. He commanded the School of Artillery for the first nine months of the year, and so was my boss while I was at the OCTU. I have the greatest respect and admiration for him, and they grow every day. He is the most considerate and most helpful superior I've been lucky enough to work under, and suffers from my well-intentioned bunglings in heroic understanding patience! We are a cheerful company in our HQ mess, and by now I think a reasonably efficient team, eagerly looking forward to the next stage of the great advance.

Diary, 26 November
A letter on security came in - this occupation of Cyrenaica is for the duration, and on no account will HMG allow it to be handed back to Italy after the war. I wonder who the lucky ones will be? Us? The Greeks? Or the Gyppos, in reward for their contribution to victory?

Letter, 14 December
We're all feeling pretty depressed and frustrated. The chief reason is the weather. We've been having a lot of rain, which makes life under these conditions most uncomfortable. Our lean-tos and various weird types of shelter, mostly built out of pieces of canvas or lorry covers or tents picked up from abandoned German or Italian camps or vehicles, don't keep out heavy rain, having been designed chiefly to keep out the summer sun. The only good point about the rain is that it has produced a rich crop of grass in the hollows among the patches of scrub and in the small wadis. The desert hasn't yet blossomed like the rose, but just outside our mess I have counted two types of small purple violets, three yellow varieties like very small dandelions or gowans, and three other bluish nondescript flowers. It is pleasant to see so much life - a great change from the entirely barren desert round Alamein and on the Egyptian frontier. There are plenty of butterflies, too, even some Red Admirals. One night I was woken up by a frog jumping onto my pillow. Some time ago I startled a flock of bustard from

under my truck - absurd turkey-like birds with a surprising turn of speed. Our quartermaster has 'acquired' an Italian shotgun and goes out before dawn on warm mornings. He claims to have sighted some duck on one of the rainpools, but so far his total bag has been one very lean skinny hare.

We live a very uneventful monotonous life. Mama's latest guess in the letter that has just arrived was, as usual, pretty near the mark. I don't know how she does it; maternal intuition, I suppose. Enough to say that we are not fighting just now, but training, and chafing a lot as a result: particularly the last two days with the Afrika Korps retreating west from Agheila. I still think Rommel will fight for Tripoli. No doubt we'll soon see.

On 18 December our Corps Commander, General Horrocks, visited us and gave us a comprehensive review of the present situation. He told us we would start moving to the Agedabia-Agheila area in early January, and promised we will be in the hunt. Horrocks struck me as a charming and enthusiastic man and we all felt more cheerful after his visit. On 19 December, to my great regret, Hugh Cowan left us for a Cairo hospital, having for some time suffered what turned out to be dysentry. On the 28th Major Dick Harding-Newman arrived as 2nd-in-command and in the absence of a colonel took over command of the Regiment.

Letter, 24 December

This is Christmas Eve. We are all sitting round the long table in our mess, having had a most excellent dinner, empty Canadian beer bottles strewn around, the wireless singing carols to us and blaring forth BBC nonsensicalities. We tried to get the Kings College carol service, but our sergeants turned up that very moment outside and started serenading us with Good King Wenceslas. Half an hour later a party of gunners appeared and treated us to what was intended to be the First Nowell. Now we are awaiting the signallers, and wondering whether our stocks of beer will last out the evening. This evening a lorryload of turkeys and thrilling Christmas titbits arrived, and a fabulous dinner is being roasted in our sand-brick oven. Our padre has been rehearsing carols in the canteens every night for the past week, and we expect a brave show at our service tomorrow morning.

We've been taking advantage of this period of rest to get quite a lot of amusement. Last Sunday we had a regimental sports meeting which was a roaring success. Some stylish running and jumping, besides a comic obstacle race which reduced all the spectators to hysterics. And an officer's tug-of-war which laid me prostrate after a marathon pull of a minute and a half.

Continued, Christmas Day

It has been a very memorable Christmas. Now, with the somnolence of repletion settling upon us, we are sitting in a circle wondering where we will spend next Christmas, and puffing contentedly at our cigars in the dim light of a hurricane lamp, set on the sandy floor in the middle of us. We heard a recording of the King's speech – the best royal utterance I've ever heard. I thought it was admirable.

But our Christmas cheerfulness didn't last long. I described the frustrations of the following weeks in two retrospective letters of 7 July and 2 August 1943:

It was a dreary, trying time, as you will have realised from my many querulous and impatient letters. We sat on the same dull featureless piece of desert for three and a half months. Towards the end I knew every patch and clump of scrub, every tiny bump on the desert skyline. We trained hard, of course, and that training stood us in good stead afterwards. But we were unable to move more than the bare minimum of trucks required to feed us and keep us functioning. Petrol was most strictly rationed. No leave to the Delta was allowed and there was just nowhere to go, no amenities, no amusement beyond what one could make for oneself - books, and an occasional dinner party with pleasant guests, some games of football and light-hearted sports, and a regimental concert party which proved a great success. I used to spend day after day in my adjutant's office, making work for myself. At frequent intervals we were assured that we were not being left out of it, and there would be plenty of work for us yet. But the day of our departure was constantly postponed. And as the rest of the Eighth Army passed Benghazi, then Agheila, then Sirte and the Wadi Zem Zem, then Tripoli itself[1] and so across the frontier into Tunisia, our restlessness and exasperation grew and grew. Before we finally moved we were 1,200 miles behind the fighting, and over 1,000 behind Tripoli, which was full of base pay offices and depots and administrative organisations. It was most ignominious for the RHA to be further from the battle than the Base Paymaster!

The reasons for our immobility were of course quite obvious. At that time only half the Eighth Army could be kept supplied in the forward areas. And Montgomery had decided after Alamein that he wouldn't have to fight another battle on a major scale before Mareth. He was right of course. So we had to stay hundreds of miles back until the port of Tripoli was working and enough supplies could be dumped across the Tunisian frontier to allow the whole army to launch the big attack. We had to send away almost all our lorries in January to form improvised supply columns, ferrying petrol and bombs for the RAF from Tobruk to Benghazi and beyond. They did not return to us till the end of February. The new year was a tricky time, with Rommel back on the Wadi Zem Zem, and Benghazi, our port to the front line, about 500 miles away. They repaired the damage to Benghazi harbour very quickly, but just the day before it was due to start working at highest capacity, a terrific storm smashed one of the moles, drove ships ashore inside, and practically put the port out of action. So Tobruk, 250 miles further back, still had to be used as the main port, and improvised supply columns like ours had to ferry the stuff forward.

Although we were certainly helping the war effort all that time, you can understand how we grumbled and protested at being General Transportation Companies. And being pinned down to a very dreary piece of desert made it far

---

1. On 23 January.

worse. I got away twice during those three and a half months, once for the day to Derna, and once for five days, duty and pleasure combined, to Benghazi. Derna is a delightful little place, the first Italian colonial town I'd seen, and I've seen nothing to beat it since. The main road runs for miles over a particularly dreary flat desert, and then suddenly, without any warning, lands you on the top of a 600-foot escarpment overlooking the sea and the dazzling white houses and villas, set among olives and palms and flowering trees, and grouped round a tiny toy harbour with two stone moles and a miniature lighthouse. The residential quarter had gardens ablaze with bougainvillaeas, hydrangeas and the first fruit blossoms: the streets are shady, with neat pavements and lamp-posts: the houses looked cool and comfortable, and even the flamboyant public buildings, adorned with fasces, have a certain dignity and good taste.

H Battery Fair, Tmimi

I thoroughly enjoyed my trip through the Jebel or 'Green Mountains' to Benghazi. All the country in the Cyrenaican bulge is as great a contrast with the desert as one could imagine. Much of it reminded me strongly of Greece. The hills are not high, but they are very rocky and full of precipitous ravines, with the slopes covered with stumpy pines and the valleys full of rich green grass or scrub, and clumps of thyme and thorns. And scattered every few miles along the road are the Italian colonists' houses. Cyrenaica was a sad sight in February. All the Italians had gone, and the Arabs were back in possession of the farms, and of course quite incapable of putting them to their proper use. One could see what had been ploughed already choked by weeds, drainage systems blocked, and the land everywhere going back. It will be a big job to educate the Senussi to the same level of agricultural knowledge as the Italian peasant colonist. Meanwhile the country will inevitably relapse. It was a strange venture, that Italian colonisation. The small white houses scattered over the green hills give a very homely look to the countryside that is most unusual in Africa. Some of the community centres, tucked away in wooded valleys, are most attractive. Church, cinema, Carabinieri barracks, local party headquarters, post office, etc., are all grouped in plain white stone buildings round a small square, with a market in the centre. A particularly charming little village was named D'Annunzio, and lies at the bottom of a long winding valley full of pines and patches of cultivation, and with immense caverns in the precipitous rocky sides. And yet, ten miles further on, where the road comes out into the Barce plain, you see Italian colonisation at its worst. The plots and houses are set out in long straight lines, every house with identically the same number of windows and outhouses, and the same shape of door and chimney: and they are all dressed up by the right in meticulous military fashion, the same interval between the houses in each row, the same sized plot, probably measured to the nearest square inch. And of course every house front proudly adorned with some fascist slogan, or perhaps with a long quotation from the Duce's speeches, 'Duce vinceremo' or 'Il Duce ha sempre ragione' written above the door in large plain black lettering.

Letter, 2 January

As you can imagine, the long evenings are a problem. I have been helping to organise quite a series of entertainments, some serious, some frivolous. Not long ago we had a debate on the subject, 'Which of these three statesman will be considered by historians to have been the greatest of their day, Churchill, Roosevelt or Stalin?' Roosevelt won easily, in spite of some fiery persuasive pleas for Stalin, mostly from our fitters and mechanics. It seems to be an army tradition that fitters should tend to Bolshevism. It was surprising that Churchill got so compartively few votes; he came third.

At last, on 3 March we set out on the long march to Tripoli, where we were told we would reorganise and rest for a while before marching on. I described my journey in my letter of 18 August:

We had only got halfway when our orders were changed: the move was accelerated, and instead of stopping near Tripoli we marched on without any break to Medenine, 50 miles across the Tunisian border, and only a few miles short of the Mareth Line. It took us 11 days' driving at just over 100 miles a day - and most of the way what a dreary drive. The run through the Cyrenaican Jebel was delightful, but after Benghazi civilisation is quickly left behind. The trees come to an end within ten miles of the town, grass slowly gives way to camel

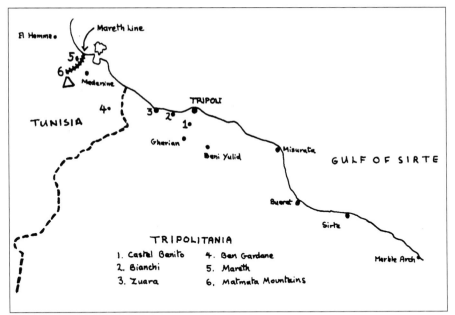

Tripolitania

scrub, and scrub to bare, rocky, desolate desert. Agheila has been described as a busy metropolis in some British newspapers, and I've seen imaginative drawings showing wide streets and shady gardens, mosques and crowded markets. In fact it is a huddle of dirty shell-splintered Arab hutments and a shabby tumbledown fort. For hundreds of miles the famous 'Via Balbia'[1] runs straight and uncompromising round the Gulf of Sirte. The physical effort of driving was exhausting enough, but the mental exhaustion of seeing for hour after hour nothing but sand and rock and the sun's glare was far more noticeable – I felt my brain almost numb at the end of the day. In all those dreary miles, which took us five days to cover, there were only two 'sights' to see. One was the town of Sirte, with a few imposing buildings and a palatial hotel in the Mussolini style: but sightseeing was sternly discouraged by notices on the roadside in typical Eighth Army style – 'Sirte is dirty with mines and booby traps. Kill yourself if you want to'. The other sight was the Marble Arch erected by Musso on the border between Cyrenaica and Tripolitania. It is a vastly tall and ugly structure of gleaming white marble, visible for fifteen miles or more on all sides. We didn't see it as Mussolini had intended us to see it. Round it were circling clouds of Spitfires and American Kittyhawks: and on the broad bronze back of one of the classical Phileni brothers (to whom the ancient Roman arch, long since disappeared, had been dedicated) was rudely chalked 'Merry Christmas 1942 from Wigan'.

1. Named after Balbo, Governor of Libya 1934-40, it ran along the coast for over 1,000 miles between the Tunisian and Egyptian frontiers.

We left the main road [on 10 March] at Buerat, where the coast curves northwards to Misurata at the western end of the Gulf of Sirte, and struck across country to Tripoli. I never want to travel such a penitential route again. For two days we banged and crashed over the raw ribs of the stony desert, till every muscle ached with clutching on to the sides of one's madly lurching truck. Inland from the coastal belt *nothing* grows, not even a withered clump of camel scrub. Nothing but an endless undulating waste of waterless, glaring sand and stones. Then one afternoon Arabs suddenly appeared, walking to meet our snake-like column, in the middle of a desolation where not even the hardiest Bedouin could have found a living. Not only men, but pot-bellied children and women, some of them witch-like and weather-worn and croaking like hens. Others were coal-black, I suppose the descendants of Nubian slaves. All lined our route and attacked every truck with a shrill chorus of "Beeskit, Beeskit, Beeskit Mister, Baksheesh Mister, Baksheesh, Beeskit, Beeskit". We were not the first column to go through and they will still be living on army biscuits long after the war has ended. Then suddenly we reached a slight rise and saw in the distance reddish mud-brick walls: a few hundred yards further and a vast gash appeared in the monotonous smooth desert. Slowly there unfolded a fantastic scene. Our track ran along the edge of a precipitous ravine 300 to 400 feet deep and half a mile wide, cut clean as if by design and invisible until we were right above it. In the bottom were green grass and cultivation, clumps of palms, wells and irrigation channels. The sides of the chasm, wherever they were not precipitous and sheer, were covered with a honeycomb of tumbledown houses and steep filthy streets, with here and there a whitewashed tomb or saint's shrine to break the monotony of the dull brown sand-mud bricks. Round the edge of this amazing town flocks of goats and sheep nibbled at the refuse heaps and the edge of the cultivation. A mile further on, on a small knoll on the edge of the cliff, and beside a waterlogged landing ground made by clearing the boulders away, stood a battlemented toy stone fort flying the Union Jack. This was the modern town of Beni Ulid, which boasted a garrison of Italian Sahara troops in the days of Musso's imperial glory, but is now one of the district capitals of British Military Authority. The road wound down the cliff side, passing through the Piazza del Generalissimo Graziani, and after climbing the far escarpment plunged northwards again into the desert towards Tripoli. It was a fantastic sight, that fertile gorge in the middle of desolation, and reminded me of an imaginative purple passage in a Foreign Legion sixpenny thriller, describing some hidden Arab fastness in mid-Sahara.

After those dreary days you can imagine how we felt when one morning we drove over a hill and saw the green trees and smiling farmsteads of Tripolitania below us. I shall always remember that first night under the tall gum trees, alive with small birds and whispering in the breeze.

Our location that 'first night', 13/14 March, was near Castel Benito areodrome, ten miles south of Tripoli.

Diary, 14 March

Moved off at 0730, lovely run between the eucalyptus and tall graceful thin-leaved trees. Through Bianchi, rows of well-spaced farms, olives and fruit trees all growing out of the sand. The Italian colonists lined the road in places, waving, holding out their hands like Arabs. Gunners from 4RHA ahead of us tossed cigarettes out to them. I was harder hearted, as they looked plump and well-fed. At places one really could not say one was not in England. Notices in Sabratha, and later in Zuara, warning against typhus - all towns out of bounds to all troops. Tarmac ceased as we crossed into Tunisia. There were notices saying 'Douane', a few ruined houses, French kilo-stones, but little else to indicate our crossing. Through Ben Gardane, completely deserted and shuttered, in the dark. Leaguered at 2145.

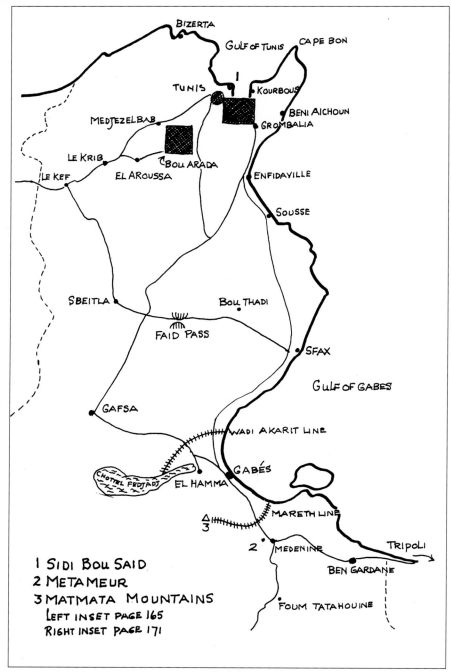

Tunisia

CHAPTER FOURTEEN: VICTORY IN TUNISIA
March – May 1943

By the evening of 15 March the regiment was in action at Metameur, just west of Medenine, behind the 'Mareth Line' where Rommel had taken his stand at the end of February. 1 Armd Div was holding a front stretching southwards from the 'huge wide well-surfaced military road' running north-west from Medenine to the village of Mareth. The division was thin on the ground, but we were told that 'there was little against us'. On 17 March the regiment participated in a 'demonstration in force' by 2 Armd Bde, as a diversion from an attack by 201 Guards Brigade on our right. Despite the fact that the whole operation was carried out in open country, in full view of the enemy on the Matmata hills, not a single casualty was suffered. It was adjudged a success, and Horrocks was impressed by our performance: "Your regiment has maintained its reputation", he told us, "no greater compliment is needed".

Next day Colonel David Welsh arrived to take over command.

The main attack was to be launched on the night of 20/21 March by 30 Corps on our right, between us and the sea. We were told that our 10 Corps was 'to be kept in cotton wool, ready to break through to Sfax and go flat out to Bizerta'.

Letter, 22 March

Your maternal intuition, having let you down badly over my triumphal entry into Tripoli, has now returned to its usual form, and your recent guesses have been most creditably near the mark. I need and can say no more. I am frantically busy again and enjoying it. I was very inexperienced when I was pushed into this job three days before the Alamein battle began. During our recent long period of training I have had time to think things out in the light of my experience in October and November, and I have got my office properly organised and the routine administration running smoothly. So I'm hoping I'll be much less harassed and overworked than last time.

I sympathise with your feelings about Eisenhower and the Vichy-Darlan appeasement in North Africa.[1] The Americans are immature, yes – militarily and

---

1. General Eisenhower, Supreme Allied Commander-in-Chief in North Africa, had recognised the authority in Algiers of Admiral Darlan, formerly Chief of State of the Vichy regime – an act which embittered de Gaulle and the Free French.

politically. They are learning quickly and painfully on the military side. It's hard not to feel just the faintest glimmer of spiteful satisfaction when they withdrew in Tunisia [at Kasserine Pass in February]. It's not that I wish them ill in any way. I think the American army, given time to train and learn, will be magnificent. We know what they did in Bataan.[1] And we all have to learn – a bitter experience. I've heard a whisper now and again that even the 'invincible' Eighth Army has been known to retreat. But our American allies were so sure of it all – so sure that the British Army was strangled by red tape and mismanaged by effete aristocratic officers, so convinced that the British soldier was soft and demoralised, and that the American army had only to appear on the scene and raise a big cheer for the Nazi hordes to turn tail and flee and not stop till they reached Tunis and Bizerta. Well, we'll see. Will the Eighth Army or the First Army get there first? I wonder.

30 Corps's attack on 20/21 March had only limited success, and on the afternoon of the 23rd came sudden orders that 1 Armd Div was to move thirty miles southwards, then sweep west in a 'left hook' through "Wilders Gap" to join the New Zealanders in their northward push and 'roll up' the enemy's Mareth Line from behind.

We moved off at 2045 on 23 March and drove all night and most of the next, reaching our assembly area close behind the New Zealanders at 1600 on the 25th, having covered about 150 miles. They were ten miles short of the Tebaga Gap between Djebel Tebaga and Djebel Melab, two rocky hills rising precipitously 200 feet above the valley. Much of the going was very rough and some of our vehicles were beginning to show serious signs of strain. At 2315 that evening our guns went forward to take over from 4 NZ Field Regiment, a night occupation being necessary because the positions were overlooked by the enemy established on Djebel Halouga to our north. At 1600 on 26 March we fired a heavy programme, with the RAF joining in in force, in support of a NZ attack which successfully opened the gap for 1 Armd Div to pass through. We got moving just before last light, 2 Armd Bde leading, with ourselves just behind 7 Motor Bde.
Diary, 27 March

At first light we were still moving in clouds of dust along the road [leading to El Hamma] up a broad valley two or three miles wide. Into action in a flurry, and the division formed a 'box' with backs against the steep hills on both sides. Regiment found a decent position in small wadis and depressions among scraggly barley and wheat fields, a good deal of cultivation. Much litter on the road, familiar post-Alamein sight. We had only done 20 miles since previous position. Enemy tanks and infantry were reported behind us, across the road by which we had come. Visits by ME 210s and JU 88's. Our OPs engaged enemy MT and tanks withdrawing north-east into the hills, but our tanks were held up by 88-mms. Visibility bad owing to dust, but general impression was that a force of some size was piling up into Hamma.

1. The peninsula in the Philippines where American troops held out against superior Japanese forces until 9 April 1942.

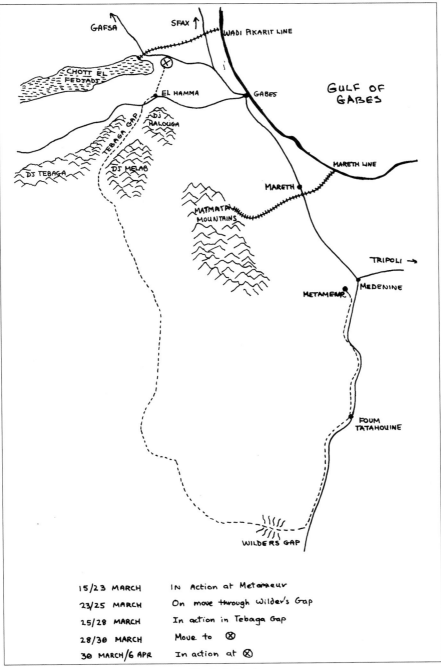

15/23 MARCH	IN Action at Metameur
23/25 MARCH	On move through Wilder's Gap
25/28 MARCH	In action in Tebaga Gap
28/30 MARCH	Move to ⊗
30 MARCH/6 APR	In action at ⊗

The Left Hook

28 March

At first light came news of our 'relief' by 8 Armd Bde and NZ Division, which moved into area south-east of us and freed our lines of communication. CRA ordered nine divisional concentrations on Hamma and district between 1100 and 1530. A lot of shelling on the ridge just above RHQ, aimless harassing but none the less frightening for that.

Soon after first light on 29 March 'came report that enemy evacuated Hamma last night'. Gabes also had been captured and the Mareth Line abandoned by the enemy, 'I'm afraid with success'. We moved forward twice beyond Hamma during the next two days and on 30 March went into action just south of the Gabes-Gafsa track. During that day it became clear that the enemy intended to hold what became known as the Wadi Akarit line, running 18 miles south-westwards from the sea along the high ground of the Roumana-Meida-Rass Zouai-Haidoudi features to the great Chott El Fedjadj salt lake. This was the last natural barrier against access to the Tunisian coastal plain.

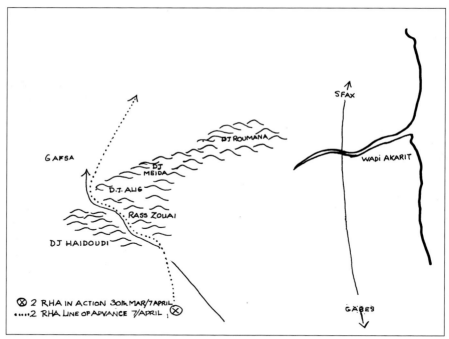

The Wadi Akarit battlefield

Diary, 31 March

At first light heard that 7RB had pushed well ahead during the night and now found themselves in an exposed position overlooked on almost every side, shot at by machine-guns, mortars and artillery. I hope our fire helped, but they had heavy casualties, 23 officers, and had to withdraw. John McMinnies [I Battery] put up a grand fight, stayed under heavy fire, was wounded in three places by shell splinters, only came back when infantry withdrew and calmly went into an Advanced Dressing Station – the first indication to his crew that he had been hit. He was sent straight back, but I hope it's not too serious. We moved forward a few miles in the afternoon. OPs out with armour reported steady stream of traffic behind Roumana, including tanks on transporters. One company of 1KRRC arrived in evening to protect us: but as the tanks pulled back to leaguer behind us, and there was no one else in front, we felt a bit naked, and made cautious plans for pulling out in hurry in case of trouble.

1 April

Heard we are here probably till 4th – a full scale attack will have to be mounted.

Letter, 1 April

Today has not lived up to its name. The sun is shining brightly, there is a fresh breeze blowing and a lovely view to look at. All very peaceful, and I have had time to wash myself – several weeks' dust and grime and sweat. And now a few hasty letters and a valiant attempt to get the regiment's war diary up to date, one of the duties I most enjoy, but it takes much time and effort.

The next four days were relatively calm. There was much air activity and some hostile bombing and shelling, but little firing by ourselves. We watched the area all round us gradually filling up with the preparations for a big attack. On 5 April I drove down to Hamma for a bathe in the hot sulphur baths, 'dozens of soldiers washing their clothes in the hot stream, some of the pavement obviously Roman'.

Diary, 3 April

Some interesting intelligence summaries recently. German morale shows signs of deteriorating, POW confess they dislike our artillery barrages, they are asking interrogators about Dunkirk and are keenly aware of limitations of Italian navy. War weary and frustrated about Africa but still optimistic about Russia – all will be over by the autumn. Italians since Alamein are nicknamed 'Strassenverstopfer' [road blockers].

The big battle started very early in the morning of 6 April: 30 Corps attacked on a three-division front. In its initial stages we were in support of 4 Indian Division, and our guns fired pretty continuously from 0415 to 1300. By that time the Division had secured all its first objectives on the summits of Zouai, Alig and Meida, and opened up the central pass through which the main Gabes-Gafsa road ran. It had also taken 4,000 prisoners. That evening we got our orders to move, at an hour still unknown: we were to follow 2 Armd Bde through the pass in single file, then open out when we reached the plain and drive on. It was not until well into the afternoon of 7 April that the order came.

A tank of 2 Armd Bde moves forward to pass through the Wadi Akarit Line, 7 April.

Diary, 7 April

The pass most attractive. Zouai was a formidable mountain, sheer precipices of 500 feet or more, deep gloomy ravines, strange pimples of sheer crumbling rock, Indians sitting calmly on the tops and watching us pass. Shadows very deep, and it was cold – the rocks a deep velvety purple against the sunset. Road climbed perhaps 200 feet, there were several hastily patched demolitions. Then down into what seemed an endless expanse of absolutely flat desert. We drove about five miles northwards in the dark, then close leaguered.

Over the next three days we moved steadily forward as the enemy retreated, fighting only small rearguard actions. The going became worse and worse, with a series of wadis ten to twenty feet deep running across our line of march, with consequent bottle-necks at each crossing. Behind the ridge of hills on our left were the Americans of First Army, visible from time to time, though we made no contact. As we got further north, prosperous farms began to appear, some in clumps of trees – a dream valley of plenty after Akarit and Wilder's Gap. On the 10th we heard that Sfax was clear of the enemy, and we went into action at Bou Thadi, fifty miles north-west of the town. But the enemy by then was far away, making for the Enfidaville line, and at Bou Thadi we came to rest for four days.

Diary, 10 April

Our wadi has very recently been the home of a Luftwaffe repair shop. Countryside is littered with skeletons of Messerschmidts, battered engines and bits and pieces of fuselage, and the very thoroughly-dug trenches and dugouts are full of *Voelkischer Beobachter*[1] of two weeks ago (full of Stalingrad heroes)[2] and *Afrika Post* (published in Tunis) of a few days ago. So I started polishing up my German.

Letter, 12 April

All is sleepy and peaceful. The only sounds I can hear are my driver rinsing the soap suds out of his filthy shirt on the far side of the truck, a very distant lorry changing gear at the soft wet patch at the mouth of our RHQ wadi, and the buzzing of the flies – this last is an ominous warning of what is to come. I have just had a bath in my wash basin and have put on a clean drill shirt and slacks, to celebrate the coming of summer. It is wonderful to have said goodbye to the sand – I hope forever – and to be surrounded by green again. When I woke today the air was full of larks. One morning a big fat goose flopped lazily over my head. If I had had my tommy gun handy I would have had no scruples – think of roast goose for dinner after weeks of bully and stew. But our menu has been much brightened the last few days – eggs, dried figs that make an excellent sweet after stewing, and even – rare and wonderful prize – fresh fish not twelve hours out of the sea: mullet I think, but delicious, whatever it was.

On 13 April came a warning order that 1 Armd Div was being 'lent' to First Army and would shortly move round to the Medjez El Bab sector where the main attack on Tunis will be launched. We were told to expect a paint spraying team from U.S. Army which would camouflage all our guns and vehicles in European instead of desert colours.

Diary, 15 April

The operation order for the move came in in evening, and I got our orders out. We drive all night and should get to Le Krib, twenty miles short of Medjez, in afternoon of next day. Only one halt of one hour is to be allowed to us. For part of the way U.S. Signal Corps vehicles will travel with us, sending dummy radio messages to encourage the enemy to suppose that we are 2 U.S. Armd Div. A magnificent letter signed by G2 arrived, bidding us adopt as far as possible the looks and habits of First Army – admittedly we can't abolish our suntan, but we musn't give the 'V' sign or talk Arabic, we must sit at attention in our vehicles, and above all not shoot a line about Eighth Army, for 'First Army are very sensitive and some formations, especially 46 Div and 6 Armd, have fought very well'. What tact, what incredible stupidity! I shall keep a copy of that letter as one of my most treasured souvenirs.

1. The daily newspaper of the Nazi Party.
2. The German 6th Army of 100,000 men had surrendered to the Red Army at Stalingrad on 1 February.

16 April

The paint – about eight gallons of it, our share, to do the whole regiment – arrived about 1100, together with a dozen tough looking Americans glued to their tin hats, with two most efficient sprayers run by a small engine. George [Broomfield, our Quartermaster] produced some black paint from his hidden stock, and some red and blue powder, which he looted from a house in Sfax. With all this and much petrol we brewed a mixture that turned out a tolerable greeny-brown, and by spraying it thinly over our most yellow and conspicuous trucks (to the Americans' disgust, who thought it a botched-up job) we produced a rather dirty mottled effect which was reasonably effective camouflage and delighted the Colonel's heart. The sergeant in charge was a bluff blunt little man who believed in getting on with the job and didn't understand about saluting or showing respect to senior British officers or other such waste of time. Amusing to watch the Colonel waste his oiliest charms on him.

We moved off that evening at 2115. A nice farewell message to the Division from Horrocks in which he referred to the tank history we made on the way through to Hamma. We climbed perhaps 200 feet to the top of Faid Pass, then for many miles passed camps and vehicle parks on both sides of the road with American sentries curiously watching us go by. A cold cheerless dawn found us halted just short of Sbeitla. We dove on all day, in fits and starts but on good roads: north to Le Kef, then east towards Tunis, and turned off the road five miles short of Le Krib for the night. We learnt that we were under command of 9 Corps, which was staging the forthcoming big offensive. We had travelled 150 miles since Bou Thadi.

17 April

At Le Kef we really reached civilisation: there was a train in the little branch terminus with steaming engine. Much traffic on the main road from Algeria which we joined just below the town. Cars and lorries in green and brown colours with unfamiliar signs and soldiers with pale complexions, their web equipment blancoed green, wearing tin hats with netting over them. But they were not sitting sternly to attention, nor was their march discipline as impeccable as we had been led to suppose. The elaborate policy of deception was hardly what it should have been: RASC lorries drove in and out of our column with 'Monty's boys' and 'Alamein to Mareth' scrawled over them. We were greeted by French urchins with 'Vive la huitième armée'. Plenty of life in the narrow winding streets – Americans in plenty, many British troops wearing brown and pink berets (the latter are Army Air Corps), French girls smartly dressed, cafés and hotels apparently well patronised.

On 18 April we moved another 25 miles to an assembly area near El Aroussa station, where maximum concealment and minimum movement were enforced. On the night of the 20th, in heavy rain, we went into battle positions in a narrow wadi just north of Bou Arada.

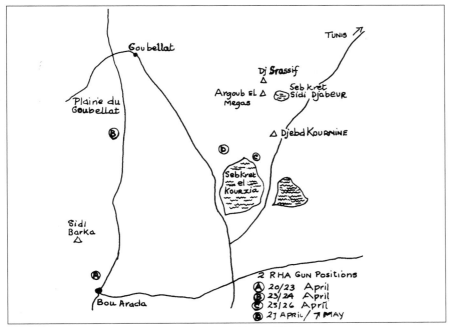

Area of operations, 20 April/7 May.

20 April

We received our first First Army rations, fabulously good, compo pack, containing all sorts of goodies, including steak and kidney, marmalade, rice puddings, boiled sweets, and Players. Compo tea is a a snag, a powder which when mixed with hot water provides tea, milk and sugar combined, but it doesn't taste the same.

The big battle began at 0330 on 22 April. In the initial stages we were under command of 46th Division and supporting 16th Battalion Durham Light Infantry. Their objective was a hill named Sidi Barka, held by the Hermann Goering Division. We fired almost continuously until 0645.

22 April

I tried to sleep through the barrage but messages soon started to come in, and I had to get up about 0430. First two phases of the attack seemed to go well. At 0645 Brian Teacher [Commander of I Battery] reported several of our concentrations had had excellent results, 16 DLI were now in possession of almost the whole of Sidi Barka. But we soon heard that they had had heavy casualties. At 1000 the enemy put in a counter-attack which Brian engaged with the whole Regiment. Geoff Neale [of L Battery] had his armoured car put out of action by a mortar shell which landed alongside and killed his driver. But he got another armd OP up and continued the good work – a great effort. Much quieter

165

afternoon. At 1800 we reverted to command of 1 Armd Div. Lack of orders made the Colonel fuss, but in the middle of the night Bunny Cowles arrived from Div, woke me up and read out a long order to me, asking every other sentence whether I was awake and listening. I just kept my eyes open long enough to realise that we were not moving before 0730 tomorrow, so dropped off to sleep again. An unsatisfactory battle, it seemed to be out of control from the first, and I missed that quiet feeling of confident efficiency which was so prevalent throughout Wadi Akarit. The rain was unfortunate and certainly contributed to holding up our infantry. But there's no doubt that the Hermann Goerings are a tough crowd.

At 0715 on 23 April we started moving northwards behind 2 Armd Bde along tracks through wooded hills and down into the cultivated Goubellat plain. Into action at 1130 on its western edge.

23 April

RHQ did a stout piece of roadmaking and filled up a small wadi with water in the bottom, making it passable for guns. Everyone very happy chucking rocks and mud into the water and splashing round. Our Air OP contacted us, an energetic, very pleasant gunner officer on a motor bike. He selected a suitable field and then buzzed off back to fly up his Taylorcraft plane, which we christened Cuthbert. I found myself left all on my own all day, sitting on my two sets, coping with information from CRA and 2 Armd Bde, the Colonel's constant queries, constantly changing OP locations, regimental shoots on a few occasions towards end of the day. A whole day on the wireless is too much for any human, and at times I came very near to breaking point.

That afternoon we moved forward twice, as our OPs reported the tanks were still pushing slowly ahead. They met little opposition except from mines until the evening when they reached the eastern edge of the plain under low bare foothills. Many of the farms were reported booby-trapped, but we were lucky in avoiding them.

24 April

Thick white dripping mist for most of morning, visibility nil for almost two hours after first light. The Armd Bde groped forward very cautiously, moving eastwards through the hills into another plain full of marshes, stretching north-east from the Sugar Lake [Sebkret el Kourzia] towards Tunis. Regiment did fair amount of shooting as day wore on. Tanks were worried by well-sited 88-mms, and about 1230 Bays lost six Crusaders in less than a minute. I suspected many of the 88s were really Tigers [the latest, very formidable German tank]. Brigade later admitted their existence, and the Tiger menace was soon quite to eclipse the 88. Regiment moved forward 2500 yards in the afternoon. About 1700 came a scream from Brigade that one of their patrols was being shelled – so I quickly stopped the shoot. After dark the Colonel was summoned by CRA and given orders for a change of plan. We are said to be up against a dead end, with the enemy holding the hills and wadis to our east in strength. So we are to move round to north shore of Sugar Lake and reinforce and pass through 6 Armd Div. We pulled out at 0100 when the moon was up and drove back three miles into the middle of the Goubellat plain, where we close leaguered for the rest of the night. Got to bed about 0330.

25 April, Easter Sunday

By 1430 the Regiment was in action on the northern shore of the lake, tucked under a step hill rising to 100ft. To its north there opened up a flat open plain lying under the sensational knobbly isolated peak of Kournine, a high sugar loaf 1200 feet high with rocky top knot, completely dominating the surrounding countryside. As we came in, we passed two 88mms knocked out by 6 Armd Div with crews still lying dead around them, and several burnt out Shermans and a knocked out Tiger, a huge massive creature with its vast lopsided gun at a forlorn crazy angle, looking very dejected and quite out of its element. We hadn't been in position for half an hour when a solitary ME 109 came flying in 200 feet or so above the lake, making right over my truck and skimming the top of the ridge above us. I saw him, realised I was plumb in the line of fire, and lay down in a shallow depression feeling very naked. Lester, one of our batmen, manned the Bren and opened up. The plane replied at once, put a cannon shell thro' Lester's leg and sprinkled the hillside with bullets as he went over. A very stout effort on Lester's part. Our tanks pushed slowly forward, but Srassif and Kournine are going to be big obstacles, and it doesn't look as if we'd be able to move far without getting onto their tops. 6 Armd Div are all round us but will shortly be pulling out. Their infantry have had a hard battle; all afternoon weary Guardsmen came trickling back through us from their forward positions in the wadis and foothills south of Kournine: they lost much of their transport there early this morning, and have been shelled without respite. Ben's RAP [Regimental Aid Post] full of them, he says it is sheer physical exhaustion, but it's difficult for him to evacuate them, as all sorts of technicalities about desertion begin to crop up.

26 April

Busy day's shooting, most of it towards Srassif and on the lower feature immediately in front of it, a green ridge called Argoub el Megas; on its right-hand end is a brilliant poppy field, covering its slopes, a vivid splash of crimson in the surrounding bright green, and in front of Megas is a small still shallow lake with green shores, Sebkret Sidi Djabeur. OPs reported enemy positions on Megas and Kournine strongly held. On Megas Tigers moved constantly up and down behind the ridge, at intervals drove up to the summit, turret down, fired two or three rounds at our tanks and in less than a minute had disappeared, to reappear in a different place and repeat the procedure. These tactics were difficult to deal with.

I was sitting with Bobby [Warren, Regimental Signals Officer] in the truck, each of us with a pair of earphones on our head, about 1215, in a comparative lull, when there was a sudden shattering bang just outside and fragments of metal came through the sides and roof. At once there were shouts and groans outside. A

75-mm shell, fired quite at random, had landed a few feet from where Gunter [my clerk] and Binz [my driver] were sitting watching the tea boil. I shall never forget those groans. The shell hole was not more than fifteen yards from where I was sitting. Gunter never had a chance. His stomach and back had been torn away and he was lying in pools of blood by the time I got out of the truck and round to him. Ben gave him morphine and he gradually quietened down. Binz was amazingly cheerful though his left wrist and right leg were a nasty mess and some splinters had penetrated his chest, which worried Ben most. Gunter died in the ambulance on his way to hospital. It was a big shock to me, it was so unexpected and such infernally bad luck.

During the night of 26/27 April we moved a few miles to a new position north-west of the lake.
27 April
My truck was tucked into a natural depression with walls five feet high, good protection. But by taking six steps backward I was in full view of Kournine, which commanded a magnificent view over the whole divisional area, and in particular overlooked all tracks leading into the regimental area and the wadis connecting the battery positions.

On the night of 26/27 April 7RB had carried out a silent attack on Srassif, which failed. We fired a great number of rounds in their support during the following day. Next night the Yorks & Lancs attempted to capture Kournine, but failed: and the Lincolns tried on the night of the 28/29th, but again without success. At frequent intervals throughout three days our whole regimental area was sprayed with concentrations of enemy shelling, including 210-mms which made huge craters on the hill just above my truck. But RHQ escaped unscathed. On 29 April shells put Cuthbert out of action, so we were deprived of the Air OP upon which we were beginning to rely.

On the night of 29/30 April a larger-scale operation was carried out: 1KRRC successfully attacked Megas with the support of a divisional barrage, but 2RB's silent attack on Kournine failed.

1 May
Very quiet day. Our infantry pulled back a little off Megas last night. In evening 74th Medium Regiment put an airburst stonk over top of Kournine, a most impressive sight. We were to hear a fortnight later from Gen. von Broich, Commander of Hermann Goering Division, that this was one of most uncomfortable half hours he'd ever spent in his life. After many rumours about the new plots being hatched, we were given all the dope. The main attack, which they hope will finish off Tunis, is to be launched by 9 Corps round Medjez. We are to be left here on this miserable sector of which we are all getting pretty tired, and are to hold it for meantime.

The next five days were a quiet period of waiting. On 4 May two enemy fighters flew high over our gun area: they turned out to be the last enemy planes we were to see in Africa. The news of the big battle in the north, which started on 5 May, was uniformly good.

Letter, 6 May

This will be an unsatisfactory letter again, I'm afraid, for I can't write what you most want to hear: but I'll do my best to give you a general idea of how we are faring.

It is getting really warm now, and we are all in drill for the summer. We have had a good bit of rain in the last week, especially at night. The climate is very different from the desert with its dry winds and clear starlit nights: instead, much haze and mist in the early mornings, mid-day often close and muggy, but usually a cool breeze blowing down the valleys. And at nights heavy dew and often thunderstorms – sometimes it's difficult to distinguish the lightning from gun flashes in the distance. The flies are getting bad again – this country has at least that in common with the desert. But on balance what a blessed change in scenery. Our HQ here is perched on the green slopes of a deep gash in the hills, deep cleft running down into the main valley a good 100 feet below. In the distance all around us are the real mountains, lovely-shaped peaks, their lower slopes thickly covered with pines and tall scrub. We spent one night in a valley that might have been taken straight out of Greece: fragrant mountain smells, the sound of the wind in the pines, and a cuckoo shouting his head off to wake us up at 5.30 in the morning. Then between the high hills and the rolling grassy downs are broad flat valleys, richly cultivated. The villages in the plains are delightful. We passed one one day which had a wayside railway station, a stone church and a small canning factory – all so French that I could have screamed with delight.

As I said in a recent letter to Hugh, in spite of all their follies and meanness, their unprovoked hostility and indifference to the war that most Frenchmen, especially in this country, have shown in the past two years – even so I find myself at the least possible excuse ready to forgive and welcome them. Even the Frenchness of the roadside signs and telegraph poles delights me. I have spoken to a few Frenchmen, not of politics, for they are very reserved – it will be thin ice for a long time in Tunisia, I think. But their one topic of conversation is the war, and their hope that the war is over for them. It is, of course, in one way. But it will be a long time before they taste the full delights of peace, in spite of the arrival of la huitième armée which the small boys still troop round mimicking and saluting. I came across a small village shop run by an old Madame who might have lived all her life within sight of Notre Dame: she had only dried figs and salted mackerel to sell, and she sighed sadly as we looked around the walls and read the advertisements for Brazilian coffee and Danish Karlsberg beer and Lyons woollens. There are places, if one looks hard and sharpens one's nose sufficiently, where local homemade bread can be bought, and sometimes fresh vegetables and eggs, well within reach of the front line. And the local red wine is both palatable and potent. Those are the advantages of fighting in a civilised county. But there are disadvantages too. I remember writing almost my first letter from the desert, in August 1941, and saying that at least one need have no scruples in shelling and digging up the sand, for no one would suffer except the armies involved. But I have seen things recently that reminded me sharply of France and Greece: worse sights, for the destructive power of the bomber has increased many fold since 1941, and both sides have learnt how to use their guns and tanks with more shattering effect. In the desert we used to dream of Tripoli, our goal, and imagine it as a city full of comforts and pleasures. Well, it's hardly that. And we have only a long trail of destruction and desolation to look forward to, both sides of the Mediterranean, and worse and worse as we push up into Europe. Then we'll see not only the results of the shelling and bombing, but of starvation and disease, and persecution, and perhaps civil wars. My heart fails me sometimes when I think of the ruin and destruction we are going to bring on Europe – on top of the ravages of Hitler and Mussolini the results will be ghastly. What a God-sent chance we shall have when it all ends. But if we don't seize that chance to heal and rebuild, will we ever be forgiven?

At first light on 7 May Srassif was reported clear of the enemy, and 2 Armd Bde started advancing. That same evening we heard that Bizerta and Tunis had fallen. During the next three days we occupied in quick succession one position after another, in pursuit of the enemy's rearguard. Our line of advance was eastward from the Plaine de Mornay through the hills about fifteen miles south of Tunis. At midday on 9 May the Bays were held up by 88-mms on the eastern edge of Creteville, and it was clear that the enemy intended to offer serious resistance in the pass leading through to our objective, Grombalia. We suffered a number of casualties that day from shelling, and were busy engaging vehicles and infantry in retreat. A hundred prisoners, mainly Italian, were taken.
2 RHA War Diary, 10 May

About 1200 two German officers from Hermann Goering Grenadier Regiment had approached tanks of the Bays with white flags and offered to surrender with 700 men if a short truce could be arranged. The envoys were given 45 minutes from 1400 to bring their men in, and all regiments were ordered to stop firing into the pass for this period. Between 1400 and 1500 a steady trickle of Germans came down the road from the top of the pass.

But that evening, after the truce had ended, the Brigade ran into trouble in the pass, which was dominated to its south by the rocky peak of Djebel Ressas. Heavy and accurate concentrations from the enemy's 105s and 210s made it impossible for the regiment to move forward until dark. Italians meanwhile were still coming down out of the hills, and one Italian officer pointed out a German OP and MG post on top of Djebel Ressas, which we immediately engaged.

At 0730 on 11 May our tanks entered Grombalia and there met units of 6 Armd Div which had made 'a sensational dash last night and early this morning across the neck of the Cap Bon peninsula to the sea at Beni Aichoun'. The regiment went into action north of Grombalia at 1000 and engaged tanks and guns: but these were the last rounds we fired on African soil.

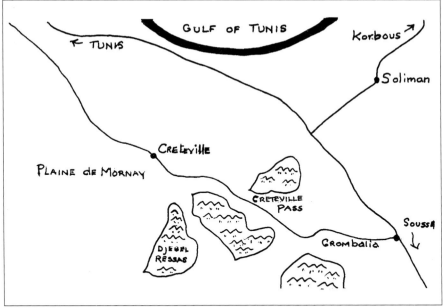

Area of operations, 7/10 May.

11 May

From midday onwards a constant stream of German and Italian lorries and cars of every size and make, crammed with surrendering soldiers and airmen, was passing down the road into Grombalia, where the scenes in the POW cage and the huge car park outside were reminiscent of peace-time bank holiday crowds.

12 May

The last sounds of battle were heard about 1430 far to the south, where it was learnt that 90 Light Division were surrendering. The battle of Africa was over.

Letter, 13 May

All day I have been sitting quietly working and writing under an old knobbly olive, watching the prisoners stream by. They are going past in an unending flow, six-ton and ten-ton lorries piled high with Germans and Italians, an occasional Italian sailor, thousands in Luftwaffe uniform, officers in their staff cars sitting stiff and reserved, sometimes a row of medals and Iron Crosses on a general's breast. It is an amazing, incredible sight. Some of the lorries have the signs of those crack divisions of Rommel's which the Eighth Army has been fighting without a break since that first contact with the Afrika Korps at Agheila in February 1941 – 90th Light division, 15th and 21st Panzer, old friends whom we had got to know very well. And now they exist no more. They are driving in in their own lorries to the prisoners' cages to give themselves up. Few of them are under guard as they pass us: they will pick them up later. They are bringing their own field kitchens and watercarts, and piles of rations. Some of the Italians are laughing, one gave the V sign, another a moment ago was playing a banjo. But most of them are tired and dejected. The Germans are smart and well turned out. Some of the faces and arrogant bearings typify nazism. I wish I could think that their term as prisoners will change those looks and spirit: but I doubt it. On the whole the Germans seem interested by what they see, quiet and rather subdued. Interested, I hope, to see the vast quantities of dumps and equipment that they have had to leave intact for us, and the lorries and cars with German registration plates that are buzzing up and down the roads. I hope they realise that all this will be used against them, quite soon perhaps. And I hope that they are subdued for the right reason, and that they know they have been soundly and squarely beaten. Goebbels will say, probably has already said, that they were overwhelmed by numbers and weight of metal. There's much truth in that. The army they despised so much in 1940 for its out-of-date, inadequate machines and organisation, has at last produced superior equipment and tactics, and shown that it understands both. And all this was done under Hitler's very nose. They fought well, these Germans, not quite to the very end, but almost. And where they fought best and hardest we outfought them. I hope these lorry-loads of young, well-built, blonde Aryans realise that also. I think they do.

The Afrika Korps surrenders, 12 May.

172

It has not been a picnic, this last battle. We have had our full share of hard knocks. There are some blank spaces which will never be filled again, some 'old familiar faces' which I shall always miss. I don't feel deliriously triumphant. In fact, it's still rather difficult to believe. This is what we have been thinking about and discussing and looking forward to since long before Alamein. Now it has happened, so smoothly and 'inevitably' that I find myself watching these scenes almost in a detached and matter-of-fact way. I have to say to myself now and again, 'This is a victory that will make history: the Afrika Korps is finished: and Africa is free'. It *is* thrilling, of course. And yet, just at the moment, I'm more inclined to think of what it has cost – to us, to this country, to all of us, in terms of loss and waste and suffering. I hate this war more and more every day. Let's pray it will soon be over.

CHAPTER FIFTEEN: TRIPOLI, CAIRO, ALGIERS
May – November 1943

On 13 May the Regiment moved to an area north-east of Soliman, in the middle of a huge German ammunition dump, for rest and maintenance. Our immediate task was to collect, list and guard all enemy equipment in the area which was worth salvaging. Daily leave parties to Tunis started at once.

Diary, 15 May

Allan Harvey and I set off at 2 pm in his Volkswagen for Tunis and beyond. Much traffic on the road, one in every four vehicles a captured German or Italian staff car or lorry. We drove straight through the city to Sidi Bou Said, a delightful and unexpected place, just like an Italian or Riviera village, perched on a round headland, very narrow cobbled streets. From the top, where French coast defence 6-in guns in concrete turrets, covered with Italian scrawls, were being manned by British gunners, a glorious view. Across the water fifteen miles away the peak of Kournine and behind, far higher and craggier, its sensational precipices in silhouette, Djebel Ressas. It was strange to stand there in the complete tranquillity of Sidi Bou Said, so far from war, and see that wicked mountain that meant so much to us those last three days of battle. Then back to Tunis. I wandered down the main boulevard, overshadowed by trees, complete with kiosks and pissoirs, grandly French. *La Tunisie Liberée* on sale, with news of Giraud's deposition of the Bey,[1] a speech of de Gaulle printed in full, an announcement that six Frenchmen have been condemned to death for high treason. So it begins. Big group of civilians listening to news through loudspeakers, the latest count of 160,000 prisoners, big RAF raids on the Ruhr etc. Allan and I walked round looking at the posters, pictures of Churchill and Roosevelt everywhere, 'Justice must be done', Giraud's motto – 'Notre seul but – la victoire'. Proclamations calling up Frenchmen for the army posted over notices in German, French and Italian requisitioning all vehicles. Here and there, peeping out from under the red, white and blue of liberated Tunis, a picture of pathetic, grey-haired Pétain,[2] and

1. General Giraud succeeded Darlan (see p. 157, note) on the latter's assassination on 24 December 1942: de Gaulle reluctantly approved the appointment. The Bey of Tunis had collaborated with the Italian and German occupying forces.

2. President of the Vichy State, signatory of the armistices with Germany and Italy in June 1940.

underneath 'les paroles du chef'. Almost all the shops shut, some small bread queues, chemists and knick-knack shops open, one big cafe on the corner of the boulevard full of troops and, I suppose, beer, or at least some wine. Some of the civilians looked just as if they were from the Quartier Latin, especially one old man with grey hair in black beret, a frail little lady on his arm, talking away in serious solemn tones. A great many smartly dressed girls, Parisian in their looks and manner, and interesting to see that in spite of six months of enemy occupation, supplies of lipstick were still holding out.

17 May

At 2.30 a great parade of all our captured enemy vehicles, staff cars and 10-tonners, a grand convoy – all to be handed in to Divisional Reception Park. Sad but inevitable. I went bathing with George Broomfield and Padre and large party, up the Korbous road. No beach, and going in and out a bit tricky, fair-sized waves breaking on the slippery boulders. We swam out to a sunken Italian destroyer lying fast on the rocks 400 yards off shore, a huge bomb-hole in her centre. She lay at so steep an angle that walking along the decks was painful and awkward, the metal burning hot to the feet. The wardroom, engine-room etc. all awash, and all manner of eerie splashings, gurgles, bangs and creaks and suckings coming from inside. A sad sight, and I felt quite frightened by the weirdness of the noises.

On 20 May there was a victory parade in Tunis, in which 35 representatives of the Regiment took part. Next day we started on the long journey back to Tripoli, driving 485 miles in four days. There we settled down once again to a static period of training as part of 10 Corps of the Eighth Army. There were practice camps and exercises and demonstrations in scorching heat in the barren hills around Gharian, twenty miles to the south. We were situated first at Suami Ben Adem, then at Castel Benito, about ten miles inland on the edge of the Tripoli oasis. We had to hand over a great deal of our transport and equipment.

Diary, 6 June

All officers in to Tripoli to attend Monty's talk in the Miramare Cinema. He was in colossal form, briefly surveyed the world. Softening process in Italy had begun with a vengeance. Eighth Army will not spend summer bathing in Med. We are here for rest, overhaul and maintenance, and so is Desert Air force. Training for close country is our chief job. So it looks like Italy (or Sicily?) for us.

Letter, 5 June

I have now been released from the adjutant's job and am back in a battery. It is a pleasant change and considerable relief. I think seven months as adjutant is quite enough for anyone in wartime, especially if those seven months contain two long battles during which one had to work continuously at maximum pressure. I must confess I was getting very very tired towards the end, and also a bit stale. I came to H Battery on 31 May as Battery Captain, that is 2nd in command, and took over command as the battery commander [Chris Vesey] had been wounded while we were with the First Army in April, and was reported to be in hospital in Algiers. Then one evening the Colonel told me he had decided to promote me to major. By the day before yesterday I was beginning to get into the swing of it and really enjoying 'running my own show', when the wounded battery commander returned quite unexpectedly from Algiers. So here I am, battery captain for a bit of time yet, half disappointed and half relieved.

23 June

I have little news for you except for one big event, and that was the King's visit. It was a very quiet, perhaps almost dull, visit: but I was glad of the absence of bands and marching and ceremonial. One of my biggest bugbears is marching past celebrities on ceremonial parades. We all turned out in our best clothes and lined a long stretch of road between the olives and under the tall gums and eucalyptus trees. He drove down quietly in a open car, stopping to talk to each Colonel, with the usual cavalcade of Generals and Brigadiers, ADCs and press photographers and all the trail of small fry. I thought he looked ill, and heard afterwards he was suffering from 'gyppy tummy'. He must have had a miserable time, driving down mile after mile of troops. But it was a great idea to come out and see us – I suspect it was his own – and he did us all a lot of good. We saw his big plane fly over us when he left, with a vast escort of fighters thundering past, twisting and turning and watching all the time. It was a great sight.

Otherwise life goes on placidly. We have started training again to replace our losses in the last battles. But we are not over-exerting ourselves. We get up early, work from 6 to 12.30 and finish for the day, except for occasional lectures and discussions in the evening. We are being well looked after: rations are excellent, comforts for our canteen are all that one could ask for in the circumstances, and we get a bottle of beer a week, each of us, the most welcome luxury of all in this hot weather. We are unfortunately some way from the sea, tho' near enough to send lorry loads of bathers in the afternoons. I have had some lovely swims on two very pleasant beaches. Our tents are pitched between very small young olives, but along every road and lane are planted the graceful tall gums, and sometimes a rank type of desert pine: these make long shady avenues, full of small finches and singing birds and lizards and crickets. And beside every farmhouse is a high wind-pump over a well, out of which the water is pumped into a cistern about 30 feet square, before draining into the irrigation channels and flowing on to flood the fruit trees and plots of maize and vegetables. These cisterns make perfect swimming pools in which to take off the sweat and dust of the day and get an appetite for dinner. They are about five feet deep when full, and the one I swim in most is covered with a roof of vines. I wish it were the right season: I should then spend all evening floating in the warm water and plucking fat grapes from above my head.

This is an exciting, but tantalising period. The old formations are being split and reorganised, old faces disappear. As you can imagine, everyone is ceaselessly asking the same questions, 'When?' and 'Where?'. I shan't speculate here, but I don't think we'll be left out of it for very long.

On this last point I was proved wrong. On 10 July came the news that Sicily had been invaded. Once again we had been left behind. But there were consolations. At the beginning of July I had four days' leave in Tripoli at the Del Mehari Hotel on the seafront. It was very cool, 'its many inside courts surrounded by colonnades of pleasant whitewashed stone, with attractive lily ponds and shrubs.'

On 22 July the Regiment moved to a location right on the sea near Zuara, 25 miles west of Tripoli, We were told that we would shortly move to the Bizerta area, 'to guard prisoners of war for probably three months, equipment expected to start arriving in September but we were unlikely to be in action before November.'

Letter, 21 July

All my thoughts and energies for the past fortnight have been wrapped up in desperate schemings to get down to the Delta. I consider I have a strong case, having last seen Cairo at the beginning of October. Three days ago I was told I was being sent on a course at the School of Artillery. You can imagine my rapture. In a flash my grumpiness and gloom vanished and I wrote off to Hugh, commanding him to be in Cairo for the whole of August. To-night I hear the course is cancelled. But I am not yet contemplating suicide, for I have been promised a job which will take me to the Delta on duty.

My job was to take 70 drivers from the Regiment to Cairo, to collect vehicles and drive them to Algeria. Charles Kauntze and Oscar Rose were to be my assistants, and we would be part of a divisional party of 1100, commanded by Lt Col Gerald Grosvenor of the 9th Lancers.

Diary, 26 July

Heard sensational news on last night's BBC that Musso has resigned.[1] Into Tripoli in afternoon. Notices posted on the streets and buildings – "Il Fascismo ha cessato di esistere", and announcing Badoglio's succession as prime minister. Maddeningly little news or explanation yet available – we must be patient.

The regiment started moving back to Tunisia on 4 August. My Cairo party had meanwhile moved into Tripoli, the officers to the Del Mehari, the other ranks to the rest camp. There we hung around until 12 August when we finally embarked at 6.15 on H.M.T. Talma, B.I. trooper of about 10,000 tons.

Diary, 12 August

Troop decks more than usually crowded. *Talma* in peace-time was on Calcutta-Hong Kong run, converted to trooper at outbreak of war, her accommodation

---

1. Mussolini was dismissed by the King and immediately interned on 25 July. Badoglio, Italy's senior soldier, formed a non-fascist government and started to negotiate secretly with the allies for an armistice.

gradually extended to cope with tightly-squeezed 1200 in place of originally intended 800 – but we now have 1600 aboard. Contrast with officers' accommodation, as usual, glaring. It is a very slow boat, 12 knots maximum when unmercifully flogged, and submarines can catch her: so blackout especially important, as also prevention of throwing of rubbish overboard. Sailed at 11.30. Two of us in the convoy, our fellow – traveller being a small Polish freighter, unladen, towing a balloon. Our escorts are one small destroyer and a dumpy, business-like little corvette.

We spent most of 13 and 14 August anchored off Valetta, and were 'at once surrounded by a swarm of boats with Maltese of all ages and both sexes, some with grapes to sell, but all begging for food and cigarettes.' We sailed again on the 14th, 'two destroyers racing out from Valetta to escort us.' About 5 p.m. we joined a convoy of thirteen freighters from England, four of them with ballons, and settled down to a steady course eastwards.

We disembarked at Alexandria at 4.15 p.m. on 19 August and travelled by train overnight to Cairo. I arrived in time to have lunch with my brother, who had booked a double room for us at the Metropolitan Hotel. Originally the divisional contingent had been told to expect three to four days' leave before collecting the vehicles and setting off for Algeria. But as it turned out, they were not ready for us, and my regimental party were able to enjoy the delights of Cairo until 2 September. 'Life in Cairo is same as ever', I noted in my diary on 21 August, 'perpetual round of sleep and eats'. Besides re-establishing contact with old army friends, I met several of my brother's SOE and Embassy colleagues.

Letter, 19 September

I made the most of my ten days. Cairo is a horrible city, and yet it is civilisation. And after ten months in the desert or in countries disorganised by war, it was sheer joy to see shops full of every imaginable article, streets full of fast noisy cars, well-dressed people and lights and good food. While Hugh worked in his office, I used to potter round the shops or look up old friends of OCTU days or simply wander aimlessly and enjoy the sensation of being able to get just exactly what I wanted at almost any time of day – a taxi or a cool drink or my soft hotel bed. The last had an irresistible attraction after lunch.

You will have heard of me already, of course, from Pan.[1] I do hope he didn't refer to me as 'the simple-hearted warrior'. What a joy to get away from endless military 'shop' and domestic gossip. That's what I most value about those then days. I feel I've got in touch with the outside world again, and regained a certain sanity and mental balance which was fast disappearing during the early summer, smothered by the irritation of inactivity, discomfort and uninspiring daily routine. I've now enough 'background' (the wrong word), quite apart from my suitcase of delightful books, a most catholic selection, to keep me going for many months, if need be.

---

1. 'Pan' Panigian, one of my brother's SOE colleagues, had recently returned to London and seen my father.

On 1 September I gathered my convoy together at Mena Garrison, on the outskirts of Cairo near the Pyramids. It was composed of 40 water carts, 28 15-cwts and one 3-tonner, with a draft of 10 officers and 120 men of the RAOC bound for Tripoli. We started on our long drive next day, and reached Tripoli on 15 September, having covered 1380 miles. It was a monotonous journey, but on many evenings we were able to park our vehicles near the sea and enjoy reinvigorating bathes. We also fed ourselves well, having stocked up with delicacies and liquor in Cairo.

Letter, 17 September

It's just a fortnight since I said goodbye to Hugh, and here I am again on the terrace of the Tripoli 'Lido', drinking iced lemonade and just about to swim in a rough dancing blue sea. It's almost as if I had never been to Cairo and were back in the dull days of routine of last July. But tomorrow I'm off again with my convoy of vehicles, heading westwards and northwards, and should rejoin the Regiment within about 10 days.

I have thoroughly enjoyed the long drive from Cairo so far. But it has been tantalising to be cut off from the world for so long. We heard the news that Italy had been invaded[1] at a lonely, sandy petrol station twenty miles west of Alamein. At Benghazi came the news of Italy's surrender.[2] For the past week we have been asking at every isolated desert post for the latest news of Naples, and here in Tripoli, when we arrived, we found a good bit of gloom. But that has all gone with the latest report of the turning of the scale at Salerno[3] and the linking of 5th and 8th Armies and 5 Corps. What magnificent prospects. And this morning's *Tripoli Times* says the Jugoslavs have captured Split. Can it be true?[4] It's like watching the walls of Jericho crumbling: Hitler's fortress showing the first serious cracks. It's only a beginning no doubt, but what a magnificent beginning. I should dearly love to know what's happening inside Italy, and particularly in Italian politics. I do hope we don't make a mess of it. I don't like the complete silence on the subject. It is so important to support the right people and say the right things *now,* for all the peoples of Europe (and especially the Russians) will draw their own conclusions from our actions in the next few weeks as to what sort of peace and what sort of future for Europe they can expect from us.

Having dropped off our RAOC contingent, acquired seventeen truck-loads of tea for transport to Tunis, and had all our vehicles greased, oiled and repaired as necessary, we set off again westwards on 18 September. We had also acquired an aged staff car, in which I rode in great comfort between breakdowns,

---

1. A small British and Canadian force landed on the Italian mainland opposite Sicily on the night of 2/3 September and advanced up the toe of Italy almost unopposed.

2. Italy's unconditional surrender was announced on 8 September.

3. A large British-US force landed at Salerno on 9 September, meeting fierce German resistance.

4. It was true, but Tito's partisans were almost immediately ejected by German forces.

which were frequent. At last on 24 September, having covered another 600 miles, we reached our destination, Bone, a port fifty miles inside Algeria. There we handed over our vehicles and 'got receipts for them – they didn't even count them' – and were then transported to the station. About 6 pm a train of cattle trucks came in, full of pioneers, and as soon as they unloaded we took possession – twenty men to a truck, with one for us four officers. But the train never reached our destination, Bizerta, as the engine broke down on the evening of the 25th at a junction named Mastouta. 'The Railway Transport Officer told us that there was no immediate prospect of getting another. The station absolutely filthy, tins and melon skins and every kind of unpleasantness littering the tracks and sidings'. Fortunately we were able to get through by telephone to the Regiment, which sent three 3-tonners to pick us up. And so at 4 p.m. on 27 September I arrived back with H Battery. 'Everyone was in exceedingly good form, though bored with running transit camps for Americans embarking for Italy'.

Diary, 28 September

The battery is responsible for about twenty of the 'Houston' areas, into which units, with or without vehicles, are sent from the 'Texas' concentration area, to wait until they are called forward by the embarkation authorities to their own ship lying alongside at the docks. Italian prisoners work all day in the cookhouse and on cleaning up vacant areas. On the whole the system is working magnificently, and the fame of 2 RHA's good work has spread over Tunisia. We eat stupendous meals in the mess, the greatest advantage of the present job being that one can't help 'making' rations, however honest one tries to be – hence the tomato and fruit juices, spam, sausages, boned chicken, excellent tinned vegetables and fruit, and above all the coffee.

3 October

In the evening I was summoned by the Colonel, who told me that Frizz Fowler has decided to promote Roy Seel to command F Battery [in 4 RHA], not me, in spite of his remonstrations. He gave me a personal letter from Frizz, assuring me that I haven't been passed over, and that in normal circumstances I would have been his no.1 choice, as I am of the Colonel, but that he considered Roy the type of commander 'for filling a rather unorthodox hole'. So that is that. My feelings are as always mixed.

On 30 September we had learnt that the Division was to move very shortly to the Algiers area. I left with the regimental advance party on 4 October. It was a four-day, 500-mile drive, through a mixture of rugged mountains and rich cultivated plains. 'All the small villages gaily decorated with tricolours, to celebrate the liberation of Corsica, as we afterwards were told'. On the evening of 7 October we reached our destination at Rovigo, a small town set among vineyards and orange groves fifteen miles south of Algiers.

Diary, 8 October

The location allotted to H Battery is a large prosperous farm on the Sidi Moussa – l'Arba road. It has two large yards, big stables, fat geese and turkeys and hens everywhere, dozens of sheds and garages, several cottages and detached houses. But all the accommodation they are offering us at present is the huge 'cave', three rooms in a wing of 'la grande maison', and an open shed that will make a good gun park.

9 October

Had a long chat with the directeur and persuaded him to give us a henhouse as kitchen for the officers' mess, part of a garage and a third small room as stores. But only reluctantly.

10 October

To the farm in morning with whole battery party, and they started on thorough sweeping and washing down of the 'cave'. I hope they get rid of the rancid sour stench of wine lees – though I find myself getting used to it.

Letter, 11 October

I am exploring the countryside, requisitioning billets and making all possible arrangements so that our troops, when they arrive, will be able to settle down in comfort and without fuss. I enjoy being semi-independent and spend my days running round 'scrounging' simple amenities like chairs and tables and tents. I realise now how lucky I have been in getting down to Cairo and so escaping the seven weeks of drudgery the rest of them have been through. The job I found them doing had as much connection with gunnery as knitting or playing the violin. I can't say I'm in any violent hurry to rush into Europe in mid-winter and fight what would certainly be a most uncomfortable, and probably very dangerous campaign. There's a lot to be said for the ancient habit of going into winter quarters, and starting again in the spring. As I told you before, you needn't worry about me yet awhile.

I did a bit of snooping while in Cairo, and talked to Hugh about PICME [Political Intelligence Centre, Middle East] and various other possibilities. Hugh was actually rather discouraging and said he didn't think PICME was the thing for me. I can't really make up my mind. The prospect of an office job in Cairo, particularly at this stage of the war, when Cairo is becoming more and more of a backwater, quite frankly does not appeal to me much. If I was offered something definite in the way of political intelligence or military liaison, I should take it, especially of course if it touched the Balkans. And I am keeping my eyes open this end. Part of my hesitation was due to the fact that I didn't exactly know what my prospects were in the regiment. I now know that I am next on the list for a battery, and should get one soon, – H, I hope. That being so, I am tempted to wait.

It was delightful to get your Skye letter. How I wish I could have been with you. The pleasantest part of this place is that it is right under a range of hills that rise to 3,000 feet, and wherever one walks or drives one sees that lovely background, blue in the sunshine with the cork trees and scrubby oaks and pines making large dark blotches: and on the wet days the clouds come right down and the hills put on their nightcaps, and the rain drives down in visible, soaking mist into the green fertile plain – just like in that happier land.

The battery arrived from Bizerta on 25 October, by which time a reasonably comfortable camp had been prepared under my direction. Training began as we received our new equipment, and we were told we were to be ready to fight again by 31 December.

Letter, 4 November

It is raining hard outside as I write this. But how nice to be able to ignore it, and sit comfortably and warm indoors again. We have established our mess in two delightful upstairs rooms in the old wing of 'la grande maison'. They are bright and clean, with our own homemade sofas (made from the seats of German lorries looted in Tunisia last May), and in our sitting-room we have installed a stove, also looted from the battlefields, set in a red brick grate, which gives off a fierce and soporific heat.

Three days ago we decided to produce a battery pantomime for Christmas. We have an excellent hall with plenty of room for a stage, and of course an expert gang of carpenters and electricians and stage managers. I have been inveigled into being the producer.

This will hardly give you the impression of intense military activity. But we are not exactly marking time and I have enough to do to prevent me becoming bored.

De Gaulle seems to have pretty complete control of affairs now. Every town and village is plastered with the cross of Lorraine. I'm told the enthusiastic demonstrations in Casablanca, Algiers and Tunis when de Gaulle arrived the first time were worth seeing.[1] A pretty comprehensive purge of French officers is going on, particularly of those who ordered their units to resist the Americans a year ago. Periodically prominent citizens are locked up for 'sentiments collaborationistes'; this happened recently to two judges and the headmaster of the municipal school in a town less than twenty miles from us, and as you can imagine it caused something of a local sensation. I don't think royalism has any future, now that the influence of Algerian 'bien pensants' has been so much reduced by the introduction of de Gaullists into key jobs, and by the arrival of leaders of the resistance movement in France. All the talk now, at political or 'cultural' meetings, and in the papers, is of the 4th Republic.

Letter, 9 November

Most of the battery is in camp 50 miles away through the hills, next to an

---

1. De Gaulle had recently moved from London to Algiers as head of a French Committee of National Liberation which was granted official allied recognition.

182

artillery range, and busy firing the guns and giving officers practice in shooting once again. I have been left behind to hold the fort in our farm, guard the baggage and improve its amenities for the worst of the winter that will soon be here. A battery captain's job is not a thrilling one. Being second-in-command of the battery he has no 'command', and therefore no direct responsibility for looking after a particular number of men, and few opportunities of getting to know any of them well. To-day I supervised the construction of a wire-netting enclosure into which we will put the 25 live turkeys which we are shortly being given, to be fattened for Christmas. And my chief concern now is thinking out ways of heating the hilly, draughty corridors of the 'cave' where 150 of our men sleep. All materials are scarce in this country, especially timber, nails and corrugated iron. There are no battlefields where one can pick up unlimited quantities of salvage, and the civilian market was exhausted months ago. So it's improvisation, improvisation, improvisation, even more than usual. But it's wonderful what can be done with the tins and drums that bring us our petrol. We have converted a tent into a bath-house, with four baths, cement drain, duckboards and clothes pegs complete. Water is unlimited and we heat it in yet more drums on an oil-and-water stove. I had a luxurious bath this afternoon. And so the days roll by.

Thank you for sending me *Wind of Freedom*[1]. It is a graceful and heartfelt tribute to Greece and he doesn't exaggerate. You have often asked me about the day I got my M.C. And your guess was right. The exact incident is described on page 184 lines 14 and 15. It was just south of Ptolemais, on Easter Sunday, April 13th. One day I'll write about it at greater length. I can still remember every detail very vividly indeed. But don't expect a tale of dazzling heroism. It was very far from being anything of the sort. In some book or magazine I've read recently I came across a phrase by a correspondent who was in Greece during the campaign. He said that, for anyone who was in Greece, that war would always be '*the* war'. And how true that is. In spite of all my varied and interesting and exciting experiences since, I doubt if I'll ever again feel the exhilaration and enthusiasm I felt in Greece. And that in spite of the anxieties and doubts and misery, which, God knows, were many.

1. By Compton McKenzie, who included in his book extracts from my letter of 28 March/27 April 1941 (see. pp 66-7 and 79-80) a copy of which he had received from my father.

CHAPTER SIXTEEN: RETURN TRIP TO ENGLAND
December 1943 – March 1944

On 30 November I received a bombshell even greater than that of 14 November 1941.

Letter, 30 November

I may see you before this reaches you. How odd that looks on paper. I'm so excited I can hardly yet collect my thoughts. Here are the cold plain facts.

I was told one hour ago that I have been given a vacancy on a course in England beginning 15th December. I believe it's at Oxford. It lasts about a month. And I don't suppose for a moment that the course carries on without a break over Christmas.

This is all as certain as anything can be in this Army. So keep your ears glued to the telephone.

I took off from Maison Blanche airfield at 4.30 p.m. on 3 December in a DC3 'with most comfortable peacetime seats'. All my pockets were crammed with oranges as gifts for the family and friends at home. My fellow passengers, besides eight other officers going on my course, were a full colonel in the ATS (whom we named the Queen AT), two French civilians, a French lieutenant bound for Marrakesh, and an American major and a captain bound for the USA via Dakar and Brazil.

Diary, 3 December

We flew low, about 5000 ft. I imagine, and I read my 1/2,000,000 map and looked down on the toy farms, toy lorries and horses crawling along the straight ribbon-like roads. Fascinating scenes. Touched down at La Sénia airport, outside Oran, just before 6, as it was too late to go any further. Lorry took us to hostel in the pre-war Air Force barracks. A vast meal of B rations. I sat next to the Frenchmen who speculated how the Germans would feel if they could see the 'spread'. One of them had recently come from Paris.

Next day a four hours' flight took us to Fez, where we landed in a 'howling bitter wind and driving rain. The weather reports spoke of continuous rain at Casablanca and Marrakesh, likelihood of thunder-storms, impossible to fly on to-day'.

4 December
Found ourselves at the Hotel Palais Jamai, an old Moorish palace, now converted to luxurious modern hotel owned by the Compagnie Transatlantique. Delightful courts, lined with blue, white and red-brown tiles, a fountain, hanging trees and palms. Unfortunately not enough rooms to go round, so I found a comfortable divan in an upstairs salon and had it made up into an excellent bed, the only snag being the lack of privacy. Four of us took a guide down into native city, an incredible rabbit-warren, like Jerusalem but even more puzzling. Between the four walls live 260,000 Arabs. We wandered for what seemed miles through endless crowded passages, donkeys and Arabs and sheep all jostling their way past. Back to the hotel in the dusk, every shop ablaze with electric light.

Next day the weather reports said no change, so we were stuck. But on the 6th our pilot 'told us met. reports were bad, but he'd have a shot at it'. He succeeded, and we reached Marrakesh that evening.
Diary, 6 December
A colossal airfield, the American Mediterranean Air Base, with rows of Liberators and huge hangars. Full of hope we entered the Traffic Office, to be told no plane for the UK to-night. Majors and above billeted in the town, the rest of us in bungalows next to the aerodrome, peacetime French airforce officers' quarters.

7 December
At the Traffic Office they said there would be no plane to-night. So spent morning getting a pass into the native town (it's out of bounds to all troops because of bubonic plague). Then down to La Mammounia Hotel for admirable lunch. As we came back to hotel American MPs stopped us and told us every man must be in the Base or in his quarters by 4 p.m. It looks as if Roosevelt and party are returning this way[1] and this might account for the lack of planes to UK.

8 December
At 10. the now inevitable answer to hopeful enquiries – no plane for UK to-night. In evening for a brief half hour the rain stopped. Quite by chance I looked to the south on my way back to camp and saw a sight that took my breath away – the jags and snowy peaks of the summits of the Atlas clear at last. When I got back to my house I was dragged into the room where live four American bomber pilots, with a huge log fire. I talked, watched them play bridge, ate oranges. They should have taken off for England last night but the co-pilot was sick. And they offered me a lift when they go to-morrow night, if no plane goes by official ways.

9 December
Round to Traffic Office for the familiar answer, no plane for UK to-night. So

1. Roosevelt had attended the Teheran Conference with Churchill and Stalin from 20 November to 2 December. After a further conference with Churchill in Cairo, he left for home on the 7th.

down to the hotel. Streets of the town full of MPs, two standing at every road junction, looking both ways. The state of alert is still on and in theory everyone confined to barracks, though they let me through the gate without questions. The airfield stood by all day to receive Roosevelt, but the only dignitary who did alight was Humphrey Bogart. At 6. back to the airfield to eat and find the Liberator crew. Thrilled to hear they take off to-night and have room for me. Spent the rest of the evening with them by their roaring fire, and went with them at 8. to see Tarzan wipe out a Nazi battalion in darkest African jungles. They are a most amusing crowd. Chase, the pilot, whose mother comes from Glasgow; Johnson, the co-pilot; Baskett, a tiny little fellow, the liveliest and noisiest of them all, reading economics at college before the war, the navigator; and Bienapfl, the bombadier, affectionately referred to as Beanawful. At times I found myself confessing to a slight anxiety when I reflected that this quartet of bridge-mad, playful,quarrelling schoolboys was that very night to fly me from Morocco to England. At 2330 they took me along to their briefing in the operations room. Detailed weather reports. They were given clear descriptions of St. Mawgam aerodrome in West Cornwall, and how to recognise it. A revelation to me of the careful and efficient organisation built up to make this ferry service so safe and reliable. I was next taken to the stores to draw a parachute and a Mae West, and we drove out in a 15-cwt to the waiting plane. We all stood amidships for the take-off at 0140, then when we were up and away everyone crawled into their stations. I had plenty of space to lie down on the top of baggage in a long alley, the flight deck, leading from the entrance to the forward turret. We climbed steadily to 9500 ft. and it soon got very cold. Breathing at first was a little difficult, but after a few hours I got used to it. Absolutely steady, not a suspicion of a roll or bump,the monotonous hum of the engines and feeling of immense, perfectly-controlled power giving a great sensation of complete confidence.

10 December

Dozed till about 8, then roused myself and wriggled forward to Baskett's navigation 'cabin'. An unforgettable sight out of the windows, we were above all the clouds, brilliant sunshine all round. Baskett showed me his instruments. About 10.20 we first sighted the English coast and started to go down through dense rainclouds. It got colder and colder. We all retired amidships for the landing, which took a long time. Then the bomb doors opened and I set foot again on English soil after 3 years, 1 month and 9 days.

After various inquisitions from American and British authorities, whom I finally convinced from my documentation that I was not a deserter, I was driven to the Penmount Hotel in Newquay, reserved for RAF and USAAF transients, with a railway warrant for London in my pocket. I arrived at Paddington at 8.15 next morning and phoned my parents in Wimbledon.[1] The housekeeper answered.

1. My father had retired from the Political Intelligence Department of the Foreign Office in September 1942 and returned to his chair of Central European History at the School of Slavonic and East European Studies. He and my mother moved back into the family home at 1 Parkside Gardens, Wimbledon.

'I told her who I was and said I was speaking from Paddington: she said "Oh yes, wait just a minute", in so ordinary a voice that I imagined I was expected, and called my mother.' On the way to Wimbledon I was 'half surprised to find trains and buses still run just the same, half wondering whether I had been away at all' A huge breakfast awaited me, and I found that 'my phone call had come right out of the blue, just as after Dunkirk, perhaps even more unexpected. Half an hour later my letter [of 30 November] arrived'

On 15 December I reported to the RAC Officers' Tactical School in Oriel College Oxford. Little did I know that almost exactly two years later I would become a Fellow and Tutor of the college.

Letter, 18 December

It's just like old times to be sitting at a desk in an Oxford room, writing a letter home, with the rain and wind beating at the windows and those well-known chimes ringing out every quarter of an hour. I share this room with a major from the other gunner regiment in our division [John Charles of 11HAC], whom I know very well. We eat in Hall, waited upon by ATS. Our 'ante-room' is not the JCR, but part of the SCR. One sees very little of the College dignitaries – most of them of course will be away. A few undergaduates and students in uniform sit at the long central table, while we occupy the two side tables. The high table is unoccupied except on Sundays. There are 50 of us on the course, including a dozen Canadians, two Americans, a Pole and seven Czechs. Most of the British officers have been in England the whole war, but there are nine of us from North Africa and at least two from Italy. So there is plenty of variety and much interesting military gossip. So far we have attended lectures, but next week will start driving out into the countryside for the exercises. The programme is comprehensive, and I shall enjoy it while learning much.

The course lasted until 14 January, with a four-day break at Christmas which I celebrated with the family at home. I had time to call on several of my pre-war tutors, and on 6 January lectured on the Balkan situation, on the basis of information acquired from my father. 'As a result', I wrote to him the next day, 'Tito's banner now flies triumphant over Oriel College.'[1] It went off very well, though I say it as shouldn't, and there were lots of questions afterwards. I hope I said the right things. The Czechs seemed especially pleased'. Meanwhile I had received a letter addressed 'Major S-W' from Bill Blacker, whom I saw several times (he was now 2nd in command of 63 Medium Regiment R.A.): he had heard that I was to get I battery when I got back to the Regiment.

On calling at the War Office on 15 January I was told, to my great delight, that there would be no convoy to Algiers before mid-February, so I could take four weeks' leave. Despite the blackout, frequent sirens and the deafening noise of

---

1. In the dispute over British support for Mihailović or Tito, my father took the side of Tito, despite his communism, because he was fighting the Germans effectively, and advocated a Yugoslav, not Greater Serbian, policy.

anti-aircraft guns, wartime London offered an amazing range of entertainment, and I indulged in an orgy of theatre, film and concerts, ate surprisingly well in restaurants, and visited many relatives and friends. On 1 February I was summoned to an investiture at Buckingham Palace to receive my Military Cross from the King. Finally on 18 February I embarked on H.M.T. Ormonde, *a P&O boat of about 20,000 tons, at Princes Pier, Liverpool.*

Letter, 25 February

5th day at sea. It already seems months since we parted, and England and London and the family drawing-room are fading slowly into the misty distance of soothing lovely memories. During that quiet restful month with you, I had grown some pretty deep roots. But now I'm already reconciled again to that strange state of rootlessness which the Army enforces upon one. Rootlessness, of course, in space only. For I'm going back to people I know and like, and to a Regiment for which I have the greatest affection and where my roots have been growing for a long time.

I realise now that three months ago I was stale, very stale. Now I feel completely rested and refreshed and ready for anything that may come along.

So much for the waffle. Now for a little about this trip so far. For four days now we have been rolling and pitching in a respectably rough sea. All this time, I'm proud and surprised to say, I haven't felt a qualm. We are very crowded, and some captains and subalterns sleep in hammocks in a vast dormitory. I've luckily got a bunk in a cabin with five others. Getting up in the morning is a bit difficult, but so far we have all remained friends. About 9 p.m. one is driven to bed, for the atmosphere of fug and tobacco smoke in the lounge becomes intolerable. The food is excellent and I spend most of the day reading.

We docked at Algiers at 1230 on 1 March. I disembarked with Dick Harding-Newman, and to our delight we found a staff car and Liaison Officer from 1 Armd Div HQRA waiting for us. He told us that 2 RHA left Algiers for Italy on 17 February. At HQRA Dick and I parted – he was to command 76 Anti-tank Regiment. I was carried off by Nigel Wingate, O.C. 42 Light Anti-Aircraft Regiment, old friends from desert days, to stay at his RHQ as a transient guest. A few days later Peter Bishop turned up, having attended the Oxford course after mine, got married and obtained an air passage back. He proved a good companion.

Letter, 5 March

Over a fortnight since we saw each other, and I haven't yet reached the Regiment. I'm actually staying at the moment with a sister regiment trying to kill time as pleasantly as possible while waiting for transport.

As you can imagine, wherever I go I am overwhelmed by questions about England. I have been incredibly lucky, and realise it more and more in talking to men who have spent the last three months out here, in the same place week after week. With time on their hands they inevitably start worrying about their families and get all sorts of crazy ideas about conditions at home. I can at least help there to some extent. These latest air raids add to the worry, and of course the question of Americans in England is always cropping up. It's not easy to answer some of their questions. When the Second Front opens and the American casualty rates are published, I think there will be a lot less worrying and discontent. I don't want to exaggerate, but with every week that passes the problem of keeping up morale becomes more difficult. And it's only too easy for me, who have been home, to say the wrong things.

On 10 March Peter and I received telephone orders to report to the Racecourse Reception Camp. On saying good-bye to the 42nd LAA, they 'wouldn't let us ask for a mess bill, let alone pay for a drink.' We found we would have to spend a night in the Camp, so 'decided to say good-bye to Algiers with enough liquid refreshment to ensure that we slept'. There followed a deplorably drunken evening, ending up in a RASC mess on a beach somewhere outside the city, from which we were driven back to Camp at midnight by 'an unfortunate batman who seemed quite resigned to his job'. Next morning I 'got very shakily to breakfast at about 8.40' and at 1030 we set off to the docks in a large party, including a dozen men for 2RHA. By 1230 we were aboard the Derbyshire, *a pre-war trooper. Peter and I had a comfortable cabin between us. On the morning of 12 March we joined a convoy of a dozen ships and made for Naples. Next day we spotted 'the bulk of Kournine on the far side of the Bay of Tunis', our last glimpse of Africa, and disembarked at Naples on the afternoon of the 14th.*

While on board the Ormonde *I had heard rumours that the Regiment had been sent to Anzio,[1] but at Algiers I learnt that the plan had been changed at the last moment and that it was instead settled in a very much less formidable role, that of 'demonstration regiment' at the Central Mediterranean Training Centre, located at Benevento forty miles north-east of Naples.*

1. An allied force had landed at Anzio, 30 miles south of Rome, on 23 January. It failed in its object of cutting the enemy's line of supply to the battle front 70 miles to the south-east, and remained confined to a small bridgehead until May.

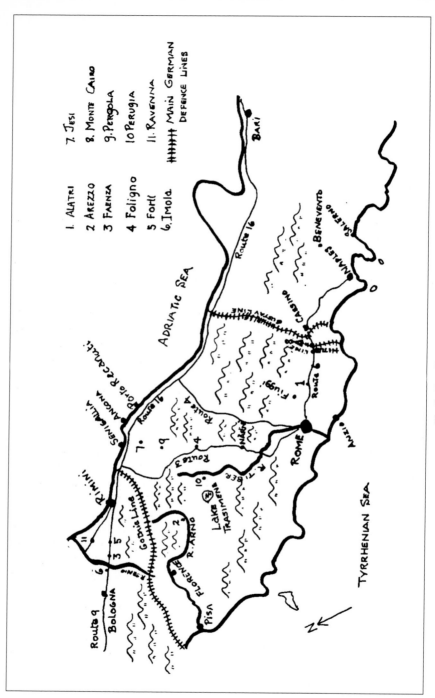

The Italian Campaign, 1943-5

CHAPTER SEVENTEEN: MARKING TIME IN ITALY
March – May 1944

Letter, 16 March

Here I am at last, at my journey's end, and thankful for it. I arrived two days ago, and by a stroke of luck met an officer of the Regiment within half an hour of leaving the ship. So I was spared any more nights in depots or transit camps, and was here the same evening.

Things here are extremely quiet. I found the Regiment doing much the same things as they were doing when I left in December. I had hoped I had brought the fine weather with me, but last night it poured with rain all night and this morning the snow was right down low on the mountains which surround us on all sides. As you can imagine, my head has been in a constant whirl since I arrived. Taking over a battery is no simple job but I'm finding my feet slowly. Luckily I know the officers, all the senior NCOs and a reasonable proportion of the men. Some of them are real old friends, having been in H/I in December '39.

At the moment our chief battle is with the mud. I plod round all day in gum boots. It is appalling, far worse than that winter in France.

1 April

I am writing this in our mess, a large, rather bleak room in a solidly built farmhouse. The north wind is blowing down on us straight off the snow, and whistling and moaning eerily round every corner and up every passage. But we have a home-made furnace fed by diesel oil and the local white wine to keep us warm. And judging by the chatter and noise all round me, I can't say we are depressed. The local inhabitants tell us that this is most unseasonable weather, that by the first of April it should be warm and balmy, that the rain should be behind us and spring in full swing. But today it sleeted and I brought my gumboots out again. Wherever I have been this war, the locals have always said the weather that year has been exceptionally hot or exceptionally cold. Our padre has a strange mystical theory about it in which he has almost persuaded himself to believe. I doubt whether Providence has had anything directly to do with it. There is a rival theory that the recent fantastically heavy bombing of Cassino[1] and the steady intensity of artillery fire has somehow shaken the heavens and forced them

---

1. Most recently on 15 March.

to unload upon us the waters that they would have preferred to store up for next winter. But whatever the reason for it, this rain is trying.

This is an interesting country. I can't say I've progressed very far in my studies of the language. So many Italians speak such good English – or American. But occasionally I buy and read the local paper, *Risorgimento*. I haven't tried to talk politics – it's probably unwise. But driving thro' the villages I make a point of reading the slogans rudely scrawled in black or red paint on the blank white walls. Some villages are covered in hammers and sickles. Most have 'A basso il Re'. A very favourite inscription is 'Si volete pane, cacciate il re'. In the port where I landed I saw this one, which pleased me: 'VV Churchill Roosevelt Stalin Tito'.

The poverty of these peasants is appalling. And the contrast between their abject misery and hunger, and the smug oily prosperity of the merchants and shopkeepers, who exploit both us and the Americans and their less fortunate countrymen who have fewer strings to pull, is quite revolting. The misery is worst, of course, in the large towns.

AMGOT [Allied Military Government of Occupied Territories] has been much abused, but their problems were vast and they haven't put up a bad show. Food is being distributed on a large scale. Driving home the other day after dark I passed a long stream of women trudging patiently along the road with half-full sacks of American flour balanced on their heads. Even so many are hungry. I was visiting the cookhouse of a neighbouring unit in a local town the other day. As a soldier walked away to the table to sit down and eat, a spoonful of potatoes fell into the mud at the entrance to the shed. An old woman darted forward, grabbed the spoonful off the path, with a fistful of mud, and gobbled it all down together. Food is not the only problem. The undamaged houses are full of refugees from the battle zones, and in many cases each room is occupied by a different family. Our local town has been badly knocked about by the RAF and USAAF: and there are many others as bad in this part of Italy. Most of the damage was done in attempts to destroy two important bridges across the broad river. The irony of it all is that the bridges have been destroyed all right – the heavy traffic now crawls in single file across narrow temporary wooden structures. But the Germans did the destruction, just before they withdrew. Our bombs left the bridges untouched, though they made a shambles of all the houses along the river and reduced a fine church to a shattered shell. From the far bank of the river the town looks as bad as the worst pictures of Ypres in the last war or Guernica in Spain of 1937. In many places the streets are merely muddy lanes between shapeless piles of rubble, out of which stick twisted girders and broken beams and rafters at crazy angles. The old houses are so flimsily built, solid though they look from the outside: the stone is soft and the cement has powdered with the years. Many of the modern buildings are mere shells though the walls remain standing. The railway station is another scene of desolation. Rusting engines sit there, riddled with bomb splinters; all around are overhead electric cables trailing along the ground, and Italian and Deutsche Reichsbahn goods wagons overturned or derailed or burnt out and reduced to twisted steel. The people of the town wander round calmly, rather apathetically. Outside ruined shops sit women with fruit or trinkets or pots and pans on improvised stalls. Desultory road-making or demolition or rebuilding goes on. Refugees scrape in the rubble for their belongings. Many corpses are said to be still lying underneath the ruins. In the evenings the streets are crammed with people, civilians of both sexes, soldiers in British or American or Italian uniforms. And a queer wartime life of gaiety and false prosperity has grown up. But what a price the Italians have paid for their folly.

7 April

I'm over the worst of the rush now, and have had time to look about me, and to make two excursions which very pleasantly combined duty and pleasure. The first was into Naples for the day. It had to be a rush visit and there was little time for pottering. But I did a little shopping, and have sent off a humble little food offering which I hope will arrive safely – just a few titbits: a box of figs, a few sugar almonds and a big, rather evil-looking hunk of what I think should be called candied peel. I hope in spite of its appearance that it will be useful for puddings or cakes. And I've slipped in some razor blades from Germany. Naples is an odd place just now. The devastation round the docks is pretty thorough – I had seen nothing like it till I arrived in this country. If the ruins were tidied up and the walls patched like in London, it would probably look much better, and less desolate. But as it is now, with rubble and dust and filth over acres, it's not a pretty sight. But away from the docks and further into the town many of the streets are almost untouched, the pavements are so jammed with civilians and soldiers that one has to fight one's way along, and the shops are doing a roaring trade. The profiteering had become so scandalous that AMGOT has been forced to do something about it. Many shops have been put out of bounds to troops and some stiff penalties have been handed out. It's strange how in one country one thing is unobtainable, but in the next supplies are unlimited. Razor blades are an example – there are still huge stocks of them in Naples, even after six months of occupation. In Algiers pencils or notebooks or any kind of stationery were unobtainable. Here the stationers' shops are almost as well-equipped as Rymans in Victoria Street was two months ago. And I'm told there are several restaurants where, for a price, one can get as good a meal as anywhere between London and Cairo. Yet in the next street there are people half starving.

I spent the afternoon at the Opera, which is in full swing, and saw Verdi's *La Forza del Destino*. The whole atmosphere of formality and solid good taste was pleasing. Before the overture they played the Marseillaise, the Star Spangled Banner and God Save the King – the last very quietly, on strings alone, with no trills or embellishments, and it sounded very impressive. It was well worth going to see the opera house alone: it's certainly a grand sight, with the wide sweep of the boxes all round, tier above tier right up into the roof, gleaming with gilt and huge mirrors inside and red plush chairs. Four of us sat in the stalls, and in the intervals we wolfed down cream cakes and chocolates – such cakes as London hasn't seen for many a month, and only Messrs Groppi of Cairo could surpass. It was a thoroughly enjoyable outing, gay and irresponsible.

As we drove up the hill out of the town we saw Vesuvius belching clouds of black smoke, and from time to time in the middle of the smoke a vivid flash of flame. One night soon after the eruption began we saw a glare in the sky even from our camp, which was far away over the snowy mountains. A few days later I had to drive right down to Salerno on business and again passed near Vesuvius. The smoke was still pouring out, though the volcano had almost died down. Only two small trickles of lava were still to be seen, giving off columns of white steam, just below the top. But Salerno and the countryside for miles around were grey in volcanic dust – choking dust which blinded one as one drove along the traffic-laden roads. In the villages the streets had mostly been cleared and the dust was piled in great heaps against the walls of the houses. In places it must have been quite two feet deep; many of the vineyards and orchards were completely silted up and only quite long grass had survived and pushed through. The wretched peasants had finished much of their spring hoeing, and were patiently at work again starting the job all over a second time. As we drove into one small town, I really though we might be entering a drab North Country mining town, covered in its film of smuts and coal dust. It was a sight I'll never forget.

On 2 April the Regiment set out from Benevento on a two-day drive to the front line at Cassino. We had to occupy our gun positions by night as they were overlooked by the monastery, which had been reduced to rubble by British and American bombers in February. We were under command of the 6th Armoured Division, which was in process of taking over our sector of the 'Gustav Line' from the New Zealanders. Immediately on our left was a French Moroccan Division, beyond whom were the Americans filling the gap down to the sea. Opposite us were 1 Parachute Division, Hitler's heroes, 'who seem to revel in hanging on by the skin of their teeth, without food or water, almost without ammunition it seems – with the eyes of the world upon them'.
Diary 4 April

Up before 7. to walk round the gun positions in daylight. Pits well dug and camouflaged, and some trenches already dug in the gulley behind. R Troop and one gun of S Troop overlooked by the monastery. We shall have to restrict movement by day to an absolute minimum and try to lie as low as possible. I hope they won't make us do too much firing, as there is nothing to stop the enemy fixing us accurately to a matter of almost inches. The Battery Command Post is in a house inhabited by a decent Italian family – father, mother, daughter and two small boys, one wearing a sergeant's stripes and gun on his arm. The family live in one room downstairs, well protected with strengthening baulks of timber and efficiently blacked out. We are in possession of the rest of the house. Beside the well are the graves of two unknown German soldiers. Behind the house are small plots of vegetables between the vines and fruit trees, which the family are busy hoeing. The area is not clean – pits of half-buried tins, paper everywhere. No vehicles allowed on the positions, except my jeep which will live in a shed, beside the house: and of course motor-cycles for a despatch-rider service to the wagon line.

In evening went up to our OP on Monte Trocchio, slowly climbing through two small villages to a track junction immediately below the summit where OPs have to start walking. We have two maintenance points on our OP line (about 2 miles of cable); the second lives in top village, Santa Lucia, in 'OP House': three rooms, kitchen range and roaring log fire. Bob Banks [R Troop Commander] has decided he will live up there even when off duty, and certainly he is comfortably established. Italians are still living in both villages – within 800 yards of FDLs [Forward Defended Localities] and frequently under shell-fire – it's a fantastic situation, but I admire their attachment to their home and vineyards. So the maintenance parties get their clothes washed and food cooked for them. They are delighted with their jobs and have no desire to come down to the guns.

Our OP is on the ridge well below the rocky peak which rises steep and craggy up to 1300 feet. It's merely a crack between the rocks, built up with boulders in front, a tiny olive bush hiding the entrance, no roof and little protection, and very uncomfortable – I can't think how 4 NZ Fd stuck it out for two months, especially

View from Monte Trocchio OP.
The ruined monastery in the centre background, Monte Cairo in clouds behind. Part of the continous smokescreen, protecting our infantry, on far right. In the foreground are Bdr Gray and Gnr Holley of R Troop.

during the last Cassino battle when things were very lively. I sat with Bob until dark: a marvellous view of the town right below us, dominated by the monastery and the high mountains beyond. To their left one looked up the broad Liri valley, along which ran Route 6, the main road to Rome. To the left again, more high mountains through which the river Garigliano flowed towards the sea. At first sight the Liri valley looked flat, but after a few minutes of map reading one realised that there are many little valleys and gulleys and ravines – and in these the enemy lies low all day. A dream OP, with enemy FDL's only 1000 yards away on the far bank of the river Rapido – yet not *one* sign of a moving living creature.[1]

The next six weeks were strangely peaceful, even though we were in constant contact with the enemy. I described them in a later letter.
Letter, 20 May
I think I told you in one of my letters how unreal the war often seemed – the birds, and the trees bursting into leaf, and the frogs and crickets at night seemed more real than the guns and the noises of sporadic skirmishing along the infantry line. I could sit at my table in my room busy with routine administration, or perhaps reading or writing letters, as quietly and comfortably as if I were in camp at Cairo or in barracks at Aldershot. Yet I had only to stretch out my hand, pick up the phone and speak to one of my troop commanders in his observation post within 600 yards of the enemy. We didn't do much firing, got little enemy shelling back, and saw unfriendly planes only two or three times in the whole six weeks; and in all that time eight Germans and a dozen vehicles were all that was seen from the OP – occasionally some mortars firing, very rarely a few gun flashes. It is amazing how low the Germans can lie, and how disciplined they are.

One of our occasional, and more trying, tasks was to fire the continuous smoke screen which concealed our infantry from the monastery. It meant 'each battery firing for 15 minutes, followed by a half hour's rest, and no gun to fire more than two consecutive rounds, in order to fox the enemy flash-spotters'. We also had to do propaganda shoots: firing shells to burst over the enemy lines which were filled with Frontpost, *the weekly 'straight' news-sheet produced by Psychological Branch, Allied Forces HQ [which I thought 'too dull'] and safe-conducts for deserters.*

On 23 April we came under command of 8th Indian Division, which was relieving 6 Armd Div, and we had to find a new OP in order to give the 19th Indian Brigade more effective support. It was situated on a small lump named La Pietà, to the south of Trocchio.
Diary, 24 April
The OP is in a solid though battered house, overlooked by the monastery and

---

1. A vivid account of 'Forty-eight Hours on Trocchio' by Bob Banks may be found in *The Royal Artillery Commemoration Book 1939-1945*, pp. 309-12: and the photo here reproduced appears on p. 318.

so much in view of the enemy that movement out of the house is impossible in daylight. We poked our heads into a black hole of Calcutta with blankets slung across the entrance, where in the light of a guttering candle we could see a circle of dusky Indian faces grouped round a petrol stove on which gypatties were being made. As all doors open onto the enemy, we had to clamber the length of the house through holes in the walls dividing the rooms, rather like progress in a submarine. At the far end met Chuck Wilson, the Canadian officer lent to the Mahrattis as instructor, with whom we will share the OP. The nearest enemy are just across the river, only 600 yards away. When we started to gossip and laugh, the Indians hushed us up very severely. The whole place littered with filth and stank – sanitary arrangements necessarily primitive. One looks out through a narrow slit. The whole effect rather eerie.

26 April

Woken at 0430, left in the jeep twenty minutes later in steady soaking drizzle. Met Bob in the black hole, full of slumbering Indians and a thick atmosphere of oil and petrol fumes from the stoves, stale food and tobacco smoke. Also met again Chuck Wilson. It was light by 0540, but so misty that one could see practically nothing. Bob and I spent practically the whole day map reading, a difficult business with so many false crests, so many houses looking much the same, and most deceptive distances – though whenever the mist did disperse, the view was incredibly clear. Chuck's Mahratta assistant occasionally emerged from the black hole and asked for the phone. Then there would be a ten-minute flood of Urdu – obviously all the company gossip: 'jeep' had taken so-and-so sahib somewhere that day etc. And every three words was 'Tik-hai', said in an immense variety of expressions and accents, and every conversation ended with 'Ram-Ram'. In middle of afternoon I was horrified to see an Indian standing outside the house at a time of best visibility. He turned out to be an orderly from Company HQ, not knowing the form. Chuck tried to give him a heavy rocket, but his four-and-a-half words of Hindustani soon failed him. Altogether, in spite of the cold, the dripping roof, the discomfort and the monotony, an amusing day.

Charles Kauntze [S Troop Commander] arrived at 2100 to take over in a vile temper. And when we got down to the track, we found a complete shambles – four jeeps floundering in the ditch, yards of cable wrapped round their axles. It took us two hours to get down the 400 yards to Jeephead, and when we got onto the road it was so pitch black that we could only travel 5 mph. Various Indians in full martial array looked up out of the darkness to challenge us, but with a casual wave of the hand and a confident 'Tik-hai' we got past them all without ever being examined. A lot of harassing fire, heavy shells falling on Trocchio and round Santa Lucia. But none troubled us. The fireflies dancing in the air in thousands, a most lovely sight.

As April wore on, the signs of an impending offensive became increasingly visible.

Letter, 20 May

All that time we had been watching the preparations and every time one drove back from the front to the back areas one saw more equipment piling up – more tanks and lorries, bigger ammunition and petrol dumps, more bridging material stacked ready for the river crossings, roads being widened, guns moving up by night into carefully camouflaged positions where they lay doggo and silent till the barrage opened up at 11 pm on the night of the 11th. It was fascinating to watch.

CHAPTER EIGHTEEN: THE ADVANCE TO ROME
May – June 1944

It was on 6 May that the Colonel told us that the 11th would be 'the day'. The objective of the Allied armies would be to reach the Pisa-Rimini line, 200 miles ahead, as soon as possible. Our immediate task would be to break through the Gustav Line, then the Hitler line, prepared but as yet unmanned eight miles up the Liri valley on the road to Rome. On our sector there was to be a set piece attack, and 'we are to crack on and accept casualties'. I commented in my diary, 'If we can't get to Rome and beyond this time, I think we'd better pack up and go home'.

My own role in the initial stages of the battle would be to act as 13 Corps' artillery liaison officer with the 1ére Division de Marche d'Infanterie [1DMI] on our immediate left. On 7 May I visited its divisional HQ, where I was 'introduced to the artillery staff officers' and 'shown the whole plan of attack in their operations room'. Next day I attended a conference of CRAs, presided over by the CCRA, at the artillery HQ of the Corps Expéditionnaire Française [CEF] at Sessa Aurunca, a small town untouched by the war. Afterwards 'a colossal lunch in a pleasant small restaurant taken over as a mess, with bevies of French colonels, and the General presiding jovially and noisily over the gathering. Excellent Algerian wine, which they bring over half-dehydrated, and cognac to end up with. I found I could understand most of the military and gunner terms'.

The task of the CEF would be to capture the peaks of the Aurunci mountains overlooking the Liri valley from the south, then sweep downwards and northwards behind the German defences, while the 4th British and 8th Indian Divisions launched a frontal attack up the valley. The French were 'tickled to death at the prospect of our LOs and immediately wanted to know how many guns we could offer them and for how long and when'. I had to explain that they could count on no continuous artillery support from 13 Corps artillery, that they were 'low on our priority list, but we will be delighted to help if we can'.

Diary, 10 May

Reached 1DM1 at 1500 – complete with pigeons[1] Saw White, the senior LO at div. HQ, who introduced me to the Chief of Staff, St Hillier, the G2, Mirkère, and

---

1. Carrier pigeons, for use in the event of a breakdown in telephonic or wireless communications.

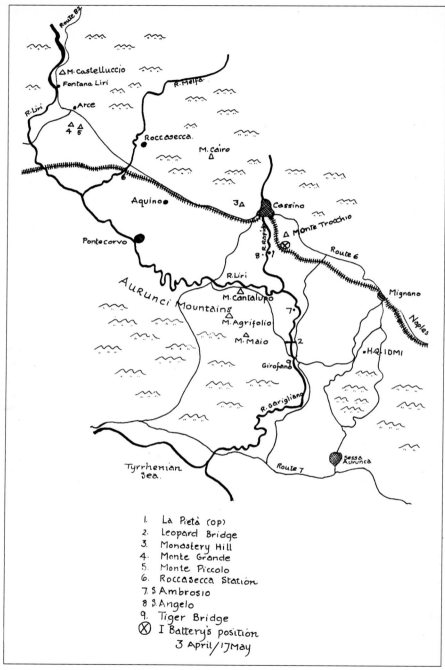

The Gustav and Hitler Lines battlefields

the divisional commander, General Brosset – a hearty confident impressive man of 46, very young for a French general. Dined in his mess. He commanded a brigade at Enfidaville [in northern Tunisia] and in one battle captured 800 prisoners. But as he said rather grimly, he measures the success of his battles by the number of dead, not the number of prisoners. They are very bitter, these Frenchmen, and no wonder.

11 May

A glorious fresh day. Spent morning finally mastering codes and maps and orders. Wireless worked splendidly to RHQ till 2000, then got progressively worse. When we opened up on the 78 Div liaison net at 2045, fifteen minutes before zero hour, all we could hear was the LOs with 2DIM [2e Division d'Infanterie Marocaine], like us forlornly calling control. I've never known the air so full of cracklings and whines, Morse and music and distorted voices in English, French, American and German. The guns went off with a big bang at 2300.

12 May

At first light began to get small scraps of information. Soon became clear that Girofano, just inside 2DIM's right boundary, was the key to the whole sector, over-looking the whole of 1DMl's front. A harassed morning, running to and fro between my wirelesses and the operations command vehicle. At last at 1100 we got through to 78 Div via a relay station sitting somewhere near Mignano – this was thanks to a despairing note I wrote to BMRA via the French LO with 8th Indian Division. At 1200 despatched a pigeon to 13 Corps with a long codex message saying that little advance was to be expected by 1DMI until 2DIM had taken Girofano.

13 May

By 1200 Girofano was reported entirely clear. At 1200 we had to send off the other two pigeons, their time limit having expired, and I could produce no message. They fluttered away, circled round once or twice to get their bearings and then made off confidently in the direction of 13 Corps HQ. The pace quickened with 2DIM's capture of Monte Maio at 1530 and of Agrifoglio at 1700, which meant that it was downhill for them all the way to the Liri. The whole HQ thrilled, and I'm glad it has been the French to have the first successes. Meanwhile my own division pushed steadily forward.

14 May was a day of sensational news: advances by both 1DM1 and 2DIM along the ridges of the Arurunci summits. Advances by the British and Indian divisions in the Liri valley were much slower.

14 May

Mirkère went down to the prisoner-of-war cage to interrogate Germans. He is Russian-born, speaks fluent Russian, German, French and English. On looking through papers and letters he found a photograph of seven Russians (four men and three women) strung up on a pole, one of the women obviously not dead as one could see from the way she was hanging – the first such photograph I've actually seen. And standing round within a few feet with their hands in their pockets and grinning were a dozen German soldiers. The man Mirkère was interrogating thought it was a good joke, said some of his friends were in the photo. So Mirkère told him to lie down in the dust, rub his nose in the dirt and kiss his boots – and he did.

I gave my parents further details of my four days with the French in a retrospective letter of 12 November:

I was doing a temporary liaison job between our British Corps and the French division on our immediate left, to ensure that both knew where the troops of the other had got to, and to provide additional artillery support for the French if they got into a tight corner. I was determined to engage something, and just as the enemy were getting out of range in their retreat, a target cropped up – a strong point on a high ridge called Monte Cantalupo, overlooking the Liri. So we ordered the Regiment to fire on it, and scored a great success – the Entente Cordiale was very securely cemented. What pleased them most was that our fire enabled their Senegalese troops to reach the craggy summit of Cantalupo before the Moroccan Goums of the neighbouring division on their left, with whom there was a healthy rivalry. So fervent messages of mutual congratulation passed between the French Brigadier and our Colonel. Living in their mess was a most interesting experience. The General, Brosset, was a young energetic professional soldier, and an appalling snob. He loved talking to me of the baronets and milords that he had met in Paris and Algiers before the war. He also had an embarrassing habit of suddenly quoting Keats or Tennyson or Swinburne and asking me – or the resident British LO, who was far more illiterate even than I – where the lines came from. I was constantly being caught out, to the great enjoyment of the General's staff. But in spite of his snobism he was a very fine soldier and an ardent de Gaullist, as indeed they all were. The division was one of the original Free French divisions and fought at Bir Hakeim. They now have American equipment, but a profound mistrust of the Americans – how bitterly they talked of the Darlan affair,[1] and of the whole American outlook to European problems. But they were more interested in fighting than in talking at that time, and their performance really was brilliant. Several German reports and documents have since been captured which distinguish between the dynamism of the French, their energy and quickness to exploit success, and the slow unimaginative methodical plodding of the 'Anglo-Americans' – and there is a lot in the distinction. The way those Frenchmen scaled precipitous mountains and fought on and marched on, in spite of the complete inability of their supplies to keep up with them, was really inspiring. And the fighting was particularly ferocious, with no mercy shown on

1. See p. 157.

either side. About the second day a story got round a Senegalese brigade that a Senegali had been found nailed to a tree with his head lying between his feet. I don't know whether it was true or not – I shouldn't be surprised, for the Germans have done such things in Italy. But what was undoubtedly true was that when the story got round, a party of Senegalese cut off the heads of about 50 German prisoners – and I don't think their French officers ever tried to stop it. I heard that from the Chief of Staff of that division himself, for he had just returned from that brigade, having carried out an investigation. And of course when I showed a certain shocked surprise, they all rounded on me, and said, "You English, you are too soft, you forgive too much, but of course you haven't suffered". And no doubt they are right.

On the afternoon of 14 May I was told that I was being relieved in the next 24 hours by a captain and subaltern from a Canadian medium regiment.
Diary, 15 May
My relief took over after breakfast. A good order of the day from Juin[1], saying that they had broken the line that Hitler called impregnable in spite of ferocious resistance, and asking every soldier to redouble his efforts and hasten the liberation of la Patrie. We got some wine, bread and milk off the General's cook as a parting gift – a delightful little man, four times wounded as a parachutist in Africa at Tobruk, Alamein, Benghazi and Tunis. Now graded and enjoying his job.

Left at 0915. We crawled down the dusty road from San Clemente, the tracks getting rougher and narrower, with the last steep descent a succession of hairpins cut out of the hillside. And so across the Garigliano by the Tiger Bridge pontoons. Traffic incredible, anti-tank and AA guns going forward, empty supply echelons coming back. POW digging slit trenches under watchful eyes of N.African infantry, looking as if they thought it was their own graves they were digging. Back across river by the northernmost bridge, Leopard, recently-built pontoons. Had to wait 20 minutes for a heavily loaded convoy driven by Indo-Chinese drivers, coming in opposite direction. Furious arguments between French MPs and sappers as to weights and speeds of vehicles crossing. And when our turn came we swamped the first pontoon, howls of fury as I disappeared.

Got back to the Battery about 1500. Found the Regiment still sitting pretty, at four hours notice to move. The big barrage had gone off well with not one unfriendly shell landing in our area. But G Sub. had a tragic accident: as they were loading a shell, it exploded just outside the breech, the cause still a mystery. McIlvaney and Hamilton were killed outright, Heggie so badly wounded that he's unlikely to recover, Bdr Scarr pretty bad and unlikely to return to us. Sgt Harrison miraculously quite unhurt but very shaken.

16 May
We fired a two hour barrage at 0900 in support of 38 Bde [of 78 Div] who

---

1. Commander-in-Chief of the French Forces.

pressed well forward. We have no OPs out and are purely in an Army Field role. A few odd POW trudging back under escort – our Italian family rushed out every time to stand on the top of the embankment and shout abuse, especially the two small boys. Oscar [Rose] tells me that the first time a POW passed, one of the boys rushed out with scissors and had to be held and prevented from attacking the Tedeschi. Meanwhile the great attraction for the whole of the Command Post during the battle has been the twelve chickens successfully hatched by the solitary hen, almost as the first salvo of the barrage went off. Several sittreps came in during the evening. 90th Light are coming down hotfoot and being thrown in by odd companies and battalions to stop the gaps. This may mean we go slower, but in the long run it's a good thing to engage his reserves and destroy them here.

17 May

Fired yet another barrage at 0700 in support of 38 Bde. Moved forward at last, at very short notice, at 1730 – through the Gustav Line. A mad rush, down to the river Rapido by admirably policed and signposted tracks, across London Bridge through a smokescreen, San Angelo looking grim above us through the smoke, and when we drove through it I've never seen such desolation. Into action 1000 yards beyond the village. Everyone out of practice in mobility, but we gradually got organised in the pitch black. We are reasonably out of sight of the monastery though if the enemy look hard they'll see two guns.

We moved forward again up the Liri Valley on 18 May to get within range of the village of Aquino, a central strongpoint of the Hitler Line where the Germans were making a stand. Movement heartbreakingly slow owing to congestion on all the roads and tracks. We passed many of the targets which we had engaged in previous weeks, and 'all along the route at intervals the smell of death contrasting strangely with the green trees and hedges'. Everyone heartened by the news that the Poles had captured Monastery Hill. On the 19th we had our first heavy rain since the battle had begun: it reduced the roads to deep mud. On the 20th 'slow digging by gunners and drivers, and pits gradually went deeper. Our fighters go overhead in fours and fives almost continuously, the taxi cab rank system'.

Letter, 20 May

Your letter of the 13th reached me yesterday night – six days from London to the battlefront of Italy is not bad is it? And I am taking advantage of today's lull to answer it immediately. This battle is what we have been waiting for for six weeks. Now that we have overrun the country over which we used to look before the battle began, I have seen some of the German dugouts, deep solid affairs, constructed with strong baulks of timber and often concreted foundations. Inside most of them have beds and tables, electric light fittings, even crude stoves. The furniture is mostly looted from Italian farms, I imagine. But sitting down there they could afford to laugh at anything but the heaviest barrage. The British soldier is a good digger, but he can't be induced to take war as seriously as all that. And as for sitting in a dugout all day, well, he just gets bored and starts walking around – if the enemy sees him, it's just too bad, but it's worth the risk. It isn't of course – I've often watched our infantry pottering around a ruined house, just exploring, or perhaps getting wood for their dinner fire, in full view of the opposite side. And they will continue to do it however well trained. I suppose that's the difference between a nation with war and military discipline in its bones, and a nation that can outfight and out-manoeuvre its opponents and at the same time laugh, and be careless and refuse to be crushed and dehumanised by the seriousness and starkness of it all. And thank God for those very differences!

It is good to be on the move again, and we are all confident this time of going a long way. We gunners are very lucky and how often I feel thankful that I am not an infantryman (strangely enough the infantry often say how glad they are not to be gunners!). We rarely have to walk, can carry enough kit to be comfortable when we halt, yet can pull out of action and be on the road and in pursuit of the enemy in a matter of minutes. I travel in an armoured command car – much quieter and with far more room in it than a tank, and it has the advantage that it refuses to be beaten by the roughest going or the deepest squelchiest mud. I have two wireless sets in the back – on one of them I control my guns and observing officers, on the other I report information and targets and progress of the battle back to Regimental Headquarters. When the battle is fierce I more or less sit on these two sets, listening and giving orders. When things are quiet I wander round the gunpits chatting to the gunners, or visit the vehicles and drivers in the 'wagon lines' behind the guns, or drop in on the Command Post where the Battery team of surveyors do the computing and all the technical gunnery calculations. The Battery Staff-Sergeant Equipment Repairer – a real old soldier, a saddler in the days when the RHA had horses, has made a magnificent canvas lean-to which

R Troop Command Post, May 1944.

travels rolled up on the side of my command car, and can be let down and converted into a snug little bivouac in a few minutes. It rained hard last night, but I was perfectly dry inside. So you must imagine me at this moment sitting on my camp bed beside my truck, in the privacy of my lean-to, using my mapboard as a table on my knees, looking out along a green hawthorn hedge which surrounds the orchard where our trucks are parked. The vehicles are hardly visible, for the drivers have competed with each other in turning their own truck into a haystack or a large thorn bush or perhaps just a patch of standing corn. This country is ideal for camouflage, and the ditches and runnels that criss-cross the orchards and vineyards provide ready-made slit trenches if shells or bombs come down.

I had to break off for fifteen minutes, for my batman, Gnr Simmons, an ex-boilerman from a Sheffield ironworks, brought me a vast dinner produced by our indefatigable cooks – fresh roast beef, fresh cabbage, tinned peas, dehydrated potatoes and brown gravy, followed by a large raisin dumpling and a mug of tea. We eat like lords – and what admirable organisation to get fresh meat right up to the front. How different from the early desert days, when it was bully and biscuits day after day. And this afternoon a worthy lady from Manchester appeared driving a mobile canteen, and stopped in the middle of our gun position during a shoot to dispense tea and cakes. War is indeed full of strange contrasts.

This is certainly a beautiful county, but how it has suffered. Every village we have passed through since we started advancing is just a heap of rubble or a row of gaunt shapeless walls and gables, sometimes a more solidly built house with the shell of a room inside and perhaps a staircase half undamaged. The isolated farms have suffered less though none have escaped untouched: most of them are full of signs of a hurried German retreat, and underneath them are these amazing deep dugouts. Every field and vineyard is pitted with shell holes, vines and trees are smashed, and now our waves of tanks and guns and lorries are beating down the tall crops and completing the desolation. Yet even so, nature seems to triumph, and I dare say in a few months, when we have passed on, the grass and crops will have grown again and only battered houses and blown bridges and bulldozed tracks will show where armies have passed.

I hope this has given you some idea of my present surroundings and occupation. Places and names I cannot give as yet.

Diary, 21 May

Some shelling in the afternoon and I discovered my slit trench was quite inadequate. It was only harassing by 105s, but some shells dropped close. Wandered round some German gun positions which are in a valley over a hill 400 yards from us. Brought back copies of *Südfront* and *Völkischer Beobachter*, full of the British coal strike and declining English morale. A few planes over in the middle of the night, much AA fire. A spent bullet suddenly came through my tent, tore my mosquito net, penetrated one blanket and stuck me sharply on the backside. I got under my truck and lay there very chilly until the fire stopped.

*On 23 May a major setpiece attack was launched on the Hitler Line, led in our
sector by the 1st Canadian Infantry division.*
Diary, 23 May

Up at 0515, walked round all the guns before the barrage started at 0557. Little
information, the infantry got to the first objective with less opposition than they
expected, but there ran into heavy shelling and met troublesome mines. A
Churchill regiment in support of the Canadians was dead on our regimental
frequency and we got a depressing impression of the battle from them – a
squadron wiped out, 88-mms everywhere. But all along it was a tough grim fight.
At 1000 there was an unforgettable roar of planes overhead, and we saw at least
200 Liberators fly over, their noses and fuselages catching the sun and looking as
if they were silvery tin fish afire, a lovely sight. About 1200 we had a William
[army] target, I should expect the first in history. There was a strong point in
Aquino full of mortars and mgs and SPs which was pasting the Canadians further
south. So the Canadian CCRA took every gun off the barrage and other tasks and
for two minutes there was silence – then the whole Eighth Army's artillery
opened up with a crash – I should have liked to see that target. A few minutes
before 1650 came a sudden order to fire the second half of the barrage. Many
reports came flooding in of the enemy pulling out in a hurry. Good news of an
attack from the Anzio beachhead, starting at 1100. At 1900 I relieved Tom

Pontecorvo, on the Hitler Line, after the battle.

Mathias [my battery captain] at Canadian Corps HQ. Found their tails right up. They claimed not only to have smashed the famous Hitler Line in a day, but to have annihilated 361 and 576 Panzer Grenadier Regiments in the process.

On 24 May we again came under command of the 6th Armoured Division.
25 May

Another day of waiting. Aquino declared clear in the early morning. Great news at 1130 that Fifth Army on our left had linked with the Anzio beachhead. Suddenly we were told we had been given high priority, moved off about 1700 but had to pull off the road at last light to let the Coldstreams go through. I sat on my scout car and drank a bottle of beer as it grew darker and darker, and the fireflies began to dance. Got going about 2130, crossed the Forme d'Aquino, very steep hill on both sides, double Bailey bridge at the bottom, a bulldozer standing by with engine ticking over, to winch our vehicles up when they got stuck. Reached new gun position at 0230, about 2000 yards west of Aquino.

Early on 26 May 10RB crossed the river Melfa. At midday the Guards started moving forward up Route 6, but ran into stiff opposition from enemy positions on Monte Piccolo and Monte Grande, which dominated the road from the west. We moved forward again during the night of 26th/27th, taking four hours to cover four miles, and went into action close to Roccasecca station.

27 May

A hot airless, exhausting day. Everybody was very tired and spent most of the day resting, though it was too hot to sleep and the flies were appalling. The Guards attacked in the afternoon, and the Coldstreams got one company onto Piccolo, but had to come off it. We fired a large number of Mike [regimental] and Uncle [divisional] concentrations on both Piccolo and Grande and on the hills east of Route 6.

28 May

The Guards attacked again at 0015 and we fired a programme from then till 0350 in their support. They got onto both Grande and Piccolo, but at very first light the German parachutists counter-attacked and pushed two Grenadier companies off Grande. Bill Hutley was FOO with one of them, and enemy infantry appeared suddenly within ten yards of him. They riddled his signaller with bullets, but Bill miraculously got away. The Guards came down that hill in a hell of a hurry, leaving their wireless sets and some of their arms behind them. At 0830 the Colonel summoned me to him at Grenadiers HQ in a sunken lane right under Piccolo. Between 0900 and 1100 the Regiment fired many concentrations on the two hills, and the enemy pressure eased. The Grenadiers were very weary and a bit thin on the ground, their morale extremely low. In the afternoon I visited Charles in his forward OP, together with the company commander. In the evening Battalion HQ moved down the hill into the deepest bottom of the wadi, and I spent the night there next to the Colonel.

29 May

Very early it became quite obvious that the enemy had withdrawn off both hills. The Guards were very slow to exploit, and our OPs couldn't get patrols to go forward with them. The Guards later sent up burying parties and brought their dead back to a large cemetery near Battalion HQ in a green field – I should think twenty to thirty graves from each battalion. They found Bill Hutley's signaller among them. The Colonel went off and left me as LO at Grenadier HQ. In the afternoon Charles and I walked up Grande. The whole hillside pitted with shell holes, field and medium, and almost every sangar had had a hit. And towards the top we started coming on corpses, very grisly ones, lying in pools of blood, mangled and covered in swarms of flies. It made me realise very forcibly the effect of concentrated shell fire on rocky ground without cover. In the evening the Guards became non-operational and I returned to the Battery, which had moved forward in the morning to a position just short of Piccolo.

For some days we had been receiving reports that a new M Brigade was shortly to be formed as the third brigade of 6th Armoured Division. It was to be composed, beside ourselves, of the 2nd, 7th and 10th Battalions of the Rifle Brigade and 7th field Squadron RE. 2RB and 7RB, old friends from desert days, had recently arrived from Egypt. The Brigade, now numbered 61st Infantry, became operational on 29 May. For the moment its role would be purely defensive: mopping up isolated enemy pockets to the north and covering the sappers working on the blown bridges across the Liri. I commented in my diary on 30 May: 'The enemy has started going back in earnest, I think: if we can gather momentum we will go a long way.

31 May

To 7RB at 0800 for conference on next move. I felt seedy, headache and pains all over, and on return decided to retire to bed till the afternoon. But was not left in peace. At 1330 the Battery moved forward up Route 6 to Arce, then turned onto Route 82, the road badly blown; long diversions through river beds and vile choking dust. Into action on far side of Fontana Liri Inferiore, a modern town badly smashed and looted. Not a civilian to be seen. The Command Post in a large mansion complete with ornamental garden, which had been used as a German hospital, very comfortable and cool. 7RB had had an officer and seven men wounded on booby traps in the town earlier in the day, so all were warned to stay put. I still felt most seedy and was just retiring to bed when BSM Blanch arrived with the news that Driver H. had been found in a house killed by a booby trap. We at once organised a rescue party. He was lying in a small furnished room, in complete chaos after the explosion, amid a jumble of furniture, clothes and knicknacks. We worked very carefully, first removed all the rubbish, chairs etc. between H. and the doorway, using telephone cable and pulling from a good 50 yards away outside. Then I tied the cable round his middle and pulled him out – no further explosions. He was quite dead, and a horrible sight, face almost unrecognisable. He had evidently been looting and had a crucifix stuffed inside his shirt. He must have been bending forward over a suitcase and the mine was set to explode when he opened it. A terrible instance of the results of disregarding warnings and orders to stay put. We fetched some 6 Armd Div sappers and they had a good look at the house, found at least three other mines on doors and windows. I watched them remove and dismantle one – a 'beauty', they called it.

1 June

Slept twelve hours but woke up not feeling much better. Am praying it is not malaria, having been a bit slack with my mepacrine. Went up to Bob Banks's OP on Monte Castelluccio and sat with him for three hours. A lovely view but desperately hot, the only shade came from a few scraggly thorn bushes on the rocky slope. No sign of the enemy in our vicinity. Retired to bed at 2000, having eaten practically nothing all day but drunk with gallons of tea.

On 2 June we really started moving forward, an advance which was to continue, with fits and starts, for the next thirteen weeks. Back onto Route 6, 'a chaotic march as no one knew where we were going to'. After about fifteen miles we pulled off the road into a peaceful valley, where at 2100 we received our orders from the Colonel. He reported that the Canadians were racing forward to meet the Americans breaking out of Anzio, and the Germans were retreating rapidly to avoid being trapped. 6th Armoured Division was to pass through 78th division, which was already in Alatri, and push on through the Apennine foothills to Fiuggi, Palestrina and Rome. 61st Brigade would lead the Division, and 7RB would lead the Brigade, with a squadron of the Derbyshire Yeomanry, a squadron of 17/21st Lancers and I Battery RHA under command.

Night 2/3 June

Off we went at 2200 at terrific pace. 7RB certainly moves once it starts. The route was very roundabout, a big circular detour north of Frosinone, as the town was impassable owing to blocked streets and blown bridges. Drove into leaguer five miles south of Alatri about 0100. To bed at 0230 – I confess I had slept on the march.

3 June

Up at 0345, after just over an hour's sleep. Drove fast up the hill into Alatri town, where found Bob, 7RB Tactical HQ and hangers on, all halted while a bulldozer dealt with a demolition and removed burnt-out German vehicles which blocked the road. OPs from 57th Field and a medium regiment reported to me, also a rep. who could call on all 78 Div artillery if required – a fantastic amount of artillery for 7RB group. The town not much damaged, modern and laid out nicely, but quite deserted. About 0700 all moved on. Soon 7RB bumped opposition round 'Middlesboro', the junction of the Guarcino and Fiuggi roads. Bob at once engaged Spandaus and a few men moving about in the trees and hedges. Douglas[1] called me forward and he made his plan – to push Peter Shepherd-Cross's company right round to the left to cut the Fiuggi road and come

---

1. Lt. Col. Douglas Darling, 7RB's CO.

down on Middlesboro' from the west. I sat on Bob's tank while we registered two points where the enemy was suspected, and at 1030 all was ready for the fire plan. It went well and the company got round behind without oppositon. All this time the troop of tanks had been loosing off with 75mms and Brownings, and occasionally a burst of Spandau would come back. The riflemen got into the houses on the road junction and took a dozen POW. But when they pushed on east of the road and across the valley they got badly mortared. So our Observation Group moved 1000 yards forward, and in a little wayside halt on the railway made the plan for Battle No. 2. Bob and I saw movement round a house, so we plastered it, and the Shermans put half dozen rounds right through the roof and sides, firing right alongside the station building and bringing down slates and plaster perilously near my head. Then I spotted perhaps twenty men moving up the hill on the far side of the valley, slinking along the stone dykes and through the olives. so we had a Battery gun fire target, while the medium OP plastered the slopes higher up. We enjoyed our shooting. John Leonard [adjutant] on the air upset about the ammunition situation, but I refused to be limited, and in the end H and L sent over some of theirs. Meanwhile RAF fighters were straffing houses on outskirts of Guarcino, perched on the high crest to our north. About 1330 the riflemen pushed on across the valley, found several dead round the house we had engaged, and rounded up more than 30 Germans hiding in culverts and ditches, all very shell-happy. The RBs very pleased with our support and almost embarrassing in their compliments. In the evening 2RB took over the lead, and I returned to 7RB Battalion HQ. Went early to bed, feeling at peace with the world and dog tired. One of the most satisfactory days of battle I've ever had – open mobile fighting, visible targets, a respectable advance and opportunities for really directly helping the infantry, and knowing that they appreciated it.

4 June

The Colonel called in about 0900 and suggested I should swan ahead and find possible gun areas, as whole Regiment was out of range. So off I went, lovely drive, smiling countryside almost untouched by war, except for the growing number of burnt-out trucks abandoned by the roadside. The RAF have been doing a good job. Then suddenly there was Fiuggi, huge hydros and hotels in the modern spa down in the valley, many of them painted over with large Red Crosses. Met six Italian patriots on the outskirts, in civilian clothes with armbands, carrying American tommy-guns and bandoliers fiercely fastened round their middles. But they dived pretty quickly for the ditch when shells fell half a mile away. Set off back to meet the Regiment. Two miles east of Fiuggi discovered the road was being most accurately shelled. In a lull drove furiously past, found most of I Battery halted on the far side and shooed them on. Heard that the Americans have got into Rome, splendid work. The shelling of the road stopped in the afternoon, and the patriots, commanded by a local Italian colonel, gave useful help in rounding up stragglers. I was allowed to spend the night with the Battery. We never had to fire. Various transport troubles, and with one

3-tonner off the road we have had to dump all our cooks and cookhouse equipment near Frosinone and go onto vehicle cooking. By last light our tanks were reported beyond Serrone, which meant we were out of range.

Airgraph, 4 June

For some days I've been hoping for a chance of writing a letter, but tonight it will have to be an airgraph. This battle has gone better than any of us dared to hope, after so many disappointments in this country. We have't covered a vast distance, but the damage we have done has been enormous – there are visible traces of it within 400 yards of me, a burnt-out tank and two abandoned lorries. A few miles down the road I passed three 88-mm guns, also abandoned and burnt-out It will be interesting to see how the next phase goes. Either Hitler will have to send down considerable reserves to stop us – which will directly help the Second Front or Tito or the Russians or all of them: or he will lose the whole of Italy – and then what? We have had an energetic battle and few quiet days since 11th May. When we haven't been firing we have been moving, along narrow tracks jammed with traffic and enveloped in one continuous choking cloud of dust. I have had some bad days with hay fever. So often we have put our guns into action in standing crops, and with vehicles and men crushing the pollen all round, you can imagine my misery – I find hay fever far more of a struggle to cope with than the enemy.

Diary, 5 June

Battery received orders to move at 0700, I rushed off to join 7RB. Owing to demolitions had to take winding sideroads, extremely steep and dusty, but finally tuned into a beautiful villa garden at La Forma, just beyond Serrone. Douglas installed himself in a palatial mansion complete with oak tables and chairs, shady and cool, and lunched in state. Two South-African ex-POWs, dressed as civilians, turned up with fascinating tales of their life in the mountains north of Serrone during last three months, amongst other things said the owner of DD's mansion was the notorious local Fascist – which seemed more than likely: he was well-fed and well-dressed, and hovered obsequiously in the background, very reluctantly acting as interpreter between us and a varied loquacious enthusiastic group of partisans who gave us much information about small groups of enemy left in towns of Olevano and Roiate to the north, mines on the roads etc. I looked for cherries in vain in the Fascist's garden – riflemen are too quick.

DD gave us exciting orders at 1230. The Division is to push ahead hard to-day and to-night, and our orders are to hustle the enemy. Terni is our objective. We moved off at 1315. Smooth run to Genazzano, through smiling green fields and orchards, then over four hours' wait while sappers fixed demolitions ahead in Cave. The peasants brought us huge branches laden with cherries and we gorged ourselves. The road was littered with burnt-out German vehicles, lorries, half-tracks, mules, a dozen Panthers at least, four or more 88-mms, bales of propaganda leaflets, bundles of abandoned kit, ammunition, all the jumble of a hurried retreat. Shortly after Palestrina we turned left along the via Prenestina, running roughly parallel to Route 6 – a Roman road with the original Roman paving still in use, which didn't do our trucks any good and jolted us all up. About 10 miles short of Rome we stopped for a brew, then on after dark, and I lost myself on the map in spite of a good moon. Open country, rather bleak, the Campagna. 7RB went a tremendous pace and several times I found myself out of contact both in front and behind. We finally pulled off the road about three miles outside the city, on the 'northern by-pass' next door to the Roman Agricultural College, and bedded down about 0100.

6 June

Lazy day. I walked to the top of a grassy ridge behind the leaguer and saw the sprawling outskirts of Rome stretching away to the south, with the dome of St. Peter's in the far distance rising majestically above everything. Terrific sensation was the morning news with German announcement that we have landed in France somewhere near Le Havre. Within 100 yards of my half-track was the beginning of a French leaguer, and I couldn't help enjoying making the dramatic announcement, 'On a débarqué en France'. No details but it set everyone speculating excitedly. The King broadcast in the evening and confirmed it.

CHAPTER NINETEEN: FROM ROME TO FLORENCE
June – October 1944

6th Armoured Division's route northwards from the eastern outskirts of Rome started up Route 4 on the eastern bank of the Tiber. The role of 61st Brigade was to protect its right flank in the rolling hills which bounded the valley. During 6 to 9 June the Germans carried out a series of daytime rearguard actions, withdrawing at night. The Regiment moved forward four times, and its OPs accompanied the leading armoured and infantry units, which made periodical requests for artillery support. I noted on the 8th, 'The trouble is the same as for several days past – very effective demolitions covered by shell-fire, and the enemy is using his guns concentrated and unpleasantly, having ammunition he wants to get rid of'. Route 4 ran close to the main Rome-Florence railway line,

The Rome – Florence main line. Route 4 can be seen on the right.

which was 'an amazing sight. The line is cut at least every half mile, either by RAF or German demolitions. There are scores of burnt-out wagons, scuppered engines, both steam and electric. And oddest of all, whole loaded trains full of military stores, in Italian, German, French and Jugoslav wagons, just marooned and sitting on the track. Operation "Strangle" must have presented the enemy with fearsome supply problems – the railways just ceased to function'.

On 9 June the Grenadiers and 17/21st Lancers ran into more determined resistance on a line between the hill town of Poggio Mirteto and the Tiber.
Diary, 9 June

In evening got orders from the Colonel: Division's objective is Narni tomorrow: the Guards make the crossing of the river Farfa and the next stream north of it (at Poggio Mirteto station) tonight, then 7RB, with I Battery close behind, leads the Division.

10 June

Moved off at 0330. As it slowly grew light we crossed the Farfa by the amazing Ponte Sfondato – the road crossed by a vast natural archway of rock through which the river flowed boiling and swirling, grey and cold and clear. The Guards had not reached their objective at Poggio Mirteto, so we found a snug little battery position, rather too far forward for my liking, but completely out of sight, in a deep green hollow north of the Montopoli road and east of the divisional axis. I sat in the hot sun under an olive listening to the 8 o'clock BBC news on the CRA's set. Very soon afterwards the shelling began, a few odd rounds at first, then a good stonk slap in the valley, which caused quite a number of casualties in 7RB. They scattered to the four winds, vehicles starting up and careering in all directions, stretcher bearers running, riflemen tearing after their trucks shouting, "Wait for me, chum". Not very dignified but very sensible. Then down came more, six rounds whistled just over my half track and our deep slit trench. So Bn HQ moved back over the brow of the hill in some disorder – it took me an hour to find them, and while wandering with a medium OP I once more got soundly shelled for my pains, this time in a house full of peasants – an old woman stood in the corner muttering and bringing down curses on Mussolini's head. When I found HQ I dug hard again, in the broiling midday sun, and we were reasonably far down when the next shelling came. About 1600 down into the Farfa gorge where DD set up his HQ right under the cliff face where no shells could reach him. Heard over the air that our chief cook, Frost, and five of his assistants had been wounded by a stray shell – very unlucky but only Peel at all serious. Had glorious bathe in the Farfa, cold but invigorating, and deep enough to be able to swim. It was hard to reconcile the beauty of the valley, the rocky archway of the bridge, the peaceful woods on either side with the shambles of two hours before and the occasional shell passing overhead to harass the road behind us.

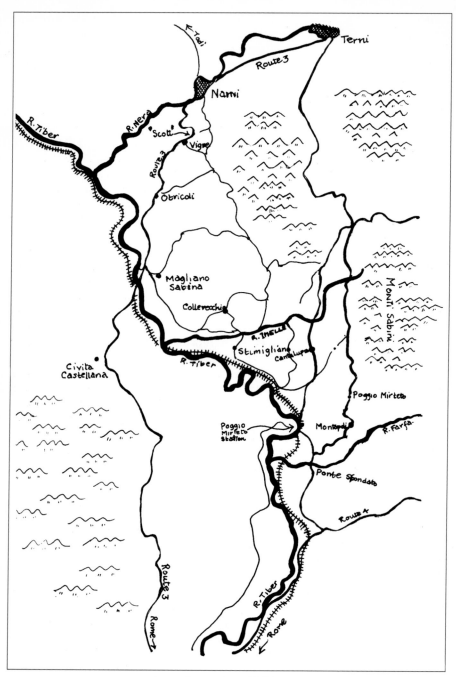

Area of operations, 10/14 June

At 1800 to DD's orders. Guards to attack at 2100, then 2RB to go through to Cantalupo. 7RB will advance as far as possible along western route towards Route 3 – but no start this time until Guards are actually on their objectives. Summoned my jeep on the air to come down and fetch me. Jones appeared after some delay, having stopped to pick up two badly-wounded Welsh guardsmen hit on the roadside on their way forward to assembly area for to-night's attack. We got up to the Battery unmolested. Found the Command Post well established in vast cave-like shelters dug under the house where I had left them in the morning. Vehicles dispersed down towards the valley, and drivers had more very safe shelters down in the wagon line. Very lucky, for the whole slope of the hill was being plastered intermittently, not at all healthy. I walked in to find Oscar [Rose] had just been wounded by a single shell, in the neck, not too nice, and he was coughing up blood at an alarming rate, but amazingly plucky, and just before he left in the stretcher jeep said to me, "I *do* hate the Germans just a bit now" referring to his many arguments in the past about imperialist wars and not hating the German people. Ben [our MO] was there, cool and fearless as ever. I had just begun to give out orders when a phone call came from S Troop asking for Ben and stretchers urgently. Till then the guns had had nothing near them to really worry them, and had been sitting comparatively peacefully in their deep little dell, hearing the Guards being mortared and shelled all day. Then one solitary shell dropped slap beside the ditch in which two subsections had been brewing up, wounded four men. At once Cliff [Hollingworth] and others ran down to help, a second solitary shell landed a few yards away, killed Cliff outright and wounded nine more. Johnston and Hodds died of wounds later in the evening at the Field Ambulance. BSM Riley and Sgt Bevan among the wounded, but they at least were not at all serious. Gnr Martin rushed off to return with two ambulances and in 20 minutes we had got them all away. Ben amazing. When I got back to the Command Post, RHQ were shouting for me for orders. So off in the jeep back across the Farfa to RHQ to tell my tale of woe and ask if H or L could support 7RB tomorrow when they move forward, as we are now considerably disorganised. The Colonel wonderfully helpful and a soothing influence, and we agreed that S Troop should pull back after dark behind the rest of the Regiment, and rest awhile on the banks of the Farfa and reorganise. So back after dark to the Battery to sort it all out. Meanwhile R Troop fired some harassing tasks for the Guards. All a bit shaken, especially S Troop, and I found myself in the evening worrying morbidly over responsibility and asking myself over and over again whether it had been right to put the Battery into action just there and whether we shouldn't have moved earlier. Fortunately shelling died down about 2130 and peace returned – the enemy obviously once again pulling out in the nick of time. S troop started moving back about 2230. I then returned to Bn HQ dog tired, had a stiff whisky and dropped off to sleep. One of the blackest days in the Battery's history since Knightsbridge – three killed and fourteen wounded by three shells – and one of the worst days I've experienced during the war.

11 June

Woke late, still feeling tired and rather loath to face the problems that awaited me. A gentle drizzle soon started, and reduced the tracks to mud and slush. Got to the Battery about 0900 and visited S Troop, all looking more cheerful. Padre buried Cliff in the morning beside a guardsman. The rain and mist made the ceremony more than usually dismal. By midday we had sorted ourselves out, and when the Colonel came round I said we wanted to go with 7RB, that we wouldn't allow others to think we were licked and that it would do us good to be on the move. So off we went at 1300. Came out on the Tiber again at Poggio Mirteto station which was completely shattered, the railway line blown to smithereens. The narrow muddy road ran flat and straight for three or more miles near the river, then turned sharp right over a ridge and down into the valley of the Imelle. The head of 7RB's column reached the crest behind the village of Stimigliano and got promptly shelled. The Battery did a crash action on the roadside, but its support was not required. By evening two squadrons of tanks had crossed the Imelle, so 7RB was ordered to provide protection for them during the night. I arranged DF tasks with DD, but we were not called upon to fire them.

12 June

Up late, a glorious sunny fresh morning after yesterday's rain. Drove across the Imelle and joined 7RB Battalion HQ on the other side at Collevecchio in a palatial country mansion, completely deserted.

Letter, 12 June

I write this sitting at the head of a long oak table surrounded by high-backed leather armchairs in a cool tiled dining-room built in 'baronial' style, complete with Chinese lanterns electrically lighted, a vast open brick chimney and a Latin inscription round the top of the walls. The latter is a quotation from Esdra about sowing in tears and reaping in joy. Not very apt for the owner of the house who, I hope, will very shortly be reaping in tears, if he has not already done so. It is a pretentious building, quite modern, perched on a grassy hill and surrounded by lovely rolling country quite reminiscent of English parkland, dotted with tall shady trees and covered with ripe corn and occasional vineyards or vegetable patches. At the moment it presents the usual war-like aspect: under every tree tanks or lorries are parked, the vineyards and gardens have been churned by tracks and wheels, and there is a gun position just behind the house with all its attendant mess and noise and turmoil. It seems a pity that this lovely country should be so battered – but I feel it only in a very distant impersonal way. One gets callous and hard about such things. And about this particular house I feel no scruples or pricks of conscience whatsoever. The owner is evidently an ambassador of some distinction: I have just been looking through the Italian diplomatic handbook for 1937. The rooms are full of official Fascist pamphlets and correspondence. And I reckon he is fair game. On the whole our troops are marvellously well-behaved, considering that we were at war with these people until nine months ago. They loot very little, and show an extraordinary respect even for rich houses and estates like this. I'm afraid I assume that anyone with wealth in this country must have been a Fascist, and am prepared to turn a blind eye. Ten minutes ago I was delighted to see my driver appear with a sandbag full of new potatoes and another of young lettuces. I don't think the worthy ambassador will miss them. A useful rough indication of the degree of Fascist enthusiasm of any householder whose property we come across is the extent to which the Germans have left it intact. As they retreat they seem to be systematically looting the farms: they take the livestock and chickens, often all the furniture. And usually what they leave they wantonly smash. There is plenty of evidence that in many places they have just run amok. One of my troop commanders was among the first of our tanks to enter a certain village four days ago. In the main street were lying nine corpses, civilians, horribly mutilated. And for nearly an hour he and the other tanks were unable to move for the crowds around them. The whole population rushed out, in spite of the few odd shells still landing, swarmed round our vehicles pelting and smothering them with roses, and the women sobbing and kissing any soldier they could get at. It is on such occasions that one realises what the well-worn word 'liberation' really means. The peasants are magnificent – almost always. They give us unlimited information which usually turns out to be accurate. And not long ago, as I passed a small farm, the family ran out to greet me with cherries and eggs, and pressed a small crumpled piece of paper into my hands. It had a message written in English, signed by a Dvr Beeson, and said 'This family has hidden and fed me for seven months; please do all you can for them'. I could do nothing except give them some cigarettes and bully, but I hope that piece of paper will eventually get them the reward they deserve. There are active Italian partisans all over the country, and I have seen several groups, picturesquely attired, with rifles or tommy-guns, bristling with cartridge belts slung round their waists or over their shoulders, very dirty and unshaven, in tattered civilian clothes. I should doubt if their methods of fighting have much resemblance to those laid down in the Geneva conventions. A shot in the dark or a stab in the back is the usual story, I suppose. and that partly explains the civilian corpses that are found in some of the villages. But not the mutilations. For that there is only one horrible explanation.

Don't let me give you a false impression of this campaign by writing of cool oak-beamed houses and a smiling countryside and cheering rose-throwing populations. Those things are true and they give one hope and courage and sanity in the middle of the beastliness of battle. But this is not a picnic. The enemy is going back, going back a long way. And we are doing our best to hustle him. But he is a cornered rat with a lot of fight still left in him, and we are paying a price for our advance. I had meant to write two days ago, but didn't because I was in a mood of black depression and I would have said distorted things. We had had a bad day. One of my young officers, of whom I thought the world, was killed, and another, my right-hand man, badly wounded. We had 14 men wounded in the battery, some of them severely. That is the testing-time for a commander, and it is a test I do not enjoy – something inside one's brain keeps on hammering out 'Was I right, was I right, could it have been avoided, did I take every precaution, was I right?' That hammer means sleepless nights and black depression. I confess that two days ago I was near to despair, and sorely tempted to shrink from the responsibility. But the mood passes. I know in my own mind that I *was* right – and one has to harden oneself and not take one bad day too tragically. I found then, as I have found before, that with the loyalty and courage and cheerfulness of the men in the Battery, one can shoulder any burden. They are magnificent (what a trite inadequate word) and to discover that they have confidence in oneself and are determined to help to the utmost gives one an exhilaration and strength that makes one's spirit almost invincible. Today we are enjoying a lull and after yesterday's rain the air is fresh and the smells are glorious. We are advancing and likely to continue advancing – though slowly maybe. And our spirits are soaring. So think of me just now as completely happy and not one little bit depressed. The news from everywhere is magnificent. And we are thinking of you at home, in the thick of it now, with battle raging just across the Channel. How frightening it is to be so powerful, to have the means of such complete destruction. Please God may it end soon.

In the afternoon of 12 June the Battery moved back into action, tucked under the steep hill on which the town of Magliano Sabino stands. We fired on several divisional targets around the village of Otricoli, where the Germans were making a stand. Bob Banks and I did a preliminary reconnaissance of positions suitable for occupation before first light next day, when 7RB were to launch a company attack. We found 'the best tracks had ominous holes in them with wooden mines lying beside them'.

The guns moved forward at 0345. S Troop was safely in action by 0520. But two quads of R Troop blew up on mines which the sappers hadn't lifted: front wheels blown off, engines shattered, quads set on fire. Two gunners 'had their ears damaged and had to be evacuated. But very lucky it wasn't worse. Tribute to good sandbagging[1]. Meanwhile Bob had reported Otricoli clear, so I followed DD up the road.'
Diary, 13 June

Found Otricoli a gay sight, ecstatic inhabitants still cheering every vehicle that entered, flowers being thrown, flags waved, vino at every door. In the municipal hall at the far side of the village a huge dump of German rations, nominally guarded by two riflemen. But we did well and filled lockers with German M & V, tinned peas and carrots. A stack of fodder burnt and smoked merrily in the main square. An atmosphere of carnival. About 1130 7RB was ordered to push on and I followed. Slow progress and many diversions. Drove through the tiny village of Vigne, finally held up by a really serious blow at 'Scott', where a high bridge across a deep narrow cleft had been truly demolished. Jeeps, vehicles with

1. Sandbags were placed on the floor of the quads, over the front wheels and under the front seats.

4-wheel drive and tanks could make it, but the long column of 7RB in front of me came to a halt, and were saved by 2RHA. Charles and Ray [Simpson] used their tanks to tow vehicle after vehicle up the precipitous slope – 3-tonners, 15-cwts, ambulances, most of the battalion. I sat and watched idly, occasionally helping to fasten together the long series of tow ropes, and encouraging the motor-cyclists as they came slithering and bouncing and skidding up towards me – particularly the MPs, who kept falling off and having to be rescued and helped up by a crowd of jeering and highly delighted riflemen. As good as a gymkhana, never a dull moment. The Battery started moving forward about 1500, at a maddeningly slow pace, and 7RB established their HQ on the southern edge of Narni. Only one troop of H Battery had got across 'Scott', the rest of the Regiment was not allowed forward until the Bailey bridge had been completed. So all of I Battery had to hang about half the night. I spent the night up at Narni castle, a massive square keep full of refugees, on the top of the hill dominating the town and the Nera gorge – a glorious view, the loveliest scenery we've seen for a long time. And from the town below rose the sound of continuous cheering, speech-making, the town band marching to and fro playing martial airs, singing and rejoicing. Between the houses I caught glimpses of processions, red flags, the whole town filling the small square in their Sunday best to celebrate their liberation. And on the walls of almost every house, in a matter of minutes after our arrival, were printed posters, "VV gli alleati, VV gli stati uniti, VV gli inglesi" etc. – big praise too, for the Red Army.

14 June was a day of rest and maintenance. New vehicles arrived to replace our many casualties, and our cooks rejoined us from the rear. On 15 June we moved forward again with 7RB. The bridge across the Nera gorge had been blown, so we started with a difficult seven-mile diversion; but after that we had a fast clear run in a northerly direction.
Diary, 15 June.

Between Capitone and Montecastrilli we drove for at least five miles through a continuous ammunition dump. The RAF had made hay, its bombs had sent thousands of shells sky high, the vineyards blackened by burnt-out cordite and HE, trees blasted and in several places huge bomb craters in the middle of the road. Tremendous reception in all the villages and at every farm – vino held aloft, flowers thrown, riflemen grinning. After Dunarobba we left all semblance of a hard road and twisted along a narrow soft track unmarked on any map. I got completely lost, and the lovely view was so wide and distant that it helped very little. At last we reached a village and I asked the inhabitants its name – it was Montenero, very picturesque, perched on a peaky hilltop. A few hundred yards beyond, Todi suddenly came into view: a lovely sight, tall massive buildings clustered together on a hilltop, palazzos and solid stone houses inside a formidable town wall, and all dominated by a high graceful spire, the most 'northern' town I've yet seen in Italy. It gave me a thrilling feeling of nearing more familiar lands – and home. By 1700 the town was confirmed clear of the

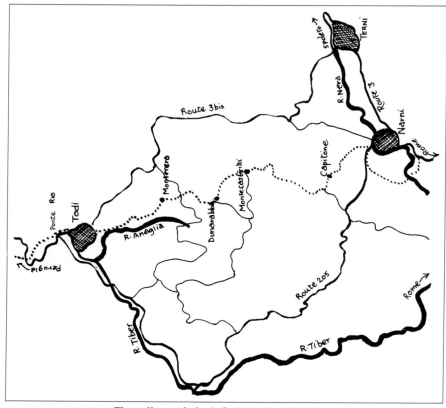

The gallop with the Rifle Brigade, 15/18 June.

enemy, so I ordered the Battery forward to a delightful position just short of the blown bridge across the Anaglia stream, right under the town. 7RB dashed on down the main Todi-Perugia tarmac road and took up defensive positions round Ponte Rio, captured intact by the Lothians. Latter were held up a mile beyond by a second blow, mines, sniping small arms fire and shelling – contact at last with the rearguard, after our exhilarating gallop. 7RB were heavily shelled all round Ponte Rio. Bob had half a dozen successful shoots, which I hope helped them. Back to the Battery just before dark to have a drink to the return of mobile warfare – it had been a really enjoyable day. And it increased our enjoyment to be out of touch completely with RHQ – even with two relay stations out. Much celebration in Todi, and we passed an MP sitting in a jeep looking very merry, surrounded by lovely girls pouring vino down his throat. Big notices in German, 'Eintreten verboten, Todi – Lazarettenstadt'[1]. Apart from the damage caused by a few dozen shells this morning, the town untouched.

1. 'Entry forbidden, Todi – hospital city.'

16 June

Battery moved in the morning to a position 1500 yards NE of Todi. 7RB received orders that they were to stay put. In late morning I had a look around the town. Very clean. Crowds of inhabitants just standing round excitedly. Saw a German soldier being marched up the main street to prison with a rope round his neck and middle, hands tied behind his back, jeering crowds. Notices on every wall in bright red and yellow posters, exhorting the populace in the name of the Committee of National Liberation to remain calm and work hard: and bands of youths wandering round the streets painting up VV Matteotti[1] etc. The Colonel arrived in his jeep about 1600, walked round the guns and apologised for the arrival of the Regiment to upset our independent battle. The main body of the Div. pouring up, endless streams of traffic. Saw DD in evening but there was nothing to be arranged. Heard an Italian interrogating a prisoner in German and translating into English, a stout effort. But he turned out later to have been the chief requisitioning officer for the Germans – the FSS [Field Security Service] were onto him in a flash and locked him up. General view seems to be that the enemy will try to hold a line round Perugia, then fall back to Florence and the main Apennines.

On 17 June the rain, which had been threatening for the past two days, fell in earnest. During the next two days the Brigade advanced slowly into the southern outskirts of Perugia, fighting a series of brief actions. On the 18th the Regiment moved forward three times, and that night supported a successful attack by 10RB on Monte Lucignano.

Battery History, 19-20 June

The next obstacle proved more formidable: Monte Malbe, a steep hill rising over 1000 feet above Route 75, the main road running west from Perugia to Lake Trasimene. The first 300 feet were cultivated, but immediately above the small village and palatial villa of Fontana dense woods began, intersected with ravines which gave excellent cover for snipers and made very hard going for the infantry. After Fontana the road degenerated into a rough cart track with sharp corners and bad gradients, impassable to wheeled vehicles larger than a jeep. At La Trinità the woods stopped and the summit was rocky and bare. La Trinità itself consisted of a red farm house and a large yard behind, with the small chapel which gave it its name in one corner.

7RB attacked during the night of 19/20 June, in steady rain. They were initially successful. In Fontana twenty prisoners were taken while asleep, and C company reached La Trinità. But it then became clear that the enemy was holding the reverse slopes of Monte Malbe in strength. From 0730 onwards the forward infantry positions became increasingly uncomfortable. Mortar fire was heavy and there was sporadic shelling. Spandaus on the flanks made movement on the summit impossible. Charles remained with C Company HQ in the Red House, with a wireless working back to his jeep 400 yards down the track. The view from

1. See p. 88, note 1.

La Trinità was extremely limited, and it was possible for enemy infantry to lie unobserved within less than 100 yards of Company HQ. I took my jeep up and parked it alongside Charles's, in order to give an extra link over the regimental net.

I Battery moved during the morning, with great difficulty owing to the rain-soaked fields and tracks, past Perugia station and into action north of Route 75 at l'Olmo. While it had been moving, the enemy had counter-attacked. Charles called for fire on his registered targets, and for 20 minutes H and L Batteries were firing almost continuously. The riflemen held their ground and about 1330 the enemy withdrew.

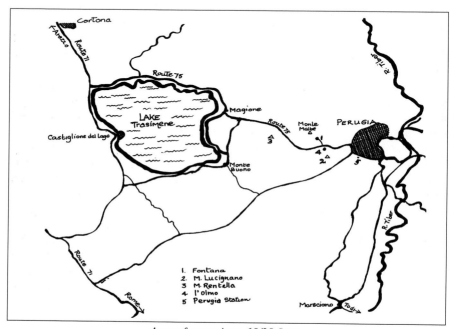

Area of operations, 18/28 June.

At 1715 came a second counter-attack, even more determined than the first. The enemy very nearly succeeded in recapturing La Trinità, and for fifteen minutes it was touch and go. The leadership of Major Fyffe, company commander, was inspiring. Charles and I called for concentration after concentration on to Trig point 652, the summit of Monte Malbe, and its reverse slopes. During the counter-attack H and L Batteries were both on the move, so practically all the firing was done by I. The range from S Troop was only 2300 yards, and some of the targets were closer than this. Ammunition supplies sank very low, but when the situation was really serious, two loaded 3-tonners arrived, amid cheers from the whole gun position. The Colonel set to with everyone else to hump the boxes from the road over the muddy field to the guns. The mediums also joined in with, as we learnt later, devastating effect. Major Fyffe and his platoon commanders kept howling for more and more fire, and sent over the air the most bold and alarming corrections – 'Drop 200, drop 400, right 300, drop 200 . . .' I edited these orders before passing them on, and usually halved the corrections. The only possible explanation seemed to be that the infantry were bringing the rounds down upon themselves. This in fact proved to be the case, and it probably saved the day. The price was two riflemen killed and three wounded by our own shells, and a gaping hole in the side of the Red House caused by a direct hit from a medium shell.

During the whole day Charles's OP signaller, Bdr Gilchrist, had given a magnificent example of courage and efficiency. During both counter-attacks he transmitted the vital fire orders and messages as calmly and faultlessly as if he was taking part in a peace-time signals exercise. His contribution to the success of the battle was immense and for his action he was subsequently awarded the Military Medal.

After 1800 the battle died down and the enemy retreated to lick his wounds. So ended the battle of Monte Malbe, one of the most important I Battery had fought in this war. The day had proved one thing – the value of teamwork and mutual understanding based on personal contact between gunners and infantry. The battle quickly passed into legend. Already in the middle of July I heard a rifleman describing to the rest of his section how 1000 German corpses had been found in a wood behind Malbe after one of our stonks. When I tried to interrupt, I was accused of false modesty and howled down.

We later had the opportunity of walking over the Malbe battlefield. 'As on Grande, there was plenty of visible proof of the lethal effect of concentrated artillery fire: about 50 corpses left on the ground, and these were probably only a proportion of those killed, for the Germans have always made great efforts to recover and bury their dead. The finding of a corpse in a bramble bush only 35 yards from the Red House showed how near the enemy came to recapturing it on 20 June'.

At first light on 21 June patrols of 7RB found the summit of Malbe unoccupied. I spent the next two days at the Red House, watching the periodic signs of enemy movement in the valley below through a slit in the wall at the back of the chapel, and trying to locate and engage the mortars and artillery which continued to trouble our infantry. On the night of 21/22 June 10RB reached the summit of Monte Rentella, a prominent feature on the opposite side of Route 75, but were pushed off it in a fierce counter-attack just before first light. Our guns had a busy morning. In the afternoon patrols found Rentella clear, and by evening the KDGs had reached Monte Buono, directly overlooking Lake Trasimene. The next five days were a static period, with a good deal of observed shooting but no major actions, and after the 28th the Battery was silent. That day the enemy's harassing of Route 75 between us and Perugia ceased, and it became possible for day leave parties to visit the city where amenities for the troops were being rapidly organised.

Letter, 28 June

We are at the moment enjoying a lull and sorting ourselves out for the next phase. We are still in action and still in contact with the enemy, but the battle has died down on our sector and we are content to let it remain like that for a short while. What we really need in the Regiment is a good rest. We have been in action for just under 3 months, and during that time we have been manning our guns every minute of the 24 hours, except for the time we have spent on the road moving forward. We have had some strenuous shooting, some days firing our ammunition as fast as it arrived and reducing the RASC to something near despair. Other days we have fired practically nothing and have just sat round waiting. But by day everyone has to be ready and at a minute's notice to answer calls for fire; by night at least one man has to be awake on each gun. So that even on the quiet days the men get little relaxation. What they want is a fortnight right away from the guns and a complete change of atmosphere. We are all a little weary and I hope we will get our rest sometime soon. We look hopefully at the villages we pass through and make a mental note of the billets and concert halls (usually the local Fascist HQ), the fields suitable for football pitches and the best rivers for bathing. Anyway it's something to look forward to. We are all in very good heart otherwise – as indeed we should be – and pretty pleased with ourselves. And when people complain of being weary, I find the best answer is to compare ourselves with the enemy. Most of the prisoners we have taken recently were in a miserable state. Not all of them of course: some units still fight with an amazing determination and morale. But the countryside has been full of stragglers, many of them found drunk and asleep in farmhouses, dejected with apparently no further interest in life. Practically all of them are filthy – louse ridden and flea ridden. That I think is significant, for although they may be short of soap, this country has as much water as anyone could wish. I heard one young German being interrogated – a fine, well-built specimen of 'Aryan manhood', about 22 I should think, and a member of what was once a crack fighting unit. He had 'allowed himself to be left behind' by his company, as he put it. He was only too ready to give information about his unit – until recently very rare among German soldiers. When asked whether there were many others who allowed themselves to be left behind, he produced a weary attempt at a smile, said 'Ja, viele' and shrugged his shoulders. And when asked where his unit had gone to, he said 'zurück, immer zurück'. The Italians say they had talked to hundreds in the same frame of mind during the last days before they pulled back. It's a most encouraging sign – one day the German Army *will* crack, if we keep on hitting hard, and giving it no rest – shelling and bombing by day and night, smashing his communications and harassing his line of retreat. Well I know that bitter desperate feeling when one is retreating: the air full of enemy planes, one town after another and dumps and vehicles abandoned, and no future to look forward to. But our retreats were nothing in distance compared to the length of that weary road back to Berlin.

I have had a little time for sightseeing, and hope to do a lot if and when our rest period comes along. This country is full of weird contrasts. One can spend the morning at an OP, looking out over the enemy lines, probably sitting in a shattered house surrounded by mines and shell craters and all the usual desolation of battle. When one leaves the OP one drives cannily, listening for the whistle of the shells and keeping an eye open for handy slit trenches. Then a 20 minute drive and one is in the centre of a lovely old town, almost untouched by war, full of civilians strolling as if there had never been a German within thousands of miles. The shops are a bit empty, it's true, and one can't get a meal except through the Army. But the narrow streets and alleys, the squares and piazzas full of statues and surrounded by noble Renaissance facades, the lovely doorways, the towers and churches and archways transport one to an entirely different world. Even so, hob-nailed army boots and tanks parked in the public gardens bring one down to earth. And sightseeing, even with a Baedeker which one of my troop commanders cleverly had sent from home, is apt to be disappointing. The best facades and monuments are bricked up, and the famous paintings are hidden away in cellars. And yet not even war can suppress that thrilling atmosphere of 'living' history.

The weather here is very changeable. The last two days have been extremely hot, roasting sun and no breeze. But before that we had had five days of rain, Scotch mist on the hilltops soaking through the pines, and several torrential downpours with the thunder drowning the gunfire. Those wet days turned every mountain track into a watercourse, and the stubble fields became soggy expanses of mud and water. Luckily there are plenty of farms in this country – dirty, it's true, and fly-ridden, and left by the Germans in a revolting state, but better than nothing against the rain. Moving our guns became a nightmare – progress one day was 100 yards every half hour for a whole afternoon. Only jeeps could get along unaided.

I wonder where we'll be when winter comes on us again. Chasing across the Hungarian Puszta, or inside the Bohemian fortress? Or perhaps all will be over and we shall be champing and shouting to be taken home? It's just as well one can't read the future. But what wonderful possibilities there are.

On 30 June we were relieved by 154th Field Regiment (Leicestershire Yeomanry) and moved to a harbour five miles south of Lake Trasimene, where we enjoyed our first night out of action since 2 April. Our move was part of a major reshuffle: 6th Armoured Division was being switched westwards from 10 to 13 Corps to relieve 78th Division, which had recently fought a stiff battle on the western shore of the lake. After taking over, 6th Armoured Division's task would be to push on steadily up Route 71 to Arezzo, then north-west along Route 69 down the Arno valley to Florence. It would guard the right flank of 4th Division which was expected to do the hard fighting.

On 5 July our leading tanks were halted by strong opposition ten miles short of Arezzo, and it became clear that two hills dominating Route 71 from the east, Monte Castiglion Maggio and Monte Lignano, would have to be captured before further progress could be made. We left our harbour early on 3 July and went

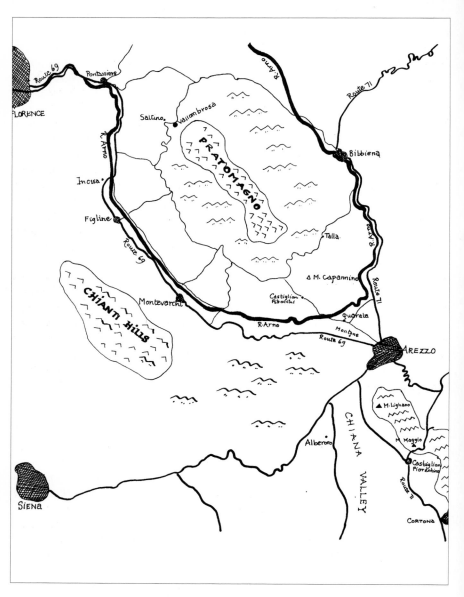

Area of operations, 5 July/18 August

into action on the 5th in the flat fields of the valley three miles short of Castiglion Fiorentino. Almost the only source of our information about the enemy was 'civreps' from the local inhabitants, which often proved most accurate and reliable. The general impression, confirmed by a talkative German prisoner, was that the enemy intended to defend Arezzo and stand on his present line as long as possible. On the night of 6/7 July 2RHA supported an attack by 7RB on Monte Maggio.

History, 7-8 July

The riflemen got to within 100 yards of the summit, Point 756, but failed to dislodge the enemy and had to dig in and consolidate before first light. In the early morning two counter-attacks were repulsed, with the help of us and 57th Field Regiment. But at 2215 on the 7th the enemy attacked again, and were over the ridge and in among our platoon positions almost before anyone realised what was happening. The forward positions immediately became untenable and as the two companies withdrew in the dark down the steep hill, all their communications failed. I withdrew with them in some haste. The help we could give was limited, and in one area our own and the enemy's troops were so hopelessly mixed up that our shells were undoubtedly responsible for a few casualties among the riflemen. At first it seemed that the casualties had been extremely heavy, but all through the night stragglers came in, some of them after lying up for hours in the enemy's lines. Fortunately he did not press his attack home.

During the evening of 9 July the 57th Field Regiment took over our responsibilities at Monte Maggio, and next day we moved into the 4th Division's area on the far side of the Chiana valley. The distance was not more than eight miles as the crow flew, but in order to avoid the attention of the enemy, who was heavily shelling Route 71, we had to travel nearly twenty miles. Our new position was on the edge of the scattered township of Alberoro, well concealed from the east. We spent the next three days awaiting the major attack which was being prepared to capture Arezzo.

Letter, 13 July

Things are going slower here now, and we have had our disappointments recently. But it was to be expected, and Kesselring[1] can hardly expect to be left alone for long. As I write the RAF are turning and tumbling over each other in the sky above, and the guns bark from time to time. But we ourselves are enjoying an ideal respite, in a delightfully peaceful little valley, surrounded by shady woods that are full of magpies and woodpeckers and finches and lizards. Also of mosquitos, the biggest nuisance of this time of year. I think we must be out of the bad malarious belt by now, but even so we take all precautions and sleep under nets every night. The weather is amazingly variable. A day of thunder and drenching rain will be followed by a day of roasting cloudless heat, which reminds one of desert days. It's quite different heat, of course, much damper and therefore more oppressive. The temperatures don't compare with Africa. But

---

1. Commander-in-Chief of the German Forces in Italy.

sometimes one is reduced to sitting in the shade of one's truck, just panting and sweating and longing for the evening.

I was lucky a week ago to get enough time to drive over to Assisi. The town is absolutely undamaged. The Germans had used it as a hospital and leave town entirely. Many of the large convents and hospices were covered in Red Crosses. I loved the town with its narrow steep streets and paved squares, so clean and quiet, and such a contrast to the noise and dust and petrol fumes of every town and village on the main roads behind our lines. I'll also remember Assisi for its cherries. Quite by chance the two of us (I was spending the day with Bob Banks, one of my troop commanders, and incidentally an architect, which makes him an interesting sightseer) walked into a small cafe and found on the counter the largest barrel or cask of cherries I've ever seen. We bought eight kilos, and then drove up the narrow stony track in our jeep right up to the Citadel. There we sat, the two of us with our driver, dangling our legs over the edge of the grassy walls, gazing at the view over the Tiber valley to Perugia and northwards into the hills, making ourselves ill with cherries and spitting the stones down onto the town far below. It was a lovely break in the routine of battle.

I think the most annoying thing about battle is being cut off from outside news. It's true we hear the BBC, but only once a day, and probably only the headlines at 9 am, which a signaller can take down as they are read at dictation speed. One never gets an opportunity really to listen to talks and commentaries, and anyway one never knows the times of the programmes. The *Eighth Army News*, a well-run little paper, vigorous and 'progressive', comes up spasmodically. We get the military news, but hardly ever the political background to the war. I should like to know something more of the Italian political situation. The peasants we meet are for the most part completely apathetic. The usual reaction, when asked about Badoglio or the new coalition government[1], is a shrug of the shoulders – 'Just one more gang of politicians'. The priests often express great concern at the unhealthily close relations between us and the Bolshevists. That is not surprising – I think the outlook of the Catholic Church in Italy and Germany will be very far from benevolent towards the idea of the United Nations.[2] In the towns one gets a different impression. In several we have recently passed through, within a few hours of our arrival, flamboyant posters have appeared on the walls with Vivas all round for Churchill, Roosevelt and Stalin, and long appeals from the local committees of the Communist Party or the Committee of National Liberation. The sceptical say that these posters are carried forward by special political officers with our leading troops. This is not true, and I think there is no doubt that the posters have in many cases been prepared and printed before our arrival. This confirms the existence of well-organised underground movements. Opinions differ as to the usefulness of the partisans. Their chief concern is certainly to protect their shops and houses and women from the retreating Germans. And who

1. After the capture of Rome the Badoglio Government was replaced by an anti-fascist coalition under Bonomi.
2. The alliance of Britain, the Soviet Union and the USA.

is to blame them? Blowing up German lorries or capturing bridges to prevent their destruction, and other similar jobs, come very low down on their list, and I've yet to come across an instance of local partisans actively harassing the Germans. Though I'm told in Northern Italy partisan activity is on a far greater scale – and of course in Istria there are Tito's men to help them to organise themselves. But undoubtedly they do useful work in rounding up German stragglers, and we get a lot of information from them. The Communists seem to be much the best organised, as apparently is the case everywhere in occupied Europe. I have heard several AMGOT officials in Southern Italy say, with bitter regret, that the Communists in the towns they adminster are the only people who can be relied upon to get anything done at all. No one else has any 'go' or initiative, or takes the war and the colossal administrative problems of Italy at all seriously. In the first few hours of liberation one sees amusing scenes. The main square fills with people, of all ages and classes and sexes: Red Flags are produced, speeches made, the band parades up and down, the local Fascist's windows are broken (he himself has usually fled), walls are covered with slogans (*Viva Matteotti*[1] is the favourite), and any English soldier who appears on the scene is carried shoulder high to the nearest café and plied with vino. All the while a prodigious amount of drinking goes on. Youths appear in gleaming red shirts and scarves, and silly little 'partisan' caps like paper hats out of a Christmas cracker, with a star set in the middle of the peak. Long stories are told of heroic deeds in the face of vast German armies. The gullible are persuaded that every mountain in Italy was for three long years covered with Italian soldiers refusing to fight for Musso. What children the Italians are. It's impossible to hate them. And yet I often wonder how many of these cheering youths were only a few weeks ago parading enthusiastically in shirts of that less respectable colour, black.

Monte Maggio and Monte Lignano were captured by the New Zealanders on the night of 12/13 July. The Guards Brigade then took over the lead, and at 0100 on the 15th launched the big attack. 'The artillery support bordered on the fantastic', and 2RHA fired long timed programmes on two successive nights. The Guards met tough opposition, but the Germans pulled out before first light on 16 July. By 0700 the armoured cars of the Lothians were in Arezzo, and by midday had captured the bridge over the Arno at Quarata intact: the demolition charges and fuses were found in position, but the Germans had had no time to set them off.

I Battery moved on the evening of 16 July into the southern outskirts of Arezzo. 7RB was given the task of protecting the crossing at Quarata, and targets for defensive fire by the Regiment were fixed from the map. 'Lt. Col. Fyffe insisted on naming two of them SETON and WATSON, then drove off with the Brigadier, leaving me helplessly protesting'.
History, 17-18 July

Our tanks, followed by 10RB, crossed the Arno soon after first light on

1. See p. 88, note 1.

17 July, but at once encountered opposition from small groups of infantry. But more serious was the extremely heavy shelling which followed the least movement of either our infantry or tanks. Enemy OPs had perfect observation over the whole of the Arno valley from anywhere they liked to establish themselves on the huge mountainous mass of the Pratomagno. This fact was to dominate the whole of 6th Armoured Division's operations for the rest of the time we fought with them. It was a perpetual problem to find gun positions out of sight of the mountains on our right. and the pattern of the fighting remained the same all down the Arno to Pontassieve: as the enemy slowly withdrew, he blew all the bridges and cratered the roads at least once every half mile; and when we advanced, every diversion in turn would be shelled with unnerving accuracy by OPs well sited on our right flank.

The guns moved forward in the morning of 17 July to a position in the ravine of the Castro stream, behind Montone village, two miles west of Arezzo. They were greeted by two hours of severe shelling. At 1800 7RB were ordered to prepare for a night attack on Castiglion Fibocchi. A company moved off from Quarata bridge at 2200 and reached its objective; but when B company took the lead, it ran into heavy machine-gun fire. Major Meldrum, commanding the Battalion in the CO's temporary absence owing to malaria, decided to pull back into a defensive position and dig in before first light. I reached their position, together with the jeeps of Battalion HQ, at 0400 and got cracking on the digging without delay.

Daylight on 18 July found the Battalion on a slight slope among crops and vines, with a view of not more than 50 yards to the front. It was overlooked by high hills not more than 2000 yards away, and it was impossible to move without being observed. The road back to Quarata was particularly bare and conspicuous. Moreover, it was soon obvious that the enemy knew exactly where we were, and about 0630 the shelling and mortaring began which was to continue, with very few quiet periods, for the whole day. Fortunately most of the shelling was by 75s, though 88s and 105s joined in from time to time. One shell fell on the very edge of my slit trench: I felt it penetrate the earth touching my right shoulder, but miraculously it was a dud and didn't explode. It proved impossible to locate the enemy guns, and all that we gunners could do was to stonk Castiglion and the likely valleys where there was a chance that the mortars might be. It was a day of great strain and discomfort for the whole battalion. Casualties had not been light, and the men were tired and dispirited by not being able to hit back. They were also so thirsty in the hot sun that in spite of the certainty that it would be observed, a jeep had to be sent up loaded with water. When orders came over the air that the battalion was to hold its position overnight everyone was reduced to something near despair. Major Meldrum protested so energetically, however, that these orders were cancelled and we were told to pull back to the bridge at last light. Every man undoubtedly shared my feelings of relief at getting away from a position where I had spent quite the most unpleasant day of my life.

Over the next ten days 6th Armoured Division advanced slowly astride Route 69, which ran north-westwards down the Arno Valley from Arezzo to Florence. 61st Brigade's role continued to be to fight on the right flank along the lower slopes of Pratomagno. The 2nd, 7th and 10th Rifle Brigade took turns to provide the necessary infantry support, and I spent much of my time at 7RB battalion headquarters. The battery moved five times between 19 and 28 July, each time for a distance of about five miles. The most serious resistance since the Castiglion battle was met on 29/30 July, in the hills east of Figline Valdarno, from the 1st German Parachute Division.

R Troop's Sherman OP crossing the Arno, 25 July. Gnr Marr in turret, Dvr McCann driving. Photograph by Bob Banks.

History, 23 July

It was weird country, cut by a succession of narrow valleys impossible to climb and covered with a thick tangle of trees and thorns and brushwood. These were ideal for defence by a minimum number of well-sited Spandaus, bazookas and artillery OPs. Farmhouses were thickly scattered along the valleys, surrounded by orchards which provided an unlimited supply of superb peaches, pears and plums. The quantity of fruit we consumed was phenomenal, and digestions were in a perpetual state of disruption throughout July and August.

On 31 July I Battery received orders to go off on its own next morning to support the KDGs back north of Arezzo.

1 August

It was an odd experience to retrace our footsteps over 20 miles and to find Arezzo changed out of all recognition: roads jammed with maintenance traffic, ammunition and petrol dumps spread all over the countryside, and big gangs of Italians working on the railway. Between this vital base area and the enemy on the heights of the Pratomagno stood only Lindforce, which we now joined. It consisted of squadrons from the KDGs, Warwickshire Yeomanry and Central Indian Horse and a battery of the 5th Anti-Tank Regiment, and was under command of the 4th Indian Division, part of 10th Corps. Its task of filling the gap between the extreme right flank of 6th Armoured Division and the left hand brigade of 4th Indian Division was not arduous, as it amounted merely to maintaining standing patrols to watch the slopes of the Pratomagno, and arranging a little harassing fire from time to time.

3 August

Bob went up to his OP on Monte Capannino [2200ft] at first light. It had a magnificent view down into the deep Talla valley and across to the 3500ft ridges of the Pratomagno to the north-west. R Troop moved into a forward position just north of Castiglion for a day's shooting. With 6th Armoured Division we had recently been restricted to 15 rounds per gun per day except for emergencies. Having now changed Corps, and with no RHQ or BMRA to worry us, we decided to enjoy ourselves. Bob harassed Talla, a gun position previously reported by partisans, and about a dozen other likely areas of enemy occupation. That evening we fired two concentrations in support of an attack by 11th Indian Infantry Brigade, starting from Capannino. This was the preliminary to a full-scale attack by 10 Corps which it was hoped would carry us northwards astride Route 71 as far as Bibbiena and right up to the Gothic Line which stretched across Italy from Rimini to Pisa.

But that same afternoon the CO paid us a visit, bringing the news that we would return to the Regiment next day.

4 August

We were extremely sorry to leave Lindforce. It had been a welcome change from routine plodding down the Arno Valley. The atmosphere with the KDGs was typically 'cavalry' and charmingly informal. They believed in doing themselves well and lived in the greatest comfort: when their HQ moved up to Castiglion, the CO's two pedigree chargers brought up the tail of the column, with groom in charge. They were in the happy position of not being required to fight serious battles or even to gain ground. Their method of operating was very reminiscent of the 'columns' of desert days. No night patrols, only routine guards. We gunners got a lot of shooting. The main gun position was quiet and shady, with bathing in the Arno just behind. And the OP on Capannino couldn't have been more delightful. The ridge was thickly wooded, and to sit in the shade of a massive oak, in the fresh mountain air, shooting a troop at random targets, was a delightful way of spending a summer's day. Whether it inflicted any damage on the enemy is quite a different matter.

On 5 August we were back in action with the Regiment a few miles north of Incisa in Valdarno. On our immediate left, across the Arno, 4th Division was fighting hard in the Chianti hills, and further west the New Zealanders and South Africans that day reached the Arno at Florence and occupied the part of the city south of the river. 6th Armoured Division's role was very minor: just to 'prod on', exerting constant pressure and inflicting maximum damage without suffering unduly ourselves. We were delighted when the German 1st Parachute Division was replaced on our front by less aggressive formations.

Between 5 and 8 August we fired a lot in support of the Guards, who made slow progress in the foothills of Pratomagno. On the 9th 7RB took over the lead. 'The days passed gently and pleasantly – a very gentlemanly war'. There was no infantry activity by day, but night patrols went out, often 'accompanied by one or two partisans who were delighted to act as guides, particularly as they were given a suit of battle dress to wear and a tommy-gun to carry. They were well organised and brought back much information about enemy gun positions and outposts in the hills'. Our main targets were on the slopes below the holiday resort of Vallombrosa, including the very prominent Grand Hotel at Saltino.

Letter, 12 August

Out here things are much the same as when I last wrote. We advance slowly, nothing sensational, but useful all the same, with a growing feeling that we are now near the end of the campaign which began on 11th May, and that another phase may open at any moment – with perhaps even more sensational and far-reaching results. The enemy fights hard and I can't help admiring him for it. I don't think his resistance is inspired either by belief in victory or by fanatical determination to defend the Fatherland – or Hitler – or anyone else. I think most of these Germans fight on in weary, bewildered, grey desperation, chiefly because their fogged mechanical minds are incapable of thinking up any practical alternative. A few desert, and the prisoners we take are almost always depressed and worn out and dirty. But we must assume they will continue to fight, both bravely and skilfully, as at present, and base our calculations on that assumption. And I have every hope that the poison of doubt and disintegration will seep downwards from the top. At present there are few signs of any serious disaffection among the rank and file. But one can't bump off very many field marshals and generals before even the dumbest German – incapable of thinking though over 90% apparently are – realises that something must be wrong.[1]

Bill Blacker's death, of which we got news on 5 August, was a great shock. It appears to have been a desperate piece of bad luck. One stray lone shell landed on his truck in Normandy and blew it to bits. How often in this war has the stray

---

1. This is a reference to the abortive plot to kill Hitler on 20 July, which was followed by savage reprisals against the military and civilian plotters. One of them, Rommel, committed suicide.

shell done more damage than a deliberate concentration from 20 guns. There are too few soldiers like Bill and the Army will need them long after the war. He was 2nd in command of H/l when I joined it in France and I'll never forget what I owed him for helping a very green, rather bewildered subaltern – a civilian in the midst of soldiers – to settle down and learn Army ways and master the mysteries of gunnery. He was a brilliant battery commander in the Desert and in Greece (where he got the DS0 almost the same day I got my MC), and his influence and inspiration will be felt in this battery for a long time to come – even, I think, after the last man to serve under his command has passed on elsewhere. Time and time again, when confronted with a problem, perhaps of tactics, perhaps of discipline, I find myself thinking, 'What would Bill have done in a case like this?' And usually that provides the answer.[1]

On 12 August we were told that we were to leave 6th Armoured Division and move across to the Adriatic to rejoin 1st Armoured Division, which was already concentrated south of Ancona and waiting to take part in the grand assault on the Gothic Line.

On 18 August we handed over to 57th Field Regiment and started on a three-day journey across the Apennines which ended on the sea one mile south of Porto Recanati. We had been told that we would be left in peace for the lsongest possible period, in order to rest and reorganise ourselves. A major reorganisation had been made necessary by the impact upon the Regiment of the Python scheme, under which all men who had completed more than 4½ years service overseas would qualify for repatriation.

Letter, 5 September

We have been in a feverish state of upheaval. All the men in the Regiment who served in France (34 in I Battery) were summoned home – to their immense delight of course, sorry though almost all of them were to leave the Regiment. And so we were plucked of all our senior NCOs in one fell swoop, and ever since I have been worrying out all the promotions and swapping round involved, interviewing dozens of new reinforcements, explaining to some why they were not being promoted, persuading others to accept promotion, and staring hour after hour at my fat ledger with all the men of the battery in it, with their histories and trades and crimes and idiosyncrasies. We have it all sorted now, except for a few blank spaces still to fill. But it's a different battery and I miss all the old faces I've known through France and Greece and the Desert, and lately from Cassino to Florence. It was a sad parting. And now it will be a hard struggle, breaking in the new arrivals to our ideas, training and nursing and driving them, till we get back to the old standards of efficiency and nearly perfect teamwork. We'll do it, of course, but it will be hard work, good though the material is.

I also qualify for posting home, having served four years and nine months

1. I wrote an appreciation of Bill Blacker for *The Royal Artillery Commemoration Book 1939-45* (pp. 667-9). He was killed on 11 July while commanding 179th Field Regiment RA.

overseas. My two breaks, in 1940 and last Christmas, were only of five and two months respectively, and so are not considered to break the continuity. I have signed a certificate saying I don't want to return to England at the moment. I can cancel this certificate whenever I wish, merely by the stroke of a pen, and will then be put back at the top of the waiting list for a passage home. My reasons are these. Firstly, if I came home, I should come as a captain. And if I were lucky enough to be given a battery at home to command, I should never get another like this. Secondly, I want to be in at the kill. I want to see the Germans in Italy smashed as I saw them smashed in Tunisia. And I want to experience the thrill of crossing the German frontier as a member of the Eighth Army. Perhaps I won't – who even now can foretell the course of the war, and where we shall go from here? But with victory rushing nearer every hour and the news so overwhelming that one can hardly take it in, I think I should feel very much left out of it sitting in some depot in England – much as I'm tempted by the thought of another month's leave with you all at home

How thrilled you must be, with Rumania an ally (how farcical the somersaults can be),[1] Bulgaria dropping out,[2] the Czechs fighting in the Tatra,[3] and Tiso[4] wailing about treacherous partisans. Then Tito hobnobbing with Churchill in Rome.[5] And the pace in France is just dizzy. By now the British tanks must be in Seclin and Roubaix and Allennes-les-Marais and all the other dingy ugly little towns I got to know so well in 1940. And in Lille too, I expect. I hope the Audras [French friends of the family] are there and well and getting the last ounce of excitement and exhilaration from the noise and shouting and singing and rejoicing. When we left Lille in May '40 I remember how some Frenchmen ran up to us and patted the sides of our little whippet tanks – very sadly and very bewildered and frightened. They will enjoy watching the unending dusty roaring columns of Churchills and Shermans and Cromwells and self-propelled guns racing through their cobbled streets on the way to the Siegfried Line.

I try to be humble and not to exult – but it's hard. May the end come as soon as we now dare to hope.

Our hopes of a few weeks out of action, to enable us to get men away on leave to Rome and absorb our reinforcements, proved vain. However we were able to make the most of Porto Recanati.

1. Romania had been Germany's active ally in the war against the Soviet Union. On 23 August 1944, with Soviet troops already on Romanian soil, King Michael staged a military coup d'état and declared war on his former ally.

2. Bulgaria, following the Romanian example, declared war on Germany on 6 September.

3. Some Slovak (not Czech) forces rose against the Germans at the end of August in the Tatra, part of the Carpathian mountain range, but were quickly repressed.

4. Pro-fascist ruler of Slovakia 1939-1945.

5. 12/13 August, in Naples, not Rome.

History, 21 to 26 August

The weather was glorious and we were within a few hundred yards of a beach of clean dazzling white sand which stretched in both directions as far as the eye could see. The Battery lived in bathing dresses and took more exercise in five days of swimming than in the past five months of fighting. Elaborate steps had been taken to conceal the presence of the Division in the area, and an order had even been issued that not more than 20 men from one unit could bathe on the beach at the same time. However, for us veterans, who had the dust of battle fresh on our faces, these restrictions were somewhat relaxed.

On our last evening we had a gigantic party, a farewell to the Python veterans and the Drivers' Day celebrations (postponed from 5 May)[1] combined in one. Tom Mathias [Battery Captain] had scoured the countryside for eggs and poultry and vino, and had returned with truck loads of food, and we were able to borrow enough tables and chairs from the local Town Hall to seat the whole Battery. It was a great send off for the veterans with a battle record which could be equalled by very few others in the British Army today.

1. Drivers' Day celebrated the Battle of Fuentes d'Onoro in Spain on 5 May 1811, during which a section of Bull's Troop RHA, having been cut off, charged back to the British lines through the French Cavalry. I Battery RHA retains to this day the title of Bull's Troop.

CHAPTER TWENTY: THE BATTLE OF THE GOTHIC LINE
August – October 1944

While at Porto Recanati we had learnt of the plan for the assault on the Gothic Line. The objective, General Oliver Leese, Eighth Army Commander, told us, was Vienna – an announcement which, when I passed it on to the assembled Battery, provoked a good deal of derisory and sceptical laughter. By 25 August the Poles had reached the river Metauro, which runs into the sea at Fano. That night the attack began, with the Poles on the coast, the Canadian corps in the centre, and 5th Corps, which included 1st Armoured Division, on the left in the foothills of the high Apennines. 1st Armoured Division was to be kept fresh until a breakthrough had been achieved. If the infantry attack met stiff opposition, 2RHA would go into action to give additional support; but whether we were required or not for the big battle, we would fall behind 1st Armoured Division when it passed through the gap on its way to the Po.

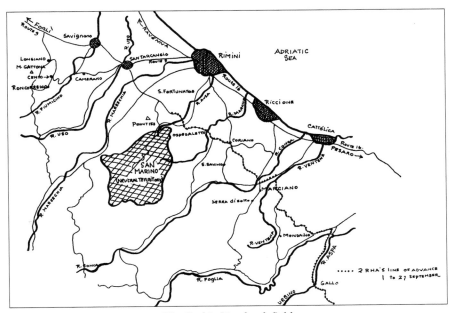

The Gothic Line battlefield.

239

On the night of 27/28 August we left our seaside resting place and started on a difficult four-day 80-mile drive northwards, passing through Jesi, Fabriano and Pergola. Early on the morning of 1 September we went into action at Gallo, eight miles north-east of Urbino, on the northern slopes of the Apsa valley.

History, 1-2 September

Remained in action without firing a round. From the crest 200 yards in front of R Troop's guns the main enemy positions could be seen with alarming clarity. Fortunately we were left alone. The two days were the hottest we had yet experienced in Italy, and the warm gusty wind was reminiscent of the Egyptian khamseen. There was not a scrap of shade in the whole Battery area, and down in the valley the Germans had systematically felled every tree. What news we got was amazingly good: by the evening of the 2nd it seemed that the Gothic Line had been broken, and we were told that we would move early next morning to rejoin 1st Armoured Division, who were being hurried up from Recanati straight into the battle.

3 September

Pulled out of action at 0600 and drove eight miles down the road into harbour in 1st Armoured Division's concentration area. 46th Division were across the river Conca and almost in Coriano, shouting for us to come up and exploit the 'break-through'. It looked as if the chase had begun and we started speculating how soon we would be in the northern plains.

Letter 3 September

It has been lashing with rain while I have been writing this, and little puddles of water are forming at the bottom of the walls of my snug little tent. We are all delighted that it has come at last, and that the thunder is rumbling right round the sky and in and out of the deep valleys. The last five days have been intolerably hot – stuffy and airless, with thin mist and haze diffusing the sun and making true shade impossible to find, and a warm wind laden with dust parching the throat. I didn't know Italy in September could be so unpleasant. And if anyone ever talks to me about Musso's road-making, I shall have a very tart reply. The main roads are magnificent, but the secondary roads are shocking. Never have I seen such dust. When the tanks churn by, it is reminiscent of some of the worst Desert tracks. At sunset a dense pall of dust settles over every valley up which the winding roads run, and for 50 yards either side the grass and vines and trees are white with the fine silting powder. But now the sky is clearing, the rain has laid the dust for a few hours, and the breeze is fresh and cool.

On the night of 4-5 September we moved forwards, 'a heartbreaking march' which took 12 hours to cover less than 12 miles, and occupied a position in the Ventena valley a mile east of Marciano.

Sextons (self-propelled 25-pdrs) near Mondaino in the Ventena Valley, 4 September.

History, 4 September

The news got steadily less rosy all day: our leading tanks were meeting fierce opposition on the Coriano-San Savino ridge. The 46th Division had miscalculated and the breakthrough was still to be made. The enemy was becoming more aggressive, and even shelled the tail of our regimental column as it came down the hill to the Ventena valley.

On 5 September we engaged targets throughout the day in support of 1st Armoured Division, but our tanks made little progress. The Battery moved across the Conca in order to support a night attack by the 18th Lorried Infantry Brigade on the San Savino ridge. Bob marched with the 14th Foresters' CO and I spent the night with their adjutant. As soon as they reached the outskirts of San Savino, they met determined opposition from Germans well established in the houses and hedges and small gardens. Just before first light the Yorkshire Dragoons passed through to lead the attack.

6 September

When light came all was in incredible confusion. The two battalions were hopelessly mixed on the ground, and the enemy proceeded methodically to plaster the slopes of the ridge and the bottom of the valley with mortars and artillery. It was impossible to get observation from anywhere, and neither tanks nor gunners could do much to help. The Foresters were pulled out at last light, by which time they had had 3 officers and 13 ORs killed, 5 and 65 wounded, and 1 and 43 missing. The Yorkshire Dragoons took over all positions on San Savino ridge.

The period from 7 to 12 September was uneventful, although our guns were busy answering calls and firing small programmes for 56th Division on our right as well as on our own front. On the night of the 12th/13th Eighth Army launched a second massive attack, the task of 1st Armoured Division being to capture the whole of San Savino-Coriano ridge. At 1800, 1945, 2140 and 2306 the artillery of three divisions fired gigantic stonks on San Savino. 'The effect was terrific – a huge cloud of dust and smoke rising hundreds of feet into the air'. H-hour was 2300.

13 September

This time the attack had been most carefully prepared, and a greater contrast to the first battle could hardly be imagined. The Foresters went into action at 0530. Soon reports started coming in of first 10 prisoners, then 50, then 100, then droves of them being hauled out of dug-outs and cellars. It was a pleasure to listen to the excited signallers on the battalion net. In all the Foresters sent back 600: all were bomb-happy, dirty and thoroughly demoralised. It was just what the battalion needed after their disastrous experience a week before. In the evening our tanks started passing through. The attack had been a huge success, with the Canadians, the Ghurkas and ourselves firmly on our objectives.

On 14-15 September our part in the battle, which gradually moved forward, was small and passive. On the morning of the 16th the Regiment moved up through Coriano and into action just west of the town.

16 September

Coriano, like San Savino, was a shambles. For days afterwards German prisoners were burying their own dead, and the stench was revolting. And our casualties, particularly in the first battle, had been heavy. In a house near S Troop's new position was found a whole Italian family dead except for a small boy of about four who was badly wounded but still alive. We hadn't seen the effect of such intense shelling before. But in spite of the desolation of the villages it was a pleasant position, among the vines and olives of a shallow green valley. We acquired enough glasses to equip both the officers' and sergeants' messes of the future from a wrecked shop in Coriano. And in a lane right on S Troop's position was discovered a Volkswagen quite intact, with the driver lying dead beside it. It was soon running round the countryside labelled with the Battery's sign.

18 September

The Division was marking time while the preparations were being made for the big attack by 4th division and the Canadians on San Fortunato, some way to the north of us on our right. It was 'the last ridge before the plains'. In the evening the Regiment moved forward across the Marano and into action two miles south of Ospedaletto.

A searchlight installed itself within 100 yards of our Battery Command Post, and as soon as it was dark opened up on a nearby cloud. It was an amazing sight: dozens of searchlight beams rising from behind ridges every mile or so along the whole front, all playing on the lowest clouds they could find. The effect was exactly that of a half moon, and apart from helping the infantry to see their way, was an enormous help to drivers moving along the narrow muddy roads.

On 19-20 September a fierce battle was fought for Point 153, a hill north of the Ausa river overlooking the Marecchia valley. 2RHA was continuously engaged in support of both the infantry (especially the Yorkshire Dragoons, Foresters and Ghurkas) and the tanks (especially the Bays and 4th Hussars). 20 September was a black day: when the battle moved on, the bare slopes to the south-west of Point 153 were left littered with their knocked-out Shermans and Stuarts. Heavy rain made it necessary to cancel an attack that evening, and on the following morning it became obvious that the enemy had taken advantage of it to fall back. The Ghurkas occupied Point 153 and on 22 September David Wootton, S Troop commander, occupied an OP in a house on the nearby road.

22 September

The view from the OP was staggering. At last we were on the 'last ridge'. Immediately below lay the wide shingly bed of the Marecchia, with the castle and town of Santarcangelo on its small hill dominating the far bank. Beyond stretched the plains of the Po valley as far as the eyes could see, dark green, covered with olives and fruit trees, littered with small farmhouses shining a brilliant white through their hedges and gardens and the tree-lined lanes. On the right the coastline curved away in a broad sweep to the north-east, merging in the distance with a wide expanse of white salt marshes, divided from the sea by low sand-dunes. On the horizon stood the domes and towers of Ravenna.

The Ghurkas captured Santarcangelo after a fierce fight on 24 September and pushed on down to the banks of the next river, the Uso. I Battery was placed in close support of the 4th Hussars, who crossed the river but at once ran into opposition.

25 September

The tanks, with a company of 1KRRC, spent most of the day being stonked by mortars and guns, and achieving nothing. In fact it was country as unsuitable for an advance by tanks as could be found anywhere. By the end of the day everyone had finally lost their few remaining illusions about 'the gallop to the Po'. I wasted the day sitting with the 4th Hussars' CO far back on the hill south of the Marecchia. It was a battle in which we could do nothing but hopefully strafe likely OPs and mortar areas, and it was as well that the tanks were never hard pressed. At last light they withdrew, leaving 1KRRC to guard the Uso crossings.

From midnight on 25-26 September 2RHA ceased to be under command of 1st Armoured Division and became 5th Corps troops. On the 27th we moved back to the small hillside village of Serra di Sotto, near to Marciano and close to our gun positions between the 5th and 16th. At long last our long awaited and badly needed period of rest had materialised. The CCRA promised us a fortnight out of the line if it was humanly possible. So we settled down to training and 'peacetime' soldiering.

Letter, 9 October

It was very pleasant to have an officers mess again, and to be able to get every man sleeping in a house – for the first time since the Battery left Africa in February. The inhabitants were a bit suspicious of us when we arrived, having suffered from what must have been vilely behaved units in their area when the fighting was passing over them. But we were on our best behaviour and the Italians rapidly thawed. So much so that many of the gunners refused leave in a rest camp when it was offered them – they were much happier sitting round the firesides with their Italian families in the evening, with a glass of vino and long bilingual conversations about the Tedeschi, the duration of the war, their home towns in England and the delights of peacetime – the usual soldiers' topics. We had one most successful evening when we invited the local choir to come and sing in our canteen. A piano was procured, sandwiches and coffee were handed round – many were seen furtively wrapping up slabs of cheese and hunks of white bread in their handkerchiefs to take home – and as the evening wore on and the wine flowed more freely, we treated them to a selection of good traditional English songs, the words of which it was just as well they didn't understand. It's strange to think that thirteen months ago we were at war with these people.

Another winter of war would undoubtedly be a terrible blow to our hopes, and would increase war-weariness in the Army and other services, and amongst you at home. The average soldier is living for an armistice this year. If it doesn't come, things will not be easy all round. But when one thinks back to a month ago, and reckons up what has happened in that time, it seems that anything may happen before the winter does come. We are across the Rhine in Holland and the Russians are through the Carpathians. Perhaps being through the Gothic Line will prove equally important. And so one waits impatiently for the next 100-mile advance and the next capital city to be freed. And the faster things go, the more impatient I become they are not going faster.

While we were at Serra, officers' leave started. I decided to make a dash for Bari where I hoped to find my brother Hugh, still working in the Balkan section of SOE. I set off on 1 October in my battery commander's 8-cwt with my driver and three more men in the back.

Letter, 9 October

I hadn't been able to give Hugh any warning, not having known till the day before I left that I would definitely get away. And so, although being extremely disappointed. I wasn't surprised to hear he was in Cairo. However I met several of his colleagues and many army acquaintances of my own, though unfortunately all the Jugos that I have met were away from Bari. I heard lots of gossip from the Balkans and elsewhere, lived luxuriously and enjoyed the good wines of the country. It was grand getting right away from the battle and the Battery and all the minor inconveniences and worries. Above all it was a tonic to be once again in a live town, where life, if not perhaps completely 'normal', was at least organised and outwardly civilised. After four months on end seeing every town and village battered by bombs and shells, or even when undamaged, probably almost deserted, shops shut, streets dirty, and no public services or amenities, the senses become a bit numbed. Driving back to Bari the countryside gets less and less beautiful, and the towns and villages more and more squalid. What a difference there is between North and South Italy. I drove all night, and when morning came I could hardly believe I was in the same country. But that change for the worse was amply compensated for by seeing a train again, and in Bari a real trolley-bus in working order, and Italian newspapers on sale, electric light in all the houses, posters and advertisements on the walls, and in the shops far more than I expected – fruit, wonderful grapes, thousands of bottles in the wine shops, fountain pens, shoddy clothes, even ladies' hats, glasses and saucepans – all sorts of homely things which it was a pleasure to look upon again. I went to a cinema and a symphony concert – the Pastoral Symphony played rather indifferently by the local 'Friends of Music' orchestra, conducted by a real Italian maestro with long hair. But mostly I just sat and gossiped, ate large meals and dozed afterwards.

The change in atmosphere from the front to the base is a bit bewildering at first. Of course Bari, although hundreds of miles from the Italian front, has for a long time been very near the Jugoslav front. I saw more partisan uniforms in the streets than any other uniforms – expect perhaps British. But people at a base look at the war in a completely different perspective, which I find refreshing as a change, but also infuriating. There are too many armchair strategists about who talk the wildest nonsense in the most knowing manner about operations on the Eighth Army front. It made me suspicious of their news and theories about other fronts. On one or two occasions I found myself getting angry and laying down the law. There was one RAF squadron leader – not a pilot – whose job was to inspect accommodation, arrange local purchase of stores and deal with Italian authorities and contractors. He started declaiming very loudly about all Italians being thieves and scoundrels, no better than Arabs, never having lifted a finger to help the Allied cause. I told him he ought to visit the front line for a fortnight before making wild generalisations about Italians. He was furious, and I was a bit ashamed of myself afterwards.

We were not left long in our resting place at Serra di Sotto: on 4 October we received orders to go back into action with the 2nd Armoured Brigade in support of 46th Division in a big attack across the river Fiumicino. But we were assured by the CCRA that we would be pulled out at the first opportunity to complete our rest and training period. I got back from Bari just in time to rejoin the Battery on its move forward. By 1100 on 6 October we were in action close to Camerano on the far side of the river Uso. Our guns were sited along the rows of vines in grassy fields which soon became waterlogged swamps of mud. The big attack by 46 and 10 Indian Divisions was launched at 1915 on the evening of 7 October, but we fired a continuous 'softening' programme from 1412 onwards. Both divisions made good progress until 2300, when the rain started. A ford across the Fiumicino was opened for jeeps, but no tanks had got across by the evening of the 8th.

Drying Out, 9 October.

Sgt Blackburn's gun pit (D Sub), with L/Bdr Penman, Gnr Wadd and Bdr Redshaw. Sgt Stacey's gun (C Sub) in the background.

Letter, 10 October

I am afraid the piece in your last letter about the smiling fertile plains of Lombardy only raised in me what the novelists call a hollow mirthless laugh. You should see us now. Our vehicles are bogged down, gun pits two feet deep in water, roads just a morass of mud along which a small vehicle can drive perilously at walking pace, slithering and skidding from ditch to ditch. Our tents drip, blankets are sodden, boots full of water. It does dry amazingly quickly as soon as the sun comes out, and we had a lovely warm day yesterday after three days of almost continuous rain. But this morning the clouds have settled down again low over the hills to the west, and a grey gloomy mist hangs over the plain. This month is always the rainiest in this part of the world, but I imagine the winter is pretty unpleasant. The two consolations are that the further we go, the better the roads become and the more of them we find. Secondly, there are plenty of houses where one can at least get a proportion of the Battery under cover. But ploughing through these farmyards and soggy ploughed fields to visit waterlogged guns is a depressing way of spending a day.

History, 8/19 October

In spite of everything, all our programmes were fired and all the guns remained in action. It was a great achievement of which the gun detachments rightly felt proud. The sun returned on the 9th and on the afternoon of the 10th the 46th and 10th Indian divisions captured the villages of Longiano and Roncofreddo, and tanks poured across the Fiumicino. Visibility from our OP was incredibly good in the afternoon: every house and tree in the plain clearly visible as far as the domes of Ravenna breaking the horizon. In the afternoon of the 11th the Regiment moved forward to a position half a mile short of Cento, nicely concealed from the enemy to the north by Monte Gattona. The next three days were very busy: we fired on many brigade and divisional targets, and helped to repel several enemy infantry counter-attacks.

By 14 October we were all becoming impatient and wondering what had become of the CCRA's promise. When sitreps arrived containing the news that two out of the three Field Regiments of 46th Division were resting out of action, we were tempted to conclude that the Regiment had been landed in a stooge role, not perhaps for the first time. We had been brought up from Marciano to 'thicken up the barrage', and here we were, more than one week later, having moved forward 6000 yards, now well in front of 46th Division artillery, still in action and sending OPs out with the leading infantry. During 15/16 October we fired in support of 138th Brigade, which made slow progress north-westwards through the Apennine foothills. On the evening of the 16th we received the news that we were at last to move back to a rest area really far in the rear. We reached Senigallia, a largish town on the Adriatic coast between Pesaro and Ancona, on the morning of 19 October.

CHAPTER TWENTY-ONE: A WINTER OF RE-EQUIPMENT
October 1944 to January 1945

History, October 1944 – January 1945

The Battery area in Senigallia was right on the beach at the southern end of the town. R Troop was billeted in a fair-sized *pensione* and the remainder of the Battery lived in the row of houses strung out facing the sea. Some of these were partly occupied by civilians, most of whom were not the owners but refugees. One empty villa made a good cookhouse and Battery office. There was a NAAFI Day Leave Centre right inside our area: this provided tea and buns, an orchestra, barbers' shop, vino in the evening and a very good supply of cigarettes and other NAAFI goods. We established a good liaison with the manager and were able to borrow the building after closing hours for whist drives and dances and other social functions. The officers and sergeants both found good messes, fully furnished, in houses along the main street [Route 16] and also billets with various prominent personalites of Senigallia.

I was billetted with the local Director of Schools and his wife. He supplied me with anti-fascist pamphlets and leaflets and caricatures of Mussolini.

Letter, 25 October

We are out of the line again, resting for a while and training and generally polishing ourselves up. We all have a roof over our heads. Thank God we have, for the last two days have been frightful, a howling gale turning dry streams into torrents and penetrating even into our solid houses.

Not so long ago we fired some propaganda shells, and one of the leaflets we sent over had written on it in huge block capitals: 'Die Allierten sind in Deutschland. Wofür verteidigst du noch Italien?'[1] A most pertinent question. I'm afraid, in spite of Monty's cheering speeches, it looks as if we are in for another winter of disappointing progress, and I am starting to cultivate patience in myself and others in preparation for a trying six months ahead. At least, in spite of all our grumbles, one can humbly thank the Almighty that we were not born Germans, for this winter in Germany will be something approaching Hell.

---

1. 'The Allies are in Germany. Why do you go on defending Italy?'

248

Retrospective letter

We had only been in Senigallia for a week when we were told we were losing our tractor-drawn 25-pounders and getting self-propelled guns instead – Sextons, 25-pounders mounted on a Sherman tank chassis. These were the weapons we used to dream about in moments of wild optimism in desert days. The first self-propelled guns to be used in the British army actually appeared at Alamein in October 1942. For various reasons we were not given them then, though it was not for lack of trying on our part. However, better late than never, and the news gave us a new lease of life. Many of the men had become thoroughly stale, but the prospect of having new guns to play about with

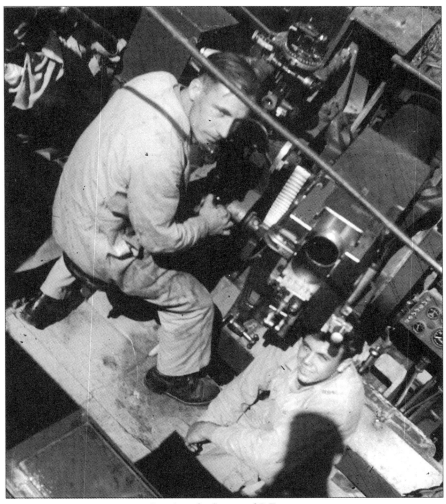

Interior of a Sexton of R Troop.

249

cheered everyone up. It meant a lot of hard work – dozens of tank drivers to be trained, new tactics and gunnery drill to be worked out and perfected. What I appreciated most was that we spent the Italian winter in billets – from that point of view we couldn't have chosen a better time for our conversion.

Our first Sexton arrived early in November, and for the next 2½ months we were training intensively. By Christmas we had our full establishment of eight guns, as well as new half-tracks to act as command post vehicles. Our equipment repairer 'converted my battery commander's jeep into a wonderful limousine – enclosed in a one-piece canvas cover, complete with talc windows and zip-fastening doors'.

History

A special allotment of vacancies at the Rome and Florence Rest Camps was made to the Regiment. By the end of January 143 men from the Battery had had a week's 'local' leave. In addition, when officers went on leave and took a truck with them, they filled up the back until it almost burst with men and kit. In this way another 93 men got to Rome, unofficially. The unofficial parties had no vacancies at the Rest Camp, but found good billets in Rome itself – strictly against the law. These private I Battery billets were also used by members passing through Rome on duty. One of their advantages was that they contained a lock-up garage.

A sensation was caused on 14 November when it was announced that a home leave scheme, Leave in Advance of Python (LIAP) was being started from Italy. Wild hopes were soon damped when it was discovered that the Battery would get only about two vacancies per month. Even so, this was a lot better than nothing.

Three extremely successful Battery dances were held. Tom Mathias and his enthusiastic staff put in weeks of hard work hiring the hall and the band, advertising throughout the town, procuring huge quantities of food and drink and sending out a host of agents to persuade the girls to come along The girls certainly turned up, though how much this was due to the prospect of 'molto mangiare' was never quite certain. They brought a formidable train of grandmas and chaperones, even a few boy friends, with them. The chaperones sat round the walls watching like hawks, and only rose to their feet to descend like vultures on the 'mangiare' as soon as it was brought in. The highlight of the first dance was the ceremonial presentation of a huge chrysanthemum to the CO by a very merry gunner.

We had a certain amount of trouble with an organisation calling itself Nembo. This posted notices in the town threatening severe punishment for any local girls who dared to associate with British soldiers, or even to accept food or cigarettes from them. Nembo had been active for some time in the coastal towns, and several girls had had their heads shaved after attending British dances. There was only one case of this in Senigallia during our stay, but the mere threat spead alarm and terror among the female population and made them very reluctant to go out after dark. The name Nembo was taken from a well-known formation of Italian parachutists, which was actually fighting in the mountains as part of the Folgore Division.[1] But it was not the parachutists who caused the trouble in Senigallia. We suspected the crews of the Italian Navy motor torpedo boats, who lived in the harbour, though we never got proof. Tom Mathias arranged an interview through an intermediary with Nembo himself, and we had visions of a meeting with sinister masked men in some murky garret. The interview never came off, but the excitement blew over. Tom, universally known as 'Capitano Tom', rapidly became a power behind the scenes in the town: and his tact and energy, and the exemplary behaviour of the whole Battery, averted any incidents. Even so, we took no risks: at the second dance there were more men picketing the doors and stairs and neighbouring streets than there were men dancing.

At the end of November I had a week's leave in Rome.
Diary, 26 November
Got away at 1100. A light-hearted party – Jackson driving, Jones, Beadle, Barnes and Holland in the back, with the Director of Schools, muffled up to the eyes and looking rather apologetic as always: he had got an AMGOT pass to Naples, for family reasons. Very bad traffic to Jesi and we just crawled. The aerodrome an incredible sight, jammed tight with Spitfires, Baltimores, a dozen types of plane hardly able to move for the crush. Brewed up just beyond Fabriano. Mine host tried to buy us some eggs from a small cottage but the woman said very firmly she had no hens: the schoolmaster's comment was, 'Ils sont vilaines, très vilaines. C'est un peuple inférieure, je le dis à mes élèves tous les jours, c'est triste, mais c'est vrai'. What hope for Italy when the educated class talks like that! On over the backbone of the Apennines, then down Route 3. The autumn tints of the trees lovely, deep russet-brown. Lights twinkling from Narni, and as we pounded down the familiar road to the Tiber bridge it got pitch black. Hard to recognise the diversions that so plagued us in June. Delayed for many miles by long columns of Italian vehicles coming up the road past us, all brand-new British equipment, headlights blazing. At last reached the outskirts of Rome, crossed the Tiber, drove on and on down a main street in what I thought was the right direction until I found we were at the Victor Emmanuel monument. So up to the main station where we dumped mine host to catch his train to Naples to-morrow. I got an authority from the Town Major and was in my room at the Albergo Eden by 2100. Jones and Jackson & Co. disappeared with the truck to instal themselves at I Battery's private billet.

---

1. On our side. After surrendering to the Allies in September 1943, the Italian government declared war on Germany on 13 October. Political objections to the reconstitution of a fighting Italian army were overcome by the growing shortage of Allied manpower in Italy, and in September 1944 six Combat Groups were formed, wearing British uniforms and armed with British equipment. The Folgore was one of them.

Letter, 6 December

This week I must give you my impressions of Rome in 1944. I spent most of last week there, and only got back here early on Saturday morning to plunge once again into the old routine of training. It's hard to believe that the great city is only a day's journey distant by road: we live in a completely different world here. I stuck pretty well to the programme which I had forecast – sightseeing in the mornings at a gentle enjoyable pace, huge meals, a little shopping – but I was very lazy – and three visits to the opera. The intervals between these spurts of energy were mostly spent at my hotel lying back in a comfortable armchair, listening to a trio playing Mozart or Carmen or Lilli Marlene, chatting with the many old acquaintances I met, and just quietly enjoying the luxury of carpets, bright lights, waiters to bring me a drink, hot baths and all the other delights of civilisation.

Rome at first sight has been completely untouched by the war. There is not a sign of bomb damage, not a house has been scratched. The streets are full of shoppers and idle promenaders, shop windows are well-filled, there are rows of bottles behind every bar. Well-dressed women discuss the latest fashions in the restaurants, crowds pour in and out of packed cinemas. But it takes little more than a casual glance, even in the centre of the city, to realise that life is far fom normal. And I fancy in the outskirts and in the working-class districts – there are 200,000 unemployed in Rome alone – the picture is quite different. The streets are plastered with notices announcing the rationing of electricity to 50% of last year's consumption. Not many trams run, and those that do function are barely visible for the swarms of passengers hanging on to the doors and windows and bumpers outside. There are no taxis, and almost every car not in khaki paint is marked 'For use of Allied Control Commission'. Curfew is at midnight, far later than in any other Italian town I've yet been in, but after dark the streets soon become deserted and the Romans retire indoors and to their beds. Prices in the shops are quite fantastic. Every shop window displays 'the best real old genuine silver' or Venetian glass or jewellery or trinkets, and I'm told that some of it really is genuine. But not being an expert I wouldn't dare to risk the thousands of lire involved. Of useful things there is hardly a sign in any shop: six months of Allied occupation has cleaned out anything that the Germans left. Even so, they were the best shops I've seen since Cairo – far better than anything in Algiers. It made me realise once again how little the Italians had put their hearts into the war, if right up to 1943 they were still gaily producing luxury goods which disappeared in England soon after Dunkirk.

I was a bit unlucky with the weather, and it poured with rain for my first two days. In rain Rome looks drab and dreary. But in spite of the rain I walked a lot, and indeed took more exercise in five days than I have taken in a month here. I stayed at the Albergo Eden, now a British Officers' Leave Hotel, on the slopes of Monte Pincio, and used to walk down into the city every morning, usually by the Scala di Spagna, and wander gently, often rather aimlessly, with Baedeker in my pocket to consult, if I really got lost. One afternoon I walked almost the whole length of the city from north to south along the Tiber. It was full of muddy swirling waters after the heavy rains in the Apennines. But it cannot begin to compare with the Seine at Paris. I wish I could get there on leave.

My first morning I went down to the Vatican,[1] and while dithering as to whether to go inside St. Peters or make straight for the Museum, I noticed a huge door open just to the right of the Church, a lot of soldiers trooping inside, and a lovely glimpse of a long lofty gallery stretching out of sight inside. So the two of us – I was with one of my troop commanders [David Wootton] – went inside out of idle curiosity, up a magnificent marble staircase and through a massive door into a richly gilded gallery, where two gorgeously dressed flunkies handed us – a photograph of the Pope. Then of course it was too late to turn back, even if we had wanted to, and so we found ourselves at a Papal Audience. We stood for 50 minutes in a seething mass of uniformed humanity, a high proportion of it merely rubber-necking like ourselves. Most of the United Nations were represented – Canada, New Zealand, USA, Brazil, France, even Seychelles and a few black South Africans – but the Poles predominated. It was a magnificent room, 200 feet long I should think, high ornate ceiling, one side all windows, and the papal throne on a dais at one end. Up the centre of the room had been set a double railing, to form a gangway, up which the Pope was carried in, borne aloft in a huge chair. As he passed slowly up the room, he blessed the rosaries and crucifixes and photographs of himself that were held up to him: an extraordinary scene, and I couldn't help being reminded of some of the newsreels I have seen of film stars being mobbed in Hollywood by swooning movie-fans. I thought I was going to be crushed alive by the mass of people all around as they pushed and shoved and elbowed to get nearer the rails. In the middle of the excitement I happened to catch sight of a huge black American standing a little detached, placidly chewing gum and watching the scene as if he had seen it every day of his life. The procession of Chamberlains and Officials of the Court, all dressed in gold-braid uniforms, silk breeches and plumed helmets, grouped itself round the throne, between Swiss guards standing rigid and motionless, and the Pope addressed the gathering, in French and English, very quietly and impressively: unfortunately the acoustics were so bad that I caught only one word in three. Then he pronounced the blessing, and the audience was over – the soldiers of many nations flooded out to the clippety-clop of hobnailed army boots.

I spent a whole morning in the Vatican museum, and paid three visits to the exhibition in the Palazzo Venezia, organised by the Army Welfare Services. It was an amazing sensation to stand in Musso's room, with the balconies overlooking the Piazza, and look at Titians and Tintorettos and Bellinis. There can rarely have been such a select exhibition – about 70 pictures, all of them outstanding masterpieces, drawn from museums all over Italy, and all beautifully hung and lighted. I spent a small fortune afterwards on photos and reproductions, and have them in my bedroom.

1. There was a wooden barrier across St. Peter's square with notices – 'Neutral territory, Vatican City: no arms or military vehicles allowed'. But one just walked in.

10 December

I told you of some of my wanderings in Rome, my morning with the Raphaels and my audience with the Pope. but I didn't mention the highlights of my leave, my three visits to the Opera. I saw Aida, Madame Butterfly, and a memorable evening of ballet – La Bottega Fantastica, Stravinsky's Petruchka, and Bolero. I don't know which I enjoyed most. I just sat back and drank in the music and the colour and the masterly skill of the production. I only wish I could have stayed another three weeks and gone to the opera every night.

After letting myself go on the subject of opera, it seems wrong to come down to the mundane subject of food. But how important a place food assumes in a five days' leave. In Italy today the British officer or soldier has two choices when deciding where to eat: either he obeys orders and dines at a club or restaurant controlled by the Army, in which case he eats spam (if he's unlucky) or roast beef (if he's lucky) with dehydrated vegetables followed by tinned fruit; or he disobeys orders – some would say risks court martial – and eats on the Black Market – in which case he can eat what he has dreamed of since his last leave in Cairo – lobster, green salad, roast duck, chocolate ices, anything he chooses to order. By adopting the first method he dines for 2/6, by the second dinner costs anything between £2 and £3. And which do you think I did? Well, a bit of both. I had three or four memorable meals. But quite apart from the fact that it is strictly against orders, I have scruples about eating on the Black Market. It made my blood boil in some of these restaurants to see young Italian men and women well-groomed and well-nourished, eating the most luxurious dishes when within a few hundred yards of them ragged children were subsisting on roast chestnuts and a meagre bread ration, supplemented recently by a few oranges. Those sleek young men had not lifted a finger to help their country, neither to fight the English nor the Germans. From one or two people who know Rome I heard stories that made me sick. Roman society with its beautiful manners, its snobism and contempt for the lower classes – especially for the 'Africans' of Southern Italy – its perfect mastery of the English language and its shameless trimming, seems to be pretty despicable. At times I felt furiously that Rome had escaped far too lightly – that it might have done these people some good to have had a few flying-bombs and a couple of artillery barrages and a little street-fighting. But now no doubt they are well in with AMGOT, and know just how to be charming to young Guards or Cavalry officers down on leave from the front, and how to tell them all about the Communist menace in Italy and reproach them gently for all those good British tanks and machine-guns sent to Russia and to that bandit Tito. I don't know who will rule Italy after the war ends, and I see little future for the impoverished demoralised divided country. But I do pray that whoever does come to power will liquidate those parasites who grew fat under Fascism and now look to us to protect their ill-gotten gains from the wrath of their own countrymen.

There is a tirade for you!

My party left Rome at 2300 on 1 December, 'mine host in the back, brilliant moon but very cold. I drove as far as Foligno, dozed on and off from then on.

Reached Senigallia at 0640 half frozen – a bleak windy morning'.
Letter, 31 December

Your Christmas greetings reached me in good time, and I hope mine did the same. We are just about recovering from our celebrations – you've no idea what a strain an Army Christmas is. There are so many people to celebrate with – first the sergeants' mess, then the junior NCO's, then the gunners; then the other two Batteries and Regimental headquarters; then the neighbouring units – plenty of them in this part of the world. And tonight there is every sign that I shall get involved in yet another celebration – there are far too many Scotsmen in this Battery to be safe on New Year's Eve.

Letter, 11 January 1945, to my sister who was about to depart from London to the British Embassy in Moscow.

I gather that you have been having desperately cold weather. It has been pretty grim here too. Fortunately where we live the snow never lies for more than a few hours, though after 20 minutes drive up into the hills one notices the difference in temperature. Life is not exciting, but we have very little to complain of. There is just one thing I do pine for – a log and coal fire in an open grate, with the flames leaping up the chimney. All these Italian houses were centrally heated in peacetime, and the central heating was operated by electricity. When the Germans retreat they blow up the power stations: so now, no electricity, and no central heating. Instead we have to sit round a miserable oil stove, the fumes of which fill the room, make the eyes smart (mine are running with tears now) and drive one to bed half an hour after dinner. But as I've said before in my letters, when I feel tempted to groan and indulge in self-pity, I just imagine myself in action in a vineyard somewhere just north of Faenza, in a couple of inches of snow, sleeping in a tent and firing at odd hours throughout the day and night. And I just count my blessings.

We have just had three Polish officers attached to us for a week, to pick up a few hints as to how they do things in the Royal Horse Artillery. One came from Poznan, the other two from Lwow. It was a whole-time job keeping them off politics, but one evening they cornered me and we discussed the whole Russo-Polish question, the Curzon Line, the Lublin Government, the future of East Prussia and all the rest of it.[1] I hate arguing with Poles for I feel so desperately sorry for them. One evening while they were in the mess the mail arrived, and we all made a wild swoop at the table, as we always do, to grab our letters and open them and read them. I was just tearing mine open when I happened to look up, and saw the expression on one of these Pole's face. He hadn't had a letter for over four years. His wife and children may still be in Lwow, they may be dead or in

1. Poland's future frontiers had been under discussion with the Soviet Government for many months. The Curzon Line had been proposed as the Polish-Russian boundary by the 1919 Paris Peace Conference, but the Poles rejected it and forcibly seized large areas inhabited mainly by Ukrainians (including the Galician city of Lwow) and White Russians. These territories were now being claimed by the Soviet Government. The Lublin Government was the puppet communist government set up in July 1944 on Polish territory conquered by the Red Army.

Siberia for all he knows. How can one argue with a man like that about the Curzon Line and the proportions of Poles and Ukrainians and White Russians in Galicia? How simple it would be if there were only pitch black and pure white in this distracted world, if all Poles were blackguards and every Russian an angel. Or vice versa.

I wonder how the world will look from Moscow. I think I shall have to come and spend my demobilisaton leave with you.

History

After Christmas we were given a tiresome 'operational role'. There had been several cases of small enemy sabotage parties landing on the coast from submarines or surface craft. So every unit along the coast had to provide a mobile force ready to go out at extremely short notice. Fortunately ours was never called out. But as the Battery lived right on the beach, it was given one more job – that of coast-watching during the hours of darkness. On the night of 15 January our mobile force had to stand to. Next morning there was a thick sea fog, and not until it cleared were we allowed to stand down. We were told later that an unidentified craft had been detected close inshore.

Letter, 19 January

We continue to live our comfortable life of routine training. The weather is extremely variable. Lately we have been driving round the countryside on schemes and exercises. One day I had to spend six hours observing our guns firing, on an exposed hilltop with snow falling almost continuously. As a result my feet are still suffering from chilblains. But days in the open air under these conditions are almost a pleasure when one returns to a hot meal in a warm house, and a cosy bed to retire to afterwards.

I find myself mentally in a state of almost suspended animation. I think the winter, with its stalemates, is having a numbing, chilling effect on me. There has been a lot of boredom, even of depression, out here, and it's true that Italy is a bit of a backwater. But lately we have been reminded of the size of the job we are doing: we are keeping 27 German divisions uncomfortably busy, and there are only 70 on the whole of the Western Front. But I do wish the spring would hurry.

While at Senigallia we received confirmation of reports which had been circulating as early as September that 1st Armoured Division was to be broken up. The official reason was that the flow of reinforcements from Britain had practically dried up, and it had become necessary to dissolve some formations to reinforce the others. We ourselves became 5th Corps Troops. 'We received the news with mixed feelings: if it meant that we would be used for all the stooge jobs, the future looked rather grim' (History, 23 September). But that is exactly what happened. From October 1944 onwards we were without any brigade or divisional 'home', and were shifted from one division to another as the need arose. The resulting variety of experience compensated only in part for the loss of any opportunity to establish close relations, as during the summer of 1944, with the tanks or infantry whom we were supporting.

On 25 January we received a warning order that we would be moving back into action very shortly to join our old friends, the New Zealanders, under command of the 5th Corps astride Route 9 beyond Faenza. We were told to expect a very dull war.

Diary, 29 January

At 1400 I talked to the whole Battery, chiefly on our immediate future and what we can expect to do for the next month, but also trying to fit our part of the war effort into the general European picture. The news of our move has come as a great disappointment to some of the Battery, who had counted on never having to fire another shot in anger, the Russians being now within 60 miles of Berlin. It has been an amazing achievement, this winter offensive of theirs.

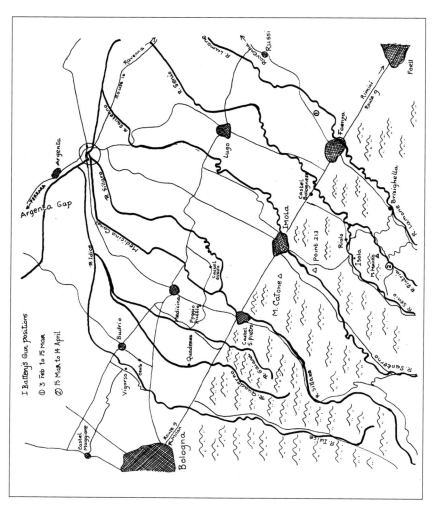

Area of operations, 3 February/22 April.

CHAPTER TWENTY-TWO: HOLDING THE SENIO LINE
January – April 1945

The Regiment started to move north from Senigallia on 31 January, and by 3 February was operational in an area out in the plain, bounded to the north by the Faenza-Russi road and to the south by the river Lamone. The front had been stationary since the New Year on a line running north-eastwards from the Apennine foothills along the river Senio. I Battery was affiliated to 19th New Zealand Armoured Regiment. Our only commitment was to keep an OP at the HQ of the forward squadron. I spent many days at Brigade HQ. Our main worry for the first month was mud, for the thaw started a few days after our arrival and much rain fell during our first week.

Letter, 13 February

Here we are back in action and already beginning to forget that we have had three months out of the line. It is a strange kind of war just now. We are doing much the same as what we did a year ago at Cassino – just sitting still and marking time and wondering how to fill in the rapidly lengthening days. It is far quieter and more peaceful than it ever was at Cassino. For hours on end not a gun fires for miles around, and back with the guns it is often hard to realise that there is a war on. Our chief preoccupation of course is the mud. The least amount of traffic wears down the narrow roads and tracks of the plain into deep ruts and potholes, and we spend much our our time towing and winching the rations and water and ammunition trucks out of the mire. Fortunately we have had a generous issue of gum boots. Apart from the boredom of being in action and confined to a small area without the satisfaction of being able to make a more active and useful contribution to winning the war, life is none too bad. We are more comfortable than I ever dreamed was possible 'in the line'. There are plenty of houses round here, and very few of them seriously damaged. The local Italians are the friendliest we've met yet, and their effusiveness is at times almost embarrassing. Unlike the district where we spent the last three months, their supplies of 'vino' seem to be unlimited. I have a huge flagon of 'bianco' put beside my bed every day. There is also plenty of firewood to be found, and most of the Battery has a roaring log fire in the kitchen chimney to sit round in the evenings. And everyone lives and sleeps in the dry except those that are actually manning the guns. In fact it could be worse.

I am writing this at a certain Brigade HQ [6th New Zealand] where I have got a temporary job as senior artillery liaison officer. It is desperately dull. Like all HQs, they live in great luxury and run an excellent and lively mess. The atmosphere is rather like that in New College Hall at dinner – the same lighthearted nonsensical chatter about the day's doings (or lack of doings), the war and the future of the world. All this within two miles or less of the Germans. And yet of course I'm deliberately giving you the wrong impression. It is one hundred to one against anything serious happening: but it is the constant struggle against becoming careless or lulled by daily routine, or assuming that 'nothing will happen tonight, I needn't bother just this once' – the constant need to take precautions and plans and counter-plans seriously in spite of all the temptations to assume the war is phoney – that is what makes life so boring and depressing. Of course no one thinks that we shall be allowed to stagnate like this indefinitely. We follow the Black Sea conference and Churchill's talk of keeping every front, in the east and west and south, 'in constant flame', with the greatest interest. I wonder what those three wise men have been hatching for us this time?[1]

I find myself in an unsettled mood. It's hard to believe that the great events which for so long we have assumed hopefully but blindly would take place, are really happening, and that the end of the war is only at the most a few months away. It's impossible to look ahead of course. If we were frantically busy like we were for most of last summer, the uncertainty and suspense would worry us less. As it is, we live from BBC news to BBC news, and groan when the Russians announce an advance of only 10 or 15 miles. Why can't they get a move on?!

History

Welfare facilities in Eighth Army area throughout the winter were absolutely first class. Forlì was the great metropolis, full of canteens and cinemas and libraries, and above all the magnificent Dorchester Club, which provided meals and music and barbers and every conceivable amenity. We sent parties regularly into Forlì for the day. Towards the end of February the weather improved rapidly. About the 10th we saw the hills beyond Faenza for the first time. The mud dried and the sun turned the hedges green and brought the young crops above the soil. Football matches were played alongside the guns. On the whole the Battery was pretty contented.

Retrospective letter

As I told you at the time, it was a ridiculous war, completely static. We were supporting the New Zealand Division who were dug in along the banks of the Senio. The Germans held the western 'stop bank' or flood bank, and also had outposts and machine-guns dug into the eastern bank. The Kiwis are always aggressive, and they used to make life hell for the Germans on the near bank,

1. The Yalta Conference between Churchill, Roosevelt and Stalin took place between 3 and 11 February.

shooting at them with every weapon they could lay their hands upon – even tanks and flame-throwers. Occasionally they would carry out a local attack and occupy one of the German positions. The enemy fought back hard, and these small actions were always fierce affairs, even though our casualties were fortunately small. But all this was only skirmishing, for the state of the ground made a large-scale attack out of the question – we could have got across the Senio any time we liked, but we would only have got bogged down on the Santerno a few thousand yards beyond

It was a very dull month for us gunners. Ammunition was strictly rationed to five shells per gun per day. Often we didn't fire for several days on end. It was just a question of sitting around trying not to get bored. We had of course been in rather the same position a year before at Cassino, but there at least the scenery was beautiful, and our observation post commanded one of the loveliest views in Italy. And even if we hardly ever saw any Germans, at least we could shoot off our rounds at positions where we knew the enemy was hiding. But the country around Faenza is dead flat. There was no observation post to go to – all the observation was done from the air, and even the artillery pilots saw very little. The only relief from boredom was an occasional 'Chinese Attack' by the Kiwis. This consisted in firing off every weapon available for about 15 minutes and making the maximum noise, in the hope of persuading the enemy that we were attacking in force, and so making him waste *his* ammunition and disclose *his* defensive plans. It was all good fun, and made a glorious firework display. The most successful were 'Operation Farouk', and 'Operation Farida' [on 2 March], carried out in honour of Egypt's heroic declaration of war!

My chief grouse at that time was that there was nowhere to walk to. The banks of the Lamone river made the only possible walk, and they were dull enough. I used to look longingly towards the hazy mountains. But I managed to keep myself amused with books, and an occasional trip to Ravenna, or down to the excellent club or cinema at Forlì. The rumours and speculations about the coming offensive were fantastic – there were hints that it would be the Eighth Army's biggest battle, and that vast quantities of ammunition and material were being stored up. This was true enough, but we all got most impatient and longed for the inactivity to end.

Letter, 9 March

Our placid rather unreal existence continues, with our thoughts far more occupied with events on the Rhine or in the Polish Corridor (or even in Mandalay)[1] than with our own little war a few thousand yards away. Since last I wrote the weather has been glorious. Today I heard and watched my first lark. And the chief noise coming through my window just now is the fierce impatient "Ah-ah-aah" of the peasants at their ploughing, as they urge on their teams of oxen down the long strips of field between their vines.

1. On the Burmese front against the Japanese.

A fortnight ago I managed to slip over to Ravenna for most of a day. I'm afraid you would be greatly shocked by its present condition. I had expected so much, but came back disappointed. It wasn't so much that it had been damaged by war – I've seen towns ten times more battered, although a big area around the canal and railway station has been reduced to chaos. But what worried me was to see what should be a sleepy, mellow town filled with dusty military traffic, workshops and bulldozers, sentries and NAAFI canteens and all the bustle of a base a few miles behind the front line. I suppose Oxford would be the same if the front lines were 10 miles up Banbury Road. I paid my homage before the tomb of Theodoric, but couldn't get in. San Apollinare Nuovo had been slightly damaged by bombing but the glorious mosaics were untouched. San Vitale had six inches of water over its whole floor: I walked gingerly down a row of narrow planks into the middle of the church and tried to imagine what it would have been like. No electric light, and the pumping machinery out of action. The best mosaics were all covered – very wise of course but very annoying.

History

On March 7th the 5th Polish Kresova Division took over the Faenza sector and the New Zealanders pulled out for a month's intensive training. We had hoped, very very faintly, that we might pull out and train with them for the forthcoming battle. But we were told firmly that we would remain where we were under Polish command and that our more remote future was completely uncertain. A week later we heard that we were to relieve 85th Mountain Regiment RA in support of the Italian Friuli Combat Group,[1] part of 10 Corps, in the hilly sector immediately on the Poles' left. By 2200 on 15 March I Battery was in action in the valley of the Sintria, a tributary of the Senio, after a westward march of about fifteen miles.

Retrospective letter

I'm afraid the comments of our gunners, on being told that they were going to support Italians, were quite unprintable. And I can't say that I felt enthusiastic. But it turned out to be an interesting experience, and we had many amusing moments. Our guns were in a quiet narrow valley dominated by the black rocky peak of Monte Mauro, 1500 feet high. It was impossible to get into our valley by day without driving for two miles over a hill [from Brisighella] in full view of the enemy. So our contacts with the outside world were limited to the hours of darkness. This was inconvenient, but had the advantage that the number of awkward visitors (such as Colonels and Generals) was cut down to a reasonable figure and we were left alone to our own devices. A greater contrast to the monotonous plain on the other side of Faenza could scarcely be imagined. Our observation post could not be reached by truck, so we had our own mule team provided for us, complete with Cypriot muleteers. They kept our OP parties supplied with food and water, wireless batteries, and all the other oddments

1. See p. 251, note.

required, doing the trip of three miles over rough tracks about four times a week. All supplies for the Italian infantry were also mule-borne along the whole sector. I used to climb the 1000 feet up to Monte Mauro at least twice a week, groaning and pouring with sweat in the spring sunshine. I very soon felt a different man, fit and cheerful. And the view from the top was glorious, right over the Senio valley and the wooded foothills, and out into the interminable plain beyond.

Letter, 19 March

Once again I must wish you [my mother] many happy returns of the day from afar. But next year I really *will* be able to deliver my birthday greetings in person, and let us hope that we will be able to celebrate the next 25th March, and all the many after the next, in a saner and happier world.

The weather here is unbelievable. Day after day brings nothing but hot sun, blue sky and cool mountain breezes. Our position here is one of the most delightful I have ever been in. I live on the first floor of a small farm perched on a rocky outcrop 300 feet above the valley floor. As I write this, I look across to four of my guns squatting ugly and resolute-looking among the pines and fruit trees. Along the bottom of the valley runs a white dusty road, crossing and recrossing the stream by a series of the ubiquitous Bailey bridges. There is a little cloud of dust moving along it now, which is my jeep going out on some odd errand. If it weren't for the uniforms, an occasional khaki truck and a very occasional bang, it would seem impossible that there should be live, aggressive, fanatical Germans only a few thousand yards the other side of that strange towering pinnacle of rock [Monte Mauro]. I was on top of it the other day, looking down on the houses and hills held by the enemy. There was not a sign of life except a flight of nine rock pigeons wheeling and swerving and chasing each other round the cliffs, and a small brown hawk hovering above an untidy copse. Wherever there is a gap in the rocks, there is a patch of spring flowers. It is a weird sensation to sit there in a cranny, panting a bit after the stiff climb, drinking in the glorious view, so peaceful and so lifeless: and yet in those quiet deserted houses sits the enemy, always watching. And then one remembers the war suddenly, takes one's eyes off the flowers and the birds and the cloud shadows on the distant hills, picks up one's binoculars and concentrates once again on that big house where a recent deserter said a company HQ was located – watching for a movement, for a target to engage, for a German to kill. And what a way to end a birthday letter – I apologise!

History

The Friuli Group consisted of two infantry regiments, the 87th and 88th, and the 35th Artillery Regiment. The infantry occupied a series of platoon and section posts, mostly in the scattered farmhouses, but a few entrenched along the knife-edged ridges, with dugouts tunnelled into the hillsides behind them. The Italians, like the New Zealanders in the plain, were not in complete control of all the ground up to the river Senio. By night German patrols were active and raids on our outposts were frequently made in strength.

I Battery was made responsible for supporting the left hand battalion, the 87th, which at night sent out patrols of different sizes and with different missions. The enemy's approach was usually up one of the deep ravines, which allowed him to get to within a few hundred yards of our post without being observed. Most nights passed without incident, but a few were lively enough: once the shooting started the whole front tended to burst into wild, frenzied activity.

I spent the first three days as LO at 87 Battalion HQ and then was relieved by Bob Banks. There was rarely anything to do except sit on the end of a telephone and wait for something to happen. The battery commander of the 4th Group of 35th Artillery Regiment, Major Ferrante, also lived at Battalion HQ and spoke French, which made liaison easier. He was a quiet, business-like little man who seemed to have the situation completely under control, and he obviously knew his gunnery backwards.

It was highly ironic that after two years of talk and discussion about 'mountain OPs', our first experience should come in March 1945. We had first begun to think about the problem near Sfax in April 1943, when we were approaching the Tunisian mountains. During the summer of 1944 we had taken part in many infantry night attacks which involved OP parties walking with wireless sets. But it was not until after we had been equipped with Sextons and trained for a fast moving tank battle on the plains of Northern Italy that we found ourselves in mountainous, roadless country, manning an OP of which no vehicle could get within two miles.

Our Cypriot muleteers were a cheery hard-working crew, who spent their evenings singing in their room at the back of the Command Post. One of their favourite songs was the Internationale – it sounds beautiful when sung in harmony in Greek. Our Command Post used to resound to it nightly, a few of our gunners joining in surreptitiously with the English words, wondering whether the Battery Commander would notice. Several of the Cypriots wore brilliant red scarves round their necks.

The main worry of the Italians was harassing fire from enemy mortars, which were extremely difficult to locate in the innumerable small valleys. Our shooting had to be a matter of guesswork. The Air OP appeared most days, but only once saw a good target.

It was interesting to see the Italian Army at first hand. All the Italians we met went out of their way to be helpful and charming to us. One of Ferrante's OP officers spoke good English and was much interested in the Sextons. He had commanded one of the only two Italian self-propelled troops in the Desert and had fought round Knightsbridge. Neither he nor any other Italian officers showed the least embarrassment in talking of their African exploits.

We heard a lot of gossip and scandal about the Italian Army from the officers of 50th British Liaison Unit [BLU], who had been training the Friuli Group for months before it came into the line. They were all agreed that the rank and file were brave fighters, who had an intense hatred of the Germans and a great desire to finish off the war and liberate the rest of their country. On the other hand, in spite of much training, they could not be classed as good soldiers. For this the BLU blamed the officers who, with a few exceptions, were completely incompetent. The junior officers were the worst.

Our small experience certainly confirmed this judgment. The Italians were more reluctant to dig in and required even more goading than the average British soldier. They walked about happily on skylines in view of the enemy, and their sentries' methods of challenging on the Sintria Bailey Bridges were a joke. To the casual eye they appeared slovenly, badly disciplined and incompetent soldiers. But this would be a superficial judgement. They were at the same time eager to learn and pathetically anxious to do the right thing and win a little bit of praise. As far as we were concerned, apart from their primitive ideas on sanitation, their chief weakness was their too fertile imaginations. One day a sensation was caused by the Italian OP officer on Monte della Volpe, who reported he could see at least 50 Germans crossing the river at Isola. This brought an indignant and sarcastic denial from David Wootton, who was 800 yards from the place where they were alleged to be crosssing, and could have seen a cat move. And indeed there was nothing there.

Meanwhile the front was becoming more active and the first moves were being made in preparation for the big attack which everyone knew was not far away. General Scattini, the Group Commander, gathered all his officers together on 21 March and gave an inspiring pep talk, which I found myself attending, half by mistake. He gave an outline of Operation Ischia, which would take place in a few days' time, the object of which was to occupy and maintain control of the whole bank of the Senio. This was followed by a terrific denunciation of bad discipline and badly dressed soldiers and of inaccurate sitreps – he wanted 'la verità, la verità, la verità', with a bigger bang on the table each time – it was lies that had brought Italy to her present state of misery. It was an impressive and dramatic speech, but according to the BLU, there had been many such before, and they had left little impression on their audiences.

Between 21 and 24 March a reshuffle of the Group took place. I Battery was placed in support of the 88 Regiment and I was attached to its HQ. I stayed there for Operation Ischia which took place on the night of 24/25 March, and afterwards Bob and our subalterns spent two or three days on the job until we were relieved of the commitment on 3 April. The Operation went smoothly for 88 Regiment and hardly a round was fired – our guns had nothing to do.

The LOs at 88 Regiment HQ found their two days' tour of duty amusing. They fed in the Brigade mess and found that at least two hours' siesta in the afternoon were required to recover from the three course lunches. These invariably included an enormous dish of rice or spaghetti which was a meal in itself. The Colonel Commanding was an extraordinary man, gross and repulsive to look at, with a phenomenal capacity for spaghetti. But he worked hard and was always to be seen touring the FDLs in his British steel helmet. The BLU's opinion of him was that he was not a brilliant commander, but that his fierce hatred of the Germans made up for all his deficiences. For a Brigade HQ their methods of working seemed a bit chaotic: news of a small enemy patrol threw everything into turmoil. On one occasion the Colonel himself arrived breathlessly in my room, having bounded up the flight of stairs, shouted "POPPEA, POPPEA" [one of our defensive fire targets], and disappeared as dramatically as he had come. A few minutes later he reappeared, waved his arms, shouted "POPPEA subito, subito" and again rushed away. We fired Scale 1 from the Battery on POPPEA and eveyone seemed satisfied.

Letter, 30 March, Good Friday, written after hearing that on the Western Front the Allies had crossed the Rhine.

I've never felt so excited, or awaited the 9 o'clock news with such impatience – certainly not since Munich Days. The next two or three days will show whether the Germans are going to be able to form one more line [of defence]. If they fail, the whole of Northern Germany should surely be overrun within the next fortnight. Then we will find out how much truth there is in these stories of the mountain fastness with its underground caverns and tons of supplies of food and ammunition. I agree with you in feeling extremely sceptical. It's rather important as far as we are concerned, for it will obviously be the 5th and 8th Armies' job to attack the fastness fron the south – the most difficult direction, I suppose. I'm not surprised that you are puzzled about our little war out here. We often feel puzzled ourselves. It will be interesting to see how much fight this [German] army will put up when the time comes. Up to a few weeks ago prisoners were still being captured who were convinced Germany would win – because the Führer had said so – just that reason, no other, but enough for their blind faith. I begin to doubt if these true Nazis will ever see sense. They will probably be convinced to their dying day that black is white, and that Hitler has won the war. We are soon going to get the answers to many questions that have been worrying us for the last five years or more. In spite of all the horror, it is a thrilling time to be alive – and what opportunities lie ahead.

Meanwhile our surroundings grow more beautiful every day. The blossom has been a glorious sight, but it is now almost gone, and the orchards and copses and straggly trees along the river are becoming rapidly, almost visibly, greener. We had a short Good Friday service this afternoon in the open air between two haystacks on the grassy slopes of the hillside above our white farm. Our padre is in many ways an estimable man, but I find his services and sermons trying. So immediately afterwards I went off by myself, found a warm sheltered hollow in a small oak coppice, and spent the whole afternoon reading the Good Friday story, in all four gospels. It was a perfect way of spending the afternoon, and no sound of war disturbed me.

On 5 April I set off for a week's leave in Florence. I knew before I left that the Eighth Army was due to attack in the very near future, but our part in the initial battle was expected to be small, so the Colonel told me to finish my leave before returning. The battle in fact started on 9 April, and I got back to the Battery only on the 12th. Next day the driver of the American Field Service ambulance, which was attached to us, burst into my office, with tears in his eyes, to announce that Roosevelt was dead.

Postcard of S. Gimignano

I spent a most enjoyable day here during my week's leave in Florence. The town was sleepy and deserted when we drove in – everyone enjoying their siesta. We were the first tourists they had seen for some weeks, and after we had done our round of the churches, seen the Pinturicchio in the Municipio and climbed to the top of the Rocca for the view, we went into the cafe in the main piazza , and over a series of glasses of bianco were told of the arrogance and misbehaviour of the tedeschi, the memorable day of liberation when the French Moroccan Mountain Division marched in, and how the purge of the Fascists was getting along. I was really sorry to get back to the bustle and uniforms and leave-town atmosphere of Florence.

CHAPTER TWENTY THREE: THE FINAL BATTLES
April – May 1945

The main battle was fought in the plains to our north, by the 5th British and 2nd Polish Corps. 10 corps had a very minor initial role: to make a feint attack on the night of 9 April and establish a bridgehead over the Senio. The enemy opposition was expected to be stiff: we had 278 Division in front of us, with 4 Parachute Regiment under its command. Immediately to its west came an Italian Fascist Republican battalion, Barbarigo.[1] 'Before the battle we wondered what would happen when Friuli met Barbarigo: but as it turned out, we were never told if they did meet or not.'

The Battery History records that at 1400 on 9 April 'our planes appeared and from then till dark there was not a moment of peace. After an hour or so, the ease and mechanical inevitability of the process, and the continuous droning and explosions, reduced us to a feeling of numbness. By 1600 the plains were covered in one vast pall of smoke and dust, and we could see nothing beyond the bottom of the valley. It was the most overwhelming display of air power that any of us had ever seen – and not a German plane in the sky'.

By the time I rejoined the Battery, the Italians had made a successful but limited advance, and after the initial timed programme which lasted throughout the night of 9/10 April, our guns had little to do. The enemy withdrew on the night of the 10th/11th, which allowed 88 Regiment to cross the Senio without fighting, and after a further withdrawal on the 13th/14th, they crossed the Santerno. Derek Thomas, R Troop Commander, accompanied 88 Regiment and on 14 April established an OP at Point 213, overlooking the valley. I visited him that day and watched the Italian infantry crossing the river and moving slowly up the far slopes towards Monte Catone.
History, 14 April

There were a very few occasional rifle shots from that direction, but there cannot have been many Germans left, and certainly no guns within range, for the Italians were presenting targets such as OPs dream about. All along the road to

---

1. A puppet Italian Fascist Republic had been set up by Mussolini at Salò on Lake Garda after his rescue on 14 September 1943 by German parachutists from the internment imposed on him on 25 July (see p. 177).

A Sexton of 1RHA crossing the Senio, 13 April.

Point 213 they were ambling along in groups of 20 to 30 on the skyline, clustering in hundreds round every house that they came to, throwing down their rifles and equipment to 'liberate' the vino and then stretching themselves out on the ground, officers and men together, to enjoy their siesta. Derek sat in his upstairs room, looking across to Monte Catone, with a milling mass of Italians under his windows, behaving as if they were at a school outing, and wondered how long the German OP officer would hold his fire. But nothing came over. The enemy was obviously too preoccupied with the battle in the plains. Our little battle seemed feeble and unenterprising, and we felt very much left out of it.

By midday on 14 April I Battery was out of range of the enemy, and next day it made two moves forward, crossing the Senio in the morning and the Santerno 'by a tricky ford' in the afternoon. We ended up in action two miles south-west of Imola. The Poles had found the town clear at first light, but we were the first tracked vehicles heavier than a carrier to pass through.
15 April

The civilians gave us a great welcome. Their shouting and cheering were completely hysterical, flowers were thrown and bottles of vino brought out. But to the gunners' disgust there were no road blocks just at that moment. The town itself had obviously been prepared for a siege; the end of every narrow street had

269

been closed by concrete blocks and there were prominent anti-tank ditches. But the houses, except round the station, were far less damaged than we had expected. Even so, it was not surprising that the inhabitants were glad to to see us and know that for them the war was over.

The Italian infantry kept pushing on well and before dark they were across the river Sillaro south-west of Castel San Pietro. By this time it was most unlikely that there were any Germans within range of us – and we hadn't fired a round all day. The night was also completely uneventful.

16 April

At 0630 there was a sudden flap; reconnaissance parties were ordered to move off at once. We were leaving Friuli Group and 10 Corps, and joining the Polish Armoured Brigade.

We were not heartbroken to say goodbye to the Italians; there was no future for us staying with them. They had been carrying out a 'stooge' role, 'exerting pressure' on an unimportant front while the battle was fought elsewhere, and had never really been given a chance to show what they could do. Such shooting and such OPs as were required were naturally supplied by their own 35th Artillery Regiment. The language difficulty meant that we were often completely in the dark as to what was going on. And most important of all, the country the Italians had been operating in was as unsuitable for Sextons as any that could be found in North Italy. So it was on the whole a relief to move out into the plains, where we should have a chance of carrying out our proper role, that of supporting armour. But we would have felt a lot more enthusiastic if we had been joining any armoured brigade but the Poles.

The battery moved off at 0700, round the northern edge of Imola again, then north-westwards into the plains. After waiting for the Bailey bridge across the Sillaro to be completed, we occupied a position on the northern edge of Castel Guelfo village.

The Polish Armoured Brigade was about to go into action, and I Battery was attached to the 4th Armoured Regiment. The Brigade's axis of advance ran north-westwards, parallel to route 9 [the main Rimini-Bologna road], towards the next major obstacle, the Medicina canal.

16 April, continued

The general impression was that there were few Germans left east of the Canal, though the odd tank and SP were being reported. The problem of liaison and language naturally cropped up at once. Fortunately there was available a Polish gunner subaltern who spoke good English and had a 15-cwt with two wireless operators with him. After some discussion we decided the best arrangement would be for him to travel on my Sherman tank and for one of his signallers to operate my second set, on the Polish Armoured Brigade's frequency. The ideal would have been for both my troop commanders also to have their LOs, but they did not exist.

Joining a strange formation is, at the best of times, perplexing. But to join a Polish brigade at half an hour's notice, and then be told that it was going straight into action, seemed likely to be a shattering experience. But gradually it was all to sort itself out in the usual self-adjusting fashion. Both troop commanders found Poles somewhere in their squadrons who could speak reasonable English. David Wootton joined 1 Squadron, Derek Thomas 2 Squadron, while I remained at RHQ. By evening the Poles had reached the Medicina Canal, where they were held up by determined resistance. The Battery fired its first rounds for three days, and during the night a fair number of 88-mm rounds fell in the regimental area; but no damage was done This was the first attention the enemy had paid us since October 1944.

We heard unofficially that our CO, David Welsh, had been awarded the DSO: an honour long overdue and immensely well-deserved, which gave the greatest pleasure to all ranks.

17 April

The enemy withdrew during the night and the sappers made a crossing of the Medicina Canal by bulldozing its banks and filling it in. The Polish tanks moved with extreme caution. The country was dead flat and visibility extremely limited. The Polish method of advance was to pump a dozen 75-mm shells into every house they came to and await developments; if the houses or haystacks caught fire, all to the good; if there were civilians inside, it was too bad. And before moving on to the next farm, a dismounted patrol, well covered by the Shermans, would search every room and barn and shed for snipers. They were very thorough and coldly efficient and were taking no chances. The only excitement occurred about midday when a corporal on the regimental HQ tank shouted that he could see movement ahead in the vines and about 100 men coming stealthily nearer. The Poles grinned and swung their turrets in that direction. When white flags were sighted, the grins grew smaller, but their fingers remained on their triggers. Finally there emerged from the vines about fifty civilians, men, women and children of all ages, some with infants in their arms, all waving sheets or handkerchiefs or something white, shouting to the Poles not to shoot and running as fast as they could. It was a pathetic sight, and an absurd anticlimax after the Poles' vision of 100 desperate parachutists stalking their HQ.

In the afternoon the leading tanks ran into heavy opposition on the river Gaiana. At midday the Battery moved forward 6000 yards to a position on the far side of the Medicina Canal, just south of Poggio Piccolo village. The Poles announced that they wanted 'the Gaiana bank destroyed' and we did our best. One of David Wootton's shoots drew warm congratulations from the 4th Regiment's CO, tactfully passed to us over the air through his Brigadier and our CO.

In the evening came the news that we had been impatiently awaiting – that the Fifth Army had launched its main attack south of Bologna on the night of the 15th/16th.

During the night of the 17th/18th it became clear that an attack on a considerable scale would be required to break the enemy on his present line.

18 April

About 0630 the news was passed round that it was to be an idle day, and that a full scale attack by Polcorps and the New Zealanders was being arranged for the evening. Most of the Poles very sensibly spent the morning in bed.

The only interest was provided firstly by Derek's liberation of a piglet under the nose of a Polish sergeant-major – this very nearly caused an international incident; and secondly by the RAF. At 0815, 1600 and 1930 low level fighter attacks were carried out by Spitfires and Mustangs on the houses along the Gaiana. They lasted about 20 minutes and the noise was deafening. During the last attack one Spitfire let his bomb go a bit wide. I saw it coming and jumped into my Sherman. It fell 200 yards from the 4th Regiment's HQ, but did no damage apart from breaking the windows. When I put my head outside again, the whole area was enveloped in a thick cloud of orange smoke [the recognition signal]. Every tank had set off its own canister. The Poles had been caught that way on the Senio and had learnt their lesson. It was a magnificently quick piece of work.

This super-close support by the RAF was new to us. About one out of every four farmhouses was attacked from the air. In the later stages probably many of them were empty or contained only Italian civilians. In fact the Italians in Castel Guelfo were complaining bitterly that when the RAF attacked their village there were only three Germans in the whole place, and they were deserters and blind drunk. But of the effect of this ceaseless, aggressive use of our air monopoly there could be no doubt whatsoever. It demoralised the Germans and made it almost impossible for them to move in daylight; if they did the results were often disastrous.

Our armoured brigade took no part in the night attack by the New Zealand and 5 Kresova Divisions which started at 2200 on 18 April; but our guns were busy. The Polish tanks began to move forward at 0700 on 19 April and quickly crossed the Gaiana. The enemy resisted stubbornly in pockets, but their casualties were heavy and as the day wore on the number of paratroop prisoners increased.

19 April

About 1500 2 Squadron started moving across an unusually wide open space, covered with low crops but without any vines or trees. Very soon four Polish Shermans were hit, two of them properly 'brewed up'. The remainder pulled back into the cover of the vines, and Derek Thomas brought down the prearranged regimental concentrations. This withdrawal evidently encouraged the enemy, for when Derek moved up gingerly to see what was happening, he saw about six groups of two to twenty Germans moving towards him about 1000 yards away. He seized his chance and gave the whole area a thorough dusting with the Regiment. After ten minutes the demands over the the air that he cut down his ammunition expenditure became too insistent to be ignored, so with great regret and indignation he finished off the good work with just the Battery. Such are the trials of an FOO when he sees his first good target in two and a half months of action.

Towards evening the excitment died down. It had been an interesting day. The distance covered had not been impressive, but the Poles had inflicted heavy casualties on the enemy with very few losses of their own. Our OPs had found their best targets of 1945 and the guns had had plenty of shooting.

At first light on 20 April the infantry confirmed that they were out of contact everywhere, and the Armoured Brigade resumed its advance at 0800. It was entirely uneventful: no resistance was encountered until the river Idice was reached. The Battery had no shooting, but moved twice, ending up in a position just beyond the river Quaderna.

20 April

During the previous night a Polish infantry officer had mysteriously disappeared in his jeep, and it was assumed that he had blundered into the enemy in the dark and been captured. In the early morning his body and that of his driver were found, both horribly mutilated. At once an order was published that no more paratroop prisoners were to be taken, except for purposes of interrogation, and even these few could be shot after questioning. This order was approved, unofficially of course, by the Divisional Commander himself – and it was carried out. David Wootton saw eight Germans being led round behind a farmhouse by determined-looking Poles, and afterwards saw their bodies in the garden. I saw a similar scene at the Polish RHQ. The Poles were completely frank and cold-blooded about the affair, and showed not the faintest qualm of conscience. Their hatred of the Germans was indeed so deep and bitter that they could not easily express it in words.

Night 20/21 April

In the evening there was the usual irritating lack of information. Once again, after telling us as late as 1930 that it would be a quiet night, the Poles suddenly announced at 2030 that a big attack across the Idice was to take place. The general situation was excellent. The Fifth Army yesterday advanced 17 km through the hills south of Bologna and was now just about to burst into the plains. Away to the north 5 Corps was at last right through the Argenta Gap. The Germans had committed their last reserves and were everywhere pulling back as fastr as they could, to get behind the Po. Here on the Idice the remnants of the 1st and 4th Parachute Divisions were thought to be fighting a desperate delaying action. Tonight's attack was being laid on in rather a hurry to ensure that they did not get away.

The Battery was busy firing a fixed programme in support of the attack, which went in at 2200. At 2300 we heard the infantry was safely across the river. The opposition had not been very heavy and no counter-attack developed. After midnight the guns had a quiet night.

21 April

Derek Thomas with 1 Squadron crossed the Idice north-west of Cento di Budrio at first light. The opposition was extremely small and the squadron's support was not required. Derek was told to report to the 8th Royal Tank Regiment, part of 7th Armoured Brigade, and in the early afternoon started moving forward with it towards the objective of Castel Maggiore.

News of the outside world was hard to come by, but there was enough to make us realise that 21 April was going to be a great day. A small mobile task force under command of the Carpathian Lancers made a successful dash to Bologna, and in the middle of the morning H Battery's FOO triumphantly gave his location as a map reference in the centre of the city. As the Poles entered from the east, American troops of the Fifth Army came in from the west, and the two Armies met in the centre amid scenes of wild enthusiasm on the part of the inhabitants.

The joining of the two Armies made a great reshuffle necessary, and Eighth Army swung its axis right-handed, to run due north instead of north-west.

I Battery moved forward in the afternoon and at 1740 fired on two regimental targets in Castel Maggiore. It would have sounded incredible if we had been told so at the time, but these were the last rounds the Regiment fired in the war. At 1930 a nebel [heavy mortar] concentration suddenly came down in the Battery area, and one round hit the side of the house in which S Troop's CP had been established, fortunately doing no damage. That was the last personal attention that the German Army was to pay I Battery RHA.

It was a very quiet night.

22 April

The enemy had withdrawn again by morning and Polish patrols found Castel Maggiore unoccupied. It was obvious that for the moment we were out of a job. Polcorps was being squeezed out by the New Zealanders and passed into Army reserve. There was vague talk of the Corps being required later to exploit beyond the Po, once a crossing had been made. But the prospect for the immediate future was rest and maintenance for at least 48 hours and possibly as much as a week. I Battery was allotted a vast sanatorium on the bank of the Idice at Vigorso, and we settled down to rest and sort ourselves out.

Letter, 26 April

The rain is falling in bucketfuls outside as I write this, and we are hoping that it won't last long enough to slow down seriously the sensational race northwards across the Adige. We have been left out of the chase for the moment – I hope not for good, for that would be a poor ending to our two months of boredom behind the Senio, and our hard-fought advance in the early stages of this great battle. We are now a long way from the front, though when we first arrived here it was only a few thousand yards up the road. Our surroundings are intriguing. We have billeted ourselves in a vast modern building which before the war was an Italian mental hospital. Recently it had been a German military hospital, and the German notices are still hanging on the doors and in the passages. When we arrived it was in a depressing state of filth and neglect. It had been shelled during the battle for the river crossing, and every pane of glass had been shattered. What little the shells left intact was effectively smashed by the German paratroopers before they pulled out. Every cupboard and drawer had been ransacked, doors broken up for firewood, valuable manuals on surgery and medicine thrown on the dusty floors. Even so, with a little work, we have already transformed the small wing of the building we decided to occupy, and for the moment we are in clover. How long we shall be left here is quite another matter. Strictly speaking I suppose we are committing a breach of the Geneva convention – fighting troops sheltering under the Red Cross that is painted all over the walls and roofs. But there is nothing to shelter from now, and my conscience is not worried.

The view over the green plain is lovely. The hawthorn and chestnut blossoms are full out. The lilac in some of the gardens along the route of our advance was glorious, and the most popular method of acknowledging liberation on the part of the local population was to throw big bunches from the balconies into passing vehicles. Some of our lorries arrived on one gun position in the middle of the battle looking as if they had just come from the Carnival of Flowers at Montecarlo.

I have had several enjoyable strolls round the fields outside the hospital grounds, armed with a pair of binoculars. The most pleasing birds here are the nightingales, which seem to sing all day and night, but particularly loudly and exultantly when the full moon is in the sky.

These days of waiting gave us the opportunity to reflect on our relations with the Poles. During the battle, in the quiet of the evenings, the lieutenant who shared my command tank used to sit his signaller down on the ground and lecture him at length. When I asked him out of curiosity what he was lecturing about, he said that he was explaining that once the Germans had been beaten, it would be necessary to fight the Russians. This annoyed and disturbed me greatly, but I kept my feelings to myself.
Retrospective letter

The Poles are thorough people and have no scruples about 'interference in internal Italian affairs'. When they were billeted around Ancona, they systematically removed all the hammers and sickles and eulogies of the Red Army from the walls. There was an ugly incident last March in Faenza. One night a party of Poles, with too much vino inside them, met a red-scarved party of Cypriot muleteers. The Poles drew revolvers and tommy-guns, and I think two Cypriots were killed – certainly more than that number were wounded. So you see the much publicised international army had its incidents and its frictions. Don't please think that I am an unreasoning Polophobe. I feel intense sympathy for them. They fought magnificently and in efficiency and aggressiveness put some British regiments I have known to shame. Their hatred of the Germans was intense, and it was well-founded. But they have a kink of megalomania in them, and their hatred of the Russians is beyond reasoning. While we were near Bologna, I was invited to a dinner party with the Polish Armoured Brigade, held in the open among the vines – and a very fine party it was. We were just finishing dinner when an orderly came in with the wireless news. Mussolini had been found and shot and publicly hung in Milan.[1] The Poles were much excited. But what really thrilled them and set them rubbing their hands with glee was the announcement that there had been a complete deadlock on the Polish question at San Francisco – Eden and Stettinius had broken off relations with Molotov.[2] The same evening I had a long talk with a senior officer of the Brigade. He was saying how much France owed to Pétain, and bewailing the fact that Poland had had no quisling to keep the country together as Pétain had done, preventing the deportations and looting of industries etc. I accused him of contradicting himself, for he had already condemmed the Lublin government as quisling early in the evening. "Ah, but that was quite a different matter". Yet I had him cornered – a pro-German quisling would have been a patriot like Pétain, a pro-Russian quisling was a traitor. Could anything be plainer than that?

History, Waiting for the end

The news kept us in a perpetual state of excitment, developing in the later stages into an acute feeling of disappointment and frustration. On 26 April I lectured to the Battery on the situation, speaking at some length on the Southern Redoubt, and at the end, half joking, remarked that perhaps the Battery had fired its last round in Europe. This raised faintly sceptical smiles; and indeed even then not one of us took the suggestion seriously. Yet that same day Brigadier Siggers, BRA Eighth Army, visited us in pouring rain and told us that as far as he could see, our part in the European war was over. The object with which the attack had started [on 9 April] – the destruction of the German Army south of the Po – had been utterly and completely achieved.

From then on one sensational event followed another. On 2 May we heard that all the German Armies in Italy had surrendered unconditionally, the capitulation having been signed at Caserta on 29 April. That evening we celebrated as best we could, having been taken by surprise, and the countryside was lit up for miles around by bonfires, verey lights and fireworks of every description. It was a great disappointment to finish the war in a backwater and to miss all the thrill of the final pursuit and triumph.[3]

1. Mussolini was captured by Italian partisans at Dongo on Lake Como on 27 April and summarily shot next day. His corpse was displayed in the Piazzale Loreto in Milan on 29 April.

2. The purpose of the San Francisco Conference, which assembled on 25 April, was to draft a charter for the projected United Nations Organisation. Stettinius represented the USA, Molotov the Soviet Union. For the 'Polish question', see pp. 255-6.

3. Later in the summer I learnt that I had been awarded a Bar to my Military Cross for my part in the Italian campaign.

Nevertheless we were in the right mood to celebrate both Fuentes d'Onoro 1811 and Victory 1945 on Drivers' Day, 5 May.[1]
History

Battery HQ and the two Troops played each other at cricket in the morning. In the afternoon a pleasantly disorganised sports meeting was held which everyone enjoyed. It was a glorious day and the sun was if anything too hot. Dinner was at 7 pm. The room which we had been using as a canteen was large enough to seat the whole Battery. The small tables and chairs, the flowers, the plates and glasses obtained from Parma, and the twenty Italian waiters hired from Bologna for the evening, all helped to create a setting really worthy of the day. After my speech we all moved out into the garden where a huge bonfire had been constructed. It contained two whole fir trees, the wrecked hulk of a German car and a generous allotment of cordite charges. It had been well drenched in petrol and was crowned by a framed photograph of Mussolini and a highly coloured picture of Hitler. I set it off by firing a verey light into the middle. After that the celebrations continued into the early hours of the morning.

Letter, 8 May

I am just emerging from a bewildered state of daze in which I have been walking around for the last week. It's impossible to take all this in at once. One sits and listens to a cool BBC voice announcing Hitler's suicide[2] or the public exhibition of Mussolini's corpse in a Milan square, and a dozen other items no less sensational, and all one can do is murmur 'incredible' and switch the wireless off. About three days later, or perhaps during those ten minutes in bed before I get up – when I do all my profitable thinking – I suddenly remember something that was on the news the night before, and wonder if it *can* be true, and then with a shock realise what it really does mean. I had often tried to imagine how the war would finish – but imagination cannot foresee the full drama of events like these. Never did I think the end would come so suddenly, like a dam bursting and sweeping away all that was left of Hitler's proud empire in the space of a few days. And now today is VE Day (horrible phrase), and the future has taken on the shape of one huge question-mark of glorious possibilties. One always used to say that in wartime one never knew where one would be 24 hours later, and that the future was quite unpredictable. But now that the war is over, the future is a hundred times more uncertain than it ever was. No one has a ghost of an idea as to what happens next. So the only thing to do is to be patient and wait till the very important persons make up their minds.

I wish we could have gone with the New Zealanders – or with the 6th Armoured Division – both of them old friends, with whom we have fought many battles. They must be having an interesting time now – rounding up thousands after thousands of Germans from the Alpine foothills and pushing on up into

1. For Drivers' Day see p. 238, note.

2. Hitler committed suicide in his Berlin bunker on 30 April.

Austria. And I gather they have had to do some delicate police work, keeping Germans and Italian partisans and Tito's merry men and Chetniks apart, all in the confined space of Trieste and Gorizia and the narrow coastal plain. I should have liked to be there. But my momentary disappointment has long since vanished in the thrill and relief of knowing that it is all over.

We have been listening to accounts of rejoicings in London and all over the world, as described on the wireless, and have had to make our own celebrations here, in the depths of the green Italian plains. We live in a backwater of country peace, far from great crowds and flags and speeches. Which I think is just as well. This afternoon we lined up our eight guns, sat round the wireless to hear Churchill's speech, then fired a salute of 21 rounds. Tonight we will listen to the King, then I shall ceremonially light our Victory bonfire, and we will all stand round it drinking hot rum punch and singing at the tops of our voices. About 11 the officers and sergeants will probably slink away to celebrate more privately, and leave the rest of the battery to their revels, which will last well into the small hours. And tomorrow the Peace in Europe begins.

I Battery after Victory, May 1945.

GLOSSARY

AA — anti-aircraft
ACC — Army Catering Corps
Ag, Agios (Greek) — Saint
AP — armour-piercing shell
armd — armoured
A Tk — anti-tank

B Echelon — the supply sections of the Battery/Regiment (ammunition, cooks, fitters, office, officers' mess and petrol lorries) located in rear areas when guns in action
Bde — Brigade
Bdr — Bombardier (rank equivalent to infantry corporal)
bir (Arabic) — well
box — all round defensive position in desert, protected by minefields
BQMS — Battery Quartermaster Sergeant.
BSM — Battery Sergeant-Major
Bty — Battery

caique — Greek fishing vessel
CCRA — Corps Commander Royal Artillery (at Corps HQ)
Cdt — Cadet
chott (Arabic) — salt lake, marsh
CO — Commanding Officer
Coy — Company
CP — Command Post
CPO — Command Post Officer
CRA — Commander, Royal Artillery (at divisional HQ)

deir (Arabic) — valley, depression
DF — defensive fire (on targets previously arranged, especially at night, with infantry or tanks in forward positions)
djebel (Arabic) — mountain
DSO — Distinguished Service Order
Div — Division
Dvr — Driver

Ed (Arabic) — the

Fd — field
FOO — Forward Observation Officer

G2, G3 — General Staff Officers, grade II, III
Gnr — Gunner (rank equivalent to infantry private)
GOC — General Officer Commanding
GPO — Gun Position Officer
HE — high explosive

inf — infantry

jebel — See djebel

leaguer — formed at night by concentrating all guns and vehicles in a close circle or square
Lo — Liaison Officer
Lt — Lieutenant

mg — machine gun
MC — Military Cross
MGRA — Master Gunner Royal Artillery (at army HQ)
'Mike' target — target engaged simultaneously by all a Regiment's guns
MO — Medical Officer
MP — Military Police
MT — motor transport

NCO — Non-commissioned Officer (e.g. Sergeant, Bombardier)
NZ — New Zealand

OC — Officer Commanding
odos (Greek) — street
OP — Observation Post
ORs — Other Ranks (soldiers other than commissioned Officers)

pdr — pounder (e.g. a 25-pdr fired a 25lb shell)

279

POW	prisoner of war
Pt	Point (trigonometric)
quad	gun tractor with 4-wheel drive
RAP	Regimental Aid Post
recce	reconnaissance
Regt	Regiment
RHQ	Regimental Headquarters
sebkret (Arabic)	lake
sitrep	situation report
SOS lines	targets previously arranged with infantry/tanks in forward positions on which immediate fire could be called, especially by night
stonk	concentration of a large number of guns on a single target
Sub, Sub-section	gun crew and tractor driver, commanded by a sergeant
tk	tank
TLC	Troop Landing Craft
'uncle' target	target engaged simultaneously by all a Division's guns
Wadi (Arabic)	rocky ravine or valley, dry except in rainy season
Wagon Line	area close behind the guns where vehicles were located while guns in action
'William' target	target engaged simultaneously by all an Army's guns

INDEX OF PERSONS
* denotes membership of 2nd Regiment RHA

283

INDEX OF PLACES

Many places of minor importance, mentioned in the text, are not included in this index, but may be identified in the relevant maps.

INDEX OF MILITARY FORMATIONS
AND INSTITUTIONS

288